Principles of Computer-Aided Design and Manufacturing

Second Edition

Farid Amirouche

The Department of Mechanical & Industrial Engineering
University of Chicago at Illinois

PEARSON
Prentice
Hall

Upper Saddle River, New Jersey 07458

Library of Congress Cataloging-in-Publication Data

Amirouche, Farid M. L.
    Principles of computer-aided design and manufacturing / Farid Amirouche.
        p. cm.
    Includes bibliographical references and index.
    ISBN 0-13-064631-8
    1. Computer-aided design. 2. CAD/CAM systems. I. Title.

TA174.A485 2003
620'.0042'0285–dc22   2003064762

Vice President and Editorial Director, ECS: *Marcia J. Horton*
Acquisitions Editor: *Dorothy Marrero*
Editorial Assistant: *Brian Hoehl*
Vice President and Director of Production and Manufacturing, ESM: *David W. Riccardi*
Executive Managing Editor: *Vince O'Brien*
Managing Editor: *David A. George*
Production Editor: *Kevin Bradley*
Director of Creative Services: *Paul Belfanti*
Art Director: *Jayne Conte*
Cover Designer: *Bruce Kenselaar*
Art Editor: *Greg Dulles*
Manufacturing Manager: *Trudy Pisciotti*
Manufacturing Buyer: *Lynda Castillo*
Marketing Manager: *Holly Stark*

© 2004 Pearson Education, Inc.
Pearson Prentice Hall
Pearson Education, Inc.
Upper Saddle River, NJ 07458

MATLAB is a registered trademark of The MathWorks, Inc., 3 Apple Hill Drive, Natick, MA 01760-2098.

Printed in the United States of America

10 9 8 7 6 5 4 3 2 1

ISBN 0-13-064631-8

Pearson Education Ltd., *London*
Pearson Education Australia Pty. Ltd., *Sydney*
Pearson Education Singapore, Pte. Ltd.
Pearson Education North Asia Ltd., *Hong Kong*
Pearson Education Canada, Inc., *Toronto*
Pearson Educaicón de Mexico, S.A. de C.V.
Pearson Education—Japan, *Tokyo*
Pearson Education Malaysia, Pte. Ltd.
Pearson Education, Inc., *Upper Saddle River, New Jersey*

Contents

4   Description of Curves and Surfaces   127

5   Solid Modeling   177

List of Figures

3   Transformation and Manipulation of Objects   69

4   Description of Curves and Surfaces   127

5   Solid Modeling   177

6   Optimization Techniques   203

7 Introduction to the Finite-Element Method   241

8 Trusses—A Finite-Element Approach   265

9   Heat-Conductison Analysis and the Finite-Element Method   293

10   Dynamic Analysis—A Finite-Element Approach   337

11   Industrial Robotics   371

12 Robot Economics   405

13 Group Technology   425

14 Computer-Integrated Manufactuing   455

15 Implementation of a CAD/CAM System   475

Preface

Principles of Computer-Aided Design and Manufacturing is the product of many years of experience teaching courses in computer-aided design (CAD). My first book, published in 1991, was a challenge—the technology was evolving and both the hardware and software were changing rapidly. Since then we have come a long way in the CAD/CAM area, and the prospects are even better for future intelligent systems that will enable engineers to design engineering products more efficiently. From design to development, we are attaining some great achievements that will engineer products that are more competitive and ready to meet the market needs. In essence, CAD will provide the engineer more time for the creative aspects in terms of concept formulation and interpretation of the results derived from the analysis.

The tools of CAD/CAM are now more standardized and most of our students today come equipped with the basic engineering graphics knowledge needed to learn advanced engineering tools. Having gone through the experience of teaching this course and at the same time trying to adapt to the changing needs in the laboratory, I have written this book under the premise of providing the students the fundamentals needed to advance their understanding of design, analysis, and product development in manufacturing. The latter is achieved through selection of appropriate topics and analytical methods in all aspects of design that are pertinent to CAD with the hope that students will embrace them with conviction. These topics are written in a clear and concise form, and are followed by examples to guide the students and engineers through a wonderful learning experience. The thrust behind learning and teaching CAD is the ability to reach a level of confidence that will enable oneself to interact with ease with the existing CAD systems to solve engineering problems.

My philosophy is to teach through examples; hence, every topic covered is followed by examples to demonstrate the concepts. The basic engineering concepts learned in this book are independent of any specific software. We are at a stage now in which CAD/CAM does not necessary have to be self-contained. Rather, students should be able to use other tools to link or provide additional information as necessary to the CAD system. Where some topics could be supplemented, I have taken the liberty in this textbook of allowing the students to perform their exercises using MATLAB for the sake of understanding that CAD is a multidiscipline in nature and some parts of the design or analysis can be programmed in other languages. This is becoming a common practice as vendors are making it simpler and easier to transport files from different systems, and in some cases even be able to integrate different analysis tools to provide the students and engineers the ability to interact with their software to meet their engineering needs. This is certainly true in the variational design and parametric designs areas in which engineering equations are the engine behind the geometrical formulation and design of certain products.

This textbook is written to satisfy the CAD requirements courses even though finite element coverage expands beyond the introduction of truss analysis. It is difficult to cover all topics in one semester. Topics should be selected to meet the course needs and the laboratory requirements that go with it. For example, at the University of Illinois at Chicago, we have a required laboratory part of the course where students are given different projects on weekly basis to become proficient in the use of CAD software such as ProE or IDEAS. The last lab projects are more involved and usually require some forms of analysis and animation. My intention is to provide additional topics in finite elements that will allow the instructor to focus not only on simple trusses but also be able to teach heat conduction, basic principles in FEM, and even vibration to broaden the scope of analysis. The idea is one that allows our senior students to be exposed to FEM by combining most of what they have learned and show how it can be done with the help of this powerful technique of FEM. This has been very successful with our undergraduate students and first-year graduate students because they are able to use this textbook to learn the basic concepts required in analysis to be able to use finite element tools such as ANSYS, IDEAS, and CATIA, among others.

The book is divided into 15 chapters and provides a unique balance of topics that cover design, 3D transformation and geometry manipulation, surface creations, solid modeling, optimization, finite elements, robotics and robot economics, and CAM implementation.

Chapter 1 provides a historical perspective of CAD and discusses virtual reality as it is used in our current engineering environment (the latter is a topic that will need to be explored further down the road). Chapter 2 addresses the different stages in design and provides concrete examples showing how these steps can be accomplished. The unique feature of this chapter is the parametric and variational design concept. In this textbook I have made an effort to enlighten the students with the need for these techniques to be taken seriously as they might become standard in the near future. The blending of man and machine is an effective tool when CAD systems are allowed to participate in the design and manufacturing process by aiding in the problem formulation, synthesis, conceptualization, and, of course, analysis. Once the students have had some exposure to CAD in general, Chapter 2 could be covered at any part of the course. I urge the instructors and readers to take the time and go over these examples and to create their own examples to appreciate the benefits of these tools.

Chapter 3 discusses 2D and 3D transformations and geometry manipulation, and provides an in-depth analysis of images in 2D and 3D, and includes isometric views. Chapter 4 explains the fundamentals underlying splines, parametric and nonparametric curves, and Bezier curves and surfaces. A number of examples are included to assist the students in understanding how the concepts are implemented. Depending on how advanced the students are, selected topics can be skipped or simply assigned as additional material for the class.

Chapter 5 introduces the concept of solid modeling and the various construction techniques and representation schemes in modeling. The students will apply some of these concepts in their lab work working with the making of solid models in CAD.

Chapter 6 covers various techniques of optimization and introduces the students to the basic concepts of how to formulate an objective function, define the appropriate constraints, and choose the analytical tools to solve the problem. This chapter also focuses on popular techniques in optimization so that senior students and first-year graduate students will have some familiarity with their use.

Chapters 7 through 10 form a unique combination of teaching the finite element method to our junior and senior students without the burden of heavy calculus. It is one of the major strengths of this textbook. If a curriculum is more focused on analysis, all chapters can be covered; otherwise, the instructor is given the choice of covering FEM by selecting the appropriate topic(s) for the class. This would include stress analysis, heat conduction, dynamic analysis, and vibration, or simply teaching the basic formulation of FEM as described in Chapter 7. The examples solved in these chapters represent real applications and will encourage the students to develop a good appetite for FEM.

Computer-aided manufacturing is introduced in Chapters 11 through 15. I have opted to focus on key topics of interest to the students such as robotics and economic impact, group technology, and computer-integrated manufacturing. These are some of the features that need to be understood in the integration of CAD and CAM.

Principles of Computer-Aided Design and Manufacturing is written for junior and senior level students and first-year graduate students who have had little exposure to computer-aided design. This textbook assumes that the students have some experience with programming and understand basic concepts in CAD found in a freshman course of graphics. This textbook is suitable for students who have had all their undergraduate requirements in their major. The latter is an incentive whereby students will fully appreciate the benefits of design techniques such as parametric and variational design and develop a deep understanding of how FEM works and how it is applied to various engineering applications.

I am indebted to the reviewers for their useful comments and suggestions, which helped shape the content and focus of this book: Dr. Heana Costea, California State University at Northridge; Derek M. Yip-Hoi, University of Michigan at Ann Arbor; and Gregory Kremer, Ohio State University. I would also like to thank Dr. M. Ayub, visiting professor in the Civil Engineering Department at University of Chicago at Illinois, for taking the time to edit several chapters and provide his insight for the book and M. Arif, associate professor in the Civil Engineering Department at University of Chicago at Illinois, for his encouragement and support. The comments and suggestions of the reviewers were instrumental in my final revision and in selecting additional topics that were missing from the original proposal. They kindly helped review my original manuscript and assisted me in looking at their course focus and syllabus to get a better picture of how the CAD course is taught at their respective institutions.

Finally, I am indebted to all my students who have assisted me in the preparation of necessary materials for this book; without their help, this wouldn't have been possible. In particular, I would like to thank Carlos Lopez for his efforts on the parametric and variational designs section of the book. I also like to thank Francisco Romero, Nagarajan Chandra, Pedro Gonzalez, and David McNeil for their genuine effort in assisting with some of the graphics of the book. I would like to thank Nikhil Khulka and Ivan Zivkovic for being there when I needed them the most to meet the publisher deadlines and organize the chapters and figures selected for the book. I also would like to thank Surya Pratar for helping with indexing of this book. Finally, let me take this opportunity to thank the editorial staff, Dorothy Marrero, David George, and Lynda Castillo at Prentice Hall, for their patience during the course of the production of the book. I had the pleasure of working closely with Kevin Bradley at Sunflower Publishing Services, who oversaw the complete publication of the book. He was kind and very responsive to all my questions. He worked intelligently to make sure I was happy with the changes and the editing of my book.

At the end I would like to thank my family, Ginger, Larby, and Anissa, for their unconditional love and support and for their understanding in the sacrifices we make in achieving our objectives. In particular, I would like to thank my mom and dad for giving me hope, guidance, and values to treasure for years to come.

FARID AMIROUCHE
The Department of Mechanical & Industrial Engineering
University of Illinois, Chicago

CHAPTER 1

Historical Perspective on Digital Computers

1.1 Introduction

Even the wisest of visionaries could not have foreseen the scope of computers' role in engineering at the end of the 20th century and the beginning of the 21st. It is an ever-expanding role that changes practically by the day. Nevertheless, we can gain some insight into its development by examining some of the first steps in the development of computers.

1.2 History of the Computer

Throughout history, humans have attempted to design mechanisms that would ease the burden of their labors. Until the 19th century, these mechanisms could help only with physical work. The first major figure in computing was British mathematician Charles Babbage (1792–1871) (Figure 1.1). His frustration at the many errors he found while examining calculations for the Royal Astronomical Society led to his search for a machine to perform the calculations. In 1822 he proposed the "Difference Engine," a steam-powered machine the size of a cottage that used a stored "program" to perform calculations and printed results without human intervention. After working on the Difference Engine for 10 years he began designing an all-purpose calculating machine he called the "Analytical Engine." Although the Analytical Engine was not completed in his lifetime, due more to deficiencies in 19th-century technology than in his designs, Babbage is considered the "Father of Modern Computing." The components of his Analytical Engine showed striking parallels with the machines of a century later,

FIGURE 1.1 Babbage's differential engine.

including an input device (a system of punch cards), a memory (he called it "the store"), a central processing unit ("the mill"), and an output device (a printer). The machine was also designed so that early results could be used in subsequent calculations. Augusta Ada King, Countess of Lovelace (1815–1842), aided Babbage in his work (Figure 1.2). This aristocratic daughter of English poet Lord Byron was also a talented amateur mathematician. Ada's immediate grasp of the Analytical Machine's workings allowed her to create the instructions for the machine, making her the first female computer programmer. Her access to all levels of society was also instrumental in helping Babbage to find governmental funding for his project. In an article published the year after her death, Lady Lovelace, every bit the visionary Babbage was, predicted that such a machine could be used to compose music, could produce graphics, and could be applied to both practical and scientific pursuits. In 1979 the U.S. Defense Department named the programming language ADA/Ed in her honor. Babbage and King were so far ahead of their time, in fact, that it would take nearly a century for technology to develop that would allow dreams like theirs to be realized.

It is generally agreed that the first generation of modern computing began in the early 1940s with the invention of the ENIAC (Electronic Numerical Integrator and Computer) at the University of Pennsylvania's Moore School of Engineering. Much like Babbage's machines, ENIAC and its descendants such as UNIVAC, EDVAC, etc. were characterized by their huge size—the result of using 18,000 vacuum tubes, the "cutting edge" technology of the time (Figures 1.3 and 1.4). In a 1941 proposal to the U.S. Army, two men from the Moore School, John W. Mauchly and J. Presper Eckert, offered to construct a machine that would compute ballistic trajectories at least 10 times faster than the differential analyzer the Army possessed. In a later modification this machine became ENIAC.

FIGURE 1.2   Countess Augusta Ada King.

ENIAC was about a block long and weighed almost 3 tons! When it was turned on, all the lights in Philadelphia dimmed. An operator was at the machine around the clock, compared to standards of today's supercomputers, which operate over 4000 times faster. Its computation speed was far greater than existing electromechanical machines and it solved problems that were beyond the reach of humans at that time. ENIAC's cost was nearly $3.5 million. Today, a microprocessor with the same computational efficiency costs less than $14.

ENIAC began a hardware revolution in computing by proving that electronic technology could be used to make fast, powerful, reliable general-purpose computers. Not everyone grasped the significance of ENIAC and its immediate successors, though. Howard Aiken, creator of the WWII decryption machine "Mark I," made this prediction while recommending that the National Research Council revoke funding for the UNIVAC project:

> We were ... misleading not only the Government agencies which had made money available for the development of such equipment, but the general public in pursuing this course of trying to develop such equipment, giving the impression that this program could be justified ... because there will never be enough problems, enough work for more than just one or two of these computers.

FIGURE 1.3 ENIAC at the Moore School of Engineering (UPI/Bettmann Newsphotos).

Popular Mechanics magazine was a bit more hopeful. They predicted, in their March 1949 issue, "Where a computer like the ENIAC is equipped with 18,000 vacuum tubes and weighs 30 tons, computers in the future may have only 1,000 vacuum tubes and weigh only $1\frac{1}{2}$ tons."

There were three major problems with the early machines: (1) communication between man and machine was difficult, (2) maintenance was high and reliability was low, and (3) the computers generated tremendous heat.

Programming the early computers required a great deal of skill and knowledge of each machine's language code because no standard programming language yet existed. All programming had to be written directly in machine languages and a different program had to be written for each task. There were no predefined functions such as math symbols to indicate mathematical operations. Programming lacked all the time-saving advantages of the symbolic representation used today. Debugging was a tedious and painstaking process—made all the more so when the occasional cleaning lady accidentally unplugged one of ENIAC's myriad wires with her mop and proceeded to plug it back in to the nearest available socket!

Second-generation computers (1956–1963) took advantage of the invention, in 1948, of the transistor. This small device made the vacuum tube obsolete; and the size of electronic machinery has been shrinking ever since. First applied to computers in

FIGURE 1.4 Technicians "programming" the ENIAC (UPI/Bettmann Newsphotos).

1956, the second-generation machines included all the components we associate with contemporary computers: printers, tape and disk storage, memory, operating systems, and stored programs. These features gave computers the flexibility to be cost effective and led to their widespread use in business.

Third-generation computers (1964–1971) were still plagued by the great amount of heat they generated, which damaged the computer's sensitive parts. In 1958 the integrated circuit (IC) solved this problem. Developed by Jack Kilby, a Texas Instruments engineer, the IC combined three electronic components onto a small silicon disk. Later, even more components were included, and true miniaturization of the computer became a realistic goal.

The fourth generation of computing applies to the years between 1971 and the present. By the 1980s, millions of components could be squeezed onto a chip half the size of a dime. Consequently, computers continued to get even smaller, cheaper, more powerful, more efficient, and more reliable. Today, the microchip stores more information, performs calculations 20 times faster, and is several hundred thousand dollars cheaper to manufacture than the block-long ENIAC. The microprocessor has revolutionized the computer world and has made computers affordable for almost everyone. IBM introduced its personal computer (PC) in 1981 and it found rapid and widespread acceptance in homes, offices, and schools. The number of personal computers in use more than doubled from 2 million in 1981 to $5\frac{1}{2}$ million only a year later. By 1991, 65 million PCs were in use.

As computers evolve from their present state, they will be able to assume more difficult tasks—tasks that require actual thought. These fifth-generation computers will contain artificial intelligence (AI) to converse with humans, learn from their own experiences, use visual input, imitate human reasoning, and perform inductive and deductive "thinking."

Hardware for the fifth-generation computers is currently being built. Examples of such computers include the psi II and the multi-psi workstation, which incorporate a high-level parallel processing language called KL1. AI features are beginning to appear in some software. Intergraph Corporation's *FreeSketch*, for example, is an intuitive tool that produces precision geometry from freehand "sketching." For example, when one moves the mouse in a circular motion, *FreeSketch* automatically recognizes the arc-like movement and places a precision arc on the monitor. Even more sophisticated engineering applications will be programmed to solve problems the way humans do.

1.3   Computer Categories

Although their internal components are basically alike, computers can be grouped into these categories:

- Supercomputer
- Mainframe computer
- Minicomputer/workstation
- Microcomputer/workstation
- Stand-alone personal computer

The supercomputer can be defined as "the computer that is currently the world's fastest and most powerful." It has a large main memory and is capable of extremely fast processing. The mainframe is often used to solve complex engineering and scientific problems, such as interactive calculations in fluid dynamics analysis, heat-transfer analysis, and stress analysis (Figure 1.5). Mainframes are also used in large-scale data-processing operations such as payroll, corporate accounting, production scheduling, and the maintenance of large databases. To be able to use computer-aided design (CAD) software on a mainframe, a special workstation is needed. All CAD processing is performed in the mainframe; the workstation is used only to display graphics. The advantages of a mainframe in conjunction with the CAD workstation are expanded memory and processing speed. However, the drawbacks are the cost and maintenance of a mainframe.

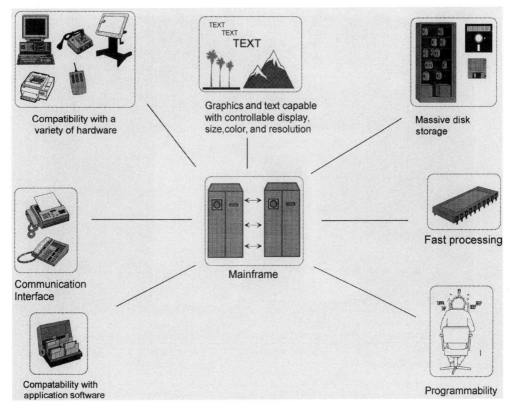

Compatibility with a
variety of hardware

Graphics and text capable
with controllable display,
size, color, and resolution

Massive disk
storage

Communication
Interface

Mainframe

Fast processing

Compatability with
application software

Programmability

FIGURE 1.5 Characteristics of a mainframe.

A CAD workstation consists of three components: the host computer, input devices, and output devices (Figure 1.6). The host computer is where all the software is located and where all processing takes place. In the stand-alone type of CAD workstation, the host computer is integrated in the machine. The others have the mainframe as a separate unit.

A workstation is superior to a personal computer because it is designed to communicate with a larger array of computers and mainframes. The standards for PCs, though, have risen significantly over the past few years to approach the capabilities of workstations.

The minicomputer is less powerful than a mainframe. Because the minicomputer is less expensive, it is cost efficient in commercial and industrial applications. Because the minicomputer is relatively small, it is often used as part of large testing equipment. Today's personal computers are becoming more powerful and represent a real challenge to mainframe computers. A personal computer is a stand-alone machine with its own processor, operating system, memory, and graphics capabilities.

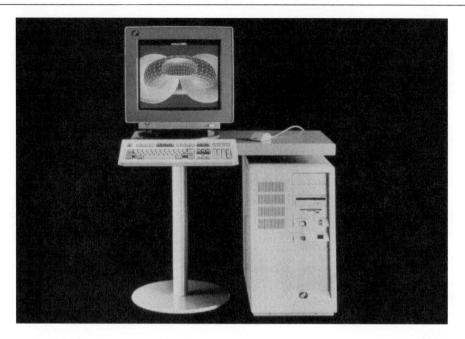

FIGURE 1.6 A typical CAD workstation (International Business Machines Corp.).

Stand-alone computers now possess processors and memory that rival the abilities of the mainframe computers of the early 1980s.

1.4 Computer Hardware

The physical machinery that makes up a computer is known as hardware. Computer hardware can be divided into four main categories: input devices, output devices, the central processing unit, and memory.

The most common input devices used for design are the keyboard, the potentiometer device (mouse, trackball, joystick), the light pen, and the digitizer. All of these control the cursor in simple executions.

Output devices are typically the monitor or various "hard-copy" devices such as plotters, line printers, and dot-matrix, thermal, ink-jet, and laser printers.

The central processing unit (CPU) is the heart of the computer. It is responsible for manipulating data from memory locations, monitoring and controlling information flow from input and output (I/O) devices and within itself, and carrying out instructions stored in memory.

Two types of primary memory are available: read-only memory (ROM) and random-access memory (RAM). Because computers must be able to access an enormous amount of data, far in excess of the main memory, other devices, known as secondary memory, are necessary to store the excess data permanently. These are typically magnetic disks ("floppies") or CD-ROMs.

1.5 Programming Languages

Computer programming instructs a computer what to do and when to do it. A computer language is the means whereby the computer communicates with humans, and vice versa, via I/O devices. There are three levels of computer languages: machine language, assembly language, and high-level languages.

1.5.1 Low-Level Languages

Machine language (ML) is the object code the computer understands. The nature of ML makes programming tedious and difficult. The makeup of 0s and 1s in a binary code causes optical confusion when reading (discerning each bit length and what it represents) and debugging the program. Assembly language was designed to replace ML with an easier-to-discern English-like mnemonic code. A program written in assembly can be translated to ML by an assembler. For each ML statement, there is an equivalent assembly statement.

Machine language and assembly are considered low-level languages because of their complexities.

1.5.2 High-Level Languages

High-level language (HLL) programs were developed to provide users with easier programming. HLLs combine several ML statements into one statement or symbol. The computer comprehends HLLs through a compiler. A compiler is a low-level language that checks for errors in programs written in HLL (source code) and translates them into equivalent low-level language (object code) programs. Let us look at some widely used HLLs.

COBOL (COmmon Business-Oriented Language) was developed in 1959 for business applications and is designed in a format that simulates composition writing. Because COBOL is relatively easy to read and understand, it is ideal for operators with no previous computer training. It is used for numeric and alphabetic data processing and file management.

The FORTRAN (FORmula TRANslation) language was developed by IBM between 1954 and 1957 for the scientific and technical field to compute complex mathematical problems. The same hierarchy of operation rules used by mathematicians is incorporated into FORTRAN's math solver. Solving complex and tedious math formulas using FORTRAN is easy because programmers write, in sequential order, the same math operations they would use to find an answer. There are several drawbacks to FORTRAN, however: (1) it has an inadequate ability to read, write, and manipulate text, (2) its program flow control commands are difficult, and (3) subroutines cannot call themselves to repeat the same subroutine function.

Named for the French mathematician Blaise Pascal, Pascal is a general-purpose programming language. It was developed by Blaise Niklaus in Switzerland during the early 1970s. Pascal can be applied in areas of intensive mathematical solution, business data/file processing, and system programming. Pascal is somewhat lacking in controlled structure flow (e.g., statement line numbers) but is strong in data structure (file) manipulation. The statements used in Pascal resemble simple English sentences.

BASIC (Beginner's All-purpose Symbolic Interactive Code) was developed in the mid-1960s by John Kemeny and Thomas Kurtsz at Dartmouth College. BASIC is unique because of its modified compiler, which automatically checks for errors after each statement line is entered. Several versions of BASIC are available, some considerably more powerful than others. The language is still used to teach computer programming to elementary and high school students. BASIC can use all the programming techniques of FORTRAN.

C was developed in 1972 by Dennis Ritchie at AT&T Bell Laboratories. C was originally designed to run with the UNIX operating system, but its popularity led to the creation of non-UNIX versions. Like BASIC and Pascal, C is easy to use, but its strongest ability lies in the area of system software.

C possesses the same mathematical capabilities as FORTRAN and the simplicity of Pascal. It does require some practice, but it can produce extraordinarily powerful applications. Its structure is much simpler than FORTRAN or BASIC, requiring a less rigid format and much simpler and abbreviated commands.

Ada/Ed was developed by the U.S. Department of Defense in the late 1970s for controlling and consolidating various computer parts and systems that essentially contain their own computer language. Ada/Ed can use the full capability of multitasking (parallel processing) computer architecture to perform several operations on several computers at the same time.

1.6   History of CAD

CAD is the creation and manipulation of pictures (design prototypes) on a computer to assist the engineer in the design process. CAD has developed over the past quarter-century into an indispensable tool for the technology, design, and manufacturing industries. CAD revolves around the integration of the best characteristics of three major elements: the CAD hardware, the software, and the user.

The blending of computers and the human ability to make decisions provides the optimal CAD system. Its primary functions are in designing, analyzing, and manufacturing. Although most novices think of CAD as an electronic drafting board, its functions stretch beyond drawing pictures. An analysis of an object drawn with CAD can be made interactively on the screen, where physical information can be extracted. In engineering, finite-element analysis, heat-transfer analysis, stress analysis, dynamic simulation of mechanisms, and fluid dynamic analysis are common operations performed with CAD.

In a sense, CAD represents the evolution of computer graphical representation of information. It was created by the aerospace and automotive industries as a method of increasing the rate of technological development and reducing many tedious tasks of the designer.

Graphical representation in computers can be traced back to the beginning of digital computers. In the mid-1950s the SAGE (Semi-Automatic Ground Environment) Air Defense Command and Control System used computer graphics (Figure 1.7). SAGE changed radar information into computer-generated pictures. It also made use of the light pen, which allowed the user to choose information by pointing at the appropriate area displayed on the CRT (cathode-ray tube).

Before 1960, "CAD" stood for "computer-aided drafting" (not "design"). At the same time as the SAGE developments, numerically controlled (NC) machines were being developed at the Massachusetts Institute of Technology. They were to find their first practical application in the designing of the complex sculpted surfaces found in the automotive and aerospace industries. Patrick Hanratty began early research in the development of computer-aided design while working for General Motors Research Laboratory in the early 1960s. A milestone in the development of computer graphics was the pioneering work of Ivan Sutherland. In 1963 Sutherland's doctoral thesis, describing the sketch pad, began laying the theoretical basis for computer graphics software. The sketch pad consisted of an oscilloscope driven by a Lincoln TX-2 computer.

FIGURE 1.7 The U.S. Air Force's SAGE digital computer (UPI/Bettmann Newsphotos).

Pictures could be displayed on the screen and manipulated by the user with a light pen. The use of systems based on the sketch pad has become known as interactive graphics. The sketch pad clearly showed the potential for a CRT as a designer's electronic drawing board, with graphic operations such as scaling, translation, rotation, animation, and simulation. (See Figures 1.8 and 1.9.)

With its dependence on large mainframe computers costing between $100,000 and tens of millions of dollars, these industries were virtually the only users of CAD until the late 1960s. Gradually, CAD applications began appearing in European auto and airplane manufacturing as well as the Japanese auto and shipbuilding industries. One estimate is that by the early 1970's only fifty companies in the world were using

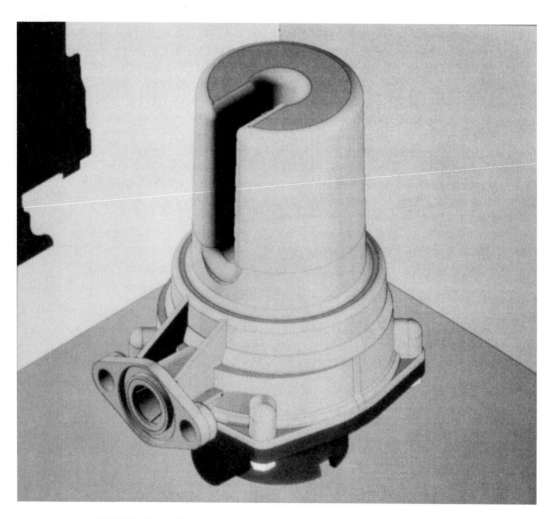

FIGURE 1.8 A solid modeling drawing (International Business Machines Corp.).

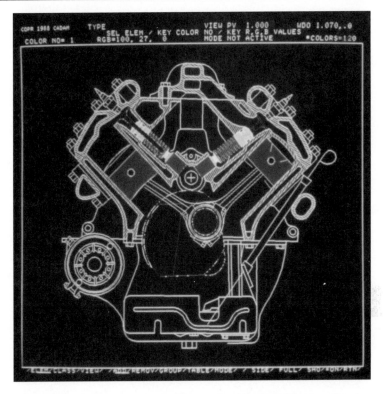

FIGURE 1.9 Wireframe drawing (International Business Machines Corp.).

CAD/CAM and that less than 1% of the parts manufactured worldwide involved CAD/CAM applications. The introduction of the minicomputer, the development of software for multiple applications, increased marketing by vendors, and decreasing prices led to CAD being used in other industries. Wireframe capabilities began appearing in the mid-1970s. Although this marked the first three-dimensional (3D) CAD application, wireframe modeling had some serious shortcomings. Wireframe views are often ambiguous, and their ability to represent curved surfaces is severely limited. Line-hiding and, later, the ability to shade surfaces greatly increased the utility of 3D CAD programs. Increasing use by companies resulted in increasing pressure for more versatile CAD software. (See Figure 1.10.)

The introduction of microcomputers with high-resolution raster screens and ever-increasing price/performance ratios led to their introduction into smaller and smaller companies. Slowly, managers began to view the CAD system as an economic necessity. By the early 1980s their use was widespread in mechanical and manufacturing engineering. Companies were virtually forced by their competitors to commit to CAD.

In January 1983 the Autodesk Corporation released AutoCAD 86 for the newly introduced IBM PC. When Autodesk went public 2 years later its annual sales topped

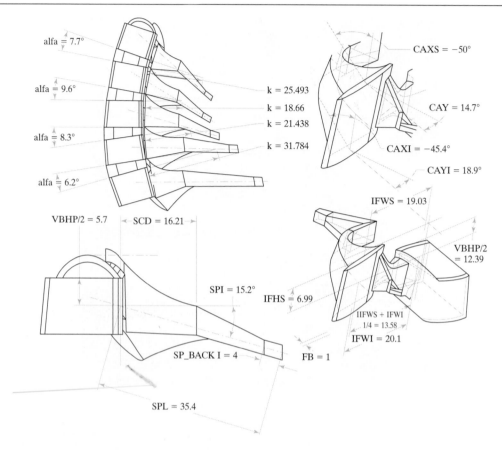

FIGURE 1.10 PC-based CAD drawings. (Courtesy of Biomechanics Research Laboratory, University of Illinois at Chicago.).

$27 million. A decade later over 1 million copies of AutoCAD were in use and Autodesk had become the fifth-largest software company in the world.

As influential as AutoCAD was and is, though, the scope of CAD/CAM has changed in recent years. Integrated CAD and CAE (computer-aided engineering) software first appeared in 1995. Until that time, engineering analysis tools and graphic design tools had been separate. A designer could generate a design based on dimensional parameters using a CAD application, then transfer the completed design to an FEM (finite-element method) application for analysis. This process was tedious, and analysis could be initiated only after completion of the design. The recent development of integrated design and engineering applications allows engineering decisions to be included in the conceptual design stage. Before a design concept has any detailed geometric features, for example, the designer can run stress, dynamics, thermal, fluid, and magnetic analyses on the design. Several software tools also provide cost/process analysis. (See Figure 1.11.)

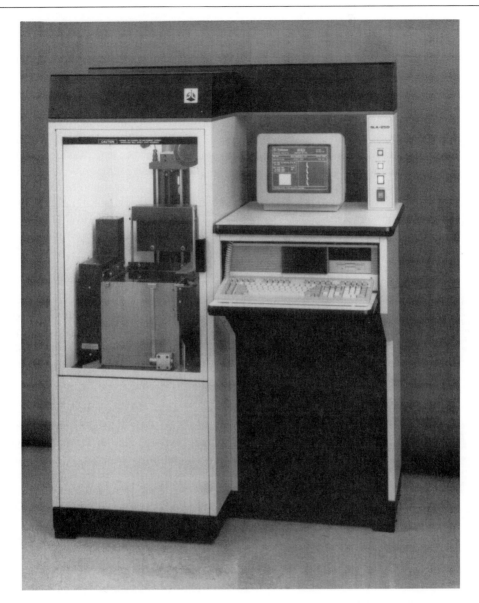

FIGURE 1.11 A stereolithography CAD system (Courtesy of 3D Systems, Inc.).

1.6.1 CAD Graphics Generator

The distinguishing characteristics of a CAD/CAM system are its use of geometric modeling, interactive graphics, and the reuse of stored information (Stark, 1987 p. 129). Geometric modeling includes scaling, rotation, translation, and geometry representation.

The lack of early computer graphics made the interpretation of computer output strenuous for the designer because it appeared in a numeric format. A means was needed for the designer to communicate with the results of the computer. This was made possible by the development of the graphic generator, which forms the basis of CAD today. A graphical program is much better at describing a design to the average user. The adage "a picture is worth a thousand words" is particularly true in this case.

General-purpose CAD graphic programs use Cartesian coordinates to organize the data for display and visualization. The x-, y-, and z-axes describe the position and space that entities occupy. By manipulating the values of the arrays, which contain the points the object occupies, one can scale (magnify or reduce) the object, rotate it about any axis, and translate (move) it to another location in the same reference axis.

To scale a drawing, the designer must supply the magnification factor. Once the computer receives the scaling size, the so-called configuration matrix is multiplied by the appropriate transformation matrix to yield the desired scaled geometry. This will be discussed in detail in Chapter 3. Some CAD systems have a ZOOM/PAN command, which allows the user automatically to magnify the geometry to either two or four times its size.

Rotating an object involves a procedure similar to that used in scaling. The user is asked to select the points or axis of rotation in addition to the angle of rotation (clockwise or counterclockwise). The CAD workstation, through its software, will then automatically display the rotated object. Although this operation seems simple, the mathematics involves the multiplication of matrices defining the geometry and the rotation. In Chapter 3, all the rotations will be discussed for two- and three-dimensional space.

Translation is moving the object from one position to another. The user defines the amount of movement on each axis. The program then moves and displays the object accordingly. Different CAD systems provide the user with several options for translation in which the new destination could be given through the absolute coordinates by providing the corresponding changes in the x-, y-, and z-coordinates. Another option is specifying a particular point position using the cursor or entering the incremental positioning of the location of the new position. The translation is done with respect to a reference point, assumed to be zero if not supplied. This option allows the user to take advantage of several reference frames to translate the object on the screen.

Early graphics programs modeled entities by wireframe drawings. Wireframe drawings are made up of lines, points, and curves representing the outline of the object. It requires some imagination for the viewer to envision the object. A function in Auto-CAD and other programs hides the lines that should not appear in a particular view, thus improving visualization of the drawing. Hidden line removal is an important feature in displaying graphics in different views. Although the computer may understand the volume inside the wireframe it occupies, the viewer may not. The introduction of solid modeling resulted in a significant improvement in design interpretation. This enhancement is vital to design and yields a conceptualized picture of how the object would look in the real world. Current CAD programs can reproduce the actual picture of the object being designed. A recent development is "rapid prototyping" in which a computer-guided laser develops a 3D model using photosensitive liquid plastic. The technique uses the same data that produced CAD drawings. The parts are made by mathematically slicing CAD designs into thin cross sections. An ultraviolet beam traces each layer in a vat of photo-sensitive chemicals that solidify as they are irradiated.

1.6.2 Objectives of CAD Programs

The computer's memory capacity and processor speed are the two top considerations when selecting a CAD software package. For example, a moderately complex detail drawing consists of about 2000 CAD entities. A good CAD package in a production environment should be able to redraw at a rate of 2000 entities per second at a screen resolution of 1024 × 768 pixels. Observations of the speed can be made by zooming, panning, or redrawing (regenerating) a large drawing of approximately 10,000 entities. Some software includes both redraw and regenerate commands. The regenerate function updates everything on disk, whereas redraw updates only a local integer base that controls the current screen image. These features are used in almost all CAD systems. Others are the ability to perform simple calculations such as areas, volumes, centroids, moments of inertia, and centers of mass, 2D- and 3D-geometry creation, dimensioning, and labeling.

Desirable features of CAD software packages are "user-friendly" communication. The criteria for such a system might include:

- that it allows the user to spend more time on the design than on the commands,
- that the number of steps necessary to activate any command be minimized,
- that any command affecting the database should have protection against accidental deletion or reorganization,
- that the menu be arranged for easy interaction with the user,
- that a set of nested commands be accessible in the midst of drawing, editing, or dimensioning without affecting the progression of the current command. That is, the user can view options during the current command, and
- that the overall appearance of the program reflects a simple and logical layout.

1.6.3 Drawing Features in CAD Software

Virtually all CAD software is capable of drawing lines, circles, arcs, rectangles, polygons, points, splines, closed curves, and double lines. CAD programs offer various other tools, including on-screen feedback of absolute, relative, or polar coordinates; rubber band lines; grid and object snaps; and parallels, perpendiculars, and tangents to existing entities.

For mechanical design, features such as automatic fillets and chamfers, automated crosshatching, the ability to construct circular or rectangular arrays of selected objects, and automatic calculation of areas and section properties must be included. Others are the ability to perform simple calculations such as areas, volumes, centroids, moments of inertia, and centers of mass, geometry creation (2D and 3D), dimensioning and labeling, and editing ability.

All CAD programs have editing features. The editing command usually includes functions such as erase, trim, extend, scale, rotate, stretch, undo, move, insert, copy, break, mirror, mirror copy, group, ungroup, and change entity characteristics. Additional features, such as zoom/window, are used to magnify specific areas for more accurate editing. CAD packages also include MACRO functions, which allow the user to execute a set of subroutines as one command.

1.7   The Role of Computers in the Future

The world of computers is going through a dynamic transition because of the low manufacturing cost and high demand. Faster systems are being built to meet the needs of computing in production. An odd situation has occurred because of the development of faster computers: operating system (OS) software improvements are beginning to lag behind hardware improvements. OS software manages computer hardware system operations and allows compatible software to interact and operate within the computer. Debates over standardization of an operating system have divided the computer industry and threaten to hinder the progress of computer technology. UNIX has been accepted as the standard operating system for multitasking. Many computer manufacturers have built their systems to run UNIX because of its flexibility and power.

Bidirectional parametric tools allow 2D profiles to be created and constrained to facilitate the creation of 3D models. Relationships can be established between the profiles and their corresponding 3D model parts so that modifications to the 2D constraints will automatically update the 3D model. Other features include photorealistic rendering and "walk-through" animation. (See Figure 1.12.)

By viewing a design as a global system of interrelated parts and functions, engineers can simplify a product concept through "part reduction strategies," in which engineering analysis highlights which parts are candidates for elimination. This encourages designs incorporating as many features as possible into each part, which results in higher quality, more efficiency, greater reliability, fewer parts, reduced direct and overhead costs, a shorter development cycle, and a more elegant and efficient design. (See Figure 1.13.)

FIGURE 1.12 An architectural "walk through".

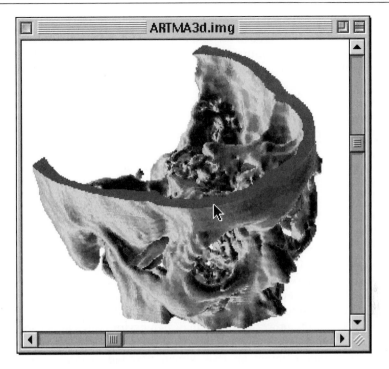

FIGURE 1.13 This biomedical application of virtual reality allows the user to rotate and tilt the piece with standard computer controls.

Predictive cost analysis is another emerging area of engineering software. It uses manufacturing knowledge for concurrent engineering to identify and reduce costs at every stage of the product's life cycle. Cost analysis can begin with preliminary estimates at the design's concept level, allowing early identification of key cost drivers. Comparing the costs of several alternative designs becomes a simple matter, and unexpectedly high manufacturing costs are easily identified. Integrated CAE products provide an effective group-oriented design environment for concurrent engineering. Team members are able to work in relation to their overall product. Changes are automatically propagated to everyone so there is no loss of model integrity or duplication of effort. This prevents unnecessary rework caused by conflicting changes.

FEM analysis can be included in the same file as the geometric design data. Analysis results, stress contours, and deflected shapes, for example, can be displayed with the original geometric model. FEM features provide sophisticated kinematic analysis and design simulation of virtually any 2D or 3D mechanical system. Packaging studies may be performed with minimum distance, interference detection, and trace envelope options. Structural analysis software furnishes linear static, vibration, and heat-transfer-analysis capabilities. Plastic analysis modules predict whether a plastic part will do the job intended, whether the part can be filled with the specified plastic, and where surface defects such as weld lines and air traps will occur.

Computer-aided manufacturing (CAM) programs allow NC manipulation of tool paths for tasks such as drilling, tapping, milling, flame cutting, boring, and lathe turning. Digital mockup, machining, visualization, and interference checking are facilitated.

Associative dimensions after each translation gives manufacturing shops the details needed to produce parts. Process documentation allows direct communication with the shop floor. The engineer is able to communicate exactly which tools to use, the assembly sequence, how it should be inspected, even what it looks like after each step, which results in increased labor productivity and reduced scrap and rework. This allows the engineer, not the shop labor, to develop the manufacturing processes.

Integrated analysis tools enable the designer to more fullly evaluate projects in the early stages, when changes are easiest and least costly. With a single command, an engineer can determine surface areas and calculate volumes, centers of gravity, and moments of inertia from a solid model.

With tolerance analysis one can simulate the manufacturing implications of specified dimensional tolerances to balance quality and production costs. Such features give the designer the power to simulate design performance under service or test conditions, reducing dependence on costly physical prototypes. With advanced technology solutions for finite-element analysis, kinematics, and dynamics, one can investigate design feasibility, implement needed changes, and optimize design models automatically. In addition to integrated finite-element analysis, design, and optimization tools, the user can generate a bill of material and a parts list from component and attribute information contained in a set of drawings.

Using software prototyping technology, the engineer is able to study the structural, thermal, vibration, and dynamic effects of proposed changes without the difficulties associated with traditional analysis tools. By testing designs in software before committing to expensive physical models, products can be produced better, faster, and cheaper than by traditional methods. Mechanical design tools can define the geometry and motion at various steps in a manufacturing process. Analysis tools can optimize cycle times and production flows, and pinpoint potential bottlenecks. Virtual reality (VR) is another area of CAE likely to gain prominence in the future. Already relatively established in the area of entertainment, VR has found many applications in the military, geological, meteorological, chemical, astronomical, and medical fields. Much like the early proliferation of CAD in the 1960s, large institutions such as Caterpillar, Lockheed-Martin, General Motors, Argonne National Laboratories, and NASA are exploring the uses of VR.

At the forefront of VR development are academic centers such as the Electronic Visualization Laboratory (EVL) at the University of Illinois at Chicago. Under the direction of Dr. Thomas DeFanti, the EVL has developed two systems that hold particular promise for engineers: the Cave Automatic Virtual Environment (CAVE) and the ImmersaDesk.

FIGURE 1.14 The CAVE (Electronic Visualization Laboratory, University of Illinois at Chicago).

The CAVE is a 10 × 10 × 10-foot structure contained in a 35 × 25 × 13-foot darkened room (Figure 1.14). Consisting of rear-projected screen walls and a front-projected floor, the CAVE is a multiperson, high-resolution, 3D graphics video and audio environment. Using special stereoscopic glasses inside the CAVE, the user is fully immersed. Images appear to float in space, with the user free to "walk" around them, yet maintain a proper perspective.

The CAVE was the first VR technology to allow multiple users to immerse themselves fully in the same virtual environment at the same time. Through a "shared" virtual experience, users can use the CAVE to find and fix problems before they occur. The CAVE can feed specialized computer files into rapid prototyping machines. Multiple users can videoconference from different locations into the same CAVE. The CAVE links with number-crunching computers to quickly and easily create a broad spectrum of complex virtual environments. Users can also link CAVE with other VR technologies to experience the same virtual environment at the same time.

The ImmersaDesk is a drafting-table style, projection-based virtual reality tool (Figure 1.15). Wearing special glasses, a user can look into the ImmersaDesk's angled 4 × 5-foot screen to view a computer-generated 3D image that is simulated with near-perfect accuracy. Both elevation and bird's-eye views are possible. The ImmersaDesk is portable yet large enough to fill a person's field of view so that it achieves the illusion of an immersing virtual environment without fully surrounding the user.

"Virtual rapid prototyping" is one of the ways engineers can take designs from concept to completion without ever fabricating prototyped models in real life. By providing

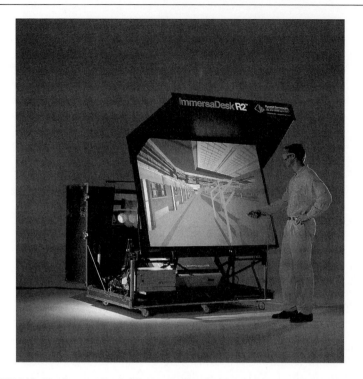

FIGURE 1.15   The ImmersaDesk (Electronic Visualization Laboratory, University of Illinois
at Chicago).

an effective way to design, test, and approve new products virtually, the ImmersaDesk
helps companies move products to market faster and, ultimately, become more competitive in today's global marketplace.

BIBLIOGRAPHY

Aukstakalnis, S., & Blatner D. (1992). *Silicon Mirage, The Art and Science of
Virtual Reality*. Berkeley, CA: Peachpit Press.

The Babbage Pages. http://www.ex.ac.uk/~rburnley/babbage.

Biocca, F., & Levy, M.R. (eds.) (1995). *Communication in the Age of Virtual
Reality*. Hillsdale, NJ: Erlbaum.

CAD/CAM Engineering Systems—Virtual Reality Library. http://www.
cadcamsys.com/IMAGELIB/VIRTREAL/VIRTREAL.HTM.

Clemson University Virtual Reality: Mechanical Engineering Research.
http://chip.vr.clemson.edu/vr/mech/mech.html.

Commercial Computing Museum—Computer History Web sites. http://granite.
sentex.net/~ccmuseum/hist_sites.html.

Computing Then and Now. http://www.nmsi.ac.uk/on-line/treasure/plan/
2ndcomp.htm#babbage.

The Day ENIAC Changed the World. http://tor-pw1.netcom.ca/~brentman/ eniac.html.

Hayward, T. (1993). *Adventures in Virtual Reality.* Carmel, IN: Que Corporation.

Heim, M. (1993). *The Metaphysics of Virtual Reality.* New York: Oxford University Press.

Historic Computer Images. http://ftp.arl.mil/ftp/historic-computers/.

History of Computing Information. http://ftp.ar.mil/~mike/comphist.

Larijani, L.C. (1994). *The Virtual Reality Primer.* New York: McGraw-Hill.

Pimentel, K., & Teixeira, K. (1993). *Virtual Reality: Through the New Looking Glass.* New York: Intel/Windcrest/McGraw-Hill.

University of Pennsylvania Archives and Records Center. http://www.upenn. edu/AR/.

Virtual Reality Lab at UM. http://www-VRL.umich.edu/.

Virtual Reality. http://www.cs.uidaho.edu/lal/cyberspace/VR/VR.html.

The VRML Repository. http://www.sdsc.edu/vrml/.

Washington State University Virtual Reality and Computer-Aided Manufacturing Lab. http://www.vrcim.wsu.edu.

Wexelblat, A. (ed.). (1993). *Virtual Reality: Applications and Explorations.* Boston: Academic Press Professional.

CHAPTER 2

Computer-Aided Design

2.1 Introduction

Computer-aided design (CAD) has revolutionized the procedures used in conceptualizing and designing mechanical parts, electrical networks, and architectural designs, among others. To understand the advantages CAD has brought to these fields, we now review the classical approach to design and study how it is done in the context of the computer-assisted approach. In this chapter we present the classical method of design, as well as the computer-assisted method, and draw some conclusions on how best to use CAD to design efficiently.

2.2 Conventional Approach to Design

To engineers, design means creating something new by enhancing existing designs, altering them to perform new functions, or simply introducing new concepts. Design is not restricted to engineers, of course, but is practiced by a large body of professionals from fashion and industrial designers to architects, sculptors, and composers.

A design is usually produced to satisfy the need of a particular person, group, or community. It is driven by the consumers, shaped by the users, and priced by the market. Therefore, to design a product, one needs to establish the problem constraints and then propose a solution that will operate within those constraints. Constraints are algebraic equations that are functions of the design parameters. They are usually in the form of equality and inequality conditions that must be met by the objective function. In the process of designing something, it will become apparent in most cases that more than one solution exists, although in some cases, no solution exists. Hence a question one would ask is, "What is the best or optimal design solution?" To answer this question, the engineer might need further information in terms of social and economic variables pertaining to the use of the product being designed. We often face decisions about factors involved in the design when specifics are not known. This requires experience and professional judgment.

Traditionally, the design process involves draftspersons and design engineers, who, once they have completed their jobs, usually present the blueprints (layouts) of the product to the manufacturing or production division. The latter employs machinists, welders, and manufacturing engineers who will try to produce the product according to the specifications given by the design group. Minor modifications in terms of dimensional precision are not referred to the design engineer, and the manufacturing engineer usually tests the product under the newly modified constraints. In many cases, analysis is limited to some basic requirements—minimum and maximum loads or ranges for certain loads, for example. Product performance failure is usually due to a lack of analysis. Professional judgment played a major role in the early days as a substitute for such analysis. It was not until malfunctions and failures had started to cause the industry to pay enormous sums of money to the victims, when insurance and liability costs were increasing at a rapid rate, that it became essential for more analysis and testing to be done before the final approval of any design. This is especially true for the automobile and commercial aircraft industries.

This ever-present possibility of litigation has profoundly affected the manner in which products are designed, manufactured, and marketed. Those involved have had to grapple with such seemingly simple issues as what constitutes a defect? What distinctions have to be drawn between manufacturing flaws and design defects? Is it ever acceptable to market a defective product? What sort of warnings would make an unacceptable product acceptable?

In general, courts have defined defects in three areas: design, manufacturing, and warning.[1] A design inadequacy is usually a characteristic of a whole line of products while a production or manufacturing flaw is usually random and atypical of the product.[2] Randomness is the defining criteria for production defects. Glass bottles that chip when the cap is removed would be a design flaw. Finding a dead mouse in a bottle of soda would be a production defect.

Consumer expectations play a large role in determining defects, the commonly accepted standard being that, in order to be legally sold, a product must be "fit for the ordinary purposes for which such goods are used."[3] The average consumer, for example, would be expected to know that ground glass in food does not meet ordinary expectations.[4] "Presumed seller knowledge" is another criteria by which defects can be defined. No reasonable person, for example, would allow a restaurant to serve salmonella-contaminated food, but we all live with the knowledge that some restaurants will, sooner or later, serve a customer tainted food. We find the risk acceptable because it is outweighed by the benefits.

---

[1]Phillips, J.J. (1988). *Products Liability*, St. Paul, MN: West Publishing, p. 11.

[2]*Ibid.*, p. 12.

[3]*Ibid.*, p. 196.

[4]*Ibid.*, p. 211.

Even unquestionably dangerous products can be marketed. Hardware stores aren't sued over axe injuries because the product carries its own implied warning: reasonable people know that using an axe can be dangerous. Similarly, a product such as a vaccine that, in some cases, is known to cause death can be marketed because of the severity of the disease it is designed to prevent. On the other hand, in *O'Brien v. Muskin Corp.* (1983), a vinyl swimming pool surface was alleged to be so slippery that it could not be safely used. As it had no redeeming societal benefit the plaintiff argued it was so dangerous that it should never have been marketed at all.[5]

Some otherwise unmarketable products can be sold by carrying a warning regarding their use. The warning must "describe the nature and the extent of the danger involved."[6] Toxic insecticides and pesticides, some of which have no antidotes when ingested, are examples.

Just the physical appearance of a product may imply that it can be used safely. A 1963 case (*Greenman v. Yuba Power Tools*) found that inadequate set screws on a power tool constituted an actionable design flaw. The fact that the product was on the market implied that it could be used safely for the jobs for which it was designed.[7]

Some manufacturing sectors have been transformed by litigation involving their products. Airbags in the automotive industries and breast implants in the medical field are two examples. Liability-driven issues in these areas are forcing companies to carry out exhaustive preliminary analysis of their products. Airbag manufacturers must prove their designs work. Breast implant manufacturers include an informational packet with each package. Their failure to include a warning of a link between implants and connective-tissue disease led, in April 1994, to the largest manufacturers agreeing to pay $4.25 billion to women with breast implants. Obviously, if they had included a warning, some of those women would not have had the implants and those who elected to receive them in spite of the warning would not have been able to claim they had been misled. The mass litigation led, in May 1995, to Dow Corning's filing for Chapter 11 bankruptcy protection.

The effect for all engineering design activities is that the possibility of litigation has become an integral part of the process.

2.3 Description of the Design Process

The steps in design are defined here as described by Ditier (1983).

1. Problem definition
2. Conceptualization
3. Synthesis
4. Analysis
5. Manufacturing

---

[5]*Ibid.*, p. 58.

[6]*Ibid.*, p. 211.

[7]*Ibid.*, p. 58.

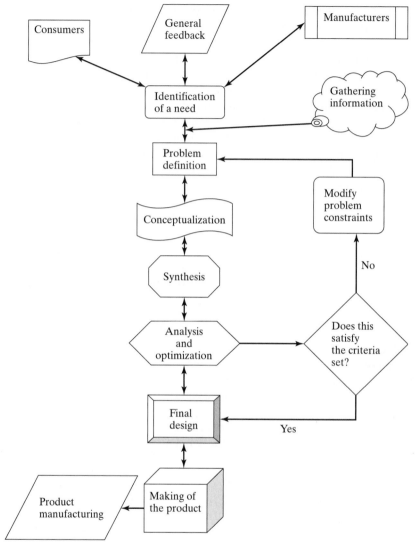

FIGURE 2.1 The steps in design.

They constitute a short summary and should serve as a guide to any project. A design module illustrating the steps in design is shown in Figure 2.1.

2.3.1 Problem Definition

A well-defined problem is the key to a successful design solution. The design process involves many stages requiring careful thinking; the problem definition helps everyone focus on the objectives of the problem and the things that must be accomplished. Engineers should not overlook the importance of this crucial first step in design, nor should they act hastily in stating the problem. The problem definition must be broadened in a reasonable fashion to make sure that the ultimate solution is the desired one. The problem definition should include the following:

1. A statement of objectives and goals to be achieved
2. A definition of constraints imposed on the design
3. Criteria for evaluating the design

Engineers will seek an optimal solution to the design problem in keeping with these requirements. Clearly stated problem definitions can foster productivity by keeping the engineer's efforts focused.

2.3.2 Conceptualization

Conceptualization is the process whereby a preliminary design satisfying the problem definition is formulated. This brings into play the engineer's knowledge, ingenuity, and experience. This phase can be either very exciting or very frustrating. The latter experience could be the result of a poor problem definition. In the conceptualization process, it is often desirable to look at some existing designs to see if they can be adapted to satisfy the problem definition. Complex problems must be broken into smaller ones in order to identify an overall design solution. In any case, conceptualization consists of generating a model in the mind and translating it back into forms and shapes to conform to a realistic model.

2.3.3 Synthesis

A successful and effective design relies a great deal on the synthesis aspect of the process which, according to Ditier (1983, p. 35), is "the process of taking elements of the concept and arranging them in the proper order, sized and dimensioned in the proper way." This is one of the most challenging tasks an engineer faces. At this stage, the information required for the proposed conceptualization is organized and a plan is devised for achieving that design. To achieve a viable synthesis decision, all the elements affecting the design, including product configuration, cost, and labor, must be considered.

2.3.4 Analysis

Analysis is concerned with the mathematical or experimental testing of the design to make sure it meets the criteria set forth in the problem definition. The engineer must test all possible factors important to the design. For instance, the engineer breaks the design problem into categories such as stress analysis, vibration, thermodynamics, heat transfer, and fluid mechanics. In each category, the design as a whole or parts of the design are tested for the ability to serve their particular function. A safety factor is usually added to make sure the design works within certain safety limits.

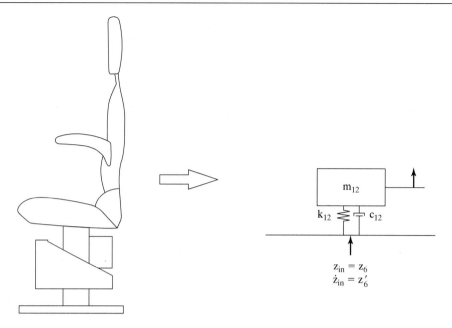

FIGURE 2.2   Vibration analysis of a car seat.

A complex design, like an automobile, is divided into realistic models. For instance, if we need to design the car suspension, we usually represent the body of the car by a mass, *M,* and the suspension by springs and dampers (linear or nonlinear). A vibration analysis is then conducted for extraction of the spring and damper parameters that yield the most comfortable ride. Figures 2.2 and 2.3 illustrate possible models used to simulate the vibration response of a car subjected to different road conditions.

Developing models (such as lumped models) requires ingenuity and experience. It is important that the models developed be realistic, simple, and mathematically testable. If a model is too complex, it is likely to take longer to analyze and hence to cost more. But if it is too simple, it might be unrealistic; that is, predictions from its analysis might not be typical of the proposed design. Simplicity is important, but the model must exhibit behavior that is close to that of the actual design, based on good engineering judgment. Ultimately, for all analyses, the models we develop must be adequate and exhibit the salient characteristics of the design under consideration.

Experimentation in analysis is another critical step in design. For instance, one might use a lumped mass model representing a car and analyze its behavior with different vibration stimuli or conduct a modal analysis experiment in which a real automobile is tested in the laboratory using shakers, transducers, and Fourier analyses. The experiment provides a true response to the model and gives a better feel for how a particular design is going to perform under the normal conditions (Figure 2.4).

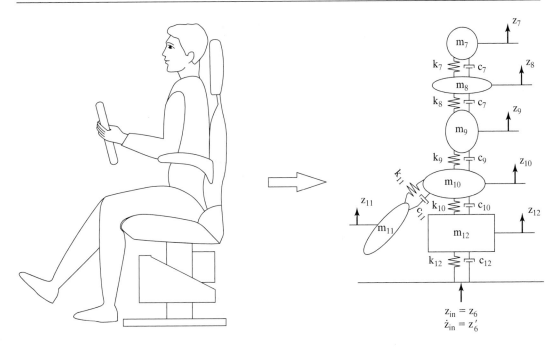

FIGURE 2.3 Vibration analysis of an occupied car seat.

In addition to mathematical and experimental verification in analysis, it is customary to examine prototypes for comfort, cushion, rigidity, and so on. Engineers use their experience to judge whether the product will meet customers' requirements.

Example 2.1 Engineering Design Process

In this section we examine four students' approaches to engineering design assignments. The design steps are followed, and a practical application is used to illustrate how the design is achieved.

Problem Definition

The assignment, to design a prosthetic leg or arm or an automatic sorting mechanism, serves as the "identification of a need." The purpose of the conveyer mechanism is to separate defective parts from those that meet the products' specs. In the case of the prosthetics, the goal of the examples given here is to achieve a design that would allow all the activities that would be possible with real limbs. In real-world applications, a project like this would be constrained by many factors. The cost of designing and prototyping such complex mechanisms would, of course, be substantial. The age of the person would be another constraint. How long will the prosthesis have to last? How would

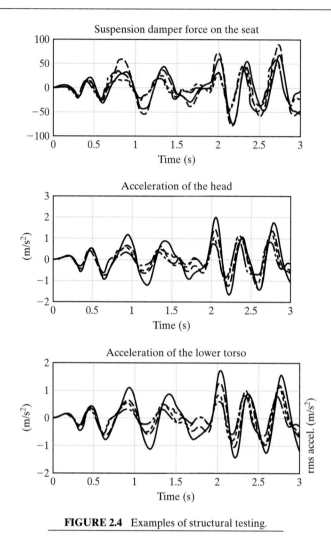

FIGURE 2.4   Examples of structural testing.

a change in the person's physique (weight fluctuation, pregnancy, etc.) affect its ability to function as designed? How would the climate affect the internal mechanisms? Will the patient be able to use improved prosthetic devices as they become available? Is there a possibility of adverse reactions to any of the materials used? How is the prosthesis affected by magnetic fields, radiation, vibration, etc.? Is it silent when in operation? Does it have to be? Should the patient expect emotional problems from the use of a prosthesis? Can the engineer design it in such a way as to lessen or eliminate them? Can its response to stimuli from the brain be rapid enough to deal with physical emergencies? Can the patient function if the prosthesis loses power? In what other ways could the prosthesis fail? How severely does this possibility of failure endanger the patient?

Obviously, many potential problems can be anticipated. Each of them should lead to a constraint; from those a comprehensive set of evaluation criteria can be created.

Conceptualization

This is the stage at which many ideas, both new ones and adaptations of existing designs, are considered. Brainstorming is an especially productive and widely used technique for creating potential solutions to problems. Most engineers find informal sketches helpful in clarifying and communicating their ideas (see Figures 2.5a and 2.5b). A common

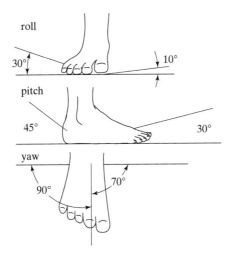

FIGURE 2.5A   Defining the range of human motion aids the engineer in conceptualizing.

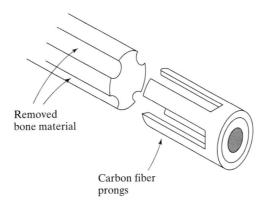

FIGURE 2.5B   Configuration of the components and the choice of materials begins at this stage.

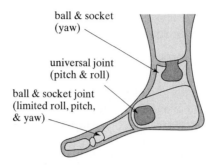

FIGURE 2.5C   The complex movements of the foot are broken down into a group of simple movements.

problem in the following design sketches was modeling the joints (see Figure 2.5c): ball-and-socket, pin, universal joints, track-and-runner arrangements, and four-bar linkages were variously considered (see Figures 2.6 and 2.7).

Synthesis

In the synthesis stage, some of the potential designs are eliminated whereas others are combined or refined until the best possible solutions are reached. Synthesis concludes with the preparation of complete CAD drawings (see Figure 2.7).

The ideas in the conceptualization stage are refined and assembled into a coherent design in the synthesis stage. The design can still be improved at this point and it may go through several permutations before proceeding to the next step:

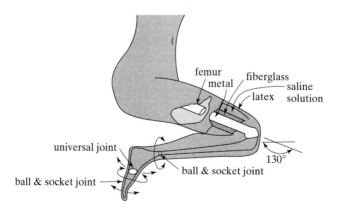

FIGURE 2.6   The mental model begins to take shape at the conceptualization stage.

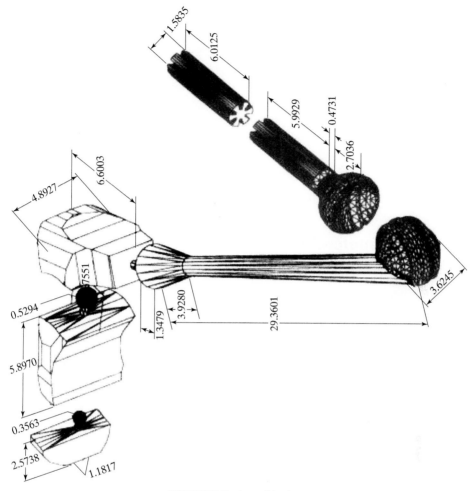

FIGURE 2.7 Assembly view.

Analysis

Our example ends here but the next step in a real design project would be analysis and optimization. The engineer would determine (either mathematically or through testing) whether the goals set forth in the problem definition step had been reached. If they had, the project would proceed toward a final design and manufacture. If those goals were not reached satisfactorily the engineer would return to the early stages of the process either to modify the problem definition or fine-tune the conceptualization stage of the design process.

End of Example 2.1

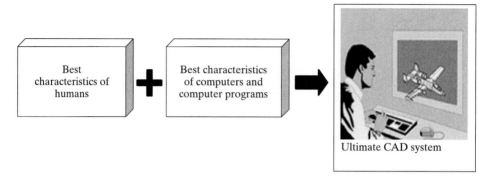

FIGURE 2.8   Characteristics of CAD.

2.4   Computer-Aided Design

CAD has gained tremendous popularity in the past decade, and it is becoming an absolutely necessary tool for any engineering task. Its application is broadening, and its success is due mostly to the mass production of powerful microprocessors and their low cost.

Computer-aided design is the blending of human and machine, working together to achieve the optimal design and manufacture of a product (Figure 2.8). The computers' graphics capability and computing power allow designers to fashion and test their ideas interactively in real time without having to create real prototypes as in conventional approaches to design.

A typical CAD system involves both design and manufacturing operations. Complex products are designed and analyzed, and their manufacturing plans are produced. The products are given the form they will have in the final stage.

How the use of the CAD system enhances designs can be demonstrated by analyzing each design step. For instance, the designer or engineer formulates the problem statement by interacting with various sources of information. From a CAD workstation, the designer can access a large body of selected information pertaining to the particular design problem at hand.

Because most companies are product-oriented and specialize in the manufacturing of certain products, it is in their best interest to build a technical library in which specific data are stored.

Complex geometries are handled with ease on a CAD workstation, allowing the user to spend more time on the design aspect of the problem.

The various design advantages CAD offers can be grouped in three areas: drafting and design, wireframe modeling, and geometric modeling.

2.4.1   Drafting and Design

Today, basic drafting and design work is done by engineers on personal computers and workstations. All drafting software operates in the same way. Points and lines that comprise a drawing are entered into the drafting system through any of the input devices available. Generally, a set of cross hairs is used to indicate the starting points of drawings. The drawing process is also aided by pull-down function menus, putting the system into different modes to construct basic elements with minimal user input. Most of the drawing packages provide a number of ways to change the drawing once it is entered into the computer. A line editor deletes lines or shows line lengths and angles. Undo commands permit the last element or specific objects to be deleted.

Most of the functions provided by drafting software are intended to increase the ease of use. For example, a specific area can be "zoomed in on" to reveal greater detail, and a drawing can be moved horizontally or vertically using the "pan" function. A grid, or series of equally spaced points, can be displayed on the screen to aid in the drawing process. The grid can help in the drawing of straight lines and give the operator a feeling of scale. The "snap" function causes entered lines to "snap" to the nearest grid point. A copy function permits an object to be duplicated anywhere else in the drawing. Another resource in computer-aided drafting is symbol libraries, which can be purchased or developed for specific applications, such as piping. A symbol library contains hundreds of predefined objects, which can be called up and placed in a drawing. Other aids are automatic dimensioning, hidden line removal, and the facility of test inclusion anywhere on the drawing using the keyboard. Layering is an important function whereby the drawing is split into distinct overlays. This function helps simplify the creation of drawings and makes plotting easier because the various separate layers can be plotted in different colors. Most of all, the design layouts or blueprints are stored in the computer and can be transmitted directly to the manufacturing division without paperwork.

2.4.2   Wireframe Modeling

Most drafting packages on the market allow the user to develop wireframe models, which represent 3D part shapes with interconnected line elements giving the simplest geometric representations of objects (Figure 2.9). Wireframe models require less computer time and memory space and provide little information about surface discontinuities. Specifying points and lines in space creates them. The interactive terminal screen is usually divided into sections showing various views of the model. The CAD system constructs lines based on user-specified points and commands chosen from an instruction menu.

The designer can temporarily erase selected lines from the screen without deleting them from the model to obtain a clearer view of the area under construction. After completing the model, the user can blank out hidden lines to give the model a solid appearance.

2.4.3   Geometric Modeling

Geometric modeling is associated with surface and solid modeling. Wireframes contain no information about the surfaces themselves, nor do they differentiate between the inside and the outside of objects. Surface models overcome many ambiguities of wireframe models. They define part geometries precisely and help produce numerically

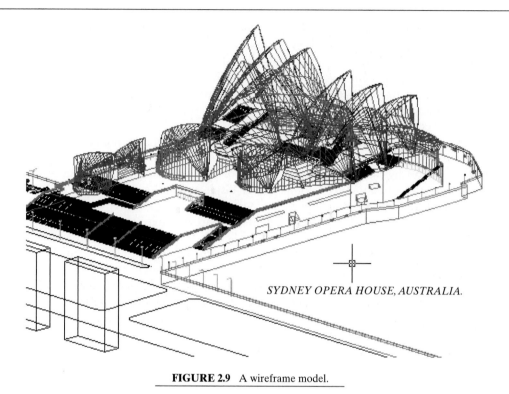

SYDNEY OPERA HOUSE, AUSTRALIA.

FIGURE 2.9　A wireframe model.

controlled (NC) machining instructions, in which the definition of structural boundaries is difficult. Connecting various types of surface elements to user-specified lines
creates surface models.

Solid modeling is used to define geometry and volume unambiguously; it provides the ultimate way to describe mechanical parts in the computer. Unlike wireframe
and surface modeling, solid modeling provides the accuracy needed for precise mechanical design. It has the potential to create a database that provides a complete description of the part to downstream applications.

Solid models are constructed in two ways: with primitives or with boundary definition. Both of these methods develop complex geometries from successive combinations of simple geometric operations. The primitive approach allows elementary shapes
such as blocks and cylinders to be combined in building-block fashion. The user positions these primitives as required and then creates a new shape with the proper
Boolean logic command. In the boundary definition approach, two-dimensional surfaces are swept through space to trace out volumes. A linear sweep translates the surface in a straight line to produce an extruded volume, a rotational sweep produces a
part with axial symmetry, and a compound sweep moves a surface through a specified
curve to generate a more complex solid. Each of these construction methods is best
suited to a particular class of shapes. Most industrial parts with planar, cylindrical, and
other simple shapes can be modeled with primitives, but complex contoured components

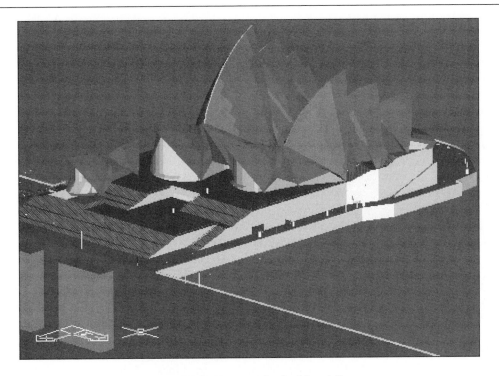

FIGURE 2.10   An example of solid modeling.

such as automobile exhaust manifolds and turbine blades are easier to model using the boundary-definition method. An example of a solid model made using SDRC's IDEAS software is shown in Figure 2.10.

The solid modeling representation of objects is discussed in greater detail, with full illustrations and examples, in Chapter 5.

2.5   Parametric and Variational Designs

Designing and drafting are the preliminary steps carried out in the manufacture of a component. Traditional mechanical CAD systems are effective tools in improving the efficiency of the drafting process, but they cannot handle the tasks of design and drafting at the same time. This forces the engineer to think simultaneously about all the design requirements and engineering relationships for each design approach.

Several new CAD systems claim to meet the needs of engineers engaged in the preliminary design of mechanical products. These systems should enhance the level of productivity of the engineers when creating or modifying designs. Two approaches that are gaining popularity for providing flexibility in the design process are parametric design and variational design.

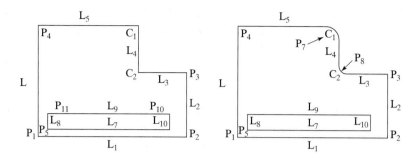

FIGURE 2.11　Parametric design of a block.

2.5.1　Parametric Design Systems

In a parametric design, the engineer selects a set of geometric constraints that can be applied for creating the geometry of the component. The geometric elements include lines, arcs, circles, and splines. A set of engineering equations can also be used to define the dimensions of the component. This simple concept of a parametric system can be explained using the following illustrations.

First, consider Figure 2.11, which represents a block with a portion removed from its side. Defining the geometries that make up the block as follows can draw the figure:

Geometric Constraints

1. Solve P_1 (origin).
2. Solve L_1 (horizontal line from origin).
3. Solve P_2 (known distance on line from P_1).
4. Solve L_2 (vertical line at 90° from P_2).
5. Solve P_3 (known distance on line from P_2).
6. Solve L_3 (horizontal line at negative 90° from P_3).
7. Solve C_2 (known distance on line from P_3 at negative 90°).
8. Solve L_4 (horizontal line from C_2).
9. Solve C_1 (known distance on line from C_2 at negative 90°).
10. Solve L_5 (horizontal line from C_1).
11. Solve P_4 (known distance on line from C_1).
12. Solve P_8 (point at a distance from C_2 at 45°).
13. Solve P_7 (point at a distance from C_1 at 45°).
14. Solve P_5 (point at a distance from P_1 at 45°).
15. Solve L_7 (known distance on line from P_5).
16. Solve P_9 (known distance on line from L_7).
17. Solve L_{10} (known distance on line from P_9).
18. Solve P_{10} (known distance on line from P_9).
19. Solve L_9 (known distance negative 90° on line from P_{10}).
20. Solve P_{11} (known distance on line from P_{10}).
21. Solve L_8 (known distance on line from P_{11}).

Thus, from a given set of geometric constraints, the basic dimensions of the component can be defined. The set of geometric constraints would be regarded as a set of instructions that when executed would create the desired geometry. Hence, any change to the known entities would yield a different picture altogether. So the objective is to create a geometric relationship between entities to minimize the time and effort spent on design.

Parametric design systems help users manipulate the length, angle, and pitch of a particular component. These systems also have the ability to record engineering relationships within a design: they enable users to pinpoint the complex relationships that exist among parts of an assembly. A simple example would be the meshing of two gears. Thus, the use of parametric design clarifies users' understanding of the engineering aspects of a component. Moreover, the parametric system can produce designs that are more meaningful than those generated by traditional CAD systems. Designers, analysts, and production engineers can work with the same solid model, extracting and adding information according to need.

The drawback of this system is that it is constrained to the set of geometric or engineering relationships provided by the engineer for creating the design of a component. The limited set of geometric constraints can make it difficult to change a parametric design model once the initial conditions have been set. These systems are best suited for design tasks that do not involve many variations in the design approach. The following are parametric models used in the design of different products.

Keypad Design *Description.* Parametric design is used to create the geometry for a keypad design because it is possible to use it for the design of any device that resembles this particular keypad, such as a remote control, pager, or mobile phone. For example, to meet the aesthetic and ergonomic design considerations, the overall contour of the keypad design is proposed as a curved surface, rather than as a simple flat design. This means that the geometry of each individual keypad is a function of where on the surface it resides relative to a provided datum. The result is a model of complex geometry that is tedious to create manually and relatively difficult to modify.

This application is a good example of using parametric design for "smart" automated geometry creation. Analysis features are created that define the relationship between the shape of the keypad and its location relative to a datum and grouped in a user-defined feature. The user-defined feature is then used to create all the individual keypads (Figure 2.12).

Turbine Blade *Description.* A traditional design begins with a set of engineering specifications, and according to these the engineer gets a set of numbers, dimensions, etc., which are then used for the modeling. Many times, the process is a progressive, iterative design, meaning one step is calculated in the design, this first step is analyzed, and based on this analysis the second step is taken; then the third step, based on results from the second, is taken. This is how the modeling tool is generally used. But if the modeling environment does not have the ability to capture these analyses, manual, iterative solving may be required on the part of the designer.

FIGURE 2.12 Keypad in the middle section of the phone.

The turbine blade shown in Figure 2.13 is a part that requires captured analyses. Many design rules for the creation of the blade are not based solely on dimensional information, but instead on measurement-type information that the engineer extracts from the model as changes are made to the model itself. For example, perhaps I need information about mass properties as the model is updated, so I can make interactive, integrated design decisions. I can now create an analysis feature, which can automatically capture this information into driving parameters, which I can use in relations.

Belt-Drive Design *Description.* This example illustrates how parametric design can be used to automate complex belt-drive design to achieve better solutions. The application, unlike any other previous example, spans a broad range of industries because many types of products require the design of a belt drive (see Figure 2.14).

The general process for designing a belt drive consists of selecting a safety factor, calculating the design horsepower, and selecting the belt pitch, center distance, sprocket combination, belt length, and belt width. The resulting design is then evaluated for qualities such as serviceability, efficiency, and compactness.

Without parametric design, an engineer must go through a great deal of trial-and-error design to fit standard part pulleys and belts to the desired belt-drive design. This process is considerably automated with parametric design. Analysis features are created to capture the lengths of the belts, clearance between pulleys, and the amount of wrap on each pulley. Analysis features also capture relations such as the pulley speed ratio and drive output speed. The results for a given belt length are then easily

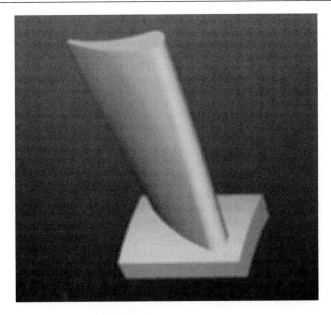

FIGURE 2.13 Turbine blade.

obtained through a feasibility study. Several independent feasibility studies can be performed for varying belt lengths and then evaluated and compared with compactness requirements, for example. If it is desired to experiment with another pulley combination, family tables can be used to make the change quickly and a follow-up feasibility

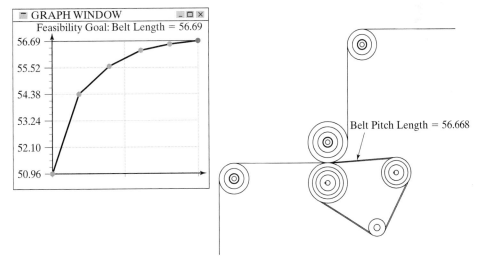

FIGURE 2.14 Design of the belt drive.

study for a desired belt length can be performed. With design exploration and solution identification so well automated, many more belt-drive designs can be tested and a better final design discovered.

2.5.2 Variational Design Systems

This technique can simultaneously solve a set of geometric constraints and engineering equations with important relationships among the elements of design. Essentially, the design is governed by a set of engineering equations relating its geometry and functions.

Unlike the parametric approach, a variational system is able to determine the positions of geometric elements and constraints. In addition, it is structured to handle the coupling between parameters in the geometric constraints and the engineering equations. The variational design concept helps the engineer evaluate the design of a component in depth instead of considering only the geometric aspects to satisfy the design relationships. This can be illustrated by the following example.

Parametric Design   In this example we will see how the geometry can be reconstructed due to the design constraints.

Consider the mechanism as shown in Figure 2.15, which consists of a rack-and-pinion gear. The rack is driven by an angular velocity applied in A to link AB. It is clear that the length of the links and the radius of the gear allow us to determine the relation between the applied angular velocity in A and the velocity of the rack. The relation between the gear and the rack is

$$R_{gear} \cdot \omega_{CD} = v_R \qquad (2.1)$$

Watch how the geometry of this mechanism is generated once the dimensions are known (Figure 2.16).

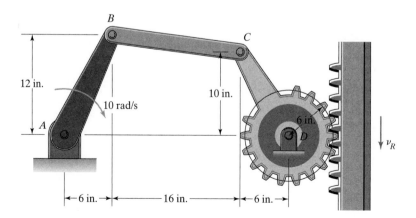

FIGURE 2.15   Design of the rack-and-pinion gear to the link.

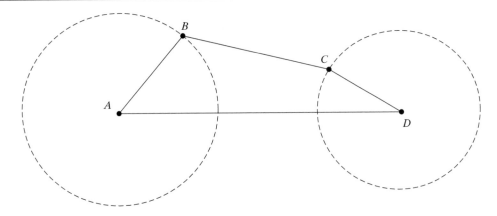

FIGURE 2.16 Geometric representation of rack-and-pinion gear to the link.

1. Position point A.
2. Position point D, knowing that it is in the same plane and according to distance $|AD|$.
3. Solve the geometric relation to position B and C.
4. Draw link AB.
5. Draw link BC.
6. Given the R_{gear} calculate the geometry and number of teeth.
7. Draw link CD.

The idea in variational design is to be able to build the mechanism based on the desired speed of the rack and the angular velocity applied to A. Because the link lengths affect the speed of the rack we should be able to use the engineering relations in terms of angular velocities and speed at a particular point to decide on the link sizes and gear radius that allow us to reconfigure the system geometry.

A change in the dimension will regenerate the drawing if the previous sequence is followed. To further see how the geometry and performances are related, let us write some geometrical relations. The following geometrical relation can be derived

$$|AB|^2 = y_B^2 + x_B^2$$
$$|BC|^2 = y_{BC}^2 + x_{BC}^2$$
$$|DC|^2 = y_{DC}^2 + x_{DC}^2$$
$$y_B + y_{BC} + y_{CD} = 0$$
$$x_B + x_{BC} + x_{CD} = |AD| \tag{2.2}$$

The velocity of point B is:

$$v_B = v_A + \omega_{AB} \times r_{AB} \tag{2.3}$$

The velocity of point C is:

$$v_C = v_D + \omega_{CD} \times r_{DC} \tag{2.4}$$

But if the velocity is expressed in terms of the velocity of B we have:

$$v_C = v_B + \omega_{BC} \times r_{BC} \tag{2.5}$$

Substituting the expression for v_B and v_C into the above equation results in:

$$y_{DC}\omega_{CD}i - x_{DC}\omega_{CD}j = y_B\omega_{AB}i - x_B\omega_{AB}j - y_{BC}\omega_{BC}i + x_{BC}\omega_{BC}j \tag{2.6}$$

If we separate the i and j components of the equation and write the geometrical relations, we obtain two equations that can be used to solve for ω_{CD} and ω_{BC}; that is:

$$f(\omega_{CD}, \omega_{AB}, \omega_{BC}, y_{DC}, y_B, y_{BC}) = 0 \tag{2.7}$$

$$g(\omega_{CD}, \omega_{AB}, \omega_{BC}, x_{DC}, x_B, x_{BC}) = 0 \tag{2.8}$$

Given the geometric relations defined by Equation 2.2 we now have a relationship between the engineering functions given by Equations 2.7 and 2.8 and the linkage geometry. Any changes to the geometry affect the solution.

Airship Design   An example in which the geometric characteristics of the design and the engineering equation are highly related is the rigid airship. A rigid airship is a steerable, self-propelled balloon that floats in the atmosphere. A low-density gas is confined in a prolate spheroid. The dimensions of the system are directly related to the payload that can be carried.

From the geometry we can say that a prolate spheroid is a surface of revolution obtained by rotating an ellipse about its major axis. The dimensions that define the spheroid are the equatorial radius of c and a longitude of a. These magnitudes allow us to calculate the area and volume needed in the equations.

$$V = \frac{4}{3} \cdot \pi \cdot a^2 c \tag{2.9}$$

$$A = 2\pi a^2 + \frac{2\pi ac^2}{\sqrt{c^2 - a^2}} \sin^{-1}\left(\frac{\sqrt{c^2 - a^2}}{c}\right) \tag{2.10}$$

Because a is bigger than c we can define a constraint relation such that

$$c = q \cdot a$$

$$q \in (0, 1)$$

In the free-body diagram of the airship shown in Figure 2.17, all the forces affecting the dirigible are shown.

From the equilibrium conditions we have

$$\sum F = 0 \tag{2.11}$$

$$E = L + S + G \tag{2.12}$$

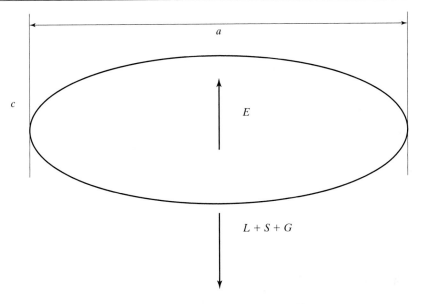

FIGURE 2.17 Free-body diagram of airship.

where the E is the force due to the difference in pressures from inside the dirigible and the atmosphere (flotation force), S is the force due to the mass of the shell, and G is the force due to the mass of the gas. Another external force to account for is the payload L. In order for the dirigible to float, the equilibrium force equation must be satisfied. This will provide us with the requirements needed between the different forces involved as well as the limit of the load that can be carried by the dirigible.

From the physical point of view the following information is needed: The density of the airship gas ρ_g, the density of the atmosphere ρ_a, the area density of the shell confining the dirigible gas σ. Therefore, we define the corresponding forces:

$$E = V \cdot \rho_a \tag{2.13}$$

$$S = \sigma \cdot A$$

$$G = V \cdot \rho_g$$

Substituting these expressions in the equations of equilibrium we obtain:

$$V(a, q) \cdot \rho_a = L + A(a, q) \cdot \sigma + V(a, q) \cdot \rho_g \tag{2.14}$$

If we analyze this equation and we know the physical properties of the problem we can see that the above equation leads to a function with three variables, that is:

$$f(a, q, L) = 0 \tag{2.15}$$

For each value of a and q we can find the maximum payload the airship is capable of carrying. The graph in Figure 2.18 shows how we can determine the payload requirement from an engineering equation, which needs the geometrical parameters, essential

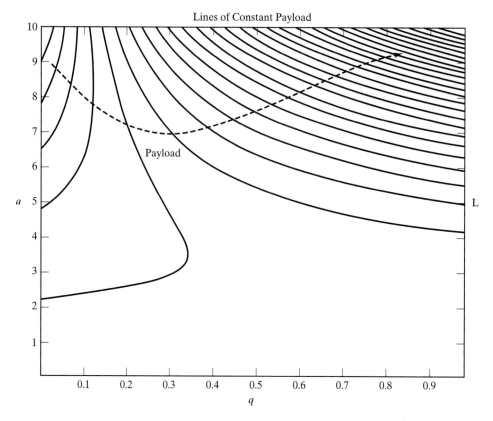

FIGURE 2.18   Load necessary for the airship.

to the design. The engineer would be quite satisfied if the airship is designed and built based on a set of engineering equations that provides the necessary information to link the load requirement to the physical shape and form of the airship.

Pendulum Design   Systems may change their engineering properties because of a change in their geometry. Consider the case of the pendulum, where its natural frequency depends on the geometry of the pendulum and its mass. Figure 2.19 shows a pendulum swinging about a hinge at point O.

The geometry depends on the parameters: a, b, α, and β. The thickness is not displayed in the drawing but it is assumed to be e. The density of the pendulum is ρ. One needs to keep in mind that the objective of this problem is to be able to provide a complete design drawing of the pendulum once the natural frequency of the pendulum has changed or needs to be changed. In the use of variational design the overall scheme must be one in which engineering principles are used to define certain geometric parameters that are needed in the CAD design of the product.

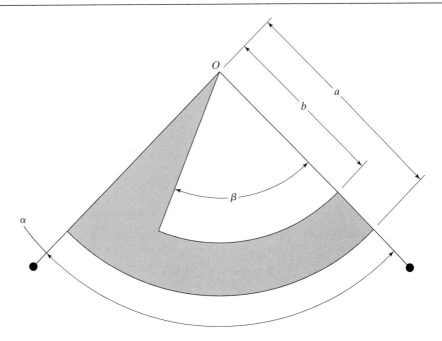

FIGURE 2.19 Movement of pendulum.

The general equation of oscillation without friction for a rigid body is given by:

$$I\ddot{\theta} + Mgl \cdot \sin(\theta) = 0 \qquad (2.16)$$

I is the momentum of inertia about O, M is the mass, and l is the distance from O to the center of the mass of the pendulum. We can see how the geometry affects not only the momentum of inertia and the mass, but position of the center of mass, and therefore the equilibrium of the pendulum.

For small oscillations the equation can be simplified further to:

$$I\ddot{\theta} + Mgl\theta = 0 \qquad (2.17)$$

The natural frequency is seen to be:

$$\omega^2 = \frac{Mgl}{I} \qquad (2.18)$$

We need to calculate the values for M, l, and I, depending on the geometrical information provided by $a, \alpha, b,$ and β. The following are the explicit relations for those parameters:

$$M = \frac{1}{2}\alpha a^2\, e\rho - \frac{1}{2}\beta b^2\, e\rho \qquad (2.19)$$

$$I = \frac{a^4\,\alpha}{4}e\rho - \frac{b^4\,\beta}{4}e\rho \qquad (2.20)$$

The coordinates of the center mass in the XY plane are found to be:

$$X = \frac{\frac{2}{3}a^3 \cos\left(\frac{\alpha}{2}\right)\sin\left(\frac{\alpha}{2}\right) + \frac{2}{3}b^3 \cos\left(\frac{\beta}{2}\right)\sin\left(\frac{\beta}{2}\right)}{\frac{1}{2}\alpha a^2 + \frac{1}{2}\alpha b^2} \qquad (2.21)$$

$$Y = \frac{\frac{2}{3}a^3 \sin^2\left(\frac{\alpha}{2}\right) + \frac{2}{3}b^3 \sin^2\left(\frac{\beta}{2}\right)}{\frac{1}{2}\alpha a^2 + \frac{1}{2}\alpha b^2} \qquad (2.22)$$

Hence, the magnitude of the length of the pendulum is obtained

$$l = \sqrt{X^2 + Y^2} \qquad (2.23)$$

From the geometry we can see how there are some limitations on the parameters where,

$$b < a$$
$$\beta < \alpha \qquad (2.24)$$

For the purpose of the analysis we define the following relations:

$$\beta = p \cdot \alpha$$
$$b = q \cdot a$$
$$p \in (0, 1)$$
$$q \in (0, 1) \qquad (2.25)$$

By inspection of the previous relations we can infer that the natural frequency will depend on the geometry. Now we have a variational design controlled by the following equation

$$\omega = \frac{Mgl}{I} = f(a, \alpha, p, q) \qquad (2.26)$$

We can set some constraints on the design of the pendulum, such as the desired mass, desired values for α, a, q, or p. For this analysis let us set a maximum value for a and α. This constraint could result from limits due to the housing of the pendulum.

$$a = 1$$
$$\alpha = 1\ radian = 57.2958^0$$

In this case we reduce the natural frequency equation to

$$\omega = \frac{Mgl}{I} = f(p, q) \qquad (2.27)$$

The values for the natural frequency are plotted for various values of p and q. The graph in Figure 2.20 will be used to relate the design parameters, which are derived from an engineering equation defining the natural frequency of the system.

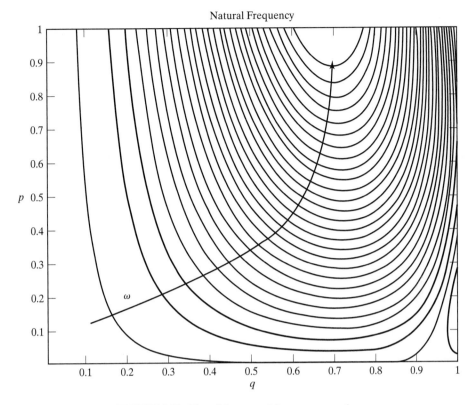

FIGURE 2.20   Plot of the natural frequency equation.

Variational design has the ability to incorporate optimization into the design environment. The engineer can specify both equality and inequality design constraints. The objective function is a set of both dependent and independent variables that are optimized (minimized or maximized) relative to one or more independent variables. Figure 2.21 shows a nonoptimized design, wherein the sides of the rectangle are not in

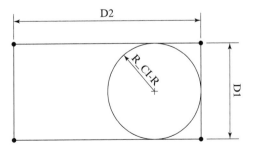

FIGURE 2.21   Design model to be optimized.

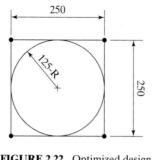

FIGURE 2.22   Optimized design.

contact with the boundary of the circle. The objective is to minimize the area bounded by the rectangle at a constant value. The optimized result is shown in Figure 2.22.

2.6   Engineering Analysis and CAD

Analysis is of two types: analytical and experimental. Both are performed to assess product performance (Figure 2.23).

2.6.1   Analytical Methods

In the analytical approach, different types of analyses can be carried out using various software in computer-aided design. These include finite-element analysis, kinematical analysis and synthesis, and static and dynamic analysis.

Finite-Element Analysis   Finite-element analysis (FEA) is a computer-assisted technique for determining stresses and deflections in a structure. The method divides a structure into small elements with known shapes for which a mathematical solution can be found; then the global problem is solved using an assembly procedure.

The first step in FEA is the creation of a model that breaks the structure into simple standardized shapes and plots it on a common coordinate grid system. The coordinate points are called nodes and serve as the locations in the model where output data are provided. Nodal stiffness properties are then calculated by the finite-element program for each element and arranged into matrices within the computer. These parameters are then processed with applied loads and boundary conditions or calculations of displacement, natural frequencies, strains, and so on.

In most cases, finite-element models are developed for prototype designs for which experimental data exist so that FEA results can be cross-checked and design modifications can be made. Modifications are also tested for actual prototypes. We will examine the finite-element method in greater detail in Chapter 6.

Kinematics and Synthesis   Mechanisms are devices used to transfer motion and/or force from a given source to an output device. The efficiency with which this transfer is

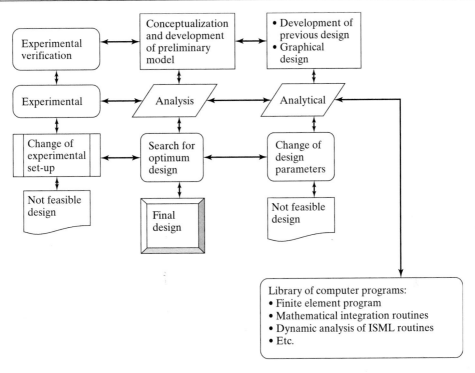

FIGURE 2.23 Process of engineering analysis in design.

accomplished depends on the mechanism design. General-purpose programs are available today to assist engineers in the kinematic analysis and synthesis of those systems. Kinematics starts with the mechanism design. It calculates large displacements, velocities, and accelerations of mechanisms without regard to the forces acting on them. The mechanism assumes zero degrees of freedom, which means that each degree of freedom (coordinate) is constrained to a particular type of motion. The advantage of combining the study of mechanisms with CAD is that it enables the design's output to be optimized and it eliminates interferences between links.

Synthesis analysis is concerned with arriving at the best characteristics of a mechanism through a set of computer iterations. The designer provides the parameters of the mechanism and the program develops the alternatives.

The first step before doing a synthesis analysis is to make decisions about various parameters of the mechanism, such as the number of links, joints, joint types, and connectivity of links by specifying which links are fixed. The basic linkage types are defined as kinematic chains within the program. The synthesis analysis is then carried out, and the mechanism structures satisfying the design objectives are determined. These programs are generally used to design four-bar linkages, although they can be used to design six-bar linkages. Some kinematic synthesis programs use graphics to make the software user-friendly. The user specifies points and motion vectors via interactive graphics that can be easily moved about the screen. After a number of points have

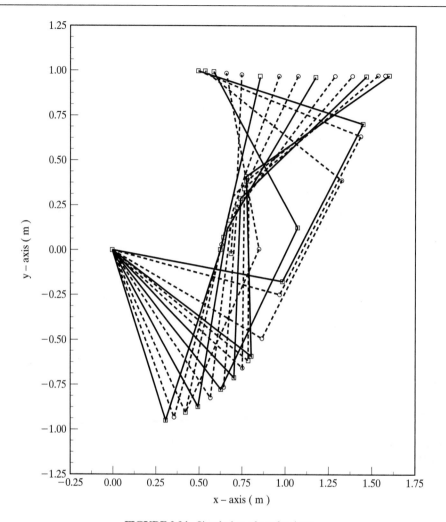

FIGURE 2.24 Simulation of mechanisms.

been specified, the program displays all possible locations of additional points to complete the mechanism. Some software also allows the user to animate the mechanism on the screen in order to check the locations (Figure 2.24).

Static Analysis and Dynamic Analysis Static analysis combines motion analysis with mass properties and force input data to determine positions and joint reaction forces of mechanisms at rest. Static analysis can also be done on mechanisms at various points in their range of movement if zero velocity is assumed. Static models can have multiple degrees of freedom. Motion and force are uncoupled in this type of analysis. In static analysis, we are mostly concerned with the reaction forces on the mechanical systems and their joints' interconnection forces. Knowing these latter forces is useful in stress analysis to determine engineering criteria such as performance, reliability, and fatigue.

Dynamic analysis uses mass properties and forces to calculate positions, velocities, accelerations, and joint and constraint reaction forces of all model parts when motion is coupled to forces in the system. Analysis is done in discrete steps within a specified time interval. Each degree of freedom in a dynamic model is associated with an independent coordinate for which the analyst has to specify both the initial position and velocity. The computer models for dynamic analysis include geometric data and mass properties of the structure as well as applied forces. The model is generally created through part, joint, marker, force, and generator statements that are input by the user.

Part statements define the geometry, mass, and moment of inertia of each rigid part of the structure. Joint statements describe contacts between moving parts that hold the assembly together. Joints can be specified as providing translational and rotational movement, including that of revolute, screw, spherical, universal, cylindrical, and translational joints. Marker statements provide a point or coordinate system fixed on each part orienting it to other parts and together defining the overall configuration of the system. Internal reaction forces are selected from a library of standard force elements such as dampers and linear springs. User-written routines can also be used to define additional parameters. Basic geometric data from CAD programs can be sent through direct interfaces. Because complete geometric description is not required, mechanical analysis can be used early in the design cycle, before the final configuration is known. Engineers can design the system knowing only mass and inertia characteristics.

The dynamic analysis output is typically available in tabular form. Graphics can be produced showing output such as force-versus-time or force-versus-displacement characteristics. In some cases, animation is reproduced from the combination of dynamic analysis data and geometry representation of the object. Software capable of performing such a task includes ADAMS, DADS, DISCOS, DYAMUS, DARS, and DYNACOMBS.

2.6.2 Experimental Testing

The second aspect of analysis deals with experimental methods in which testing is conducted on prototypes and models either to extract material properties or to validate performance characteristics of a particular design. Testing in the conventional design process is to qualify the design after manufacturing. The goal in computer-aided design is to use testing throughout the development cycle and to make better use of the test data through more advanced analysis techniques and to integrate these with other disciplines involved in design.

Initial testing can be done on a prototype or on different components to understand the model's response to certain loading conditions. Experimental data are extremely useful in the analysis of models for which analytical solutions are not reliable. This data can also be used to refine finite element models for large-scale analysis. The integration of experimental testing with analytical tools results in more effective engineering analysis. Computer-aided design provides the ultimate tool for combining such methods with graphics capabilities to allow the designer to arrive at realistic and effective designs in a minimum of time.

Additional experimental analyses include fatigue testing to estimate part life from strain gauge measurements, modal testing to extract natural frequency and mode shapes, response functions, and a number of engineering functions in heat transfer, fluid dynamics, and thermodynamics.

Example 2.2   Using CAD in Steel Frame Design

This example shows how CAD is used in the analysis and design of a tower crane. The analysis is carried out on a simplified version of the tower crane. The designer uses the computer for defining and redefining the structural attributes to control and perform the analysis and design.

The classification of the computer-aided design process is carried out first. In the problem definition section, the engineer defines the layout of the structured model—how the structure is supported, the initial properties of the structural members, and the applied loads. The steps followed during the design are the structural layout, structural properties, load combination, analysis, and design evaluation.

Because the software has interactive computer graphics, the engineer gets a continual graphic feedback. Another advantage of using CAD is the ability to change the type of unit measurement at any phase in the design. The terms used in the design and analysis of a crane are listed in Figure 2.25, which also shows the cross sections used in the construction.

The support conditions are represented clearly in the problem definition stage. So any type of support conditions, including spring and skew supports, can be assigned to any node of the structure. Defining the nodes and creating beam elements create the finite-element model of the crane. The boundary conditions are then defined in terms of restraints and loads on the tower crane.

The next phase is using the software to solve the problem. This is the process of determining forces at each finite element in the model. In the postprocessing phase an analysis data set is selected for processing. The deformed geometry plot is displayed. It is possible to modify and redisplay the deformed geometry. The force and stress diagram can be plotted on the screen. The deformed geometry plot and force and stress diagrams are shown in Figure 2.26. The designer can also study the displacements of the structure on application of different loading conditions.

Moreover, the engineer can interact with the structure at this design stage and use the alternative paths to the solution of the problem because the following facilities are available:

1. Modular generation
2. Frame combination
3. Selective addition and deletion of members
4. Distortion of dimensions
5. Isolating any substructure for analysis

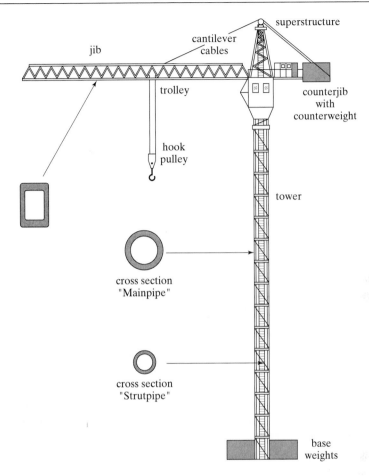

FIGURE 2.25 Terms used in crane construction (courtesy SDRC, Milford, Ohio).

Once the final design is achieved, the engineer can utilize the facility in CAD to select which drawings to make.

End of Example 2.2

2.7   Computer-Aided Engineering (CAE)

What is computer-aided engineering? According to J.R. Lemon, CAE is a product design and development philosophy that combines three key engineering elements in an integrated environment for all engineering functions within each stage of the product development cycle. These elements are applications (performance, structural integrity,

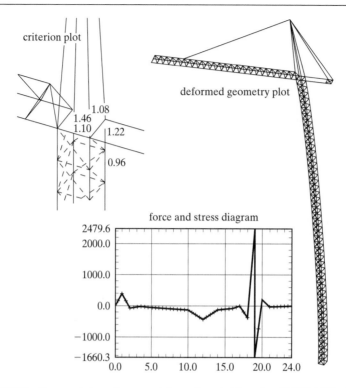

FIGURE 2.26   Force and stress diagrams, deformation plot (courtesy SDRC, Milford, Ohio).

reliability, costs, etc.), facilities (hardware/software), and technology (data and infor-mation management). Thus, the CAE approach results in the restructuring and stream-lining of the entire engineering process itself instead of the automation of specific steps in the current process, such as has been the case in computer-aided design (CAD) and computer-aided manufacturing (CAM) activities.

The CAE approach places emphasis in terms of time and money on the initial conceptual design phases. This revised allocation of resources results in extensive analysis and testing to guide product design iterations in the computer as opposed to making physical prototypes. This is a major departure from current methods in most mechanical industries, where prototype manufacture and tests are the fundamental means of evaluating product performance and quality. However, the need for proto-types is not eliminated, but the reduction in the number of prototypes needed before full production results in significant time and cost savings.

The CAE approach to mechanical product development emphasizes system ana-lytical modeling and analysis techniques at the earliest phase of design, that is, concep-tual design. The process starts with an integrated set of total system simulations of the entire product. Each alternative product concept is mathematically modeled as an entire system. At this point, overall product designers have the flexibility of defining significantly varying concepts in order to minimize weight, reduce energy consumption

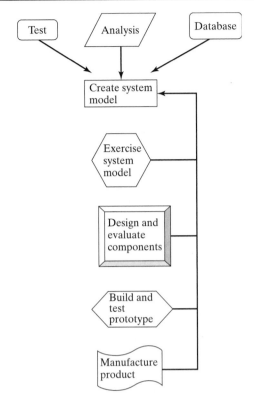

FIGURE 2.27   CAE structure as described in Lemon.

and maximize performance for acceptable product concepts.

Detailed component and subassembly design specifications are derived from system models by exercising computer simulations under severe environmental conditions and external product loadings. In addition, internal loads, duty cycles, and constraints acting on components and subassemblies at interfaces and connection points are derived from system models. System modeling and early development of product alternatives on the computer are essential differences compared with today's developments that rely on physical prototypes and build-and-test methods. The CAE approach to manufacturing new products is shown in Figure 2.27. An isolated approach to automation using CAD technology does not provide sufficient engineering effectiveness to meet most current manufacturing needs.

The new CAE approach attempts to integrate and automate various engineering functions in the entire product development process:

1. Design
2. Analysis
3. Testing

4. Drafting
5. Documentation
6. Project management
7. Data management
8. Process planning
9. Tool design
10. Numerical control
11. Quality assurance

Improved product quality, increased market share, and greater profitability depend on efficient and effective CAE integration and implementation. This is why CAE implementation has become a strategic issue in mechanical-related industries worldwide.

2.8   Integrated Database-Management Systems in CAE

Translators allow the supporting data of various other applications to interface with the central product data-management system. This capability forms the basis of effective integration of tests, analysis, design drafting, documentation, and manufacturing functions.

The application database-management systems (Figure 2.28) associated with each application workstation handle active data developed or required by the application itself. When a task is completed, appropriate data are transferred to the product computer and are used at the product level in conjunction with data and information developed by other applications. When the data are transferred from an active application status, they are processed and checked through an intermediate set of procedures and techniques to ensure that they conform to requirements, desired formats, and completeness on the product computer. Similarly, when a product development project is completed and moves into production, product data are transferred from the product computer to the corporate data-management system on a mainframe. Corporate data, of course, must be secure and protected for very long periods of time, especially in industries in which liability requirements are stringent.

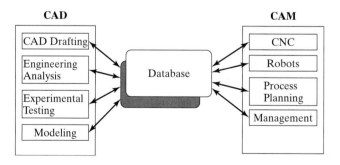

FIGURE 2.28   Database-management system, as described by Sidall (1972).

2.9 CAE Product Development

As in conventional design, CAD processes rely heavily on testing prototypes. CAE involves computer simulation of an entire system or product. Although CAD addresses only the physical description of the product, the CAE process analyzes functional characteristics such as vibration, noise, and service life—computer simulation is used to determine precise loads early so that components can be designed based on that criterion. This practice is in contrast to the traditional build-and-test approach in which component design testing relies greatly on computer simulation.

Computer simulation reduces the time and cost associated with product development. More importantly, CAE designs are optimized, in part because of the engineering effort aimed at the evaluation of alternative designs.

The heart of CAE development is the mathematical representation of an entire structure in the computer. Combining data on individual components and subassemblies creates the model. These data can come either from finite-element analysis, modal testing, or data banks, depending on which types of data are most readily available. The system model is tested and refined in an iterative process until a detailed optimal configuration is created. The first simulation is generally coarse and not necessarily intended to yield precise results. However, successive simulations suggest changes that produce an increasingly refined model. The next step is to apply loads determined from coarse modeling to model individual components. Because component designs can alter the overall performance of the system, the refined component models are inserted back into the system model, which is tested once again. These designer iterations gradually transform coarse component descriptions into increasingly optimal finite-element models. A prototype is then built and tested with modal analysis and stress-testing techniques. The results of these tests can indicate whether further changes to the system model are necessary. Prototype testing thus provides data for refinement of the system model, while the model guides the designer in understanding prototype behavior. After the prototype is redefined, the final configuration is released to manufacturing.

2.10 CAE Implementation

Implementation of an overall CAE system and its associated technologies must be planned carefully. Implementation should proceed step by step because it is not possible to switch off today's design, development, and manufacturing processes and switch on the CAE approach at the same time. As a first step toward the implementation of CAE, existing problems should be solved to gain knowledge and familiarity with the CAE system's capabilities and behavior.

A design audit is not simply a learning exercise; it is an important step toward extending a basic product to a family of new products or to fix problems that may have developed.

The next phase involves new product design and development. The CAE tools should be applied to a new and unique product design for which new concepts have the potential of providing strategic product quality and market share advantages. An optimal hardware system along with a similar integrated and distributed database-management system should be configured for in-house use and expected long-range expansion requirements. Software that performs efficiently should also be brought in house if it is economically justified.

Along with these tasks, outside CAE consultants are recommended to help guide and develop an overall CAE implementation plan. Educational programs and seminars in all aspects of the implementation of CAE are essential for all levels within an organization. Once CAE tools are implemented and the in-house organization is structured to suit the particular CAE implementation philosophy, the outside consultant's role can be reduced to solving difficult problems.

A central group to maintain and ensure the commonality of methods and facilities within various departments must be formed. This group should develop CAE capabilities and applications software only when they are essential and are not available from reputable suppliers. Because CAE is not a product or a piece of hardware but a design philosophy, corporate management must be committed to this concept and willing to expend the resources necessary to bring CAE into reality. CAE is successful only when top corporate management makes the decision and assumes a leadership role in the implementation of the CAE approach.

2.11   Simulation-Based Design and Beyond

Simulation-based-design (SBD) methods, in which a system's entire life cycle from the development of concepts and prototyping to testing and maintenance is simulated before the physical prototyping stage begins, are already being employed. The car body and valvetrain model shown in Figures 2.29 and 2.30 were created through SBD. In that project virtual prototyping ensured that the system requirements were ultimately achievable. These prototypes reflected not only the design simulations but also the scheduling, assembly, process-flow, and machine-tool simulations.

What can we expect beyond SBD? A new approach to aerospace systems design and development from NASA's Langley Research Center in Hampton, Virginia, the Jet Propulsion Laboratory in Pasadena, California, and the University of Virginia's Center for Advanced Computational Technology may provide a clue. Spurred by the demand for scientific results in a reasonable time at an affordable cost, they have developed the intelligent-synthesis environment (ISE). This was made possible by three developments: ultrafast computers, high-capacity communications, and the collaboration of diverse teams.

In what is termed an "immersive telepresence," participants will not only be in the same virtual space; they will also be able to walk around each other and exchange objects. This experience will maintain its transparency without the encumbrance of special glasses, gloves, etc. ISE also integrates parametric, variational, and feature-based solid modeling methods to produce a single, globally accessible product model (Figure 2.31).

Where as SBD allows engineers at widely remote locations to collaborate on projects, ISE will link scientists, design teams, manufacturers, suppliers, and consultants to collaborate on all stages of even the most complex systems. ISE will promote increased

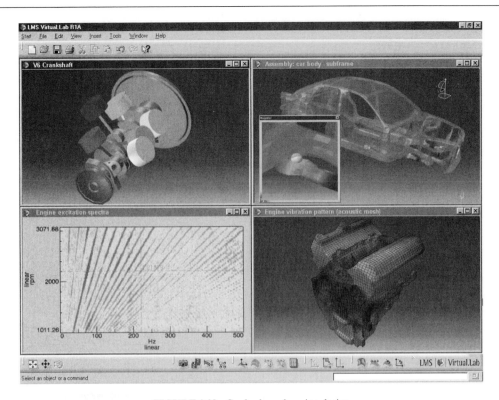

FIGURE 2.29 Car body and engine design.

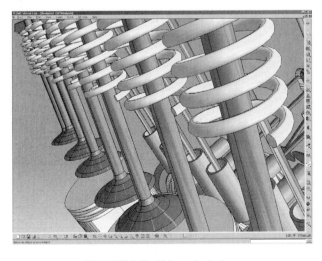

FIGURE 2.30 Valvetrain design.

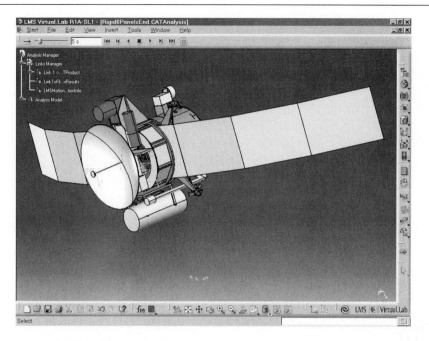

FIGURE 2.31 ISE facilitates the simulation of entire space missions.

creativity and productivity among the scientists, engineers, and technicians by allowing highly interactive multimedia information to be easily shared. Engineers immersed in virtual design environments will be able to create and modify designs in real time despite being widely dispersed physically. Ever-changing combinations of teams will be able to "plug into" a project as necessary. Because a model can be analyzed throughout the design process, it reduces both the time required for simulations and the number of prototypes that have to be fabricated (Figure 2.32).

FIGURE 2.32 With ISE, engineering teams will enjoy unprecedented freedom at every stage of a system's design.

ISE will make the translation from CAD drawings to the virtual environment seamless. The entire life cycle of a product, from assembly to disposal, can then be simulated and its long-range performance optimized.

In terms of the manufacturing process, ISE will reduce development times and costs while increasing the ease of manufacture and quality of the resulting products. For the engineer, it will nurture creativity and cultivate cultural interactivity. This increase in flexibility is almost certain to change fundamentally the nature of the engineering process.

PROBLEMS

2.1. Most drafting software packages allow the user to develop geometric models (Figure P2.1). Describe how parametric design could be used in designing the motorcycle so that it can be modified to be used for both women and men.

    The designer can temporarily change certain functions without changing the look of the motorcycle.

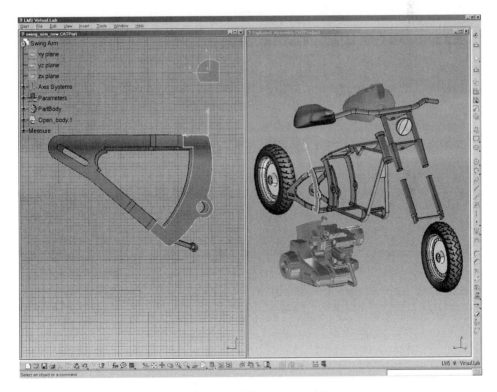

FIGURE P2.1 Motorcycle model.

2.2 Variational design. Surface models overcome many ambiguities of wireframe models, which define part geometries precisely and help produce numerically controlled machining instructions in which the definition of structural boundaries is difficult. Connecting various types of surface elements to user-specified lines creates surface models. Define the engineering functions necessary to make the airship balloon carry twice as much load in Example 2.5.2. What are the design parameters responsible for the geometry creation?

2.3. Provide the necessary design steps as shown in Example 2.1 if you were asked to design an artificial hand for someone who lost part of his lower arm including the hand.

2.4. Consider the mechanism shown in Figure 2.15 and provide the explicit form of Equations 2.7 and 2.8. Provide an equation that defines the number of teeth for the pinion gear given the radius R. Show how the rack speed U_R can be controlled by modifying R.

2.5. For the airship problem shown in Figure 2.18 we have decided that the ship takes the form of a cylinder. Provide the necessary information and derive the engineering function that allows us to determine the maximum pay load requirements. Provide a graphical solution.

2.6. For the pendulum shown in Figure P2.6, derive the engineering equations for the natural frequency of the pendulum that is a function of the geometry and mass. The idea is two-fold: (a) be able to create the design and necessary drawings using parametric design; and (b) adjust the natural frequency by changing the design parameters either l or m.

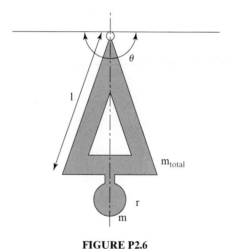

FIGURE P2.6

BIBLIOGRAPHY

An Introduction to Computer-Aided Engineering. (1982). CAE Annual.

Appletone, E.L. "Image Processing and Visualization." *DEC Professional*, July 1989, p. 38.

Angell, M. (1996). *Science on Trial.* New York: Norton.

ASMENET: home page for ASME International. *http://www.asme.org/.*

Bad Human Factors Designs. http://www.baddesigns.com/.

Beercheck, R.C. "Recreation Equipment: Engineering the Competitive Edge." *Machine Design*, June 7, 1990, pp. 58–63.

Berkely, P. (1984). *Computer Operations Training: A Strategy for Change.* New York: Van Nostrand Reinhold.

Bernstein, H.M., & Lemer, A.C. (1996). *Solving the Innovation Puzzle: Challenges Facing the U.S. Design and Construction Industry.* ASCE Press.

Birmingham, R. (1997). *Understanding Engineering Design: Context, Theory, and Practice.* Upper Saddle River, NJ: Prentice-Hall.

Buchanan, R., & Margolin, V. (1995). *Discovering Design: Explorations in Design, Studies.* Chicago: University of Chicago Press.

Chang, D., "PCs Offer More Options for Less Money." *Mechanical Engineer*, May 1989, p. 68.

Chung, J.C.H., and Schussel, M.D. (1989). *Comparison of Variational and Parametric Design.* Milford, OH: SDRC.

Computer Aided Production Engineering Tools. http://www.tecnomatix.com/.

"Computer System Design Reflects B-2's Complexity." *Aviation Week*, Nov. 28, 1998, pp. 26–27.

Crosheck, J., and Ford, M. "Simulation Takes Three Wheeler for a Spin." *Mechanical Engineering*, Nov. 1998, pp. 48–51.

Dieter, J. (1983). *Engineering Design.* New York: McGraw-Hill.

Doebelin, E.O. (1998). *System Dynamics: Modeling, Analysis, Simulation, Design.* New York: Dekker.

Dym, C.L. (1994). *Engineering Design: A Synthesis of Views.* Cambridge, UK: Cambridge University Press.

Gajski, D.D. (1997). *Principles of Digital Design.* Upper Saddle River, NJ: Prentice-Hall.

Groover, M.P., & Zimmers, E.W., Jr. (1984). *CAD: Computer-Aided Design and Manufacturing.* Englewood Cliffs, NJ: Prentice-Hall.

Holtzschue, L., & Noriega, E. (1997). *Design Fundamentals for the Digital Age.* New York: Van Nostrand Reinhold.

Hordeski, M.F. (1986). *Cad/Cam Techniques.* Reston, VA: Reston.

IDEAS (1990). *"Getting Started" Finite Element Modelling and Analysis.* Milford, OH: SDRC.

Introduction to Engineering Design. http://fulton.seas.Virginia.EDU/~shj2n/.

Jones, P.H. (1998). *Handbook of Team Design: A Practicioner's Guide to Team Systems Development.* New York: McGraw-Hill.

Karaiskos, P., & Fulton, N. (1995). *AutoCAD for Mechanical Engineers and Designers.* New York: Wiley.

Lemon, J.R. *http://www.decabe.com/Dacabe/News/corpNews2.*

Lemon, J.R. *http://www.personalengin.umich.edu/skikuchi/research/optishape1.pdf.*

Lemon, J.R., Tolani, S.K. and Klosterman, A.L., (1980). *Integration and Implementation of Computer-Aided Engineering and Related Manufacturing Capabilities into Mechanical Product Development Process*, FRG: Gi-Jahrestagung.

Medland, A.J., and Burnett, P. (1986). *CAD/CAM in Practice: A Manager's Guide to Understanding and Using CAD/CAM.* New York: Halstead Press.

Miller, A.R. (1989). *The ABC's of AutoCAD*, (2nd ed.). San Francisco: SYBEX.

Morgan, C.L., & Zampi, G. (1995). *Virtual Architecture.* New York: McGraw-Hill.

Naecker, P.A. "Workstations and Graphics Terminals: Room for Both." *DEC Professional*, July 1989, p. 48.

"New Design, Production Tools Will Play a Key Role in B-2 Cost." *Aviation Week*, Dec. 5, 1998, pp. 18–21.

Nilssen, A. "Workstations Still Hold The Edge." *Mechanical Engineer*, May 1989, p. 68.

Nobbe, T.A. "Giving Cars a Mind of their Own, Machine Design." June 21, 1990, pp. 56–59.

Ohtani, N., Duke, S., & Ohtani, S. (1997). *Japanese Design and Development*. New York: Design Council/Gower.

Pao, Y.C. (1984). *Elements of Computer-Aided Design and Manufacturing*. New York: Wiley.

Petroski, H. (1996). *Invention by Design: How Engineers Get from Thought to Thing*. Cambridge, MA: Harvard University Press.

Petroski, H. (1985). *To Engineer Is Human: The Role of Failure in Successful Design*. New York: St. Martin.

Phillips, J.J. (1993). *Products Liability* (4th ed.). St. Paul, MN: West.

Poor A. "16-Bit VGA Cards Stretch the Standard." *PC*, July 1989, p. 145.

Product Design and Development home page. *http://www.pddnet.com/*.

Ryan, D.L. (1994). *Computer-Aided Graphics and Design* (3rd ed.). New York: Dekker.

Sandler, B.Z. (1994). *Computer-Aided Creativity: A Guide for Engineers, Managers, and Inventors*. New York: Von Nostrand Reinhold.

Sidall, J. (1972). *Analytical Decision Making in Engineering Design*. Englewood Cliffs, NJ: Prentice Hall.

"Smart Cars and Highways Go Global." *IEEE, Spectrum*, May 1991, pp. 26–36.

Sriram, D., & Adey, R.A. (1987). *Knowledge-Based Expert Systems in Engineering*. Southampton, England: Computational Mechanics.

Swift, K.G. (1985). *Process Selection: From Design to Manufacture*. New York: Wiley.

Teicholz, E. (1985). *CAD/CAM Handbook*. New York: McGraw-Hill.

Teicholz, E. (1985). *CAD Handbook*. New York: McGraw-Hill.

The World-Wide Web Virtual Library. *Mechanical Engineering. http://cdr.stanford. edu/html/WWW-ME/home.html*.

CHAPTER 3

Transformation and Manipulation of Objects

3.1 Introduction

The geometrical representation of objects on a CAD workstation is based on computer graphics. Computer graphics can be defined as the generating, presenting, and manipulating of an object and the different views that can be presented with the help of computer hardware, software and graphic devices combined. The integrated system is used by the designer to create, display and store the desired database. How are graphics manipulated on the screen? What are the mathematical tools needed to visualize objects? How is an object represented in 3D?

To answer these questions we need to develop computer algorithms that will answer these questions at the touch of a button. Hence, macros are built to activate a set of commands. To generate computer algorithms we need to understand the fundamentals behind computer graphics. With a sound knowledge of the fundamentals a user can easily adapt to different CAD workstations, and use the graphics package to its full capabilities.

Computer graphics can be used in a wide range of engineering fields to increase the interaction between the user and the computer. Computer graphics is the development of a connecting bridge between the simplified visually represented output and the complex set of data and scientific calculations. The technique of integrating engineering solutions in CAD is widely used in engineering and medical sciences (Figure 3.1).

Expensive and huge equipment used in engineering applications were replaced by cost-effective computer graphics packages in which many simulations can be tried boldly without additional expenses. In medical science, the 3D visual representation of various body parts allows the doctor better diagnostics and evaluation. The inference

FIGURE 3.1 Motorcycle engine design.

will be simple with a visualized representation of output. Civil engineers use graphics to find the mistakes in very large complicated floor plans. They also view the building plan in various planes to make it more elegant in all the views.

Today the computer is serving as a processing tool that can store, retrieve, manipulate, and combine information. A benefit of this technology is that it is making our work rewarding to an extent never before possible. But as the volume of information increases, another question is asked: How can information be transferred efficiently between humans and machines? We know that the computer is a machine that generates data in a numerical form that is difficult for human beings to understand and interpret. Hence, the graphical representation of the data serves as a medium between the user and the computer, enhancing the user's ability to make quick decisions. Computer graphics is a technique used to improve the communication between humans and machines. A single graph can substitute for huge tables of numbers, allowing the user to interpret the quantities and characteristics at a glance. Thus, the use of such information can enhance productivity and provide for more effective problem solving.

Computer graphics strongly support the old adage that "A picture is worth a thousand words." Through computer graphics, we can simulate and hence predict automobile collisions, the piloting of a jet plane or space shuttle, the performance of a compressor, a turbine, or a pump at different speeds and loads, and many other engineering situations. The same graphic facilities in computer-aided design allow us to generate a detailed building (Figure 3.2), a complete automobile body layout (Figure 3.3), or any mechanical component with its corresponding drawing.

FIGURE 3.2 3D detailed building layout.

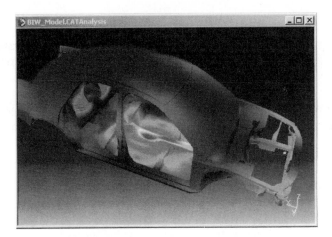

FIGURE 3.3 Automobile body display.

Up to this point, we have discussed computer graphics in general. Now we explore the methods used to project an image (described in terms of Cartesian coordinates) onto a graphic screen and then manipulate it (Figure 3.4). Often, we may want to change the scale of an image to see some details more clearly. We may have to rotate an image to a certain angle to get a better view of an object or to translate an image to another location to display it in a different environment. Dynamic movement of an assembly

FIGURE 3.4   Auxiliary view of a building.

requires different translation and orientation during each movement. These changes in orientation and scaling are done by transformation. These steps constitute geometric manipulation. These are the basic functions of computer graphics and can be accomplished by using geometric transformation techniques, which we study in this chapter. We also examine the fundamentals of mathematics for computer graphics by considering the representation and transformation of points, lines, surfaces, and objects in two- and three-dimensional planes.

3.2   Transformation Matrix

An object or geometry can be represented by a set of points in several planes. Let us represent a set of data by a matrix called C_{old}. We now define an operator R that once multiplied by C_{old} produces a new matrix C_{new}

$$C_{\text{new}} = R \cdot C_{\text{old}} \tag{3.1}$$

Hence, R is called a "transformation matrix," which could involve rotation about a point or axis, translation to a given destination, scaling, reflecting, mirror imaging about a plane, or a combination of all of these. The basic rule in transformation is matrix multiplication. It is essential to read Equation (3.1) as "operating on C_{old} by R yields C_{new}." The rule of thumb here is to remember that the product of two matrices exists only if the number of columns of the first matrix is equal to the number of rows of the second. (See Appendix A.)

3.3   2D Transformation

Consider an arbitrary point given by the coordinates (x, y). Let us operate on this point by a transformation matrix defined as follows.

$$\begin{bmatrix} x \\ y \end{bmatrix}_{\text{new}} = \begin{bmatrix} R_{11} & R_{12} \\ R_{21} & R_{22} \end{bmatrix} \begin{bmatrix} x \\ y \end{bmatrix}_{\text{old}} \tag{3.2}$$

We note here that R_{11}, R_{12}, R_{21}, and R_{22} are scalar quantities. The coordinates of the new points, that is, x_{new} and y_{new} are given by

$$x_{\text{new}} = x_{\text{old}}R_{11} + y_{\text{old}}R_{12} \tag{3.3}$$

$$y_{\text{new}} = x_{\text{old}}R_{21} + y_{\text{old}}R_{22} \tag{3.4}$$

Now let us examine what happened to the old (x, y) coordinates. Several things could be deduced from Equations (3.3) and (3.4). We first notice that if R_{12} and R_{21} are equal to 0, then the new coordinates are simply obtained by multiplying the old coordinates by scalar quantities. This, in effect, causes a stretching of old coordinates in both x and y directions. This actually produces a scaling. When the transformation matrix R has nonzero elements only in the main diagonal then R is a scaling matrix. If the elements in the main diagonal are same, that is, $R_{11} = R_{22} = a$, then the transformation matrix equation becomes

$$\begin{bmatrix} x \\ y \end{bmatrix}_{\text{new}} = a \begin{bmatrix} x \\ y \end{bmatrix}_{\text{old}} \tag{3.5}$$

In general, scaling depends on the elements in the primary diagonal of transformation matrix R. The scaling ratio can be any positive value. In the scaling of objects the relative distance between the coordinates increases by the scaling ratio. Values greater than 1 increase the size of the object; values less than 1 decrease the size of the object. Negative values will affect the final positioning, but not the shape, of the object.

On the other hand, we can let the elements of R be such that nothing can happen to the old coordinates. It can be seen that this is achieved by letting $R_{21} = R_{12} = 0$ and $R_{11} = R_{22} = 1$. Thus, if R is the identity matrix, no effect will result from the operation on the old (x, y).

But suppose we let $R_{11} = R_{12} = 1$ and $R_{12} \neq R_{21} \neq 0$; then what does R do to the old point? The transformation matrix now causes a shear-type deformation. Shear-type deformation is deformation in which the value of dimensions remains unchanged, because the element in the primary diagonal is 1. But the inner orientation or the shape alters with respect to the shear factor sh_x and sh_y. So the shear matrix is given by

$$R = \begin{bmatrix} 1 & sh_x \\ sh_y & 1 \end{bmatrix} \tag{3.6}$$

where

$sh_x =$ shear along the x direction

$sh_y =$ shear along the y direction

This is useful in applications in which the deformed shapes of object under shear load are studied.

If $sh_y = 0$ then the shear is along the x direction. The y-coordinates of all the points in the object remain unchanged. It is like sliding the horizontal layers in a uniform ratio.

If $sh_x = 0$ then the shear is along the y direction. The x-coordinates of all the points in the object remain unchanged. It is similar to sliding the vertical layers.

It is important to study and analyze the transformation techniques in two-dimensional space and then to expand the developed concepts to three-dimensional space. Now that we have some idea about the transformation matrix and its effects, we proceed to study the 2-by-2 transformation matrix and its usefulness in geometry manipulation. However, it is apparent from the foregoing analysis that a 2-by-2 transformation matrix can cause scaling, rotation, and shear deformation.

3.4   Arbitrary Rotation about the Origin

Consider the following x, y-coordinate system. The axes are perpendicular and also form a set of orthogonal axes. If we rotate both axes counterclockwise by an angle θ, we obtain a new set of axes, x', and y' (Figure 3.5).

If point P_1 has coordinates (x_1, y_1) in the x, y-plane, then its new position P_1' in the new coordinate system is defined by (x_1', y_1') after the rotation. We can write the relationship between the new and old coordinates as follows:

$$\left. \begin{array}{l} x_1' = x_1 \cos \theta - y_1 \sin \theta \\ y_1' = x_2 \sin \theta + y_1 \cos \theta \end{array} \right\} \tag{3.7}$$

Which can be expressed in matrix form:

$$\begin{bmatrix} x_1' \\ y_1' \end{bmatrix} = \begin{bmatrix} \cos \theta & -\sin \theta \\ \sin \theta & \cos \theta \end{bmatrix} \begin{bmatrix} x_1 \\ y_1 \end{bmatrix} \tag{3.8}$$

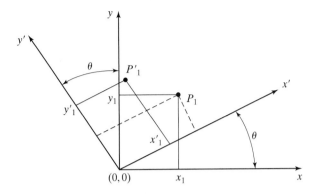

FIGURE 3.5 Counterclockwise rotation of x and y to obtain x' and y'.

where

$$R = \begin{bmatrix} \cos\theta & -\sin\theta \\ \sin\theta & \cos\theta \end{bmatrix}$$

is the rotation matrix.

To get the old point from new point replace θ by $-\theta$ in the rotation matrix, which results in R^T.

We must carefully note that in deriving the foregoing matrix equations, we rotated the x, y-axes counterclockwise, which is positive. However, if the x, y-axes are rotated clockwise by the same angle θ, we consider that angle to be negative. All other coordinates and their respective locations and matrix types (i.e., row vector or column vector type) remain the same as discussed earlier. Therefore, we can deduce the following important rule matrix $[R]$ for θ in the clockwise direction, which is equal to the transpose matrix of $[R]$ for θ in the counterclockwise direction.

3.5 Rotation by Different Angles

In cases in which the rotation of the x- and y-axes is done through two different angles, such as $\theta_1 = \theta_2$ (as shown in Figure 3.6), the relationship between the coordinates of point $P_2(x', y')$, and $P_1(x, y)$ is

$$\begin{bmatrix} x' \\ y' \end{bmatrix} = \frac{1}{\cos(\theta_2 - \theta_1)} \begin{bmatrix} \cos\theta_2 & -\sin\theta_2 \\ \sin\theta_1 & \cos\theta_1 \end{bmatrix} \begin{bmatrix} x \\ y \end{bmatrix} \tag{3.9}$$

It can easily be seen that for $\theta_1 = \theta_2$, $\cos(\theta_2 - \theta_1) = 1$ and Equation (3.9) is equivalent to Equation (3.8). Now that we see how the transformation matrix R can be used for both scaling and rotation, we can introduce the concept of concatenation.

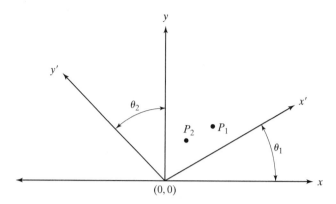

FIGURE 3.6 Arbitrary rotation of axes x and y.

3.6 Concatenation

Concatenation is defined as the resultant transformation matrix R that causes more than one transformation to a configuration matrix C. For example, if we were to scale a set of data points, namely, C, and then rotate the scaled geometry in a counterclockwise direction by an angle θ about the origin, we obtain the following

$$C_{\text{new}} = R_s \, R_r \, C_{\text{old}} \tag{3.10}$$

where R_s is the scaling matrix, and R_r is the rotation matrix. Then we define the concatenated matrix R to be

$$R = R_s R_r \tag{3.11}$$

Concatenation is a unique feature used in many CAD activities in which a certain number of transformations are to be applied to certain geometry. The advantage is in the amount of multiplication performed to get the desired picture. In the concatenation procedure, the transformation matrix R is first evaluated and then stored for future use. This eliminates the need to premultiply the individual matrices to yield the desired transformed geometry.

What remains to be studied at this point is the translation. Unlike rotation and scaling, transformation matrix R cannot be used for translation. Thinking ahead, one would need a transformation matrix in a concatenated form to cause not only scaling and rotation, but translation as well. What follows is an illustration of how that is achieved.

During the design process, when a graphic model is being developed, the use of the combined transformation is quite common. This allows changes to be made much faster.

An example in which concatenation is required is the rotation of the geometry about an arbitrary point θ followed by uniform scaling. Incidentally, the CAD systems perform only the combined scaling and rotation; translation is done separately.

3.7   2D Translation

The translation of objects in 2D is simply controlled by means of translation of the objects in the x and y directions. This function is accomplished by changing the coordinates of the points that represent the geometry. These points and their corresponding coordinates are modified by adding length $\Delta x, \Delta y$ to the original coordinates x, y defining the current position.

$$x_{\text{new}} = x_{\text{old}} + \Delta x \tag{3.12}$$

$$y_{\text{new}} = y_{\text{old}} + \Delta y \tag{3.13}$$

$$\begin{bmatrix} x_{\text{new}} \\ y_{\text{new}} \end{bmatrix} = \begin{bmatrix} x_{\text{old}} \\ y_{\text{old}} \end{bmatrix} + \begin{bmatrix} \Delta x \\ \Delta y \end{bmatrix} \tag{3.14}$$

Translation of an object is a transformation in which the relative position of all the points in the object is the same as that before translation. The displacement distance is the same for all the points.

To overcome the difficulty of causing a translation with the 2-by-2 transformation matrix R, we extend the order of the matrix to 3 by 3. Hence, R becomes

$$R = \begin{bmatrix} a & b & \Delta x \\ c & d & \Delta y \\ 0 & 0 & 1 \end{bmatrix} \tag{3.15}$$

To suit the 3-by-3 matrix introduced, the representation of any point (x, y) in 2D is represented by $(x, y, 1)$. This preserves the rules of operating on matrices. The third element could be regarded as an additional coordinate of the point. The translation process is achieved by

$$R = \begin{bmatrix} 1 & 0 & \Delta x \\ 0 & 1 & \Delta y \\ 0 & 0 & 1 \end{bmatrix} \tag{3.16}$$

where, as seen earlier, for the case of no rotation and no scaling, the 2-by-2 matrix becomes the identity matrix. For instance, if a given triangle is to be translated to a different position (i.e., destination), we simply operate on its vertices (x_1, y_1), (x_2, y_2), and (x_3, y_3) by R, where Δx and Δy take on the value of the number of units for translation of the points along x and y, respectively. That is,

$$\begin{bmatrix} x_1 & x_2 & x_3 \\ y_1 & y_2 & y_3 \\ 1 & 1 & 1 \end{bmatrix} \begin{bmatrix} 1 & 0 & \Delta x \\ 0 & 1 & \Delta y \\ 0 & 0 & 1 \end{bmatrix} = \begin{bmatrix} x_1 + \Delta x & x_2 + \Delta x & x_3 + \Delta x \\ y_1 + \Delta y & y_2 + \Delta y & y_3 + \Delta y \\ 1 & 1 & 1 \end{bmatrix} \tag{3.17}$$

3.8   Projection onto a 2D Plane

Consider the following transformation matrix:

$$R_1 = \begin{bmatrix} 1 & 0 & p \\ 0 & 1 & q \\ 0 & 0 & 1 \end{bmatrix} \qquad (3.18)$$

where p and q are two arbitrary constants.

Let us examine projection and normalization. Given the $(x, y, 1)$ point operated on by the foregoing R, the transformed point has coordinates (x^*, y^*, H) where

$$H = px + qy + 1 \qquad (3.19)$$

and

$$X^* = x, \; y^* = y$$

Thus, the new point (x^*, y^*) is projected onto a plane given by H (along the z-axis). This yields a projection.

Normalization is achieved by making the third component representing the point (H in this case) equal to 1. To plot point (x^*, y^*, H) on the x, y-plane, we divide by H to get

$$\left(\frac{x^*}{H}, \frac{y^*}{H}, 1 \right)$$

This normalization is required in order to have all new projected points expressed in a fashion similar to that of the existing points.

3.9   Overall Scaling

The overall scaling could be achieved by a transformation of the old into the new-scaled position as follows:

$$C^* = R \cdot C \qquad (3.20)$$

Overall scaling is uniform in both x and y directions by a scaling factor $n = 1/s$. Thus, the transformation matrix is:

$$R = \begin{bmatrix} 1 & 0 & 0 \\ 0 & 1 & 0 \\ 0 & 0 & s \end{bmatrix} \qquad (3.21)$$

The overall scaling is achieved by simply setting

$$s = \frac{1}{n} = \frac{1}{\text{value of the desired scale}} \qquad (3.22)$$

s causes the desired scaling only if the coordinates x, y are divided by s. This is called the normalization procedure, which makes sure all the points are in the same format.

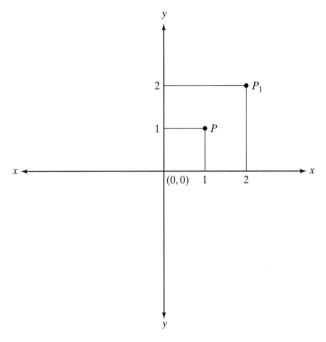

FIGURE 3.7   An example for overall scaling of a 2D object.

Normalization is achieved by making the third component representing the point (s in this case) equal to 1. To plot point (x^*, y^*, s) on the x, y-plane, we divide by s to get the scaled values.

$$\left[\frac{x^*}{s}\quad\frac{y^*}{s}\quad 1\right].$$

Figure 3.7 shows how uniform scaling is achieved when s $= \frac{1}{2}$.

3.10   Rotation about an Arbitrary Point

Besides the origin point θ, it might be important in some instances to rotate the given geometry about an arbitrary point in space. If we restrict our analysis to 2D, we first move the center of the geometry to the origin and then the object is rotated about that point in a similar fashion, as depicted in previous sections. Once the rotation is performed, the transformed geometry (object) is translated back to its original position. In reality, rotation about a point would be perceived as mathematically incorrect because it is impossible to rotate an object about a point. In 2D, however, the point of rotation represents the z-axis suppressed. Hence, rotation about a point is in fact a rotation about the z-axis with the geometry being viewed in the x, y-plane.

Example 3.1   Rotation of an Object about an Arbitrary Point in 2D

Let C describe an object or configuration of some geometry, where C is an array of data-point coordinates.

Solution   To rotate C about an arbitrary point (m, n) the following transformation is performed (Figure 3.8):

$$\begin{bmatrix} 1 & 0 & -m \\ 0 & 1 & -n \\ 0 & 0 & 1 \end{bmatrix} \begin{bmatrix} \cos\theta & -\sin\theta & 0 \\ \sin\theta & \cos\theta & 0 \\ 0 & 0 & 1 \end{bmatrix} \begin{bmatrix} 1 & 0 & m \\ 0 & 1 & n \\ 0 & 0 & 1 \end{bmatrix} [C] = [C^*] \qquad (3.23)$$

Where C^* represents the rotated object about point (m, n). The foregoing equation can be written in compact form as follows:

$$[C^*] = [R][C] \qquad (3.24)$$

where

$$[R] = \begin{bmatrix} \cos\theta & -\sin\theta & -m(\cos\theta + 1) + n\sin\theta \\ \sin\theta & \cos\theta & -m\sin\theta - n(\cos\theta - 1) \\ 0 & 0 & 1 \end{bmatrix} \qquad (3.25)$$

Here $[R]$ is the result of the product of three matrices. $[R]$ is written in a convenient form and can be used directly to perform the multiplication of three corresponding matrices.

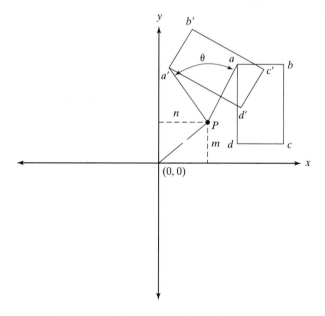

FIGURE 3.8   Rotation about an arbitrary point.

This technique is often used in CAD systems to save space and time. It can be extended for a number of other common transformations in which more than one function is needed.

End of Example 3.1

Example 3.2   Uniform Scaling in 2D

Find the transformation matrix that would produce rotation of the geometry about point A, as shown in Figure 3.9(a), followed by a uniform scaling of the geometry down to half its original size.

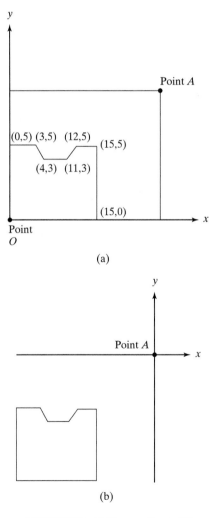

(a)

(b)

FIGURE 3.9   Uniform scaling in 2D.

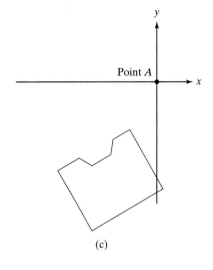

(c)

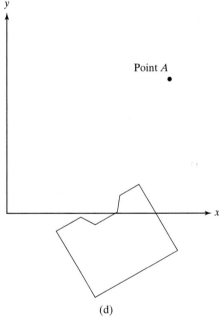

(d)

FIGURE 3.9   (*Continued*).

Solution

Step 1: Place the points into a matrix.

Step 2: Translate point A to the origin, that is, -2 along the x-axis and -10 along the y-axis, as shown in Figure 3.9(b).

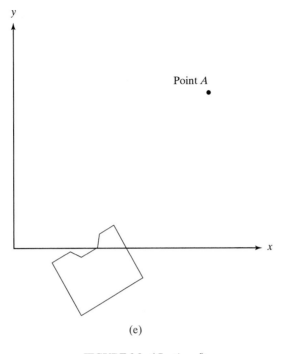

(e)

FIGURE 3.9 (*Continued*).

Step 3: Rotate the object 30 degrees about the z-axis, as shown in Figure 3.9(c).
Step 4: Translate point A to its original position as shown in Figure 3.9(d).
Step 5: Scale the object to half its original size, as shown in Figure 3.9(e).

End of Example 3.2

3.11 2D Reflection

Reflection is mirroring of an object with respect to an axis in a 2D plane. The axis line of an equation should be provided to define the line in the x, y-plane. Reflection about the y-axis is given by the reflection matrix (Figure 3.10).

$$R = \begin{bmatrix} -1 & 0 & 0 \\ 0 & 1 & 0 \\ 0 & 0 & 1 \end{bmatrix} \qquad (3.26)$$

Reflection about the y-axis is the same as reflection about the x-plane. The sign of the x-coordinates of the given object is changed. Reflection about the x-axis or the y-plane is given by the reflection matrix (Figure 3.11).

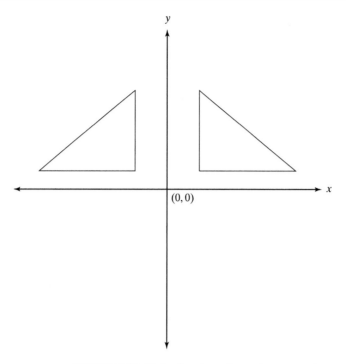

FIGURE 3.10   Reflection about the *y*-axis.

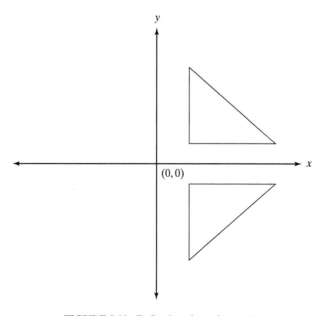

FIGURE 3.11   Reflection about the *x*-axis.

$$R = \begin{bmatrix} 1 & 0 & 0 \\ 0 & -1 & 0 \\ 0 & 0 & 1 \end{bmatrix} \tag{3.27}$$

3.11.1 Reflection about any Arbitrary Point

Reflection about any arbitrary point is done by concatenation of coordinate transformation to the given point, followed by reflection, followed by coordinate transformation back to the origin. (Figure 3.12).

The transformation matrix to move the geometry so P coincides with D is

$$T = \begin{bmatrix} 1 & 0 & -m \\ 0 & 1 & -n \\ 0 & 0 & 1 \end{bmatrix} \tag{3.28}$$

The reflection matrix about an arbitrary point is given by

$$R = \begin{bmatrix} -1 & 0 & 0 \\ 0 & -1 & 0 \\ 0 & 0 & 1 \end{bmatrix} \tag{3.29}$$

The transformation matrix required to translate the geometry back to P is

$$T\_1 = \begin{bmatrix} 1 & 0 & m \\ 0 & 1 & n \\ 0 & 0 & 1 \end{bmatrix} \tag{3.30}$$

3.11.2 Reflection about an Arbitrary Axis

To perform a reflection about any arbitrary axis defined by $y = mx + c$ we first rotate the object so that the coordinates are such that one of the axes aligns with the given axis. Then reflection about the coordinate axis is performed, and the coordinates are transformed back to the previous position.

Transformation matrices for reflection about an arbitrary axis $y = mx + c$ (Figure 3.13) are obtained through the following steps

a) Coordinate transformation to move the line so it passes through 0.

$$T_1 = \begin{bmatrix} 1 & 0 & 0 \\ 0 & 1 & -c \\ 0 & 0 & 1 \end{bmatrix} \tag{3.31}$$

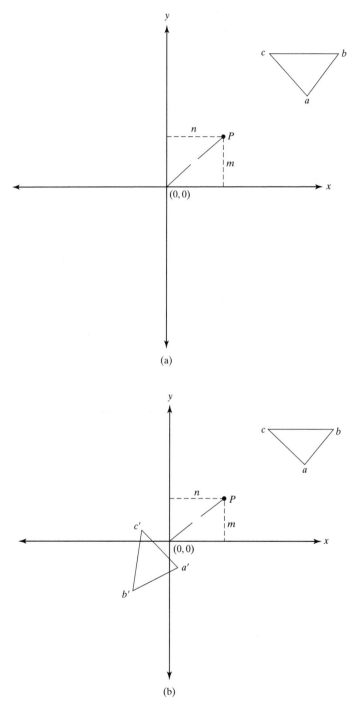

FIGURE 3.12   Reflection about an arbitrary point.

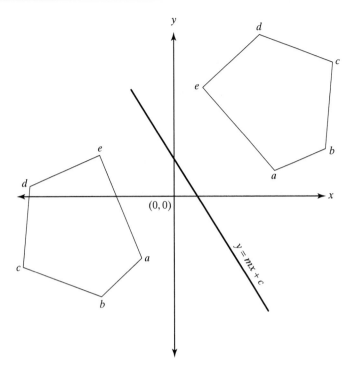

FIGURE 3.13 Reflection about an arbitrary axis $y = mx + c$.

b) Rotation to make the x-axis align with the given line

$$T_2 = \begin{bmatrix} \cos(-\theta) & -\sin(-\theta) & 0 \\ \sin(-\theta) & \cos(-\theta) & 0 \\ 0 & 0 & 1 \end{bmatrix} \qquad (3.32)$$

c) Reflection about the x-axis

$$R = \begin{bmatrix} 1 & 0 & 0 \\ 0 & -1 & 0 \\ 0 & 0 & 1 \end{bmatrix} \qquad (3.33)$$

d) Rotation back by an angle θ

$$T_3 = \begin{bmatrix} \cos(\theta) & -\sin(\theta) & 0 \\ \sin(\theta) & \cos(\theta) & 0 \\ 0 & 0 & 1 \end{bmatrix} \qquad (3.34)$$

The concatenated matrix expressing the above steps is defined by

$$C_{new} = T_3 \cdot R \cdot T_2 T_1 C_{old} \tag{3.35}$$

3.12 3D Transformation

In 2D, manipulation was with respect to a single plane. In 3D, the manipulation of an object in space is performed with respect to three mutually perpendicular axes (x, y, z). 2D transformation allows for the view of objects along a single plane. When building a realistic picture of a given object, 3D geometric manipulation is crucial to the intricate details required to produce a realistic part. 3D analysis involves more mathematical steps and provides options for 3D displays for visualizations to make the problem fully understandable (Figures 3.14 and 3.15).

To analyze drawings and designs more accurately, it is essential that they be represented in 3D. As with the 2D transformation, the 3D representation of data points should be $[x, y, z, 1]$, where (x, y, z) denotes the coordinates of a point, and 1 is a "dummy" assigned to facilitate the multiplication between the vector array representing the data and the transformation matrix. It could be viewed as a fourth dimensional vector.

3.13 3D Scaling

As demonstrated in the 2D case, scaling is achieved through two processes: (a) local scaling by using the diagonal elements of the matrix responsible for scaling and rotation, and (b) overall scaling by using 1-by-1 submatrix of the transformation matrix, which is known as s. The two cases follow:

(a) Local scaling:

$$R = \begin{bmatrix} a & 0 & 0 & 0 \\ 0 & b & 0 & 0 \\ 0 & 0 & c & 0 \\ 0 & 0 & 0 & 1 \end{bmatrix} \tag{3.36}$$

(b) Overall scaling

$$R = \begin{bmatrix} 1 & 0 & 0 & 0 \\ 0 & 1 & 0 & 0 \\ 0 & 0 & 1 & 0 \\ 0 & 0 & 0 & s \end{bmatrix} \tag{3.37}$$

In local scaling, if $a = b = c$, we have uniform scaling; otherwise the transformation yields nonuniform scaling or distortion. On the other hand, in overall scaling s ($s = 1/n$, $a = b = c = n$) causes the desired scaling only if coordinates (x, y, z) are

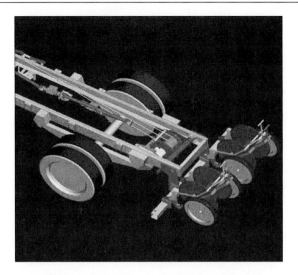

FIGURE 3.14 A trailer with a lower attachment.

FIGURE 3.15 An energy-fuel vehicle.

divided by s; this is the result of the normalization procedure that makes sure that all points are represented by the same format (Figure 3.16). For example, normalizing $[x^* \; y^* \; z^*]$, we obtain

$$\left[\frac{x^*}{s} \quad \frac{y^*}{s} \quad \frac{z^*}{s} \quad 1 \right] \qquad (3.38)$$

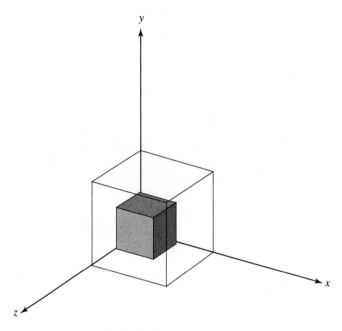

FIGURE 3.16 Overall scaling.

where

$$s = \frac{1}{\text{value of the desired scale}} = \frac{1}{n}$$

Again we have the dummy equal to 1. Thus, the coordinates are normalized and we have the required scaling.

To summarize, we can say that given a set of data points representing some given geometry and letting C represent the configuration of the geometry, then

$$R_s C = C^* \tag{3.39}$$

Where C^* is a neatly scaled C. An illustration of this can be seen in the following:

$$C = \begin{bmatrix} 0 & 0 & 2 & 2 & 0 & 0 & 2 & 2 \\ 0 & 0 & 0 & 0 & 1 & 1 & 1 & 1 \\ 0 & -1 & 0 & 1 & 0 & -1 & 0 & 1 \\ 1 & 1 & 1 & 1 & 1 & 1 & 1 & 1 \end{bmatrix} \tag{3.40}$$

Let

$$R = \begin{bmatrix} 1 & 0 & 0 & 0 \\ 0 & 2 & 0 & 0 \\ 0 & 0 & 1 & 0 \\ 0 & 0 & 0 & 1 \end{bmatrix} \tag{3.41}$$

Then

$$C^* = RC \qquad (3.42)$$

where C^* is the volume bounded by planes a, b, c, d, and i, j, k, l, as shown in Figure 3.17.

Quite often we need to magnify a portion of a model to work on intricate details. By traditional means, a designer would make several drawings of the object in different scales for different purposes. An architect, for example, routinely creates detailed drawings to clarify a feature that is not ordinarily visible on the original drawings. By using the CAD system, it is possible to construct a single model that can then be viewed at any level of magnification. This allows the designer to zoom in to refine a detail close up or zoom out to look at the model as a whole. The designer can also construct a large-scale model and then zoom in on one area in order to make sure elements do not overlay or interfere with one another (Figure 3.18). Note that the zoom function on the CAD system merely alters the size of the geometry that is inspected in order to make changes. It does not change the scale at which the drawing was created. Consequently, the original scale is that in which the drawing appears on the printed page. The matrix to describe 3D scaling transformation is given by Equation (3.26), where a, b, and c represent the scaling factors in the x, y, and z directions, respectively.

3.14 3D Rotation of Objects

In 2D rotation the direction of rotation axis is always parallel to the z-axis. But in 3D the rotational axis is arbitrary and needs complete representation of the rotational axis with respect to all three coordinate axes. There are two ways of representing rotations about an

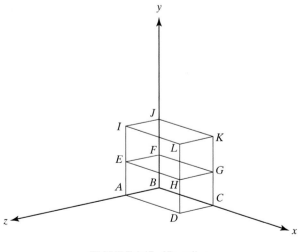

FIGURE 3.17 3D scaling.

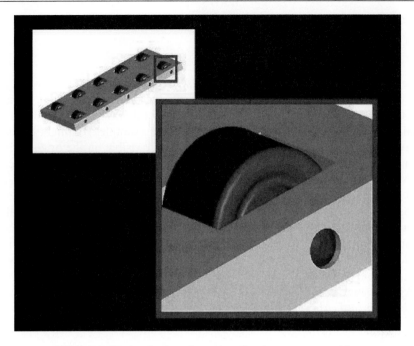

FIGURE 3.18 Application of zooming effect in computer graphics.

arbitrary axis in 3D. One method is by representing it as a rotation about the three coordinate axes *x, y,* and *z* by angles α, β, and γ, respectively. This involves more calculations.

Another method is by geometric coordinate transformation of the axis by known orientation of the rotation axis. And the transformation matrix can be represented as a single matrix (Figure 3.19).

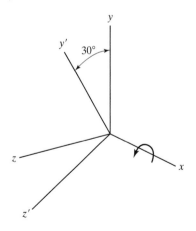

FIGURE 3.19 Rotation about the *x*-axis.

3D rotation of an object represented by a set of data points is given by

$$R = \begin{bmatrix} & & & 0 \\ 3 & \times & 3 & 0 \\ & matrix & & 0 \\ 0 & 0 & 0 & 1 \end{bmatrix} \tag{3.43}$$

Where the 3-by-3 matrix causes the given rotation. Rotation about the x-axis is obtained by

$$R_x = \begin{bmatrix} 1 & 0 & 0 \\ 0 & \cos\theta & -\sin\theta \\ 0 & \sin\theta & \cos\theta \end{bmatrix} \tag{3.44}$$

Where R_x is the result of the relationship between (x, y, z) and (x', y', z')
To show how the foregoing matrix R_x is derived, observe that

$$x = x'$$
$$y = y' \cos\theta - z \sin\theta$$
$$z = z' \cos\theta + y' \sin\theta \tag{3.45}$$

Arranging and expressing these three equations in the matrix, we get

$$\begin{bmatrix} x' \\ y' \\ z' \end{bmatrix} = \begin{bmatrix} 1 & 0 & 0 \\ 0 & \cos\theta & -\sin\theta \\ 0 & \sin\theta & \cos\theta \end{bmatrix} \begin{bmatrix} x \\ y \\ z \end{bmatrix}$$

And noting that rotation matrix R is orthogonal (i.e., transpose equals inverse),

$$R^{-1} = \begin{bmatrix} 1 & 0 & 0 \\ 0 & \cos\theta & \sin\theta \\ 0 & -\sin\theta & \cos\theta \end{bmatrix} = R^T \tag{3.46}$$

Therefore, the old coordinates (x', y', z') can be written in terms of new coordinates (x, y, z) as:

$$\begin{bmatrix} x \\ y \\ z \end{bmatrix} = \begin{bmatrix} 1 & 0 & 0 \\ 0 & \cos\theta & \sin\theta \\ 0 & -\sin\theta & \cos\theta \end{bmatrix} \begin{bmatrix} x' \\ y' \\ z' \end{bmatrix} \tag{3.47}$$

or

$$\begin{bmatrix} x \\ y \\ z \end{bmatrix} = [R_x] \begin{bmatrix} x' \\ y' \\ z' \end{bmatrix} \tag{3.48}$$

Similarly, we can obtain the transformation matrices for rotation about the y- and z-axes.

3.14.1 Rotation about the *y*-axis (Figure 3.20)

$$R_y = \begin{bmatrix} \cos\theta & 0 & \sin\theta \\ 0 & 1 & 0 \\ -\sin\theta & 0 & \cos\theta \end{bmatrix} \qquad (3.49)$$

3.14.2 Rotation about the *z*-axis (Figure 3.21)

$$R_z = \begin{bmatrix} \cos\theta & -\sin\theta & 0 \\ \sin\theta & \cos\theta & 0 \\ 0 & 0 & 1 \end{bmatrix} \qquad (3.50)$$

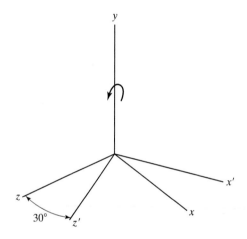

FIGURE 3.20   Rotation about the *y*-axis.

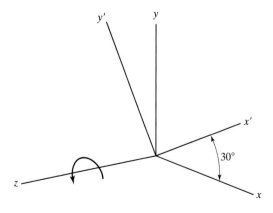

FIGURE 3.21   Rotation about the *z*-axis.

Rotation moves an object through a specified angle from its original orientation. For a positive angle, this direction of rotation is counterclockwise.

Example 3.3   Rotation in 3D Space

The box shown in Figure 3.22a will demonstrate rotation about an axis in 3D space. The box shown in the figure is at the initial starting point for all three rotations. The labeled points of the box listed in matrix format (see Sec. 3.3) are used with the transformation rotation matrices, equations (3.37), (3.39), and (3.40), to obtain the new coordinates after rotation (rotations are in a counterclockwise direction in this example).

Solution   The coordinates in matrix form are

$$[C] = [o \quad a \quad b \quad c \quad d \quad e \quad f \quad g]$$

$$[C] = \begin{bmatrix} 0 & 0 & 0 & 2 & 2 & 2 & 0 & 2 \\ 0 & 1 & 1 & 1 & 0 & 0 & 0 & 1 \\ 0 & 1 & 0 & 0 & 0 & 1 & 1 & 1 \end{bmatrix}$$

End of Example 3.3

3.14.3 Rotation about the *x*-axis for 30 Degrees

Suppose we wanted to rotate the box 30 degrees about the *x*-axis (Figure 3.22 b). We would use Equation (3.42), where the transformation matrix is defined by Equation (3.47).

$$[C^*] = [R][C]$$

$$[C^*] = \begin{bmatrix} 1 & 0 & 0 \\ 0 & \dfrac{\sqrt{3}}{2} & -\dfrac{1}{2} \\ 0 & \dfrac{1}{2} & \dfrac{\sqrt{3}}{2} \end{bmatrix} \begin{bmatrix} 0 & 0 & 0 & 2 & 2 & 2 & 0 & 2 \\ 0 & 1 & 1 & 1 & 0 & 0 & 0 & 1 \\ 0 & 1 & 0 & 0 & 0 & 1 & 1 & 1 \end{bmatrix}$$

$$= \begin{bmatrix} 0 & 0 & 0 & 2 & 2 & 2 & 0 & 2 \\ 0 & \dfrac{\sqrt{3}}{2} + \dfrac{1}{2} & \dfrac{\sqrt{3}}{2} & \dfrac{\sqrt{3}}{2} & 0 & \dfrac{1}{2} & \dfrac{1}{2} & \dfrac{\sqrt{3}}{2} + \dfrac{1}{2} \\ 0 & -\dfrac{1}{2} + \dfrac{\sqrt{3}}{2} & -\dfrac{1}{2} & \dfrac{1}{2} & 0 & \dfrac{\sqrt{3}}{2} & \dfrac{\sqrt{3}}{2} & \dfrac{\sqrt{3}}{2} - \dfrac{1}{2} \end{bmatrix}$$

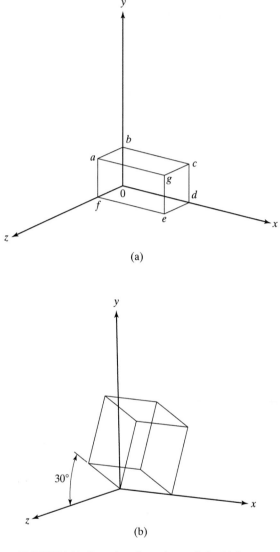

FIGURE 3.22   Rotation about the x-axis for 30 degrees.

3.14.4 Rotation about the y-axis for 30 Degrees

If the box is to be rotated 30 degrees about the y-axis (Figure 3.23), we repeat the rotation procedure about the x-axis, except we use Equation (3.49) for the rotation matrix.

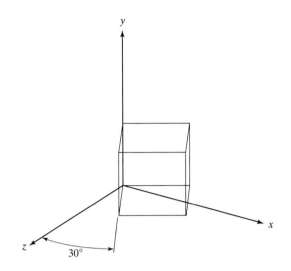

FIGURE 3.23   Rotation about the y-axis for 30 degrees.

$$[C^*] = [R_y][C]$$

$$[C^*] = \begin{bmatrix} \dfrac{\sqrt{3}}{2} & -\dfrac{1}{2} & 0 \\[2mm] \dfrac{1}{2} & \dfrac{\sqrt{3}}{2} & 0 \\[2mm] 0 & 0 & 1 \end{bmatrix} \begin{bmatrix} 0 & 0 & 0 & 2 & 2 & 2 & 0 & 2 \\ 0 & 1 & 1 & 1 & 0 & 0 & 0 & 1 \\ 0 & 1 & 0 & 0 & 0 & 1 & 1 & 1 \end{bmatrix}$$

$$= \begin{bmatrix} 0 & \dfrac{1}{2} & 0 & \sqrt{3} & \sqrt{3} & \sqrt{3}+\dfrac{1}{2} & \dfrac{1}{2} & \sqrt{3}+\dfrac{1}{2} \\[2mm] 0 & 1 & 1 & 1 & 0 & 0 & 0 & 1 \\[2mm] 0 & \dfrac{\sqrt{3}}{2} & 0 & -1 & -1 & \dfrac{\sqrt{3}}{2}-1 & \dfrac{\sqrt{3}}{2} & \dfrac{\sqrt{3}}{2}-1 \end{bmatrix}$$

3.14.5   Rotation about the z-axis for 30 Degrees

We repeat the procedure used before, except we use Equation (3.40) as the transformation matrix for rotation about the z-axis (Figure 3.24).

$$[C^*] = [R_z][C]$$

$$[C^*] = \begin{bmatrix} \dfrac{\sqrt{3}}{2} & -\dfrac{1}{2} & 0 \\[2mm] \dfrac{1}{2} & \dfrac{\sqrt{3}}{2} & 0 \\[2mm] 0 & 0 & 1 \end{bmatrix} \begin{bmatrix} 0 & 0 & 0 & 2 & 2 & 2 & 0 & 2 \\ 0 & 1 & 1 & 1 & 0 & 0 & 0 & 1 \\ 0 & 1 & 0 & 0 & 0 & 1 & 1 & 1 \end{bmatrix}$$

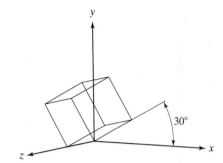

FIGURE 3.24   Rotation about the z-axis for 30 degrees.

$$
= \begin{bmatrix}
0 & \dfrac{1}{2} & \dfrac{1}{2} & \sqrt{3}+\dfrac{1}{2} & \sqrt{3} & \sqrt{3} & 0 & \sqrt{3} \\[2mm]
0 & \dfrac{\sqrt{3}}{2} & \dfrac{\sqrt{3}}{2} & \dfrac{\sqrt{3}}{2}-1 & -1 & -1 & 2 & \dfrac{\sqrt{3}}{2}-1 \\[2mm]
0 & 1 & 0 & 0 & 0 & 1 & 1 & 1
\end{bmatrix}
$$

3.15   3D Reflection and Mirror Imaging

Reflection is mirroring an object in space with respect to a defined plane or planes. Mirroring is widely used in CAD software to simplify the process of modeling. Parts that can be mirrored about a plane should be symmetric about that plane, and internal dimensions of the parts should be same. In Figure 3.25 the right and left part of the building is similar. Mirroring about the central plane can create it. This reduces a lot of modeling work for the designers, and the mirrored model can be made dependent or independent of the parent model. In the dependent model, changes made in the parent model will also make changes in the child model.

The simplest reflections occur through a plane. Reflection about the x, y-plane is given by:

$$
R_r = \begin{bmatrix}
1 & 0 & 0 & 0 \\
0 & 1 & 0 & 0 \\
0 & 0 & -1 & 0 \\
0 & 0 & 0 & 1
\end{bmatrix}
\tag{3.51}
$$

That is, for reflection about the x, y-plane element of the 3-by-3 identity submatrix (which is responsible for the z-axis), R_r is negative. Similarly, for reflection about the y, z-plane, the matrix is given by:

FIGURE 3.25   An example of symmetry.

$$
R_r = \begin{bmatrix} -1 & 0 & 0 & 0 \\ 0 & 1 & 0 & 0 \\ 0 & 0 & 1 & 0 \\ 0 & 0 & 0 & 1 \end{bmatrix}
$$ (3.52)

and reflection about the x, z-plane is given by the matrix:

$$
R_r = \begin{bmatrix} 1 & 0 & 0 & 0 \\ 0 & -1 & 0 & 0 \\ 0 & 0 & 1 & 0 \\ 0 & 0 & 0 & 1 \end{bmatrix}
$$ (3.53)

Reflection is also known as a mirror image that can be created about a specified axis/plane using the mirror option on the CAD system. It is especially convenient in terms of reducing time and effort in creating drawings.

An example of reflection is the creation of a complete model of a symmetrical model/object by drawing one section of the object and then mirroring it about a specified axis to create the remainder of the object. This technique simplifies creating models made up of symmetrical forms, such as a cast wheel.

Example 3.4   Building of a Block

Symmetry is the similarity between two objects with respect to a point or a line or a plane. Dimensions of the objects measured from the symmetric plane will be equal for both of the objects. One object looks similar to the mirror image of the other assuming that the central plane acts as a mirror. These concepts of symmetry and mirroring are widely used in the design and modeling field to reduce model creation time. Reflection is used to simplify the creation of the block shown in Figure 3.26.

Solution   The block can be divided into four symmetric parts (Figure 3.26). The entire coordinates of the block can be described using the coordinates of one-quarter of the block given by:

$$[C_1] = [a \quad b \quad c \quad d \quad e \quad f \quad g \quad h \quad i \quad j \quad k \quad l \quad m \quad n]$$

$$= \begin{bmatrix} 0 & \frac{1}{2} & \frac{1}{2} & 0 & 0 & \frac{1}{4} & \frac{1}{2} & \frac{1}{2} & 0 & \frac{1}{4} & \frac{1}{4} & \frac{1}{2} & \frac{1}{2} & \frac{1}{4} \\ 0 & 0 & 0 & 0 & \frac{1}{2} & \frac{1}{2} & \frac{1}{2} & \frac{1}{2} & \frac{1}{2} & \frac{1}{2} & 1 & 1 & 1 & 1 \\ 1 & 1 & 0 & 0 & 1 & 1 & \frac{1}{2} & 0 & 0 & \frac{1}{2} & 1 & 1 & \frac{1}{2} & \frac{1}{2} \\ 1 & 1 & 1 & 1 & 1 & 1 & 1 & 1 & 1 & 1 & 1 & 1 & 1 & 1 \end{bmatrix}$$

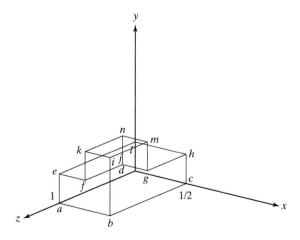

FIGURE 3.26 Coordinate description using a quarter portion of the block.

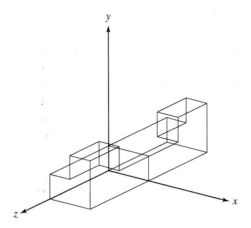

FIGURE 3.27 Half block obtained by reflection about the x,y-plane.

Step 1: Establish the transformation matrix to reflect the quarter block about the x, y-plane (Figure 3.27). Using the reflection equation, we have

$$[C^*] = R_1 C = \begin{bmatrix} 1 & 0 & 0 & 0 \\ 0 & 1 & 0 & 0 \\ 0 & 0 & -1 & 0 \\ 0 & 0 & 0 & 1 \end{bmatrix} C$$

This creates the other quarter of the block. The coordinate of one-half of the block is known.

$$[C^*] = \begin{bmatrix} 0 & \frac{1}{2} & \frac{1}{2} & 0 & 0 & \frac{1}{4} & \frac{1}{2} & \frac{1}{2} & 0 & \frac{1}{4} & \frac{1}{4} & \frac{1}{2} & \frac{1}{2} & \frac{1}{4} \\ 0 & 0 & 0 & 0 & \frac{1}{2} & \frac{1}{2} & \frac{1}{2} & \frac{1}{2} & \frac{1}{2} & \frac{1}{2} & 1 & 1 & 1 & 1 \\ -1 & -1 & 0 & 0 & -1 & -1 & -\frac{1}{2} & 0 & 0 & -\frac{1}{2} & -1 & -1 & -\frac{1}{2} & -\frac{1}{2} \\ 1 & 1 & 1 & 1 & 1 & 1 & 1 & 1 & 1 & 1 & 1 & 1 & 1 & 1 \end{bmatrix}$$

Step 2: Reflect the half portion of the block about the y, z-plane (Figure 3.28). Using the reflection equation, we have

$$[C^{**}] = R_2 C^a = \begin{bmatrix} -1 & 0 & 0 & 0 \\ 0 & 1 & 0 & 0 \\ 0 & 0 & 1 & 0 \\ 0 & 0 & 0 & 1 \end{bmatrix} C$$

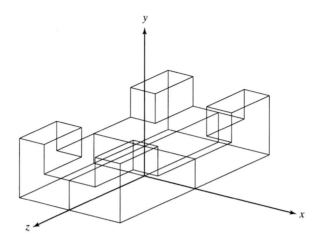

FIGURE 3.28   Reflection of half portion of the block about y, z-plane.

where

$$[C_a] = \begin{bmatrix} C \\ C* \end{bmatrix}$$

By using the coordinate matrices C and $C*$, the coordinates of the other half of the block are determined using this transformation matrix. The coordinates for the first half are

$$[C_C^{**}] = \begin{bmatrix} 0 & -\dfrac{1}{2} & -\dfrac{1}{2} & 0 & 0 & -\dfrac{1}{4} & -\dfrac{1}{2} & -\dfrac{1}{2} & 0 & -\dfrac{1}{4} & -\dfrac{1}{4} & \dfrac{1}{2} & -\dfrac{1}{2} & -\dfrac{1}{4} \\ 0 & 0 & 0 & 0 & \dfrac{1}{2} & \dfrac{1}{2} & \dfrac{1}{2} & \dfrac{1}{2} & \dfrac{1}{2} & \dfrac{1}{2} & 1 & 1 & 1 & 1 \\ 1 & 1 & 0 & 0 & 1 & 1 & \dfrac{1}{2} & 0 & 0 & \dfrac{1}{2} & 1 & 1 & \dfrac{1}{2} & \dfrac{1}{2} \\ 1 & 1 & 1 & 1 & 1 & 1 & 1 & 1 & 1 & 1 & 1 & 1 & 1 & 1 \end{bmatrix}$$

and the coordinates for the second half are

$$[C_c^{**}] = \begin{bmatrix} 0 & -\dfrac{1}{2} & -\dfrac{1}{2} & 0 & 0 & -\dfrac{1}{4} & -\dfrac{1}{2} & -\dfrac{1}{2} & 0 & -\dfrac{1}{4} & -\dfrac{1}{4} & \dfrac{1}{2} & -\dfrac{1}{2} & -\dfrac{1}{4} \\ 0 & 0 & 0 & 0 & \dfrac{1}{2} & \dfrac{1}{2} & \dfrac{1}{2} & \dfrac{1}{2} & \dfrac{1}{2} & \dfrac{1}{2} & 1 & 1 & 1 & 1 \\ -1 & -1 & 0 & 0 & -1 & -1 & -\dfrac{1}{2} & 0 & 0 & -\dfrac{1}{2} & -1 & -1 & -\dfrac{1}{2} & -\dfrac{1}{2} \\ 1 & 1 & 1 & 1 & 1 & 1 & 1 & 1 & 1 & 1 & 1 & 1 & 1 & 1 \end{bmatrix}$$

where the coordinates for the whole block (C^{**}) consists of

$$[C^{**}] = \begin{bmatrix} C_C^{**} \\ C_{C*}^{**} \end{bmatrix}$$

End of Example 3.4

3.16 3D Translation

In 3D translation the object is translated along the x, y, z-axes by values Δx, Δy, Δz along the straight-line path in each coordinate. To obtain the final position of any point in the given object the transformation matrix is applied to each point and repositioned.
New coordinates of any point in the object are given by

$$x' = x + \Delta x$$
$$y' = y + \Delta y$$
$$z' = z + \Delta z$$

The transformation matrix is given by

$$R_T = \begin{bmatrix} 1 & 0 & 0 & \Delta x \\ 0 & 1 & 0 & \Delta y \\ 0 & 0 & 1 & \Delta z \\ 0 & 0 & 0 & 1 \end{bmatrix} \tag{3.54}$$

where R_T represents the transformation matrix needed to translate a configuration matrix C to some given destination. Therefore,

$$C^* = RC \tag{3.55}$$

where C^* is the translated configuration matrix.

Example 3.5   Translation of a Block in 3D

Using the box shown in Figure 3.9(e) in Example 3.5, translate the box 2 units in the x direction, 1 unit in the y direction, and 1 unit in the z direction, as shown in Figure 3.15.

Solution   Using Equation (3.54), we substitute the numerical values into the translation matrix and apply Equation (3.55) to find the new coordinates of the points after translation. We know that $\Delta x = 2$, $\Delta y = 1$, and $\Delta z = 1$. The new coordinates of the box are

$$[C^*] = \begin{bmatrix} 1 & 0 & 0 & 2 \\ 0 & 1 & 0 & 1 \\ 0 & 0 & 1 & 1 \\ 0 & 0 & 0 & 1 \end{bmatrix} \begin{bmatrix} 0 & 0 & 0 & 2 & 2 & 2 & 0 \\ 0 & 1 & 1 & 1 & 0 & 0 & 0 \\ 0 & 2 & 0 & 0 & 0 & 1 & 1 \\ 1 & 1 & 1 & 1 & 1 & 1 & 1 \end{bmatrix}$$

$$[C^*] = \begin{bmatrix} 2 & 2 & 2 & 4 & 4 & 4 & 2 \\ 1 & 2 & 2 & 2 & 1 & 1 & 1 \\ 1 & 3 & 1 & 1 & 1 & 2 & 2 \\ 1 & 1 & 1 & 1 & 1 & 1 & 1 \end{bmatrix}$$

End of Example 3.5

3.17   3D Rotation about an Arbitrary Axis

Transformation matrix R_r could be achieved through a procedure as described below:

1. The object is translated such that the origin of coordinates passes through the line.
2. Rotation is accomplished.
3. The object is translated back to its origin.

Rotation about an arbitrary axis can be classified into three types:

1. Axis of rotation parallel to any one of the coordinate axes (Figures 3.29 and 3.30). There are only three steps in this type of rotation, because moving the line to pass

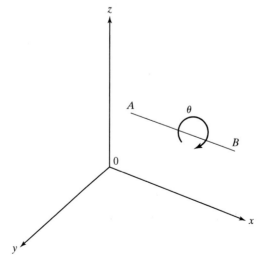

FIGURE 3.29   Rotation about a parallel axis.

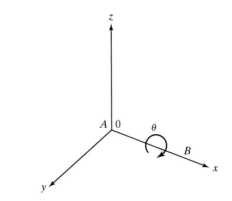

FIGURE 3.30 Translation of axis to coordinate axis.

through the origin will automatically align one of the axes with the coordinate axis for a given arbitrary line.

2. Axis passing through origin and not parallel with any coordinate axis (Figure 3.31). Rotation about the coordinate axes is performed to align one of the coordinate axes with the given arbitrary line. The number of rotations depends on the initial orientation of the given line.

3. Arbitrary line not passing through the origin and not parallel to any of the coordinate axes (Figure 3.32). It is similar to the type above with two additional steps of translating the line to pass through the origin and bringing back to the original position after rotation.

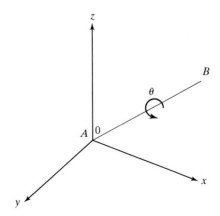

FIGURE 3.31 Rotation about an axis passing through the origin.

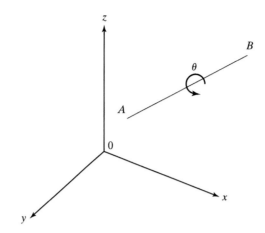

FIGURE 3.32 Rotation about an axis not passing through the origin.

If we concatenate the three foregoing transformation matrices, we obtain:

$$C^* = R_{t1}R_rR_{t2}C \tag{3.56}$$

where

$$R_{t1} = \begin{bmatrix} 1 & 0 & 0 & -\Delta x \\ 0 & 1 & 0 & -\Delta y \\ 0 & 0 & 1 & -\Delta z \\ 0 & 0 & 0 & 1 \end{bmatrix} \tag{3.57}$$

$$R_{t2} = \begin{bmatrix} 1 & 0 & 0 & \Delta x \\ 0 & 1 & 0 & \Delta y \\ 0 & 0 & 1 & \Delta z \\ 0 & 0 & 0 & 1 \end{bmatrix} \tag{3.58}$$

and

$$[R_r] = \begin{bmatrix} C_2C_3 & C_1S_3 + S_1S_2C_3 & S_1S_3 - C_1S_2C_3 & 0 \\ -C_2S_3 & C_1C_3 - S_1S_2S_3 & S_1C_3 + C_1S_2S_3 & 0 \\ S_2 & -S_1C_2 & C_1C_2 & 0 \\ 0 & 0 & 0 & 1 \end{bmatrix} \tag{3.59}$$

where

$$C_1 = \cos\alpha, \quad C_2 = \cos\beta, \quad C_3 = \cos\gamma,$$
$$S_1 = \sin\alpha, \quad S_2 = \sin\beta, \quad S_3 = \sin\gamma.$$

Successive rotations about the x-, y-, and z-axes lead to a rotation about an arbitrary axis, say $l - l'$ shown in Figure 3.33. The rotation about this axis by an angle γ can be

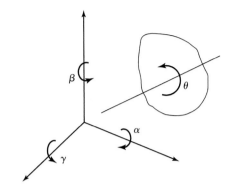

FIGURE 3.33 Successive rotation of x, y, z by α, β, γ.

achieved by the following transformation matrices:

$$R_r = R_x^\alpha R_y^\beta R_z^\gamma \tag{3.60}$$

Where R_x^α, R_y^β, and R_z^γ are rotation matrices about the x-, y-, and z-axes, respectively, by the angles α, β, and γ, as shown in Figure 3.33. This representation usually has some disadvantages associated with finding the correct angles for α, β, and γ to yield the proper rotation.

Example 3.6   Rotation of a Box in 3D Space

Using the box shown in Figure 3.9(e), find the new coordinates of the box if it is rotated 30 degrees about the x-axis, 60 degrees about the y-axis, and 90 degrees about the z-axis. (Rotations are in the counterclockwise direction.) The rotations of the coordinate reference frames are illustrated in Figure 3.20. x''', y''', and z''' indicate the new coordinate system where the box resides $[C^*]$.

Solution   Using Equations (3.32) and (3.60), we write the following

$$[C^*] = [R][C]$$

where

$$[C] = \begin{bmatrix} 0 & 0 & 0 & 0 & 2 & 2 & 2 & 2 \\ 0 & 1 & 1 & 0 & 1 & 0 & 0 & 1 \\ 0 & 0 & 1 & 1 & 0 & 0 & 1 & 1 \\ 1 & 1 & 1 & 1 & 1 & 1 & 1 & 1 \end{bmatrix}$$

And substituting $\alpha = 30°$, $\beta = 60°$, and $\gamma = 90°$ in Equation (3.59), we obtain:

$$[R] = \begin{bmatrix} 0 & \dfrac{\sqrt{3}}{2} & \dfrac{1}{2} & 0 \\[2mm] \dfrac{1}{2} & -\dfrac{\sqrt{3}}{4} & \dfrac{3}{4} & 0 \\[2mm] \dfrac{\sqrt{3}}{2} & -\dfrac{1}{4} & \dfrac{\sqrt{3}}{4} & 0 \\[2mm] 0 & 0 & 0 & 1 \end{bmatrix}$$

The final answer is

$$[C^*] = \begin{bmatrix} 0 & \dfrac{\sqrt{3}}{2} & \dfrac{1}{2} & 0 \\[2mm] \dfrac{1}{2} & -\dfrac{\sqrt{3}}{4} & \dfrac{3}{4} & 0 \\[2mm] \dfrac{\sqrt{3}}{2} & -\dfrac{1}{4} & \dfrac{\sqrt{3}}{4} & 0 \\[2mm] 0 & 0 & 0 & 1 \end{bmatrix} \begin{bmatrix} 0 & 0 & 0 & 0 & 2 & 2 & 2 & 2 \\ 0 & 1 & 1 & 0 & 1 & 0 & 0 & 1 \\ 0 & 0 & 1 & 1 & 0 & 0 & 1 & 1 \\ 1 & 1 & 1 & 1 & 1 & 1 & 1 & 1 \end{bmatrix}$$

$$[C^*] = \begin{bmatrix} 0 & \dfrac{1}{2} & \dfrac{1}{2}+\dfrac{\sqrt{3}}{2} & \dfrac{\sqrt{3}}{2} & \dfrac{1}{2} & 0 & \dfrac{\sqrt{3}}{2} & \dfrac{1}{2}+\dfrac{\sqrt{3}}{2} \\[2mm] 0 & -\dfrac{\sqrt{3}}{4} & -\dfrac{\sqrt{3}}{4}-\dfrac{1}{4} & -\dfrac{1}{4} & \sqrt{3}-\dfrac{\sqrt{3}}{4} & \sqrt{3} & \sqrt{3}-\dfrac{1}{4} & \sqrt{3}-\dfrac{1}{4}(\sqrt{3}+3) \\[2mm] 0 & \dfrac{3}{4} & \dfrac{3}{4}+\dfrac{\sqrt{3}}{4} & \dfrac{\sqrt{3}}{4} & 1+\dfrac{3}{4} & 1 & 1+\dfrac{\sqrt{3}}{2} & 1+\dfrac{1}{4}(3+\sqrt{3}) \\[2mm] 1 & 1 & 1 & 1 & 1 & 1 & 1 & 1 \end{bmatrix}$$

End of Example 3.6

Example 3.7   Rotation and Translation of a Cube in 3D Space

Given the unit cube shown in Figure 3.34, find the transformation matrix required for the display of the cube shown in Figure 3.36).

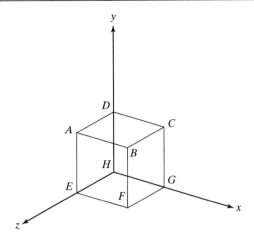

FIGURE 3.34 Initial position of the cube.

Solution

Step 1: Place the points in matrix form.

$$[C] = \begin{bmatrix} 0 & 1 & 1 & 0 & 0 & 1 & 1 & 0 \\ 1 & 1 & 1 & 1 & 0 & 0 & 0 & 0 \\ 1 & 1 & 0 & 0 & 1 & 1 & 0 & 0 \\ 1 & 1 & 1 & 1 & 1 & 1 & 1 & 1 \end{bmatrix}$$

Step 2: Rotate the cube +90 degrees about the *x*-axis (Figure 3.35).

$$[R_{s1}] = \begin{bmatrix} 1 & 0 & 0 & 0 \\ 0 & \cos 90 & -\sin 90 & 0 \\ 0 & \sin 90 & \cos 90 & 0 \\ 0 & 0 & 0 & 1 \end{bmatrix}$$

Step 3: Rotate the cube +90 degrees about the *y*-axis (Figure 3.36). Using the rotation matrix,

$$[R_{s2}] = \begin{bmatrix} \cos 90 & 0 & \sin 90 & 0 \\ 0 & 1 & 0 & 0 \\ -\sin 90 & 0 & \cos 90 & 0 \\ 0 & 1 & 0 & 1 \end{bmatrix}$$

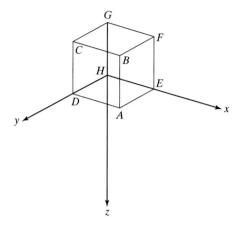

FIGURE 3.35   Rotation about the *x*-axis.

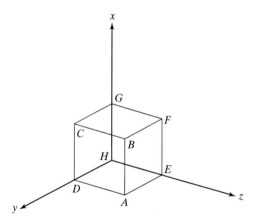

FIGURE 3.36   Rotation about the *y*-axis.

By combining the transformation matrices, we have

$$C^* = R_{s1}R_{s2}C$$

The final answer is

$$[C^*] = \begin{bmatrix} 1 & 1 & 0 & 0 & 1 & 1 & 0 & 0 \\ 0 & 1 & 1 & 0 & 0 & 1 & 1 & 0 \\ 0 & 0 & 0 & 0 & -1 & -1 & -1 & -1 \\ 1 & 1 & 1 & 1 & 1 & 1 & 1 & 1 \end{bmatrix}$$

End of Example 3.7

Example 3.8   Pyramid Rotation and Translation

Give the concatenated transformation matrix that would generate the new position of the object shown in Figure 3.37. (Face *A* given by points *ABCD* lies in the *y, z*-plane with its center along the *x*-axis.) *Note:* Show the steps you wish to take before writing the transformation matrices.

The matrix of the coordinates that contains all vertices of the pyramid is

$$[C] = [A \quad B \quad C \quad D \quad E] = \begin{bmatrix} h & h & h & h & 0 \\ -\dfrac{a}{2} & -\dfrac{a}{2} & \dfrac{a}{2} & \dfrac{a}{2} & 0 \\ \dfrac{a}{2} & \dfrac{a}{2} & -\dfrac{a}{2} & \dfrac{a}{2} & 0 \\ 1 & 1 & 1 & 1 & 1 \end{bmatrix}$$

Solution

Step 1: Determine the matrix to rotate the pyramid along the *x*-axis by 90 degrees (Figure 3.38).

$$[R_1] = \begin{bmatrix} 1 & 0 & 0 & 0 \\ 0 & \cos 90 & -\sin 90 & 0 \\ 0 & \sin 90 & \cos 90 & 0 \\ 0 & 0 & 0 & 1 \end{bmatrix}$$

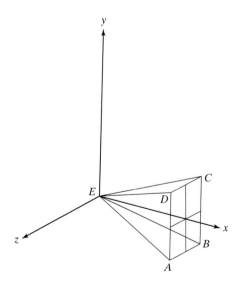

FIGURE 3.37 Initial position of the pyramid.

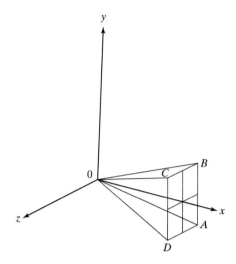

FIGURE 3.38   Rotation about the *x*-axis for 90 degrees.

Step 2: Determine the matrix to translate the object $-h$ units along the *x*-axis (Figure 3.39).

$$[R_2] = \begin{bmatrix} 1 & 0 & 0 & -h \\ 0 & 1 & 0 & 0 \\ 0 & 0 & 1 & 0 \\ 0 & 0 & 0 & 1 \end{bmatrix}$$

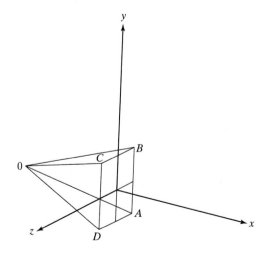

FIGURE 3.39   Translation along the *x*-axis for $-h$ units.

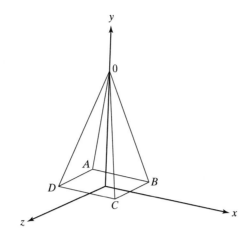

FIGURE 3.40 Rotation about the z-axis for 90 degrees.

Step 3: Rotate the object 90 degrees about the z-axis (Figure 3.40).

$$[R_3] = \begin{bmatrix} \cos-90 & -\sin-90 & 0 & 0 \\ \sin-90 & \cos-90 & 0 & 0 \\ 0 & 0 & 1 & 0 \\ 0 & 0 & 0 & 1 \end{bmatrix}$$

$$[C^*] = [R_1][R_2][R_3][C]$$

End of Example 3.8

3.18 3D Visualization

In engineering, we are often required to visualize an object in 3D space. There are two main techniques that yield such a representation. As is often the case on a CAD workstation, one can adapt the 2D representation. Such is the case in drafting, where absolute coordinates used are defined with the z-axis normal to the screen. Hence, we view the picture from it. Rotating the image by keeping the axis orthogonal is an option used for viewing and editing the graphics. On the other hand, we can work in so-called 3D space by adapting the isometric view. This option displays a 3D axis on a 2D plane keeping the axes orthogonal. This is called a trimetric projection. All the foregoing projections fall under the category of axonometric projections.

3.19   Trimetric Projection

Consider a 3D picture of an object represented by a set of data points. Let C denote such a configuration; then if we operate on C by R, we get

$$C^* = RC \tag{3.61}$$

where C^* is the trimetric projection of C if transformation matrix R causes pure rotation. Hence, the coordinate axes remain orthogonal when projecting onto a 2D plane.

A projection from 3D to 2D can be made by projecting onto a $z = 0$ plane with

$$R = \left[\begin{array}{ccc:c} & 3 \times 3 & & 0 \\ & \text{Rotation} & & 0 \\ & \text{matrix} & & 0 \\ \hdashline 0 & 0 & 0 & 1 \end{array}\right] \begin{bmatrix} 1 & 0 & 0 & 0 \\ 0 & 1 & 0 & 0 \\ 0 & 0 & 0 & 0 \\ 0 & 0 & 0 & 1 \end{bmatrix} \quad \text{(for } z = 0) \tag{3.62}$$

Pure rotation is done prior to projection and matrix R projects the object on the x, y-plane (this is done by setting the third column to 0).

Similarly, the projection onto the $z = t$ plane is obtained by

$$R = \left[\begin{array}{ccc:c} & 3 \times 3 & & 0 \\ & \text{Rotation} & & 0 \\ & \text{matrix} & & 0 \\ \hdashline 0 & 0 & 0 & 1 \end{array}\right] \begin{bmatrix} 1 & 0 & 0 & 0 \\ 0 & 1 & 0 & 0 \\ 0 & 0 & 0 & 0 \\ 0 & 0 & t & 1 \end{bmatrix} \tag{3.63}$$

The transformation matrix R is the product of two matrices. It is obtained by first performing a simple rotation of the object if needed and then projecting it onto the corresponding 2D plane. In this case, $z = 0$ or t.

If we were to project the object onto $x = 0$ or $x = r$ plane, the projection matrix would take the following form:

$$R = \begin{bmatrix} 0 & 0 & 0 & 0 \\ 0 & 1 & 0 & 0 \\ 0 & 0 & 1 & 0 \\ 0 & 0 & 0 & 1 \end{bmatrix} \quad \text{(for } x = 0) \tag{3.64}$$

and

$$R = \begin{bmatrix} 0 & 0 & 0 & 0 \\ 0 & 1 & 0 & 0 \\ 0 & 0 & 1 & 0 \\ r & 0 & 0 & 1 \end{bmatrix} \quad \text{(for } x = r\text{)} \tag{3.65}$$

In a similar fashion, the projection onto the $y = 0$ or $y = s$ plane is

$$R = \begin{bmatrix} 1 & 0 & 0 & 0 \\ 0 & 0 & 0 & 0 \\ 0 & 0 & 1 & 0 \\ 0 & 0 & 0 & 1 \end{bmatrix} \quad \text{(for } y = 0\text{)} \tag{3.66}$$

and

$$R = \begin{bmatrix} 1 & 0 & 0 & 0 \\ 0 & 0 & 0 & 0 \\ 0 & 0 & 1 & 0 \\ 0 & s & 0 & 1 \end{bmatrix} \quad \text{(for } y = s\text{)} \tag{3.67}$$

Example 3.9   Projection on a Plane

Determine the projection of the boxes in Figures 3.42, 3.43, and 3.44.

Solution   The coordinates of the box (Figure 3.41) are defined by:

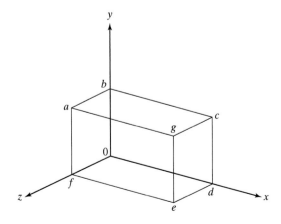

FIGURE 3.41   Initial position of the box.

$$C = \begin{bmatrix} A & B & C & D & E & F & G \end{bmatrix}$$

$$C = \begin{bmatrix} 0 & 0 & 0 & 0 & 2 & 2 & 2 & 2 \\ 0 & 1 & 1 & 0 & 1 & 0 & 0 & 1 \\ 0 & 0 & 1 & 1 & 0 & 0 & 1 & 1 \\ 1 & 1 & 1 & 1 & 1 & 1 & 1 & 1 \end{bmatrix}$$

(a) The projection of the box on the $x = 6$ plane (Figure 3.42) has the following transformation matrix:

$$[R] = \begin{bmatrix} 0 & 0 & 0 & 0 \\ 0 & 1 & 0 & 0 \\ 0 & 0 & 1 & 0 \\ 6 & 0 & 0 & 1 \end{bmatrix}$$

Therefore, the coordinates for the projection are

$$[C^*] = [R][C]$$

$$[C^*] = \begin{bmatrix} 0 & 0 & 0 & 0 \\ 0 & 1 & 0 & 0 \\ 0 & 0 & 1 & 0 \\ 6 & 0 & 0 & 1 \end{bmatrix} \begin{bmatrix} 0 & 0 & 0 & 0 & 2 & 2 & 2 & 2 \\ 0 & 1 & 1 & 0 & 1 & 0 & 0 & 1 \\ 0 & 1 & 1 & 1 & 0 & 0 & 1 & 1 \\ 1 & 1 & 1 & 1 & 1 & 1 & 1 & 1 \end{bmatrix}$$

$$[C^*] = \begin{bmatrix} 6 & 6 & 6 & 6 & 6 & 6 & 6 & 6 \\ 0 & 1 & 1 & 0 & 1 & 0 & 0 & 1 \\ 0 & 2 & 0 & 1 & 0 & 0 & 1 & 1 \\ 1 & 1 & 1 & 1 & 1 & 1 & 1 & 1 \end{bmatrix}$$

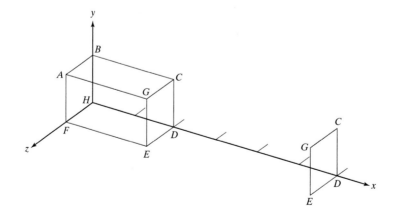

FIGURE 3.42 Projection on the plane $x = 6$.

(b) The projection of the box on the $y = 6$ plane (Figure 3.43) has the following transformation matrix:

$$[R] = \begin{bmatrix} 1 & 0 & 0 & 0 \\ 0 & 0 & 0 & 0 \\ 0 & 0 & 1 & 0 \\ 0 & 6 & 0 & 1 \end{bmatrix}$$

Therefore, the coordinates for the projection are

$$[C^*] = \begin{bmatrix} 1 & 0 & 0 & 0 \\ 0 & 0 & 0 & 0 \\ 0 & 0 & 1 & 0 \\ 0 & 6 & 0 & 1 \end{bmatrix} \begin{bmatrix} 0 & 0 & 0 & 0 & 2 & 2 & 2 & 2 \\ 0 & 1 & 1 & 0 & 1 & 0 & 0 & 1 \\ 0 & 0 & 1 & 1 & 0 & 0 & 1 & 1 \\ 1 & 1 & 1 & 1 & 1 & 1 & 1 & 1 \end{bmatrix}$$

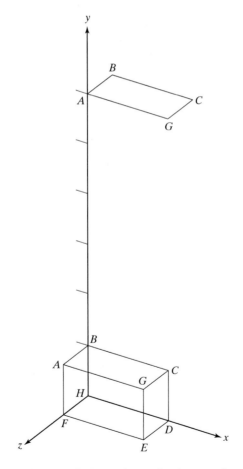

FIGURE 3.43 Projection on the plane $y = 6$.

$$[C*] = \begin{bmatrix} 0 & 0 & 0 & 0 & 2 & 2 & 2 & 2 \\ 6 & 6 & 6 & 6 & 6 & 6 & 6 & 6 \\ 0 & 2 & 1 & 1 & 0 & 0 & 1 & 1 \\ 1 & 1 & 1 & 1 & 1 & 1 & 1 & 1 \end{bmatrix}$$

(c) The projection of the box on the $z = 6$ plane (Figure 3.44) has the following transformation matrix:

$$[R] = \begin{bmatrix} 1 & 0 & 0 & 0 \\ 0 & 1 & 0 & 0 \\ 0 & 0 & 0 & 0 \\ 0 & 0 & 6 & 1 \end{bmatrix}$$

Therefore, the coordinates for the projection are

$$[C*] = [R][C]$$

$$[C*] = \begin{bmatrix} 1 & 0 & 0 & 0 \\ 0 & 1 & 0 & 0 \\ 0 & 0 & 0 & 0 \\ 0 & 0 & 6 & 1 \end{bmatrix} \begin{bmatrix} 0 & 0 & 0 & 0 & 2 & 2 & 2 & 2 \\ 0 & 1 & 1 & 0 & 1 & 0 & 0 & 1 \\ 0 & 0 & 1 & 1 & 0 & 0 & 1 & 1 \\ 1 & 1 & 1 & 1 & 1 & 1 & 1 & 1 \end{bmatrix}$$

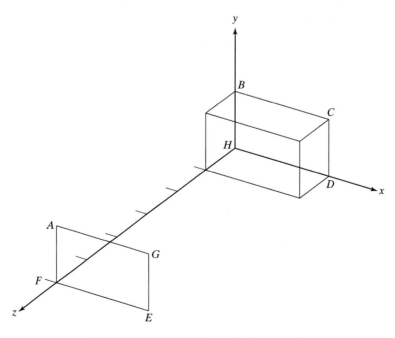

FIGURE 3.44 Projection on the plane $z = 6$.

$$[C^*] = \begin{bmatrix} 0 & 0 & 0 & 0 & 2 & 2 & 2 & 2 \\ 0 & 1 & 1 & 0 & 1 & 0 & 0 & 1 \\ 6 & 6 & 6 & 6 & 6 & 6 & 6 & 6 \\ 1 & 1 & 1 & 1 & 1 & 1 & 1 & 1 \end{bmatrix}$$

Example 3.9

3.20 Isometric Projection

Combined rotations followed by projection from infinity form the bases for generating all axonometric projections. We are familiar with the isometric view (Figure 3.45). Unlike other projections, an isometric projection is obtained by equally foreshortening all three axes when going from 3D to 2D. From the point of view of CAD software development, we are interested in finding the transformation matrix R that yields such a projection. Observe how we first manipulate the geometry and then project it onto a 2D plane by imposing the isometric conditions. For that, we perform the following:

1. Rotate about the y-axis
2. Rotate about the x-axis
3. Project about the $z = 0$ plane
4. Apply the final transformation conditions of foreshortening all axes equally
5. Get the final transformation matrix to yield the isometric view

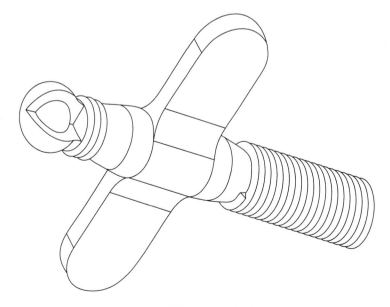

FIGURE 3.45 Isometric view.

Consider a point P given by $(x\ y\ z\ 1)$. Let us find the isometric projection of this point while using the previous definitions. Operating on P by θ and ϕ, we get

$$
\begin{bmatrix} x^* \\ y^* \\ z^* \\ 1 \end{bmatrix} = \begin{bmatrix} 1 & 0 & 0 & 0 \\ 0 & \cos\theta & \sin\theta & 0 \\ 0 & -\sin\theta & \cos\theta & 0 \\ 0 & 0 & 0 & 1 \end{bmatrix} \begin{bmatrix} \cos\phi & 0 & -\sin\phi & 0 \\ 0 & 1 & 0 & 0 \\ \sin\phi & 0 & \cos\phi & 0 \\ 0 & 0 & 0 & 1 \end{bmatrix} \begin{bmatrix} x \\ y \\ z \\ 1 \end{bmatrix} \tag{3.68}
$$

where $[x^*\ y^*\ z^*]$ represents the coordinates of the rotated point P about the y- and x-axes. The concatenated transformation matrix is given by

$$
R = \begin{bmatrix} \cos\phi & \sin\phi\,\sin\theta & -\sin\phi\,\cos\theta & 0 \\ 0 & \cos\theta & \sin\theta & 0 \\ \sin\phi & -\cos\phi\,\sin\theta & \cos\phi\,\cos\theta & 0 \\ 0 & 0 & 0 & 1 \end{bmatrix} \tag{3.69}
$$

Suppose point P denotes different unit vectors along the x-, y-, and z-axes. Hence, along x, we have [1 0 0 1], which when operated on by R given by Equation (3.69) yields

$$
\begin{bmatrix} x^* \\ y^* \\ z^* \\ 1 \end{bmatrix} = [R] \begin{bmatrix} 1 \\ 0 \\ 0 \\ 1 \end{bmatrix} \tag{3.70}
$$

where

$$x^* = \cos\phi$$
$$y^* = \sin\phi\,\sin\theta$$
$$z^* = -\sin\phi\,\cos\theta \tag{3.71}$$

If we consider the unit vector along the y-axis, it transforms into

$$
\begin{bmatrix} x^* \\ y^* \\ z^* \\ 1 \end{bmatrix} = [R] \begin{bmatrix} 0 \\ 1 \\ 0 \\ 1 \end{bmatrix} \tag{3.72}
$$

where

$$x^* = 0$$
$$y^* = \cos\theta$$
$$z^* = \sin\theta \tag{3.73}$$

Because we are projecting onto the $z = 0$ plane, we should suppress all z-components by making them equal zero. To create the isometric projection, we must foreshorten all three axes equally. One way of doing this is to equate the magnitude of the unit vectors along the x- and y-axes and then equate the one corresponding to the *y*- and *z*-axes. The latter gives the conditions of our isometric projection, which are obtained from Equations (3.70) and (3.72), respectively.

$$n_x = \sqrt{(x^*)^2 + (y^*)^2 + (z^*)^2} = \sqrt{\cos^2 \phi + \sin^2 \phi \sin^2 \theta}$$

$$n_y = \sqrt{(x^*)^2 + (y^*)^2 + (z^*)^2} = \sqrt{\cos^2 \theta}$$

$$n_x = \sqrt{(x^*)^2 + (y^*)^2 + (z^*)^2} = \sqrt{\sin^2 \phi + \cos^2 \phi \sin^2 \theta}$$

and then

$$n_x = n_y \Rightarrow \sin^2 \phi = \frac{\sin^2 \theta}{1 - \sin^2 \theta} \tag{3.74}$$

$$n_y = n_z \Rightarrow \sin^2 \phi = \frac{1 - 2\sin^2 \theta}{1 - \sin^2 \theta} \tag{3.75}$$

Equations (3.64) and (3.65) form a set of two equations with two unknowns.

Using trigonometric relationships and the method of substitution, we can solve for ϕ and θ, which yield $\theta = 35.26°$ and $\phi = 45°$. We can then conclude that given geometry in 3D represented by [C], its isometric projection is obtained by premultiplying it by R given by Equation (3.75), with θ and ϕ being equal to 35.26° and 45°, respectively. The resulting [C*] represents the projection for which we are looking.

PROBLEMS

3.1. See the original shape and position of the cube in Figure P3.1.

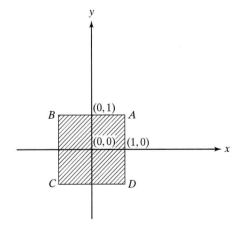

FIGURE P3.1 Cube geometry.

a. Find the configuration matrix C that represents the geometry.
b. Use uniform scaling (with respect to the origin) to magnify the object to two times its original size.
c. Find the position of vertices of the square when rotated +45 degrees (CCW).

3.2. Using the square in Problem 3.1, find the transforming matrix that produces the shear deformation shown by the dashed lines in Figure P3.2.

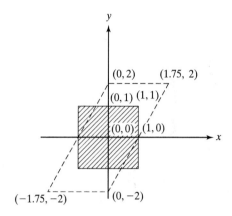

FIGURE P3.2   Shear deformation of square.

3.3. Find the transformation needed to rotate the unit cube shown in Figure P3.3 about $1 - 1'$ in a clockwise fashion by 30°. Point $0'$ lies on the x-axis, and $l - l'$ is at distance m from the x-axis and passes through the y-axis. If the cube were positioned such that $0'$ passes through 0, what changes in R would we expect?

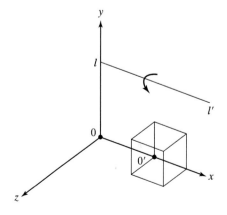

FIGURE P3.3   Rotation of the unit cube.

3.4. We would like to obtain an isometric view of an object (Figure P3.4) given in a Cartesian frame. In order to determine the desired transformation matrix, we performed the following manipulation of the object:

(i) Rotate the object about the z-axis clockwise by an angle γ
(ii) Rotate the object about the x-axis counterclockwise by an angle α
(iii) Project the object onto the $y = 0$ plane

Find the transformation matrix R that yields the isometric view.

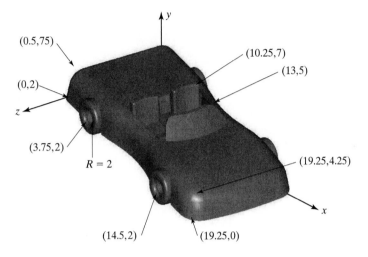

FIGURE P3.4 Coordinate and isometric view of geometry.

3.5. A strange object was found in the fields of Cincinnati and must be moved to a research center. Given the information in Figure P3.5, determine the set of transformation matrices needed to move the object to the research center.

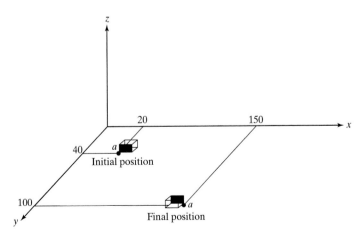

FIGURE P3.5 Initial and final positions of an object.

3.6. Automated robots, used by Widgets, Inc., operate by the use of transformation matrices to move the widgets along the production line. Given a schematic of the path (Figure P3.6) through which the widget must go, determine the transformation matrices that can make this possible.

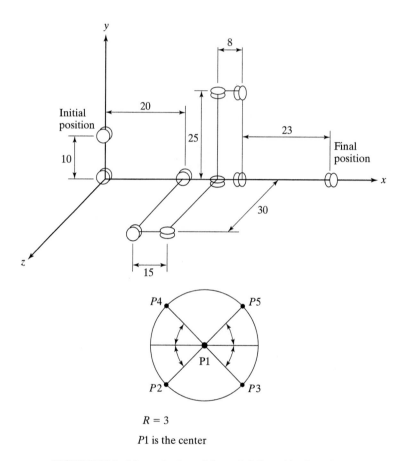

FIGURE P3.6   Schematic view of the path followed by the robots.

3.7. To draw the mechanical part shown in Figure P3.7, we need to use several transformation matrices. Suppose the only information we have is the position of the three points and the additional information on the connecting part dimensions as shown. Show how the complete geometry can be obtained making use of transformations and mirror imaging. (Check your answer on a CAD system.)

3.8. Give the concatenated transformation matrix that would generate the new position of the object in Figure P3.8 (face *eijg* in the original position lies in the *x, y*-plane). *Note:* Show all the steps you want to take before writing the transformation matrices.

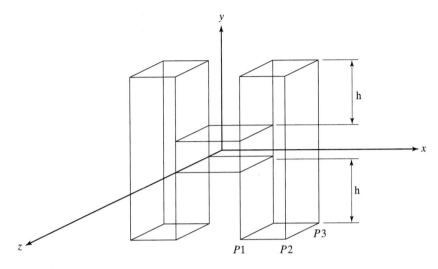

FIGURE P3.7 Geometric description of mechanical part.

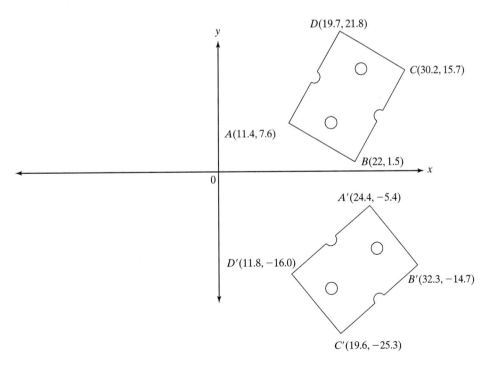

FIGURE P3.8 Coordinates of the old object position from A to D and the new object position from A' to D'.

3.9. Define the transformation matrix needed to reflect an object of rectangular shape about a line given by $y = x + 2$. The dimensions of the 2D object are $[2,2; 3,2; 2,3; 3,3]$.

3.10. Obtain the isometric transformation matrix if the steps are such that a rotation about the y-axis is followed by a rotation about the z-axis, then the object is projected onto $x = 0$. Describe the difference between these results and those obtained using the procedure described in Section 3.18.

3.11. Describe the combined steps in reflection and rotation to expose all faces of the cube in 3D.

3.12. Write a MATLAB program or equivalent of rotating an object about any axis, scale, and translate the object to any point in space.

3.13. Define a plane given by $H = 2x + y + 1$. If a triangle is to be projected onto the given plane H, give the coordinates of the triangle after projection. The initial position of the triangle edges are $[1,1; 2,1; 1,3]$.

3.14. Define the steps needed in the transformation matrices to relate the old to the new position of the object in Figure P3.8.

BIBLIOGRAPHY

Amirouche, F.M.L. (1993). *Introduction to Computer-Aided Design and Manu-facturing.* Upper Saddle River, NJ: Prentice Hall.

Farin, G. (1988). *Curves and Surfaces for Computer Aided Geometric Design—A Practical Guide.* New York: Academic Press.

Lancaster, P., and Salkauska, K. (1986). *Curve and Surface Fitting—An Introduction.* New York: Academic Press.

Rodgers, D.F., and Adams, J.A. (1976). *Mathematical Elements for Computer Graphics.* New York: McGraw-Hill.

CHAPTER 4

Description of Curves and Surfaces

It is difficult to build an elaborate system mentally without the use of computers. In engineering, sketching is a thing of the past when a detailed design is required. To construct an effective engineering system, experience with engineering software is essential. The ability of engineers to excel is best measured by their mathematical skills and education.

The objective of this chapter is to present the mathematical tools used to represent curves and surfaces. These techniques have been implemented with computers and are at the heart of CAD software. Objects are described analytically with respect to a coordinate system and are manipulated in space to obtain the desired shape, form, and view. In this chapter we introduce some general concepts relating to the representation of curves and surfaces. The goal is to address the mathematical representation of these curves consistent with the engineering perspective in design. An important part of the mathematical modeling of curves is their applications in computer-aided design with the aim of expanding the reader's specific skills. Continuous objects are best represented by curves and surfaces. To yield accurate representations of engineering models with intricate details, we need to use mathematical tools to provide a concise description of the object. In this chapter, we begin with concepts of polynomials and splines and then bridge these into existing CAD techniques in generating surfaces.

In design, most often we need to construct an accurate picture so we can learn more about an object's features and characteristics when it is subject to different environmental conditions. There are two methods of fitting curves: (a) polynomials and (b) splines. The first requirement is that a set of data points must exist; the second step is to find a function of order n that best represents the curve that passes through all the data points. Obviously, one would have to try several polynomials to achieve the desired fit. On the other hand, the methods of splines work with the basic assumption that we can pass a cubic function between any two points. By properly choosing the conditions at the end points, a smooth curve can be derived.

The significance of these representations is that they are the necessary and sufficient conditions to establish a mathematical representation of objects.

4.1   Line Fitting

To begin we should comment that some of these fitting techniques are familiar to the reader. Suppose we desire to fit a linear function to the data set, as illustrated in Table 4.1. The line fitted to a data set is called a regression line.

The linear regression function is expressed by a line function of the form

$$g(x) = c_1 x + c_2 \qquad (4.1)$$

where c_1 and c_2 are constants to be determined. Because the number of data points is greater than two, the line cannot be fitted to every point, but is determined by minimizing the discrepancies between the line and the data. It appears that the values of c_1 and c_2 that represent the distinct advantage of making the $g(x)$ function close to the y-value are most desirable. Deviation of the line from data points is clearly defined by

$$r_i = y_i - g(x_i) = y_i - (c_1 x_i + c_2), \qquad i = 1, 2 \ldots L \qquad (4.2)$$

where L is the total number of data points.

The sum of the squared deviation is derived making use of Equation 4.2 such that

$$R = \sum_{i=1}^{L} r_i^2 = \sum_{i=1}^{L} (y_i - c_1 x_i - c_2)^2 \qquad (4.3)$$

The minimum of R occurs if partial derivatives of R with respect to c_1 and c_2 are set to zero

$$\frac{\partial R}{\partial c_1} = -2 \sum_{i=1}^{L} x_i (y_i - c_1 x_i - c_2) = 0 \qquad (4.4)$$

$$\frac{\partial R}{\partial c_2} = -2 \sum_{n=1}^{L} (y_i - c_1 x_i - c_2) = 0 \qquad (4.5)$$

TABLE 4.1   A set of arbitrary data points.

i	x	y
1	x_i	y_i
2	x_{i+1}	y_{i+1}
3	x_{i+2}	y_{i+2}

Equations (4.4) and (4.5) may be expressed in a matrix form as

$$\begin{bmatrix} a_{1,1} & a_{1,2} \\ a_{2,1} & a_{2,2} \end{bmatrix} \begin{bmatrix} c_1 \\ c_2 \end{bmatrix} = \begin{bmatrix} z_1 \\ z_2 \end{bmatrix} \tag{4.6}$$

We should note that the matrix representation allows us to evaluate c_1 and c_2 and simplify by manipulation of the matrix. We have two equations and two unknowns, and the coefficient a_s and z_s are given by

$$a_{1,1} = \sum_{i=1}^{L} x_i^2 \tag{4.7}$$

$$a_{1,2} = a_{2,1} = \sum_{i=1}^{L} x_i \tag{4.8}$$

$$a_{2,2} = \sum_{i=1}^{L} i = L \tag{4.9}$$

$$z_1 = \sum_{i=1}^{L} x_i y_i \tag{4.10}$$

$$z_2 = \sum_{i=1}^{L} y_i \tag{4.11}$$

The solution to Equation (4.6) is found by Cramer's rule (see Appendix), where

$$c_1 = (a_{2,2}z_1 - a_{1,2}z_2)/(a_{1,1}a_{2,2} - a_{1,2}a_{2,1}) \tag{4.12}$$

$$c_2 = (a_{1,1}z_2 - a_{2,2}z_1)/(a_{1,1}a_{2,2} - a_{1,2}a_{2,1}) \tag{4.13}$$

Hence, Equations (4.1), (4.2), and (4.3) give the line equation for a set of L data points.

Example 4.1

Determine the regression line for the data in Table 4.2 by solving Equation (4.6). After the regression line is obtained, examine the deviation error of the line from the data.

TABLE 4.2

i	x_i	y_i	x^2_i	$x_i y_i$
1	0.1	0.22	0.01	0.022
2	0.2	0.39	0.04	0.078
3	0.3	0.57	0.09	0.171
4	0.4	0.81	0.16	0.324
5	0.5	1.02	0.25	0.51
6	0.6	1.18	0.36	0.708
Total	2.1	4.19	0.91	1.813
	a_{21}	z_2	a_{11}	z_1

Solution: First let's evaluate the coefficients of the matrices in Equation (4.6) making use of Equations (4.7) and (4.11). We calculate that the coefficients of Equation (4.6) are as follows:

From Table 4.2, we get

$$a_{1,1} = 0.91, \quad a_{1,2} = 2.1, \quad z_1 = 1.813$$

$$a_{2,1} = 2.1, \quad a_{2,2} = 6, \quad z_2 = 4.19$$

Thus, Equation (4.6) becomes

$$\begin{bmatrix} 0.91 & 2.1 \\ 2.1 & 6 \end{bmatrix} \begin{bmatrix} c_1 \\ c_2 \end{bmatrix} = \begin{bmatrix} 1.813 \\ 4.19 \end{bmatrix}$$

The solution of which is

$$c_1 = 1.98, \quad c_2 = .0053$$

The regression line is then given by

$$g(x) = 1.98x + 0.0053$$

Now we can use the regression line to find the deviation or error associated with all the data points. Table 4.3 shows that the regression line is a good fit. The graph in Figure 4.1 is an additional testimony to the accuracy of the regression line and how well it fits the given data. Note that an effort must be made prior to line fitting to determine whether the data provided do indeed represent a linear relationship between two variables.

End of Example 4.1

TABLE 4.3

i	x_i	y_i	$g = c_1 x + c_2$	Deviation (error)
1	0.1	0.22	0.2033	0.0167
2	0.2	0.39	0.4013	−0.0113
3	0.3	0.57	0.5993	−0.0293
4	0.4	0.81	0.7973	0.0127
5	0.5	1.02	0.9953	0.0247
6	0.6	1.18	1.1933	−0.0753

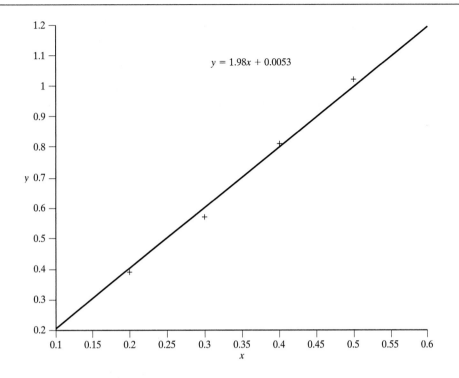

$$y = 1.98x + 0.0053$$

FIGURE 4.1 The regression line fitted to the data from Table 4.2.

4.2 Nonlinear Curve Fitting with a Power Function

It is important to know that we always seek the curve that best represents the data set. We also have learned in engineering that not all the physical properties are linear. As a matter of fact, structures under cyclic loading conditions follow an exponential function. For some data types, fitting the power function given by

$$g(x) = \beta x^{\alpha} \tag{4.14}$$

may be suitable, where α and β are undetermined coefficients. The purpose is to devise a tractable approximation of α, β for the purpose of fitting a curve through most of the data points. To determine the coefficients, we first take the logarithm of Equation (4.14)

$$\log(g) = \alpha \log(x) + \log(\beta) \tag{4.15}$$

Let

$$\left.\begin{array}{rcl} G &=& \log(g) \\ c_1 &=& \alpha \\ c_2 &=& \log(\beta) \\ X &=& \log(x) \end{array}\right\} \tag{4.16}$$

where

$$G = c_1 X + c_2 \tag{4.17}$$

Then the problem is reduced to a line regression, as described in Section 4.1. Equation (4.17) is fitted to the data set, $(\log(y_i), \log(x_i))$ and represents a mapping of the data from a simple regression line to a nonlinear power function. This technique has been adopted for years by researchers in mechanics to study the creep effect of different materials.

Example 4.2

The following data set is used to demonstrate how curve fitting of a power function can be carried out making use of the regression line technique. Consider Table 4.4, when x, y represent experimental data between force (lb) and displacement (mm). We need to find a mathematical function to describe the data, and it is perceived that a power function is most suitable.

From Table 4.4, we get the regression-line coefficients

$$a_{1,1} = 2.9524, \quad a_{1,2} = 0.6233, \quad z_1 = 1.6815$$

$$a_{2,1} = 0.6233, \quad a_{2,2} = 12, \quad z_2 = 10.35$$

Making use of Equations (4.6) and (4.7), we obtain

$$c_1 = \alpha = 0.3917$$

$$c_2 = \log(\beta) = 1.9405$$

and the power function becomes

$$g(x) = \beta x^\alpha = 6.9622 x^{0.3197}$$

TABLE 4.4

i	1	2	3	4	5	6	7	8	9	10	11	12	Total
x	0.1	0.25	0.39	0.60	1.03	1.32	1.78	2.13	2.45	3.07	3.98	4.64	
y	3.21	3.81	4.09	5.21	7.97	8.32	8.88	9.27	9.97	10.8	11.34	13.08	
$x = \ln(x)$	−1	−0.602	−0.408	−0.22	0.0128	0.1205	0.25	0.328	0.389	0.487	0.60	0.666	0.6233
$y = \ln(y)$	0.506	0.580	0.611	0.716	0.9014	0.920	0.948	0.967	0.998	1.033	1.054	1.116	10.35
X^2	1	0.3624	0.1664	0.0484	0.0001	0.014	0.0625	0.1075	0.151	0.2371	0.36	0.443	2.9524
xy	−0.506	−0.349	−0.249	−0.1575	0.0115	0.1108	0.237	0.3171	0.388	0.5030	0.6324	0.7432	1.6815

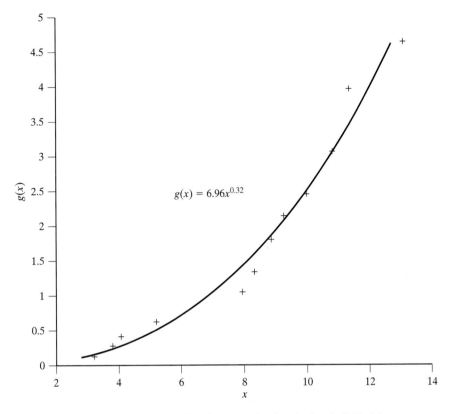

$$g(x) = 6.96x^{0.32}$$

FIGURE 4.2 The power function curve fitted to the data in Table 4.4.

The function is further plotted against the given data in Figure 4.2 to highlight its fitted approximation.

End of Example 4.2

4.3 Curve Fitting with a Higher-Order Polynomial

The principle of high-order functions can be extended to fitting a higher-order polynomial to measured data. An nth-order polynomial is expressed as

$$g(x) = c_1 x^n + c_2 x^{n-1} + \cdots + c_{n+1} \tag{4.18}$$

Where $c_1, c_2, \ldots c_n$ are constants to be determined. Obviously we need n equations to solve for these coefficients. We are faced with the task of finding the c_s values.

Deviation of the curve from each data point is

$$r_i = y_i - g(x_i), \qquad i = 1, 2, \ldots L \tag{4.19}$$

where L is the number of data points. The sum of the squared deviations is

$$R = \sum_{i=1}^{L} r_i^2 \tag{4.20}$$

In order to minimize R, we set the partial derivatives of R with respect to c_j to zero:

$$\frac{\partial R}{\partial c_j} = 0, \qquad j = 1, 2, \ldots, n + 1 \tag{4.21}$$

or equivalently

$$\sum_{j=1}^{n+1} \left(\sum_{i=1}^{L} x_i^{2n+2-j-k} \right) c_j = \sum_{i=1}^{L} x_i^{n+1-k} y_i, \qquad k = 1, 2, \ldots, n + 1 \tag{4.22}$$

or in matrix form as

$$
\begin{bmatrix}
\sum_{i=1}^{L} x_i^{2n} & \sum_{i=1}^{L} x_i^{2n-1} & \cdot & \sum_{i=1}^{L} x_i^{n} \\
\sum_{i=1}^{L} x_i^{2n-1} & \cdot & \cdot & \sum_{i=1}^{L} x_i^{n-1} \\
\cdot & \cdot & \cdot & \cdot \\
\sum_{i=1}^{L} x_i^{n} & \cdot & \cdot & \sum_{i=1}^{L} x_i^{0}
\end{bmatrix}
\begin{bmatrix}
c_1 \\
c_2 \\
\cdot \\
c_{n+1}
\end{bmatrix}
=
\begin{bmatrix}
\sum_{i=1}^{L} x_i^{n} y_i \\
\sum_{i=1}^{L} x_i^{n-1} y_i \\
\cdot \\
\sum_{i=1}^{L} y_i
\end{bmatrix}
\tag{4.23}
$$

Equation (4.23) can be used to solve for the coefficients c_j needed to obtain the higher-order polynomial function defined by Equation (4.19).

In a compact form the matrix form above can be expressed as

$$Ac = y \tag{4.24}$$

where

$$
A =
\begin{bmatrix}
x_1^{n} & x_1^{n-1} & \cdot & 1 \\
x_2^{n} & \cdot & \cdot & 1 \\
\cdot & \cdot & \cdot & \cdot \\
x_L^{n} & \cdot & \cdot & 1
\end{bmatrix},
\quad
c =
\begin{bmatrix}
c_1 \\
c_2 \\
\cdot \\
c_{n+1}
\end{bmatrix},
\quad
y =
\begin{bmatrix}
y_1 \\
y_2 \\
\cdot \\
y_L
\end{bmatrix}
\tag{4.25}
$$

When $L > n + 1$, the equation is overdetermined because the number of equations is greater than the number of undetermined coefficients. Premultiplying both sides of Equation (4.24) by the transpose of A we obtain

$$A^t Ac = A^t y \quad \text{or} \quad A*c = y* \tag{4.26}$$

from which c is given by

$$c = A^{*-1}y*$$ (4.27)

and

$$A* = A^t A \quad \text{and} \quad y* = A^t y$$ (4.28)

Example 4.3

A data set of a biomechanical experiment is provided in Table 4.5. Find a polynomial of order 12 that best fits the data.

Solution: Given the size of the matrices, we opted to leave the solution as described above as an exercise for the students. However, a solution using MATLAB is provided below. Those familiar with MATLAB will find that the function POLYFIT does exactly what is explained about the higher-order polynomial fitting technique. In this section a sample program is provided to show how the curve fits the data.

We find the coefficients of the quadratic polynomial by the polyfit command, and then plot the corresponding curve. A script to complete the answer is as follows:

```
clear, clg
x=[.1, .25, .39, .6, 1.03, 1.32, 1.78, 2.13, 2.45, 3.07, 3.98,
4.64];
y=[3.21, 3.81, 4.09, 5.21, 7.97, 8.32, 8.88, 9.27, 9.97,
10.8, 11.34, 13.08];
cc=polyfit (x, y, 2)
xx=x (1) : 0.1 : x (length (x))
yy=polyval (cc, xx)
plot (xx, yy); hold on
plot (x, y, 'X')
xlabel ('X')
ylabel ('Y')
```

The plot of the result is shown in Figure 4.3.

End of Example 4.3

TABLE 4.5   Biomechanical data.

i	1	2	3	4	5	6	7	8	9	10	11	12
x	0.1	0.25	0.39	0.60	1.03	1.32	1.78	2.13	2.45	3.07	3.98	4.64
y	3.21	3.81	4.09	5.21	7.97	8.32	8.88	9.27	9.97	10.8	11.34	13.08

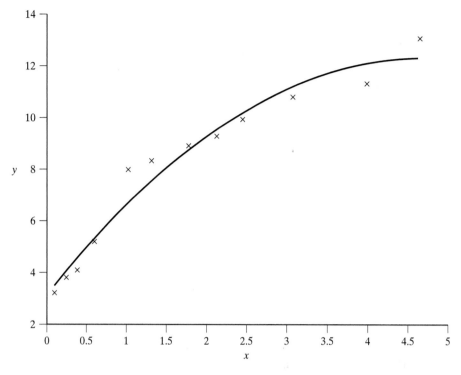

FIGURE 4.3 Plot of the quadratic polynomial fitted.

4.4   Chebyshev Polynomial Fit

Some of the difficulties with the polynomial equation approximation that may occur (such as erroneous derivatives) can be reduced or eliminated entirely by the use of Chebyshev polynomials instead of the algebraic polynomials. The definition of a Chebyshev polynomial is contained in the following rules:

1. A Chebyshev polynomial is defined over the interval $[-1,1]$.
2. The range of the independent variable must then be $-1 < x_0 < x_1 < \cdots$ $< x_n < 1$.
3. The zero-order Chebyshev polynomial is $T_0(x) = 1$.
4. The first-order Chebyshev polynomial is $T_1(x) = x$.
5. The second-order Chebyshev polynomial is $T_2(x) = 2x^2 - 1$.

A Chebyshev polynomial has a recursive formula that is used to calculate higher-order polynomials

$$T_k(x) = 2xT_{k-1}(x) - T_{k-2}(x) \qquad (k = 2, 3, \dots) \qquad (4.29)$$

For a function that has only one independent variable, the Chebyshev approximating formulation yields

$$f(x) = \sum_{k=0}^{n} a_k T_k(x) \tag{4.30}$$

Example 4.4

Figure 4.4 shows the profile of the road on which a vehicle moves. Approximate the function of the road $y = 2 \sin 22.44t$. Consider the six data points, where range of t is given by $[a, b]$

$$[a, b] = [0, 0.56] = [0 \quad 0.112 \quad 0.224 \quad 0.336 \quad 0.448 \quad 0.56]$$

Since our interval of interest is

$$[a, b] = [0, 0.56] = [0 \quad 0.112 \quad 0.224 \quad 0.336 \quad 0.448 \quad 0.56]$$

and the Chebyshev polynomials are defined over only the interval $[-1,1]$, we must transform the actual physical interval to the Chebyshev interval by using the transformation

$$I = 2\left(\frac{x - a}{b - a}\right) - 1 \tag{4.31}$$

The variable t is the independent variable in the transformed Chebyshev domain and plays the same role as x in the physical domain.

Applying Equation (4.31) to the interval [0,0.56], we get

$$I = 2\left(\frac{x - 0}{2\Pi}\right) - 1 = \frac{x}{\Pi} - 1$$

$$= [-1 \quad -0.6 \quad -0.2 \quad 0.2 \quad 0.6 \quad 1] = x'$$

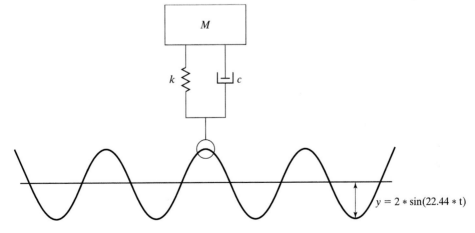

FIGURE 4.4 Free-body analysis of a vehicle on a road.

so that

$$f(x') = a_0 T_0(x') + a_1 T_1(x') + a_2 T_2(x') + a_3 T_3(x') + a_4 T_4(x') + a_5 T_5(x') \qquad (4.32)$$

where

$$T_0(x') = 1$$

$$T_1(x') = x'$$

$$T_2(x') = 2x'^2 - 1$$

$$T_3(x') = 2x' T_2(x') - T(x')_1 = 4x'^3 - 3x' \qquad (4.33)$$

$$T_4(x') = 8x'^4 - 8x'^2 + 1$$

$$T_5(x') = 16x'^5 - 20x'^3 + 5x'$$

The approximating function becomes

$$f(x') = a_0 + a_1 x' + a_2 \{2x'^2 - 1\} + a_3 \{4x'^3 - 3x'\} + a_4 \{8x'^4 - 8x'^2 + 1\}$$
$$+ a_5 \{16x'^5 - 20x'^3 + 5x'\} \qquad (4.34)$$

If we evaluate this equation at the x' data points, we get

$$\begin{bmatrix} 1.0000 & 1.0000 & 1.0000 & -1.0000 & 1.0000 & -1.0000 \\ 1.0000 & -0.6000 & -0.2800 & 0.9360 & -0.8430 & 0.0760 \\ 1.0000 & -0.2000 & -0.9200 & 0.5680 & 0.6930 & -0.8450 \\ 1.0000 & 0.2000 & -0.9200 & -0.5680 & 0.6930 & 0.8450 \\ 1.0000 & 0.6000 & -0.2800 & -0.9360 & -0.8430 & -0.0760 \\ 1.0000 & 1.0000 & 1.0000 & 1.0000 & 1.0000 & 1.0000 \end{bmatrix} \begin{bmatrix} a_0 \\ a_1 \\ a_2 \\ a_3 \\ a_4 \\ a_5 \end{bmatrix} = \begin{bmatrix} 0 \\ 1.176 \\ -1.902 \\ 1.902 \\ -1.176 \\ 0 \end{bmatrix}$$

$$(4.35)$$

The equation may now be solved to yield

$$a = [0.000 \quad -2.1839 \quad -0.000 \quad -0.3492 \quad 0.000 \quad 2.5331] \qquad (4.36)$$

and the functional approximation now becomes

$$f(x') = -2.1839 T_1 - 0.3492 T_2 + 2.5331 T_5 \qquad (4.37)$$

The desired and approximate value for the sinutoidol function as given in Table 4.6; obviously, one needs higher order polynomial to achieve the desired approximation.

End of Example 4.4

TABLE 4.6   Fifth-order polynomial curve fit (Red curve-ideal).*

Value of x in the Function $y = 2*\sin x$	Desired Results	Results from Approximation
0.1	0.1997	0.8614
0.6	1.1293	3.5580
1.1	1.7824	4.2305
1.6	1.9991	3.6396
2.1	1.7264	2.3855
2.6	1.0310	0.9226
3.1	0.0832	−0.4243
3.6	−0.8850	−1.4448
4.1	−1.6366	−2.0274
4.6	−1.9874	−2.1436
5.1	−1.8516	−1.8330
5.6	−1.2625	−1.1872
6.1	−0.3643	−0.3349

*where $x = 22.44t$

4.5   Fourier Series of Discrete Systems

Fourier series approximations are usually reserved to represent periodic functions whose analytical expressions are known. The conventional development of a Fourier series formulation is widely covered in other textbooks and is not examined here. Instead, we are concerned with the Fourier series approximation when the function is known at a discrete number of equally spaced points rather than as an algebraic equation. The data do not have to represent a periodic function. However, the choice of this approximating technique will yield better results if the data closely approximate a periodic function. By performing a variable transformation, we can transform the physical interval by using a new independent variable θ that has the range $[0, 2\Pi]$ from some given interval $[a,b]$. We then subdivide this interval into $2N$ equally spaced parts by using $\Delta\theta = (\Pi/N)$. The function y_k is then known at the points $\theta_i = (i - 1)*\Delta\theta$. There are $2N$ known values of the function through which the series will be fitted. Then we have

$$y_0 = f(0)$$
$$y_1 = f(\Delta\theta)$$
$$\vdots$$
$$y_{2N-1} = f[2(N - 1)\Delta\theta]$$

(4.38)

We define our discrete Fourier series as

$$f(\theta) = \frac{a_0}{2} + \sum_{j=1}^{m}(a_j \cos j\theta + b \sin j\theta) \tag{4.39}$$

or

$$f(\theta) = \frac{a_0}{2} + (a_1 \cos \theta + a_2 \cos 2\theta + \cdots + a_m \cos m\theta)$$

$$+ (b_1 \sin \theta + b_2 \sin 2\theta + \cdots + b_m \sin m\theta) \tag{4.40}$$

where m is the number of terms in the series and the coefficients are given by

$$a_j = \frac{2}{\tau}\int_0^\tau f°\theta/\cos j\theta d\theta \qquad j = 0, 1, 2, \ldots, m \tag{4.41}$$

$$b_j = \frac{2}{\tau}\int_0^\tau f°\theta/\sin j\theta d\theta \qquad j = 0, 1, 2, \ldots, m \tag{4.42}$$

where τ is the time period.

We can, of course, put the series through all the $2N$(interval) points. However, if we wish to obtain a smooth curve that will fit the data, we may want to revert to a least-squares approach, as delineated above. In this case, we wish to minimize the error function defined by

$$E = \sum_{k=0}^{2N-1}[f(\theta) - y_k]^2 \tag{4.43}$$

We can show that the Fourier coefficients are

$$a_j = \frac{1}{N}\sum f(\theta_k)\cos j\theta_k \qquad j = 0, 1, 2, \ldots, m \tag{4.44}$$

$$b_j = \frac{1}{N}\sum f(\theta_k)\sin j\theta_k \qquad j = 0, 1, 2, \ldots, m \tag{4.45}$$

where $\theta_k = k\Delta\theta = k(\Pi/N)$.

To illustrate this application of the above technique, let us consider four data points that are available to us by using the control function $y = 2 \sin \theta$, which indicates the forcing function for the mass (M) shown in Figure 4.5. Here, let us once again consider the data in the interval $[0, 2\Pi]$, i.e.,

θ	0	$\dfrac{2\Pi}{3}$	$\dfrac{4\Pi}{3}$	2Π
$f(\theta)$	0	$\sqrt{3}$	$-\sqrt{3}$	0

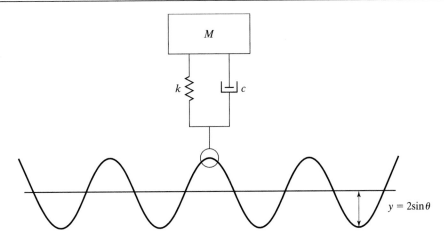

FIGURE 4.5 Mass M with support motion.

We apply the discrete Fourier series method to the above data with the four data points and use a two-term Fourier series (as the least-squares approximating curve).

$$f(\theta) = \frac{a_0}{2} + (a_1 \cos \theta + a_2 \cos 2\theta) + (b_1 \sin \theta + b_2 \sin 2\theta) \qquad (4.46)$$

Because the function is odd then all the a_2 are 0s. Hence, we obtain

$$f(\theta) = b_1 \sin \theta + b_2 \sin 2\theta \qquad (4.47)$$

where

$$b_1 = \frac{1}{N} \sum f(\theta_k) \sin \theta_k$$

$$= \frac{1}{2} \left(0 * \sin 0 + \sqrt{3} * \sin \frac{2\Pi}{3} - \sqrt{3} * \sin \frac{4\Pi}{3} + 0 * \sin 2\Pi \right) \qquad (4.48)$$

$$= 1.5$$

and

$$b_2 = \frac{1}{N} \sum f(\theta_k) \sin 2\theta_k$$

$$= \frac{1}{2} \left(0 * \sin 0 + \sqrt{3} * \sin \frac{4\Pi}{3} - \sqrt{3} * \sin \frac{8\Pi}{3} + 0 * \sin 4\Pi \right) \qquad (4.49)$$

$$= -1.5$$

Therefore the function is

$$f(\theta) = 1.5 \sin \theta - 1.5 \sin 2\theta \qquad (4.50)$$

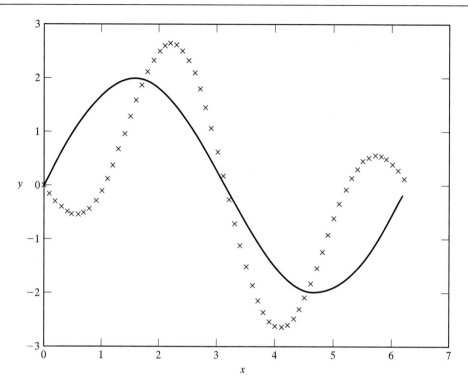

FIGURE 4.6 Graph for $f(\theta) = 1.5 \sin \theta - 1.5 \sin 2\theta$ versus $y = 2 \sin \theta$.

This equation is a poor approximation of $y = 2 \sin \theta$. The reason for this can be seen if we plot the four points graphically (Figure 4.6). The continuous curve is the ideal curve and the curve with cross sign shows the approximation. If we connect these four points by straight lines, the function looks more like a saw tooth than a sine function. In this case, the poor approximation is due to the insufficient number of data points and to the order of the least-squares approximating curve. If the number of data points available in the region $[0, 2\Pi]$ is increased to eight (with the same two-term Fourier series), then we derive the new constants b_1 and b_2 needed to approximate the function. That is,

$$f(\theta) = b_1 \sin \theta + b_2 \sin 2\theta \tag{4.51}$$

Let the values of the actual function for the eight points be given by

θ	0	51.43	102.86	154.29	205.72	257.15	308.58	360
$f(\theta)$	0	1.56	1.95	0.8676	−0.8676	−1.95	−1.56	0

$$b_1 = \frac{1}{N}\sum f(\theta_k)\sin\theta_k$$

$$= \frac{1}{4}(0*\sin 0 + 1.56*\sin 51.43 + 1.95*\sin 102.86 + 0.8676*\sin 154.29$$

$$- 0.868*\sin 205.72 - 1.95*\sin 257.15 - 1.56*\sin 308.58 + 0*\sin 360)$$

$$= 1.75 \tag{4.52}$$

and

$$b_2 = \frac{1}{N}\sum f(\theta_k)\sin 2\theta_k$$

$$= \frac{1}{4}(0*\sin 0 + 1.56*\sin 102.86 + 1.95*\sin 205.72 + 0.8676*\sin 308.58$$

$$- 0.868*\sin 411.44 - 1.95*\sin 514.3 - 1.56*\sin 617.16 + 0*\sin 720)$$

$$= 0 \tag{4.53}$$

Therefore, the approximate function is

$$f(\theta) = 1.75\sin\theta \tag{4.54}$$

The preceding equation is a better approximation, but still falls short of an acceptable approximation (Figure. 4.7). For 16 data points,

θ	0	24	48	72	96	120	144	168	192	216	240	264	288	312	336	360
$f(\theta)$	0	0.813	1.486	1.902	1.989	1.732	1.176	0.416	−0.416	−1.176	−1.732	−1.989	−1.902	−1.486	−0.813	0

$$f(\theta) = b_1\sin\theta + b_2\sin 2\theta$$

$$b_1 = \frac{1}{N}\sum f(\theta_k)\sin\theta_k$$

$$= \frac{1}{8}(0*\sin 0 + 0.813*\sin 24 + 1.486*\sin 48 + 1.902*\sin 72 + 1.989*\sin 96$$

$$+ 1.732*\sin 120\ 1.176*\sin 144 + 0.416*\sin 168 - 0.416*\sin 192$$

$$- 1.176*\sin 216 - 1.732*\sin 240 - 1.989*\sin 264 + -1.902*\sin 288$$

$$- 1.486*\sin 312 - 0.813*\sin 336 + 0*\sin 360)$$

$$= 1.876$$

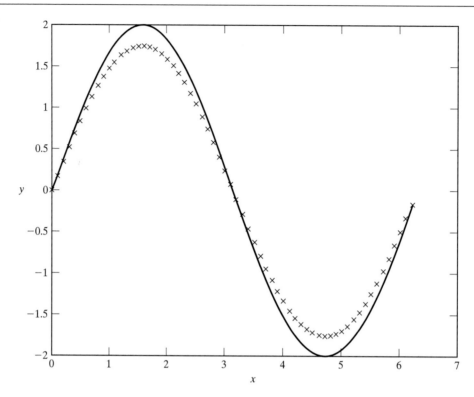

FIGURE 4.7 Graph for $f(\theta) = 1.75 \sin \theta$.

$$b_2 = \frac{1}{N} \sum f(\theta_k) \sin 2\theta_k$$

$$= \frac{1}{8}(0*\sin 0 + 0.813*\sin 48 + 1.486*\sin 96 + 1.902*\sin 144 + 1.989*\sin 192$$

$$+ 1.732*\sin 240\ 1.176*\sin 288 + 0.416*\sin 336 - 0.416*\sin 384$$

$$- 1.176*\sin 432 - 1.732*\sin 480\ -1.989*\sin 528 + -1.902*\sin 576$$

$$- 1.486*\sin 624 - 0.813*\sin 672 + 0*\sin 720)$$

$$= 0$$

$f(\theta) = 1.876 \sin \theta$ (Figure 4.8)

and for 32 data points, if we follow the same procedure as above, we get

θ	0	10.29	20.58	30.87	41.16	51.45	61.74	72.03	82.32	92.61
$f(\theta)$	0	0.3573	.70	1.026	1.316	1.564	1.76	1.902	1.98	1.998

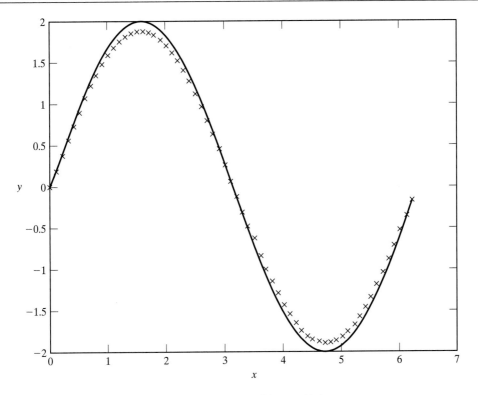

FIGURE 4.8 Graph for $f(\theta) = 1.876 \sin \theta$.

102.9	113.19	123.48	133.77	144.06	154.35	164.64	174.93	185.22	195.51
1.95	1.84	1.67	1.44	1.174	0.87	0.535	0.177	−0.182	−0.535

205.8	216.09	226.38	236.66	246.96	257.25	267.57	277.83	288.12	298.41
−0.87	−1.174	−1.44	−1.67	−1.84	−1.95	−1.998	−1.98	−1.902	−1.76

308.7	318.99	329.28	339.57	349.86	360
−1.56	−1.313	−1.022	−0.7	−0.352	0

$$f(\theta) = b_1 \sin \theta + b_2 \sin 2\theta$$

$$b_1 = \frac{1}{N} \sum f(\theta_k)\sin \theta_k$$

$$= \frac{1}{16}(0*\sin 0 + 0.3573*\sin 10.29 + 0.70*\sin 20.58 + 1.026*\sin 30.87$$

$$+ 1.316*\sin 41.16 + 1.564*\sin 51.45 + 1.76*\sin 61.74 + 1.902*\sin 72.03$$

$$+ 1.98*\sin 82.32 + 1.998*\sin 92.61 + 1.95*\sin 102.90 + 1.84*\sin 113.19$$

$$+ 1.67*\sin 123.48 + 1.44*\sin 133.77 + 1.174*\sin 144.06 + 0.87*\sin 154.35$$

$$+ 0.535*\sin 164.64 + 0.177*\sin 174.93 - 0.182*\sin 185.22 - 0.535*\sin 195.51$$

$$- 0.87*\sin 205.81 - 1.174*\sin 216.09 - 1.44*\sin 226.09 - 1.67*\sin 236.66$$

$$- 1.84*\sin 246.96 - 1.95*\sin 257.25 - 1.998*\sin 267.57 - 1.98*\sin 277.83$$

$$- 1.902*\sin 288.12 - 1.76*\sin 298.41 - 1.56*\sin 308.7 - 1.313*\sin 318.99$$

$$- 1.022*\sin 329.28 - 0.7*\sin 339.57 - 0.352*\sin 349.86 + 0*\sin 360)$$

$$= 1.96$$

and

$$b_2 = \frac{1}{N}\sum f(\theta_k)\sin 2\theta_k$$

$$= 0$$

Therefore,

$$f(\theta) = 1.96 \sin \theta$$

(See Figure 4.9).

We then see that the approximation approaches the actual function as the number of data points increases, although the number of terms in the Fourier series still remains at two. Figures 4.7 and 4.8 show the effects of the $f(\theta)$ equations on the approximation process.

4.6   Cubic Splines

A spline is a smooth curve that can be generated by computer to go through a set of data points. The mathematical spline derives from its physical counterpart—the thin elastic beam. Because the beam is supported at specified points (we call them "knots"), it can be shown that its deflection (assumed small) is characterized by a polynomial of order three, hence a cubic spline. It is not a mere coincidence that the principle of explaining the deflection of beams under different loads results in a function of a third order. The function of a spline is defined as

$$y(x) = \sum_{i=1}^{4} a_i x^{i-1} \quad (1 < i < 4) \tag{4.55}$$

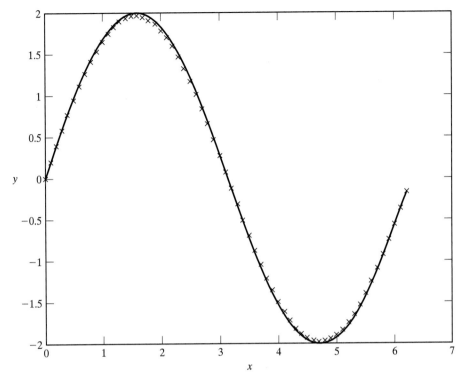

FIGURE 4.9 Graph for $f(\theta) = 1.96 \sin\theta$ versus $y = 2 \sin\theta$.

The benefits of using cubic splines are as follows:

1. They reduce computational requirements and numerical instabilities that arise from higher-order curves.
2. They have the lowest-degree space curve that allows inflection points.
3. They have the ability to twist in space.

In this chapter we will introduce two types of splines (the parametric and the nonparametric splines), where we undertake the task of explaining the basic mathematical derivation and provide examples to demonstrate their implementation.

4.7 Parabolic Cubic Splines

Consider a set of data points described in the x,y-plane by (x_i, y_i) with $i = 1, \ldots, n$. Our objective is to pass a parametric cubic spline between all these points. A parametric cubic spline is a curve that is represented as a function of one or more parameters. The parametric cubic spline equation between any two points is given in terms of a parameter t as follows:

$$S_i(t) = a_{i,0} + a_{i,1}t + a_{i,2}t^2 + a_{i,3}t^3 \tag{4.56}$$

$a_{i,0}$, $a_{i,1}$, $a_{i,2}$, and $a_{i,3}$ are constants that are determined from the boundary conditions and the continuity and smoothness of the curve. Observe how t defines a precise length between any two points. So its value goes from 0 to 1 if the length is normalized. At $t = 0$, the spline S_i is equal to the coefficient $a_{i,0}$. Hence,

$$a_{i,0} = S_i = P_i = (x_i, y_i) \quad \text{for} \quad i = 1, \ldots, n$$

$$a_{i,0} = [x_i, y_i] \tag{4.57}$$

Our objective at this point is to evaluate the constants between each interval. Parameter t cord length is defined by

$$t_{i+1} = \sqrt{(x_{i+1} - x_i)^2 + (y_{i+1} - y_i)^2} \quad \text{for} \quad i + 1 = 2, \ldots, n \tag{4.58}$$

The procedure for evaluating the other a_s constants is as follows.

Consider three points, P_1, P_2, and P_3. Let the chord length between P_1 and P_2 be t_2 and the one between P_2 and P_3 be t_3. Let S_i be the parametric cubic spline between P_1 and P_2 and S_{i+1} the one between P_2 and P_3. Because $S_i(t)$ starts at P_1 and ends at P_2, the value of t should start from 0 at P_1 and end with $t = t_2$ at P_2. In reality the constants defined in Equation (4.56) have x and y components as they are needed to define points. A general form of the parametric spline expressed in terms of both x- and y-components can be expressed as follows:

$$S_i(t) \equiv [S_{xi}(t), S_{yi}(t)] = [a_{xi,0}, a_{yi,0}] + [a_{xi,1}, a_{yi,1}]t + [a_{xi,2}, a_{yi,2}]t^2 + [a_{xi,3}, a_{yi,3}]t^3 \tag{4.59}$$

where

$$0 \leq t \leq t_{i+1} \quad \text{and} \quad i = 1, \ldots, n - 1$$

Again observe how when we evaluate S_i at $t = 0$ as well as its derivative we obtain

$$S_i = S_i(t = 0) = [a_{i,0} + a_{i,1}t + a_{i,2}t^2 + a_{i,3}t^3]_{t=0} = a_{i,0} \tag{4.60}$$

$$S'_i \equiv S'_i(t = 0) = \left[\frac{dS_i(t)}{dt}\right]_{t=0} = [a_{i,1} + 2a_{i,2}t + 3a_{i,3}t^2]_{t=0} = a_{i,1} \tag{4.61}$$

Therefore

$$S_i = a_{i,0} = P_i(x_i, y_i) \quad \leftarrow (\text{Knowns: } n \text{ control points})$$

$$S'_1 = a_{i,1} \quad\quad\quad\quad\quad \leftarrow (n \text{ Unknowns}) \tag{4.62}$$

Similarly, we write the derivatives at points P_1 and P_2 as

$$S_i'(t) = \frac{dS_i(t)}{dt} = a_{i,1} + 2a_{i,2}t + 3a_{i,3}t^2 \tag{4.63}$$

$$S''_i(t) = \frac{dS_i^2(t)}{dt^2} = 2a_{i,2} + 6a_{i,3}t \tag{4.64}$$

$$S_i'''(t) = \frac{dS_i^3(t)}{dt^3} = 6a_{i,3} \tag{4.65}$$

Our cubic spline defined by equation (4.56), when we substitute the constants $a_{i,0}$ and $a_{i,1}$ with S_1 and S_2 obtained from Equations (4.60) and (4.61), takes the following form:

$$S_i(t) = S_1 + S'_1 t + a_{i,2}t^2 + a_{i,3}t^3 \tag{4.66}$$

Continuity at the control points $P(x_i, y_i)$ $i = 2, \ldots, n - 1$ yields

$$S_i\,(t = t_{i+1}) = S_{i+1}\,(t = 0) = S_{i+1} = P_{i+1}$$

$$S'_i(t = t_{i+1}) = S'_{i+1}(t = 0) = S'_{i+1} \tag{4.67}$$

from which we solve for $a_{i,2}$ and $a_{i,3}$. Because S_i is known and $a_{i,2}$ and $a_{i,3}$ are functions of S' it is more desirable to express them as

$$S_i + S'_i t_{i+1} + a_{i,2}t_{i+1}^2 + a_{i,3}t_{i+1}^3 = S_{i+1}$$

$$S'_i + a_{i,2}t_{i+1} + a_{i,3}t_{i+1}^2 = S'_{i+1} \tag{4.68}$$

Now we can find the expressions for $a_{i,2}$ and $a_{i,3}$ as functions of S_i, S'_i, S_{i+1}, and S'_{i+1}. Using Equations (4.67) and (4.68), we get

$$\Rightarrow a_{i,2} = \frac{3}{t_{i+1}^2}(S_{i+1} - S_i) - \frac{1}{t_{i+1}}(S'_{i+1} + 2S'_i) \tag{4.69}$$

$$a_{i,3} = -\frac{2}{t_{i+1}^3}(S_{i+1} - S_i) + \frac{1}{t_{i+1}^2}(S'_{i+1} + S'_i) \tag{4.70}$$

Therefore, the spline function between P_1 and P_2 could simply be expressed as

$$S_i(t) = S_1 + S'_1 + \left[\frac{3(S_2 - S_1)}{t_2^2} - \frac{2S'_1}{t_2} - \frac{S'_2}{t_2}\right]t^2 + \left[\frac{2(S_1 - S_2)}{t_2^3} + \frac{S'_1}{t_2^2} + \frac{S'_2}{t_2^2}\right]t^3 \tag{4.71}$$

In the context of computer graphics and general-purpose algorithm development, we need to ask the following questions:

1. How can we generate a solution for S'_1 and S'_2 for all cubic functions $S_i(t)$, $S_{i+1}(t), \ldots, S_n(t)$?
2. How do we select t, t_1, and t_2 for a given set of data points?
3. How do we ensure continuity between the splines at knots $P_1, P_2, \ldots, P_n$?

In any case, the solution given by Equation (4.71) can be generalized for any two adjacent cubic segments such as $S_i(t)$ and $S_{i+1}(t)$ for $1 < i < n - 2$, where n is the number of data points. Rewriting Equation (4.71) for a general data set we get

$$S_i(t) = S_i + S_i't + \left[\frac{3(S_{i+1} - S_i)}{t_{i+1}^2} - \frac{2S_i'}{t_{i+1}} - \frac{S_{i+1}'}{t_{i+1}}\right]t^2 + \left[\frac{2(S_i - S_{i+1})}{t_{i+1}^3} + \frac{S_1'}{t_{i+1}^2} + \frac{S_{i+1}'}{t_{i+1}^2}\right]t^3$$

(4.72)

To answer the foregoing questions, we first note that to ensure continuity between the cubic segments, we need to compute the second derivative of $S_i(t)$ and $S_{i+1}(t)$ and equate them at their corresponding connecting points. From Equation (4.56), we obtain

$$S_i''(t) = 2a_{i,2} + 6a_{i,3}t \tag{4.73}$$

$$S_i''(0) = 2a_{i,2} \tag{4.74}$$

$$S_i''(t_2) = 2a_{i,2} + 6a_{i,3}t_2 \tag{4.75}$$

We also know from the boundary conditions that

$$S_i''(t_2) = S_{i+1}''(0) \tag{4.76}$$

Using Equations (4.73), (4.74), and (4.75) together with Equations (4.40), (4.41), and (4.42) we obtain

$$t_i + 2S_1' + 2(t_{i+2} + t_{i+1})S_{i+1}' + t_{i+1}S_{i+2}'$$
$$= (3/t_{i+1}t_{i+2})[t_{i+1}^2(S_{i+2} - S_{i+1}) + t_{i+2}^2(S_{i+1} - S_i)] \qquad (1 \le i \le n - 2)$$

(4.77)

In matrix form, Equation (4.77) can be written explicitly to show the important feature of the equation. That is,

$$\begin{bmatrix} t_3 & 2(t_2 + t_3) & t_2 & 0 & 0 & \cdots & \cdots & 0 \\ 0 & t_4 & 2(t_3 + t_4) & t_3 & 0 & \cdots & \cdots & 0 \\ 0 & 0 & t_5 & 2(t_4 + t_5) & t_4 & \cdots & \cdots & 0 \\ \vdots & \vdots & \vdots & \vdots & \vdots & \cdots & \cdots & \vdots \\ 0 & 0 & \cdots & \cdots & \cdots & t_n & 2(t_{n-1} + t_n) & t_n \end{bmatrix} \begin{bmatrix} S_1' \\ S_2' \\ S_3' \\ \vdots \\ S_n' \end{bmatrix}$$

$$= \begin{bmatrix} \dfrac{3}{t_2 t_3}[t_2^2(S_3 - S_2) + t_3^2(S_2 - S_1)] \\ \dfrac{3}{t_3 t_4}[t_3^2(S_4 - S_3) + t_4^2(S_3 - S_2)] \\ \vdots \\ \dfrac{3}{t_{n-1} t_n}[t_{n-1}^2(S_n - S_{n-1}) + t_n^2(S_{n-1} - S_{n-2})] \end{bmatrix} \tag{4.78}$$

It is obvious that Equation (4.78) yields $n - 2$ equations with n unknowns. Essentially we need two additional equations in terms of S' in order to solve for the n unknowns. On the other hand, if end points S'_1 and S'_n are known, as is the case in beam-deflection analysis, then the system of equations results in a consistent set of equations for which we can solve for all the unknowns. Now we can examine the boundary conditions to complete the solution to the above problem.

Boundary Conditions *Natural Spline.* Also known as relaxed conditions, natural splines are determined by setting the second derivatives of $S(t)$ with respect to time (t) at the beginning and end to 0. Thus,

$$S''_1 = S''_1 (t = 0) = 0 \tag{4.79}$$

$$S''_n = S''_{n-1} (t = t_n) = 0 \tag{4.80}$$

Writing these conditions in terms of S', we obtain two equations

$$S'_1 + 0.5S'_2 = 1.5(S_2 - S_1)/t_2 \tag{4.81}$$

and

$$2S'_{n-1} + 4S'_n = (6/t_n)(S_n - S_{n-1}) \tag{4.82}$$

Adding Equations (4.81) and (4.82) to the $n - 2$ equations given by Equation (4.49), we can then solve for all the S'.

Clamped Spline. The boundary conditions for this spline are such that the first derivatives (slope) at $t = 0$ and $t = t_n$ are specified. Hence, they form the additional two other equations needed in Equation (4.78).

4.7.1 Summary

The parametric cubic spline between any two points is constructed as follows:

1. Find the maximum cord length and determine $t_1, t_2, \ldots, t_n$.
2. Use Equation (4.78) together with the corresponding boundary conditions to solve for the $S'_1, S'_2, \ldots, S'_n$.
3. Solve for the coefficients that make up the parametric cubic splines using Equations (4.62), (4.69), and (4.70).

Example 4.5

For following data set (1,1), (1.5,2), (2.5,1.75), and (3.0,3.25), find the parametric cubic spline assuming a relaxed condition at both ends of the data.

Solution:

TABLE 4.7

i	x_i	y_i	t_{i+1}
0	1	1	1.118
1	1.5	2.0	1.031
2	2.5	1.75	0.707
3	3.0	2.25	—

We first compute the cord length

$$t_{i+1} = \sqrt{(x_{i+1} - x_i)^2 + (y_{i+1} - y_i)^2}$$

The explicit equations needed to evaluate the S' are obtained from Equation (4.74)

$$i = 0) \quad 2S'_1 + S'_2 = \frac{3}{t_2}(S_2 - S_1)$$

$$i = 1) \quad t_3S'_1 + 2(t_3 + t_2)S'_2 + t_2S'_3 = \frac{3}{t_2t_3}[t_2^2(S_3 - S_2) + t_3^2(S_2 - S_1)]$$

$$i = 2) \quad t_4S'_2 + 2(t_4 + t_3)S'_3 + t_3S'_4 = \frac{3}{t_3t_4}[t_3^2(S_4 - S_3) + t_4^2(S_3 - S_2)]$$

$$i = 3) \quad S'_3 + 2S'_4 = \frac{3}{t_4}(S_4 - S_3) \tag{4.83}$$

Using the boundary conditions given by Equations (4.81) and (4.82), together with either the above Equation (4.54) or simply making use of Equation (4.78), we get

$$[C_T][S'_i] = [C_s] \tag{4.84}$$

where

$$[C_T] = \begin{bmatrix} 2 & 1 & 0 & 0 \\ 1.031 & 4.298 & 1.118 & 0 \\ 0 & 0.707 & 3.476 & 1.031 \\ 0 & 0 & 1 & 2 \end{bmatrix} \tag{4.85}$$

$$[C_s] = \begin{bmatrix} \dfrac{3(S_{x2} - S_{x1})}{2t_2} & \dfrac{3(S_{y2} - S_{y1})}{2t_2} \\[4mm] \dfrac{3}{t_1 t_2}[t_2^2(S_{x3} - S_{x2}) + t_3^2(S_{x2} - S_{x1})] & \dfrac{3}{t_2 t_3}[t_2^2(S_{y3} - S_{y2}) + t_3^2(S_{y2} - S_{y1})] \\[4mm] \dfrac{3}{t_3 t_4}[t_3^2(S_{4x} - S_{3x}) + t_4^3(S_{3x} - S_{2x})] & \dfrac{3}{t_3 t_4}[t_3^2(S_{4y} - S_{3y}) + t_4^3(S_{3y} - S_{2y})] \end{bmatrix}$$

$$= \begin{bmatrix} 1.342 & 2.683 \\ 4.637 & 1.952 \\ 4.245 & 1.672 \\ 2.121 & 2.121 \end{bmatrix} \tag{4.86}$$

To solve for S'_i we multiply Equation (4.84) by $[C_T]^{-1}$ which automatically yields the $a_{i,1}$ constants given by

$$[S'_i] = [C_T]^{-1}[C_s]$$

where s

$$= \begin{bmatrix} 0.2792 & 1.2917 \\ 0.7836 & 0.0996 \\ 0.8776 & 0.1720 \\ 0.6217 & 0.9745 \end{bmatrix} = \begin{bmatrix} a_{1,1} \\ a_{2,1} \\ a_{3,1} \\ a_{4,1} \end{bmatrix} \tag{4.87}$$

We now use Equation (4.69) to find $a_{i,2}$

$$a_{i,2} = \frac{3(S'_{i+1} - S_i)}{(t_{i+1})^2} - \frac{1}{t_{i+1}}(S'_{i+1} + 2S'_i) \quad \text{for} \quad i = 1, 2, 3 \tag{4.88}$$

$$\begin{bmatrix} a_{1,2} \\ a_{2,2} \\ a_{3,2} \end{bmatrix} = \begin{bmatrix} 0 & 0 \\ 0.452 & -1.067 \\ -0.361 & 1.135 \end{bmatrix} \tag{4.89}$$

In a similar fashion, Equation (4.68) gives the $a_{i,3}$ coefficients

$$a_{i,3} = \frac{-2}{(t_i + 1)^3}(S_{i+1} - S_i) + \frac{1}{(t_{i+1})^2}(S'_{i+1} + S'_i) \tag{4.90}$$

$$\begin{bmatrix} a_{1,3} \\ a_{2,3} \\ a_{3,3} \end{bmatrix} = \begin{bmatrix} 0.135 & -0.317 \\ -0.263 & 0.713 \\ 0.171 & -0.536 \end{bmatrix} \tag{4.91}$$

In conclusion, we have derived all three splines joining all four data points and they are expressed in their explicit forms.

$$S_1 = [1 \quad 1] + [0.279 \quad 1.292]t + [0 \quad 0]t^2 + [0.135 \quad -0.317]t^3$$

$$S_2 = [1.5 \quad 2] + [0.784 \quad 0.1]t + [0.452 \quad -1.067]t^2 + [-0.263 \quad -0.713]t^3$$

$$S_3 = [2.5 \quad 1.75] + [0.878 \quad 0.172]t + [-0.361 \quad 1.135]t^2 + [0.171 \quad -0.536]$$

$$(4.92)$$

The display of this is given in Figure 4.10.

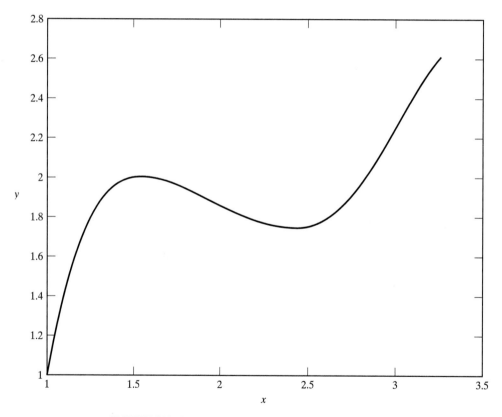

FIGURE 4.10   Parametric cubic curve given by Equation (4.92).

End of Example 4.5

4.8   Nonparametric Cubic Spline

A nonparametric cubic spline is defined as a curve having a function of only one parameter. Nonparametric cubic splines allow a direct variable relationship between the parameter value x and the value of the cubic spline function to be determined. This is seen from its mathematical representation:

$$S(x) = a + bx + cx^2 + dx^3 \tag{4.93}$$

From Equation (4.93), we see that the cubic spline is a function of x alone. Thus, we could say that for a given set of data points $P_1, P_2, \ldots, P_n$ defined in the interval in the domain $[x_0, x_1, \ldots, x_n]$, we need to construct the spline that passes through all these points. Let each subinterval be denoted by $[x_i, x_{i+1}]$; hence, our task is to find the cubic spline function for each of these intervals. Once more, we must find an algorithm to solve for the constants a, b, c, and d.

Cubic spline $S(x)$ is composed of $n - 1$ cubic segment splines. Each point has an x and y value; hence, the $S(x)$ function is defined for all points. For the interval $[x_i, x_{i+1}]$, we can write

$$S_i(x_i) = y_i \tag{4.94}$$

$$S(x_{i+1}) = S_{i+1}(x_{i+1}) = y_{i+1} \tag{4.95}$$

By considering the smoothness and continuity of the cubic splines, the following conditions are derived:

$$S_i'(x_{i+1}) = S_{i+1}'(x_{i+1}) \tag{4.96}$$

$$S_i''(x_{i+1}) = S_{i+1}''(x_{i+1}) \tag{4.97}$$

The nonparametric cubic spline function for any interval $x_i \leq x \leq x_{i+1}$ could be expressed as

$$S_i(x) = a_i + b_i(x - x_i) + c_i(x - x_i)^2 + d_i(x - x_i)^3 \tag{4.98}$$

Its first and second derivatives are

$$S_i' = b_i + 2c_i(x - x_i) + 3d_i(x - x_i)^2 \tag{4.99}$$

$$S_i'' = 2c_i + 6d_i(x - x_i) \tag{4.100}$$

Making use of the criteria of the spline given by Equations (4.94) to (4.100), we deduce the following:

$$S_i(x_i) = a_i = y_i \tag{4.101}$$

$$S_i(x_{i+1}) = a_{i+1} = a_i + b_i h_i + c_i h_i^2 + d_i h_i^3 \tag{4.102}$$

and

$$S_i'(x_i) = b_i \tag{4.103}$$

$$S_i'(x_{i+1}) = S_{i+1}'(x_{i+1}) = b_{i+1} = b_i + 2c_i h_i + 3d_i h_i^2 \tag{4.104}$$

$$S_i''(x_{i+1}) = S_{i+1}''(x_{i+1}) = 2c_{i+1} = 2c_i + 6d_i h_i \tag{4.105}$$

where

$$h_i = x_{i+1} - x_i$$

Because all the a_i values are known, we can solve for b_i using Equations (4.102) and (4.105):

$$b_i = \frac{a_{i+1} - a_i}{h_i} - \frac{h_i(2c_i + c_{i+1})}{3} \tag{4.106}$$

In essence, the foregoing equation for b_i was the result of using S_i and S_{i+1}. In a similar fashion, if we use S_{i-1} and S_i, we will get another expression as follows:

$$b_i = \frac{a_i - a_{i-1}}{h_{i-1}} - \frac{h_{i-1}(2c_{i-1} + c_i)}{3} \tag{4.107}$$

Equations (4.106) and (4.107) define the same b_i. Once we equate them they result into an equation in terms of the unknown c_s

$$h_{i-1}c_{i-1} + 2(h_{i-1} + h_i)c_i + h_ic_{i+1} = 3\left(\frac{a_{i+1} - a_i}{h_i} - \frac{a_i - a_{i-1}}{h_{i-1}}\right) \tag{4.108}$$

Once again we write the above equation in a matrix form, where the c_s coefficients are to be determined

$$\begin{bmatrix} h_0 & 2(h_0 + h_1) & h_1 & 0 & \cdots & \cdots & 0 \\ 0 & h_1 & 2(h_1 + h_2) & h_2 & \cdots & \cdots & 0 \\ 0 & 0 & h_2 & 2(h_2 + h_3) & \cdots & \cdots & 0 \\ \vdots & \vdots & \vdots & \vdots & \cdots & \cdots & \vdots \\ 0 & 0 & 0 & \cdots & h_{n-2} & 2(h_{n-2} + h_{n-1}) & h_{n-1} \end{bmatrix} \begin{bmatrix} c_0 \\ c_1 \\ c_2 \\ \vdots \\ c_n \end{bmatrix}$$

$$= 3\begin{bmatrix} \dfrac{a_2 - a_1}{h_1} - \dfrac{a_1 - a_0}{h_0} \\ \vdots \\ \dfrac{a_n - a_{n-1}}{h_{n-1}} - \dfrac{a_{n-1} - a_{n-2}}{h_{n-2}} \end{bmatrix} \tag{4.109}$$

Equation (4.109) consists of $n - 2$ equations with n unknowns; therefore, it cannot be solved. However, end points P_0 and P_n of the spline are usually known through the boundary conditions that must be supplied. By knowing c_0 and c_n, Equation (4.109) is then used to solve for the remaining c_1 through c_{n-1} values. The above equation can be expressed in a compact form as

$$[H][c_i] = [A_h] \quad \text{for} \quad i = 1, \ldots, n - 1 \tag{4.110}$$

H and A can be computed separately as they depend strictly on known coefficients.

In turn, the equation of the splines can be determined by computing the ds from Equation (4.76) followed by the bs from Equation (4.106).

$$b_i = \frac{a_i - a_{i-1}}{h_{i-1}} - \frac{h_{i-1}(2c_{i-1} + c_i)}{3} \tag{4.111}$$

$$d_i = \frac{c_{i+1} - c_i}{3h_i} \quad \text{for} \quad i = 0, \ldots, n - 1 \tag{4.112}$$

4.9   Boundary Conditions

4.9.1   Natural Splines

The boundary conditions in natural splines are found by setting the second derivatives at both the beginning and end points of the curve to 0. Therefore,

$$S'(x_0) = S''(x_n) = 0 \tag{4.113}$$

which when substituted into Equation (4.66) yields

$$c_0 = c_n = 0 \tag{4.114}$$

4.9.2   Clamped Splines

The clamped end conditions are determined by specifying the first derivatives (slope) at x_0 and x_n. That is,

$$S'(x_0) = f'(x_0) \tag{4.115}$$

and

$$S'(x_n) = f'(x_n) \tag{4.116}$$

where f' is a specified function. The following example illustrates the method used to evaluate the nonparametric cubic splines and highlights its usefulness. Note that we have introduced the concepts of splines in only a simplistic way; it is left for the reader to explore further the mathematics behind this most important curve-fitting method.

Example 4.6

Find the nonparametric cubic spline (natural spline) for the points shown in the table below.

i	x_i	y_i	h_i
0	1	1	0.5
1	1.5	2	1
$n = 2$	2.5	1.75	—

Solution:

Step 1: Control points, intervals, and a_i

Step 2: Solve for c_1: natural spline ($c_0 = c_2 = 0$)

$$h_0 c_0 + 2(h_0 + h_1)c_1 + h_1 c_2 = 3\left(\frac{a_2 - a_1}{h_1} - \frac{a_1 - a_0}{h_0}\right)$$

$$0.5 \times 0 + 2(0.5 + 1)c_1 + 1 \times 0 = 3\left(\frac{1.75 - 2}{1} - \frac{2 - 1}{0.5}\right)$$

$$3c_1 = 3(-0.25 - 2)$$

$$c_1 = -2.25$$

Step 3: Solve for b_i and d_i

$$b_i = \frac{a_{i+1} - a_i}{h_i} - \frac{h_i(2c_i + c_{i+1})}{3} \quad \text{for} \quad i = 0, \ldots, n - 1$$

$$= \frac{a_i - a_{i-1}}{h_{i-1}} + \frac{h_{i-1}(c_{i-1} + 2c_i)}{3} \quad \text{for} \quad i = 1, \ldots, n$$

$$d_i = \frac{c_{i+1} - c_i}{3h_i} \quad \text{for} \quad i = 0, \ldots, n - 1$$

$$i = 0 \begin{cases} b_0 = \dfrac{a_1 - a_0}{h_0} - \dfrac{h_0(2c_0 + c_1)}{3} = 2.375 \\[2mm] d_0 = \dfrac{c_1 - c_0}{3h_0} = -1.5 \end{cases}$$

$$i = 1 \begin{cases} b_1 = \dfrac{a_2 - a_1}{h_1} - \dfrac{h_1(2c_1 + c_2)}{3} = 1.25 \\[2mm] d_1 = \dfrac{c_2 - c_1}{3h_1} = 0.75 \end{cases}$$

The results are compiled in the following table and shown in Figure 4.11.

i	x_i	h_i	$y_i = a_i$	b_i	c_i	d_i
0	1	0.5	1	2.375	0	−1.5
1	1.5	1.0	2	1.25	−2.25	0.75
$n = 2$	2.5	—	1.75	—	0	—

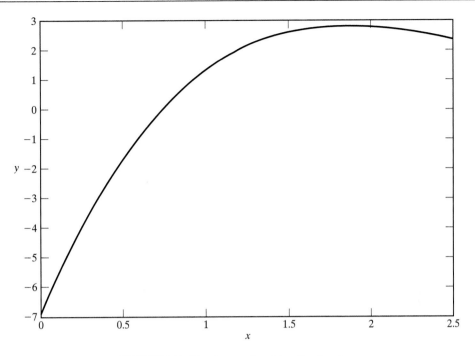

FIGURE 4.11 Nonparametric cubic spline function.

4.10 Bezier Curves

The shapes of Bezier curves are defined by the position of the points, and the curves may not intersect all the given points except for the endpoints. In certain circumstances, where there are insufficient points or awkwardly located points, the cubic spline method may not provide a smooth curve without defining more points. Bezier curves allow the flexibility of not constraining the curve to fit through all the points. One can imagine the shape of the curve to fit in a polygon defined by a series of points.

The mathematical bases (the weighing factor that affects the shape of the curve) of the Bezier curve is related to the Bernstein basis given by

$$J_{n,i}(t) = \begin{bmatrix} n \\ i \end{bmatrix} t^i (1 - t)^{n-i} \tag{4.117}$$

where

$$\begin{bmatrix} n \\ i \end{bmatrix} = \frac{n!}{i!(n - i)!}$$

and $n!$ is defined as

$$n! = n*(n - 1)*(n - 2)* \ldots \tag{4.118}$$

where n is the degree of the polynomial and i is the particular vertex in the ordered set (between 0 and n). The curve points are defined by

$$S(t) = \sum_{i=1}^{n} S_i J_{n,i}(t) \qquad (0 \le t \le 1) \tag{4.119}$$

where $i = 1$ to n, and the S_i contain the vector components of the various points.

In order to construct the Bezier curve, we need to evaluate the $J_{n,i}$, which are functions of parameter t. It is seen that the maximum value of the function $J_{n,i}$ occurs at $t = i/n$ and is given by

$$J_{n,i}\left(\frac{i}{n}\right) = \binom{n}{i} \frac{i^i (n-i)(n-i)}{n^n} \tag{4.120}$$

The following example illustrates the Bezier curve method of curve fitting.

Example 4.7

Define the Bezier curve that passes through the following points:

$$P_0 = [0 \quad 1] \qquad P_1 = [2 \quad 5]$$
$$P_2 = [4 \quad 5] \qquad P_3 = [6 \quad 1]$$

Find the Bezier curve space that passes through these points.

Solution   We note that the four points form the Bezier polygon. Because we have four defined vertices, then $n = 3$. Using Equation (4.117) we evaluate the J function, where

$$J_{3,0}(t) = (1)t^0(1-t)^3 - (1-t)^3$$
$$J_{3,1}(t) = 3(1-t)^2$$
$$J_{3,2}(t) = 3t^2(1-t)$$
$$J_{3,3}(t) = t^3 \tag{4.121}$$

Therefore,

$$S(t) = P_0 J_{3,0} + P_1 J_{3,1} + P_2 J_{3,2} + P_2 J_{3,3} \tag{4.122}$$

For various values of t, the coefficients for the Bezier curve are found in Table 4.8. The resulting $S(t)$ function is then found as

$$S(0) = [0 \quad 1] \qquad S(0.15) = [0.9 \quad 2.529]$$
$$S(0.35) = [2.102 \quad 3.733] \quad S(0.5) = [3 \quad 4]$$
$$S(0.65) = [3.904 \quad 3.733] \quad S(0.85) = [5.099 \quad 2.529]$$
$$S(1) = [6 \quad 1]$$

The results are plotted in Figure 4.12.

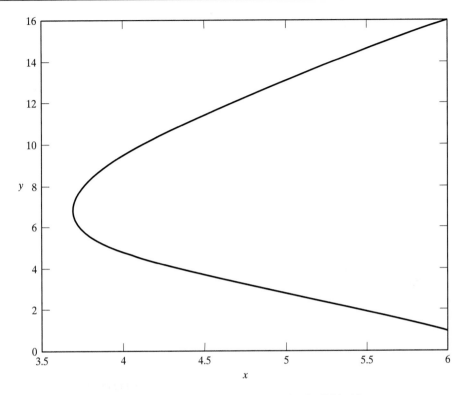

FIGURE 4.12 Bezier curve representation for Table 4.8.

TABLE 4.8 Evaluation of the Bezier function
$J_{3,1}(I = 0, 1, 2, 3)$ in terms of the parameter t.

t	$J_{3,0}$	$J_{3,1}$	$J_{3,2}$	$J_{3,3}$
0	1	0	0	0
0.15	0.614	0.325	0.0574	0.0034
0.35	0.275	0.444	0.239	0.043
0.5	0.125	0.375	0.375	0.125
0.65	0.043	0.239	0.444	0.275
0.85	0.0034	0.0574	0.325	0.614
1	0	0	0	1

End of Example 4.7

4.11   Differentiation of Bezier Curve Equation

The Bezier curve makes use of an expression that uses a factorial and a function $J_{n,i}(t)$ that needs to be kept in a compact form in order to simplify the calculation. We know that any curve function needs to be differentiated when intersection points, minimum or maximum, slopes, and endpoint conditions are sought. Let us begin with the Bezier curve as defined by Equation (4.119), where

$$S(t) = \sum_{i=1}^{n} S_i J_{n,i}(t) \qquad (0 \leq t \leq 1) \tag{4.123}$$

using differentiation by parts for Equation (4.123) we obtain

$$\frac{dS(t)}{dt} = \sum_{i=1}^{n} S_i' J_{n,i}(t) + \sum_{i=1}^{n} S_i J_{n,i}'(t) \tag{4.124}$$

Let us seek an expression for both S_i' and J' in order to complete our differentiation. Note that S_i' vanishes because it represents a value at i, and

$$J_{n,i}'(t) = \frac{d}{dt}\left[\binom{n}{i} t^i (1 - t)^{n-i} \right]$$

$$= i\binom{n}{i} t^{i-1}(1 - t)^{n-i} - (n - 1)\binom{n}{i} t^i (1 - t)^{n-i-1} \tag{4.125}$$

Substituting Equation (4.125) into Equation (4.124) yields the Bezier curve differentiation

$$\frac{dS(t)}{dt} = \sum i\binom{n}{i} t^{i-1}(1 - t)^{n-i} S_i - \sum (n - 1)\binom{n}{i} t^i (1 - t)^{n-i-1} S_i \tag{4.126}$$

Observe the left and right side of the terms of the above equation and notice how we can introduce values of S at i and $i + 1$ by simply changing the i with $j + 1$ for the left term. That is

$$\frac{dS(t)}{dt} = \sum_{j=0}^{n-1} (j + 1)\binom{n}{j + 1} t^j (1 - t)^{n-j-1} S_{j+1} - \sum_{i=0}^{n-1} (n - i)\binom{n}{i} t^i (1 - t)^{n-i-1} S_i \tag{4.127}$$

Note that

$$(j + 1)\binom{n}{j + 1} = n\binom{n - 1}{j}$$

and

$$(n - i)\binom{n}{i} = n\binom{n - 1}{i}$$

Then Equation (4.101) takes the following form

$$\frac{dS(t)}{dt} = n\sum_{i=0}^{n-1}\binom{n-1}{i}t^i(1-t)^{n-j-1}[S_{i+1} - S_i]$$ (4.128)

4.12 B-Spline Curve

B-splines were introduced to overcome some weaknesses in the Bezier curve. It seems that the number of control points affect the degree of the curve. Furthermore, the properties of the blending functions used in the Bezier curve do not allow for an easier way to modify the shape of the curve locally.

The B-spline curve is defined as follows:

$$S(t) = \sum_{i=0}^{n} S_i N_{i,k}(t) \qquad (t_{k-1} < t \le t_{n+1})$$ (4.129)

where

$$N_{i,k}(t) = \frac{(t - t_i)N_{i,k-1}(t)}{t_{i+k-1} - t_i} + \frac{(t_{i+k} - t)N_{i+1,k-1}(t)}{t_{i+k} - t_{i+1}}$$ (4.130)

and

$$N_{i,1}(t) = \begin{cases} 1 & t_i \le t \le t_{i+1} \\ 0 & \text{all the rest} \end{cases}$$ (4.131)

Again, t_i are known as the knot values and need to be evaluated in order to obtain all the N functions. Observe how $N_{i,1}$ is a constant; therefore, $N_{i,2}$ is a function of degree 1 based on Equation (4.130). In a similar fashion we can see that $N_{i,k}(t)$ has degree $(k - 1)$, where k is greater then the desired degree by 1. The value of k defines the order of the B-spline curve.

There are two types of knots:

a) Periodic knots:

$$T_i = i - k \qquad (0 \le i \le n + k)$$ (4.132)

b) Nonperiodic knots:

$$t_i = \begin{cases} 0 & 0 \le i < k \\ i - k + 1 & k \le i \le n \\ n - k + 2 & n < i \le n + k \end{cases}$$ (4.133)

When defining periodic knots the curves do not pass through the first and last points as ensured by the Bezier curve, whereas the nonperiodic knots ensure that the first and last points pass through the curve. This is due to k-times duplication of knots in the first and last ones as described in Equation (4.133).

Example 4.8

Define the B-spline curve of order 3 for nonperiodic uniform knots. The control points for the curve are given by P_0, P_1, and P_2.

Solution: When the gap between neighboring knots is always 1, this defines the uniform knots condition. From Equation (4.133) we obtain the $(n + k + 1)$ knot values as follows:

$$t_0 = 0, \quad t_1 = 0, \quad t_2 = 0, \quad t_3 = 1, \quad t_4 = 1, \quad \text{and} \quad t_5 = 1$$

$$(\text{note that } n = 2 \text{ and } k = 3)$$

From Equation (4.130) we obtain the $N_{i,k}(t)$ functions. We need to evaluate the N function corresponding to order 1, 2, and 3 as required. From t_0 to t_{n+k} we need to define $(n + 1)$ blending functions.

Order 1. Let us compute all possible functions.

$$N_{0,1}(t) = \begin{cases} 1 & t_0 \leq t \leq t_1 \\ 0 & \text{else} \end{cases}$$

$$N_{1,1}(t) = \begin{cases} 1 & t_1 \leq t \leq t_2 \\ 0 & \text{else} \end{cases}$$

$$N_{2,1}(t) = \begin{cases} 1 & t_2 \leq t \leq t_3 \\ 0 & \text{else} \end{cases} \qquad (4.134)$$

$$N_{3,1}(t) = \begin{cases} 1 & t_3 \leq t \leq t_4 \\ 0 & \text{else} \end{cases}$$

$$N_{4,1}(t) = \begin{cases} 1 & t_4 \leq t \leq t_5 \\ 0 & \text{else} \end{cases}$$

From the above we need to select the nonzero function at $t = 0$ and at $t = 1$. For that we choose $N_{2,1}(t)$ to be the only nonzero function in the range $(0,1)$ which has a value of 1.

Order 2. We obtain order 2 $N_{i,2}$ function as follows :

$$N_{1,2}(t) = \frac{(t - t_1)N_{1,1}}{t_2 - t_1} + \frac{(t_3 - t)N_{2,1}}{t_3 - t_2}$$

$$= (1 - t)N_{2,1} \qquad (4.135)$$

$$= (1 - t)$$

and

$$N_{2,2}(t) = \frac{(t - t_2)N_{2,1}}{t_3 - t_2} + \frac{(t_4 - t)}{t} \tag{4.136}$$

In a similar fashion, we obtain the $N_{i,3}(t)$ functions for order 3.

$$N_{0,3}(t) = (1 - t)^2$$

$$N_{1,3}(t) = 2t(1 - t) \tag{4.137}$$

$$N_{2,3}(t) = t^3$$

Thus, the B-spline curve is

$$S(t) = (1 - t)^2 S_0 + 2t(1 - t)S_1 + t^2 S_2 \tag{4.138}$$

where S_0, S_1, and S_2 correspond to control points P_0, P_1, and P_2, respectively.

End of Example 4.8

4.13   Nonuniform Rational B-Spline (NURBS) Curve

The NURBS curve is similar to the uniform B-spline curve except it makes use of a set of coordinates of the form $(x.h_i, y.h_i, z.h_i, h_i)$ such that

$$x.h = \sum_{i=0}^{n} (h_i.x_i)N_{i,k}(t)$$

$$y.h = \sum_{i=0}^{n} (h_i.y_i)N_{i,k}(t)$$

$$z.h = \sum_{i=0}^{n} (h_i.z_i)N_{i,k}(t) \tag{4.139}$$

$$h = \sum_{i=0}^{n} h_i N_{i,k}(t)$$

The equation for NURBS curve $S(t)$ is given by:

$$S(t) = \frac{\sum_{i=0}^{n} h_i S_i N_{i,k}(t)}{\sum_{i=0}^{n} h_i N_{i,k}(t)} \tag{4.140}$$

The advantage of NURBS comes from its flexibility to modify the curve by simply changing the x, y, z-coordinates of the control points with use of h. This convenience of a scaling factor allows for a precise change in space to develop smoother curves. In addition circular and conic shapes can be represented accurately and precisely rather than being approximated, as with the B-spline curve.

Example 4.9

Derive a NURBS representation of a quarter circle of radius 1. Let the arc be defined in the x, y-plane. Determine the corresponding coordinates of the control points, and the knot values.

Solution: We define three control points P_0, P_1, and P_2 as shown in Figure 4.13.

Let the order be 3, and the knot values are defined as follows:

$$t_0 = 0, \quad t_1 = 0, \quad t_2 = 0, \quad t_3 = 1, \quad t_4 = 1, \quad \text{and} \quad t_5 = 1$$

Following Equation (4.139), we obtain the h values:

$$h_0 = 1$$

$$h_1 = \frac{1}{\sqrt{2}} = \frac{\sqrt{2}}{2}$$

$$h_2 = 1 \tag{4.141}$$

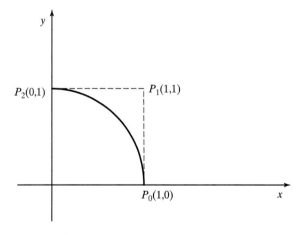

FIGURE 4.13   Control points of a quarter circle.

The NURBS equation is given by:

$$S(t) = \frac{h_0 S_0 N_{0,3}(t) + h_1 S_1 N_{1,3}(t) + h_2 S_2 N_{2,3}(t)}{h_0 N_{0,3}(t) + h_1 N_{1,3}(t) + h_2 N_{2,3}(t)} \qquad (4.142)$$

where

$$N_{2,1}(t) = \begin{cases} 1 & 0 \le t \le 1 \\ 0 & \text{else} \end{cases}$$

$$N_{1,2}(t) = 1 - t \qquad N_{0,3}(t) = (1 - t)^2 \qquad (4.143)$$

$$N_{2,2}(t) = t \qquad N_{1,3}(t) = 2t(1 - t)$$

$$N_{2,3}(t) = t^2$$

with $S_0 = P_0$, $S_1 = P_1$, and $S_2 = P_2$; after substitution, the NURBS equation is found to be:

$$S(t) = \frac{1.\begin{pmatrix} 1 \\ 0 \\ 0 \end{pmatrix}(1 - t)^2 + \dfrac{\sqrt{2}}{2}\begin{pmatrix} 1 \\ 1 \\ 0 \end{pmatrix}2t(1 - t) + 1\begin{pmatrix} 0 \\ 1 \\ 0 \end{pmatrix}t^2}{1.(1 - t)^2 + \dfrac{\sqrt{2}}{2}2t(1 - t) + 1t^2} \qquad (4.144)$$

The function $S(t)$ is strictly a function of t and can be used to generate the points that define the values of S for t. This should result in the quarter circle initially defined by three control points.

End of Example 4.9

4.14 Surface Creation

Surface creation is instrumental in visualizing objects in space. It allows the user to work with a more concrete look that shows the outer shape of the object. This feature enhances the design aspects of the problem and sets the stage for decisions on how to manufacture the components of the part.

Surface generation depends on the techniques used to fit the appropriate curves between the given boundaries. A major problem in surface fitting is defining the visual criteria for the design at hand. Therefore, selecting the appropriate methods for engineering applications is essential to a finer and more visually acceptable design. The methods should allow a certain flexibility in modifying the curve fitting for better interpolation. Some of the methods in surface fitting include the following.

4.15   Plane Surface

A plane surface is defined by four curves or lines that connect four corners. By using a CAD system, a plane is created by specifying three points. Plane surfaces are used to define planes, boundaries, intersecting planes, and simple illustrations of geometric planes when creating objects in 3D (Figures 4.14 and 4.15).

4.16   Ruled Surface

Also called a "lofted surface," a ruled surface is simple and fundamental to surface design. It is defined as follows: Given two space parametric curves c_1 and c_2, a surface S is defined that contains both curves as opposite boundary curves. (An interpolation is then carried out between c_1 and c_2; to represent the slope of the ruled surface, see Figure 4.16).

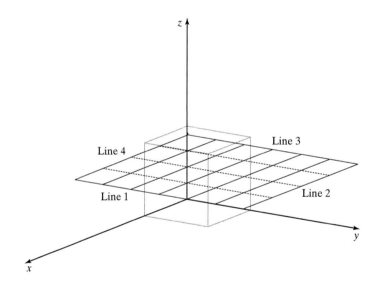

FIGURE 4.14   Plane surface formed by intersecting lines.

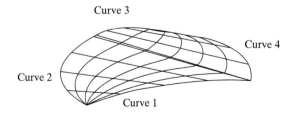

FIGURE 4.15   Plane surface formed by intersecting curves.

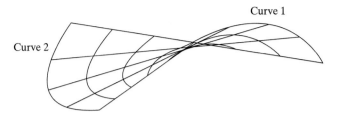

FIGURE 4–16 Ruled surface formed by two curves.

4.17 Rectangular Surface

A rectangular surface is bounded by four curves (Figure 4.17). The plane surface is a special case of the rectangular surface. Hence, ruled surfaces could also be obtained from rectangular surfaces.

4.18 Surface of Revolution

A surface of revolution is formed when a curve is rotated about an axis. The angle of rotation can be controlled; a full rotation is used to obtain the surface in Figure 4.18.

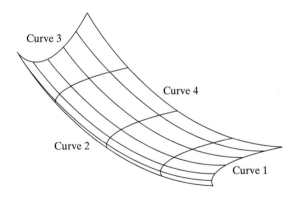

FIGURE 4.17 Rectangular surface formed by four curves.

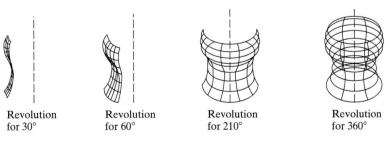

Revolution for 30°   Revolution for 60°   Revolution for 210°   Revolution for 360°

FIGURE 4–18 Revolved surface.

A grid can then be used for better visualization. Other surface creations include the Bezier surface and the B-spline surface.

4.19   Application Software

Different Ways to Create a Surface

a) Extrude—Create a surface or a quilt by extruding the sketched section to a specified depth in the direction normal to the sketching plane. When you use up to surfaces as a depth option, the new surface can be extruded to planar surfaces, or a datum plane that is parallel to the sketching plane. This is the plane surface option (Figure 4.19).

b) Revolve—Create a quilt by rotating the sketched section by a specified angle around the first centerline sketched in the section. The rotation angle can be specified as 90, 180, 270, 360. Figure 4.20 demonstrates this feature.

c) Sweep—Create a quilt by sweeping a sketched section along a specified trajectory. You can sketch the trajectory, or use an existing datum curve (Figure 4.21).

d) Blend—Create a smooth quilt connecting several sketched sections. Parallel blends can only be blind. You can also create rotational or general blends from a file (Figure 4.22).

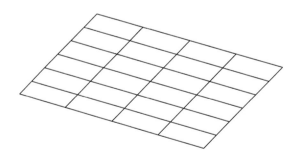

FIGURE 4.19   Plane surface.

 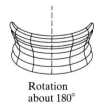

Rotation   Rotation   Rotation   Rotation
about 90°   about 180°   about 270°   about 360°

FIGURE 4.20   Revolved surface.

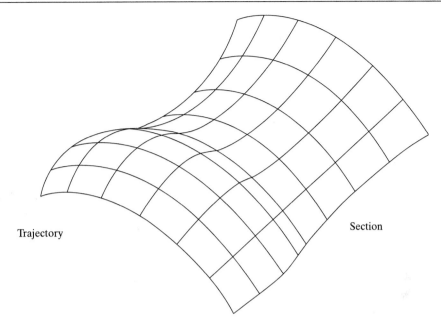

Trajectory   Section

FIGURE 4.21 Sweep surface.

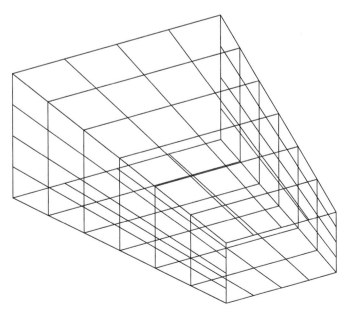

FIGURE 4.22 Blend surface.

e) Flat—Create a planar quilt by sketching its boundaries as shown in Figure 4.23.

f) Offset—Create a quilt offset from a quilt or surfaces. The quilt or surface to be offset is selected and offset direction and offset distance are to be given (Figure 4.24).

g) Copy—Create a quilt by copying existing quilts or surfaces. Specifically, a selection method, and select surfaces to copy (Figure 4.25). Most of the CAD software create the surface feature directly on top of the selected surfaces.

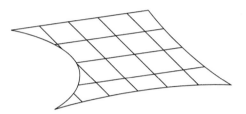

FIGURE 4.23   Flat surface.

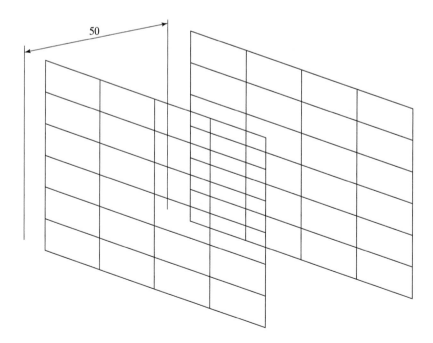

FIGURE 4.24   Offsetting of a surface.

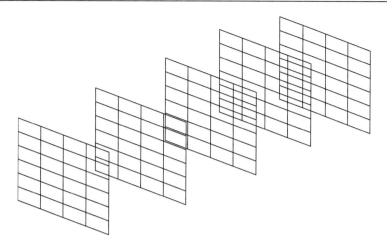

FIGURE 4.25 Copying of a surface by the selection method.

PROBLEMS

4.1. Provide the regression line equation for the following data. Explain the discrepancy of the data and the deviation error. Is the method reliable to accurately represent the given data?

x	1	2	3	4	5	6	7	8
y	1.9	4.6	5.9	8.3	9.7	13.2	13.9	16.3

4.2. An experimental tensile testing of a material resulted into the following data. What is the slope of a linear graph used to represent the data? Explain in the context of linear elasticity what the slope represents.

x	.1	.24	.31	.43	.5	.59	.69	.81
y	1000	1400	1800	2200	2600	3000	3200	3600

4.3. Data defining a projectile is given by $v = 20$ m/s, $\theta = 45$ and initial values of $y = 5$ m/s and t vary in steps of 0.1 sec from 0 to 5 seconds. Use higher polynomials to fit a curve through the data starting with a power of 2, 3, and then 4. Plot the results and provide a justification as to the degree of the polynomial that the curve is a representation of the parabola. Explain.

4.4. Use MATLAB to validate the results of Problem 4.3.

4.5. For a fifth-order Chebyshev polynomial fit the data given below and plot the results.

x	1	2	4	8	10	12	14	16
y	1.9	1.7	2	1.8	2.1	2.4	2.5	2.3

4.6. Find the Fourier coefficients and provide an explicit form of the Fourier series based on the data provided in the table. (Answer: $y = \sin x - \sin 2x$).

x	0	$\pi/6$	$\pi/3$	$\pi/2$	$2\pi/3$	$5\pi/6$	π
y	1	4	8	12	16	20	24

Compare the results to $y = \sin x - \cos 2x$

4.7. Demonstrate through Chebyshev technique how an approximation of the function $y = \cos(\pi/2)x$ can be found. How many terms in the series are needed to keep the error less than 0.001?

4.8. Construct a natural cubic spline using the non-parametric approach to fit the following data:

x	0	2	2.5	3	3.5	4	4.5	5	6
y	0	2.0	3.5	3.8	3.5	3.5	3.5	2.6	0

Compare the plot of the original data with a plot of the spline function.

4.9. For the data points selected $P_1, P_4, P_5, \ldots, P_8$ of Problem 4.3 derive the non-parametric cubic natural spline.

4.10. Write a MATLAB program to derive the cubic splines for Problem 4.9 and plot the results.

4.11. The following data points $P_0(1, 5)$, $P_1(2, 3)$, $P_2(4, 4)$, and $P_3(6, 2)$ are collected through a mechanical experiment. Derive the parametric clamped spline where the slopes at both ends are defined by $P_0'(1, -3)$, $P_3'(-1, 1)$.

4.12. Show that the Bezier curve passes through the first and last control points.

4.13. Show that the Bezier curve for the control points P_0, P_1, and P_2 is equivalent to a nonperiodic, uniform B-spline curve of order 3 defined in Example 4.7.

4.14. Expand the equation of a nonperiodic uniform B-spline curve of order 3 defined by the control points P_0, P_1, P_4, and P_5.

4.15. From Example 4.8 show that $x(t)$ and $y(t)$ coordinates satisfy the equation of a circle.

4.16. Derive the NURBS representation for a half circle of radius 1.

BIBLIOGRAPHY

Amirouche, F.M.L. (1993). *Introduction to Computer-Aided Design and Manufacturing*. New Jersey: Prentice Hall.

Farin, G. (1988). *Curves and Surfaces for Computer Aided Geometric Design—A Practical Guide*. New York: Academic Press.

Lancaster, P., and Salkauska, K. (1986). *Curve and Surface Fitting—An Introduction*. New York: Academic Press.

Rodgers, D.F., and Adams, J.A. (1976). *Mathematical Elements for Computer Graphics*. New York: McGraw-Hill.

CHAPTER 5 Solid Modeling

5.1 Introduction

The most common methods used to represent an object in computer-aided design systems are wireframe, surface modeling, and solid modeling.

Wireframe models are relatively simple to construct. They are at the heart of any CAD system; they are especially well suited for drafting. Although wireframe models provide accurate information about the location of a surface discontinuity on a given part, they usually do not provide a complete description of the part. Surface modeling is a creation of a surface, or profile, through a series of points, curves, and/or lines. It allows for more complex shapes that otherwise could not be created by solid modeling. Surface modeling is usually used in conjunction with solid modeling to create a part in CAD for analysis.

Several disparate strands of research led to the development of computer programs for the representation and manipulation of solid objects. One of these was an approach to the design of mechanical parts by treating them as combinations of simple building blocks, such as cubes and cylinders. Such programs are known as solid modelers or volume modelers, and can hold the complete unambiguous representation of geometries for a wide range of solid objects. The completeness of information contained in a solid model allows the automatic production of realistic images of a particular shape and assists in the automation of the process of interference checking.

A solid modeling system is one that provides a complete, unambiguous description of solid objects. Solid model data can be used as partial input data for analysis programs like finite-element. The output of the analysis can be represented on the solid model with centers of different colors. Once the solid object is created, one can rotate, shade, or even section the object to show interior details. Solid objects can also be combined with the other parts stored in the database to form a complex assembly of the part whose design has to be carried out. Furthermore, the solid model not only depicts the interior properties such as size and shape, but depicts interior properties such as mass as well.

5.2   Construction Techniques

Solid modeling mathematical algorithms require a certain manipulation of geometry to obtain the desired shape. There are several techniques used for the construction and editing of solid objects. Some are promising for future developments, and others are currently in use and quite popular. These techniques include

1. Boolean operation
2. Sweeping
3. Automated filleting and chamfering
4. Tweaking
5. Fleshing out of wireframes and projections

None of these techniques seems to be adequate by themselves, so the ideal solid model system should support several of them. A common feature of the techniques considered in this section is the ability to do a number of modifications with minimum user input. For example, one Boolean operation might do the work of several dozen drafting operations of the type used in traditional CAD systems.

5.2.1   Boolean Operation

Theoretic Boolean operations of intersection, union, and difference provide a useful method of constructing complex objects from simple primitives. Figure 5.1 illustrates three Boolean operations. These operations are "regularized" in some way to guarantee that valid input always produces valid output. This prevents the conversion of unrealistic features such as dangling faces and edges. Some systems that rely on boundary representation internally still allow the use of Boolean operation for input. Other systems support only special limited types of Boolean operations. For example, they do not support general union operations, but allow for the joining of two objects that have disjointed interiors that meet in a common face. Even in systems that do not support general union operations, it is useful to provide gluing as a special case because it requires little computation. Boolean operations applied to two different objects are illustrated in Figure 5.2.

Constructive solid geometry representations are often stored internally as binary trees. The system user, however, can apply the union operation to a sequence of objects in one step or subtract several objects from a given object simultaneously. Certain systems use a stack-oriented approach to Boolean arithmetic. The new object created is pushed on top of the stack, and Boolean operations are applied to the top two objects of the stack. This mode of operation is extremely flexible.

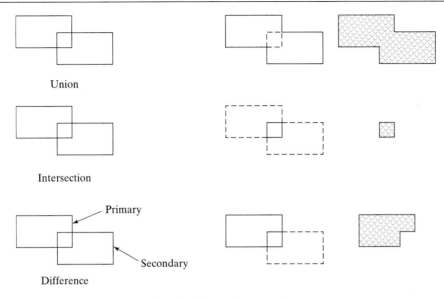

Union

Intersection

Primary

Secondary

Difference

FIGURE 5.1 Boolean operations.

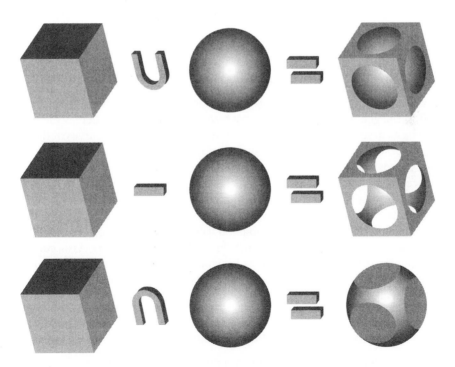

FIGURE 5.2 Boolean operations applied to a square and a circle.

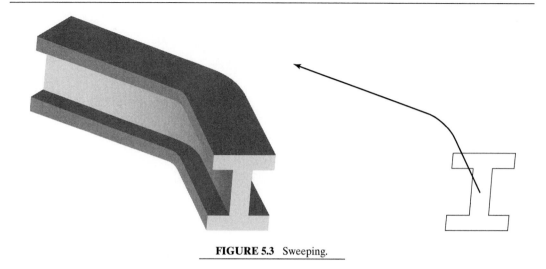

FIGURE 5.3   Sweeping.

Boolean operations form a very natural constructive technique, particularly the Boolean operation of subtraction, which is natural to people with experience in material-removal processes. The object being subtracted can be thought of as the volume swept out by a cutting tool. Similarly, the union operation is analogous to bounding processes such as welding and gluing.

5.2.2   Sweeping

In a sweep operation, an object (i.e., a generator) is moved along a curve (i.e., a trajectory) in order to sweep out a new object. Figure 5.3 illustrates a simple example in which a face representing a cross section is swept along a linear trajectory in order to create the object. The generator can be a curve, a face, or a solid object, whereas the trajectory can only be a curve or a strip of curves. The path geometry and the curves of the edges of the face operated on determine the surface geometry of the generated lateral faces. The edge curves of the lateral faces can be determined either from the path swept out by the vertices or by finding the intersections of surfaces of lateral faces.

Sweeping is a very convenient input technique. For many objects, most of the construction can be performed with just a few sweep operations. For example, intruded or projected parts can be easily modeled using sweep operations in which the trajectory is a straight line, as in the construction of tabulated cylinders. Also, curved parts can be modeled using sweep operations in which the trajectory is a circle lying in a plane perpendicular to the center line. A turned part, modeled using a rotational sweep, is shown in Figure 5.4 and Figure 5.5.

5.2.3   Automated Filleting and Chambering

In a system employing only a boundary representation, linear edges whose vertices are trihedral can often be filleted fairly easily. The edge is identified and a fillet radius is specified.

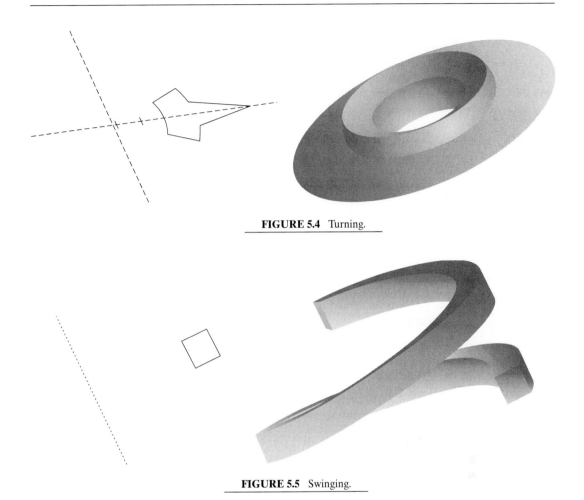

FIGURE 5.4 Turning.

FIGURE 5.5 Swinging.

The system can create a cylindrical face with its four edges and then it automatically modifies all adjoining faces and edges (Figure 5.6). Similar functions can be devised for chambering. The algorithms are very similar, but only planar faces should be created.

In constructive solid geometry–based systems, chambering and filleting are usually accomplished using Boolean operations. Sometimes special primitives are created to facilitate this operation.

5.2.4 Tweaking

Most interactions with any design tool are making small adjustments to an existing shape. Boolean operations are expensive for this purpose. An example of an operation that adjusts the geometry of the face is tweaking.

Tweaking is an editing operation in which a face of an object is moved in some way. The tweaked face and the faces adjacent to it are then adjusted to maintain the

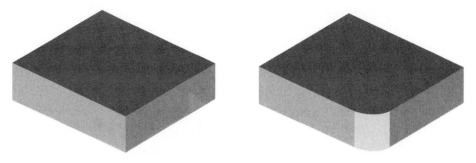

FIGURE 5.6   Filleting.

integrity of the object. The best way to perform this adjustment is to recompute the intersection of these faces, where the intersection curves become the new common boundaries. For example, in Figure 5.7, the two upper faces of the base of the object have been tweaked slightly upward.

5.2.5   Fleshing Out of Wireframes and Projections

In this method, an entire wireframe model is constructed and then surfaces are patched on using the wireframe's geometry to define the shape and position of the surfaces. Because many current users of CAD/CAM systems have extensive archives of wireframe system models, it is important that the method of "fleshing out" wireframes works in an automated fashion without user intervention. Algorithms have been developed to perform this function for unambiguous, planar-faced objects. For 3D objects, heuristic algorithms are emerging that assist the user by automatically inserting surfaces. Also, algorithms that flesh out collections of 2D orthographic projects have been developed that are beneficial in certain applications.

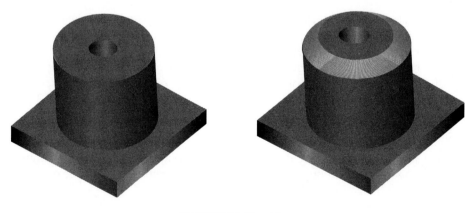

FIGURE 5.7   Tweaking.

5.3   Representation Schemes

Most solid modeling systems can create, modify, and inspect 3D solid objets. There are a number of methods that can be used for representing such models in a computer. They can be classified as

1. Instantiation
2. Boundary representation
3. Constructive solid geometry
4. Cellular decomposition

5.3.1   Instantiation

Instantiation is a traditional method of creating geometry. The usefulness of this technique depends on the range of primitives available and the number and types of values that can be specified at the time of instantiation.

In a contemporary system, the basic set of primitives includes blocks, cylinders, cones, and spheres that can be oriented arbitrarily. For the user, these can be supplemented with convenient primitives such as wedges, fillets, and truncated cones. Figure 5.8 illustrates some of the system-supplied primitives. Convenient primitives do not

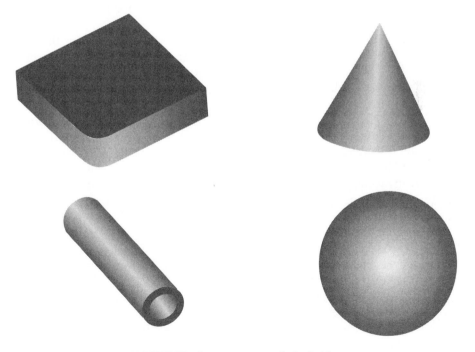

FIGURE 5.8   Some system-supplied primitives.

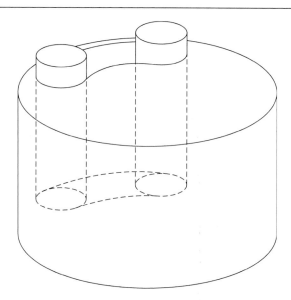

FIGURE 5.9   A user-defined primitive.

contain any new surface types; therefore, they have to be described. On the other hand, these primitives are very useful and are usually simple for the system developer to implement.

More sophisticated CAD systems allow the end user to enter the primary dimension features of primitives by defining parameterized objects. Essentially, the user writes a procedure that describes the structure of the new primitive and then the parameters needed are specified when the geometry is instantiated. These parameters include orientation and location, an overall scale factor, independent size parameters (e.g., inner diameter and wall thickness of a pipe), feature form parameters (e.g., whether a bolt should have a square or a hexagonal head), and an enumeration feature parameter (e.g., how many holes there should be in a bolt circle or a cover plate). A generic cover plate is shown in Figure 5.9, in which the user can employ the technique of newly developed primitives to create the part. This is much faster in developing solid objects compared with conventional system-supplied primitives.

In addition to base primitives, some systems can create user-defined primitives; that is, they can equip users with software to create their own set of primitives, in addition to those already defined by the system. The language used to define new primitives has enough information power that it might be possible to encode design rules within its definitions. For example, in Figure 5.9, we might write a generic definition in which only the diameter and the thickness of the plate need to be specified at the instantiation time. The number and size of holes needed in one bolt circle would then be computed internally. The user programming languages that accompany many commercial turnkey systems support a sophisticated "family of parts" of this sort.

5.3.2   Boundary Representation

Boundary representation is a scheme wherein the objects are defined by their enclosing surfaces or boundaries. This technique consists of listing all faces, vertices, and edges of an object.

Once the entity is comprised, its appropriate surfaces are then swept through space in such a way as to create the desired depths of each surface, thus creating the finished modeled representation. Mathematically, the so-called B-REP solid model is created by taking an array of data points for a given view to define the edges, faces, and vertices. Once all the points from all the views are defined and stored in the computer's memory, they are then joined appropriately to form the 3D entity. Once the entity is comprised, the computer can be instructed to use basic transformation matrices to bring out the finished solid model. The B-REP concept is demonstrated in Figure 5.10.

To interact with the B-REP modelers, the designer needs certain operating tools that assist in constructing and/or modifying the design with relative ease. Some of these operating techniques include the Boolean and sweeping operations.

Boolean operations provide a useful facility for combining and constructing solids in a B-REP modeler. They are operations that act on two boundaries and combine them into one or more new boundaries. Basic Boolean operations such as union, intersection, or difference can be used to combine different parts, resulting in a desired shape.

Prismatic and translational objects can be created by sweeping and swinging types of operations. Sweeping takes place along the cross section of the object, whereas the

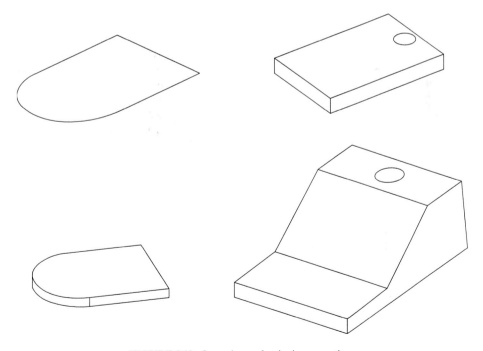

FIGURE 5.10   Sweeping and swinging operations.

swinging operations are used for rotationally symmetric objects. Figures 5.10 illustrates these two operations.

5.3.3 Constructive Solid Geometry

A constructive representation (C-REP) is a tree-like structure wherein the leaves are simple primitive objects such as blocks, cones, and cylinders and the nodes represent Boolean operations. Each node shows the set of operations that should be applied to the two subsolids below it on the tree.

C-REP is based on the principle that any complex part can be designed by adding or subtracting basic shapes such as cubes, cylinders, and cones by putting them in appropriate positions. A simple example of basic Boolean operations such as union, difference, and intersection is given in Figure 5.11.

The constructive solid geometry representation of a solid is very compact and can be generated quickly when two solids are combined by a set of operations. Figure 5.12 gives an idealization of C-REP representation.

Each of the two approaches just discussed has its relative advantages and disadvantages. The C-REP method usually has a significant procedural advantage in the initial tabulation of the model. It is relatively easy to construct a solid model out of regular solid primitives by adding, subtracting, and intersecting components. As a result of the building-block approach, the C-REP method has a more compact file in its database.

One of the biggest advantages of the B-REP system is its capability of constructing unusual shapes that would not be possible with the available repertoire of C-REP systems. Aircraft fuselages, swing shapes, and automobile body styling exemplify this.

A B-REP scheme uses faces, edges, and vertices to define an object. As a result, the 2D shapes of the object are assembled to form the component. This in turn requires

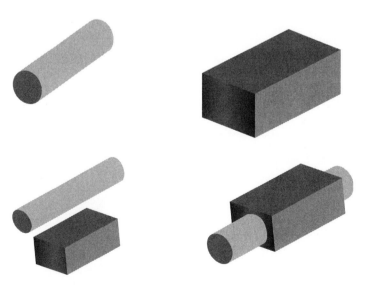

FIGURE 5.11 Boolean operations (solid objects).

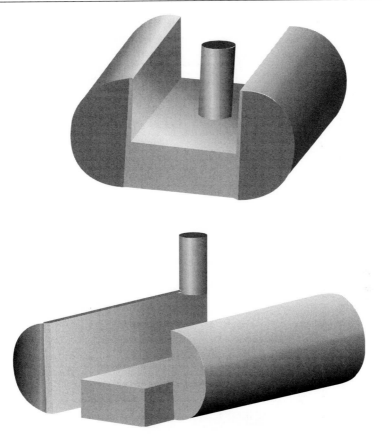

FIGURE 5.12 Constructive solid geometry.

more storage but less computation time to reconstruct the image. On the other hand, the C-REP is a scheme wherein solid shapes are combined to form a part, which requires less storage but more computation. What follows are two examples to demonstrate further the utility of the C-REP and B-REP of solids.

Example 5.1   Construction of a Wrench

Using boundary representation, construct the part shown in Figure 5.13.

Solution   The basic Boolean operation, union ($\cup$), intersection ($\cap$), and difference ($-$) are used to construct the part. This is shown in Figure 5.14.

End of Example 5.1

FIGURE 5.13　Wrench.

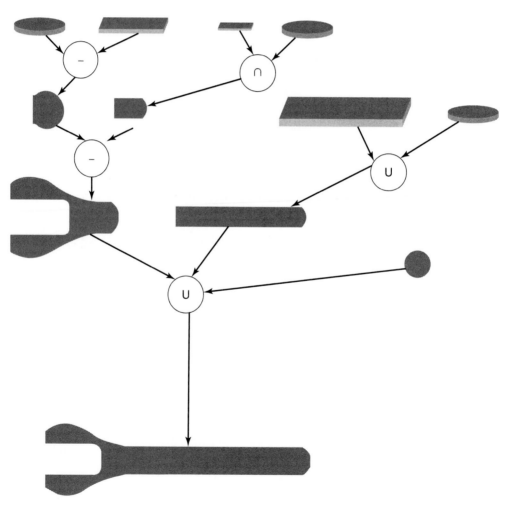

FIGURE 5.14　Boolean operation.

FIGURE 5.15 A solid model.

Example 5.2 Construction of a Solid Model

Using constructive solid geometry representation, construct the solid model shown in Figure 5.15.

Solution Similar to B-REP, the Boolean operations are carried out on solid objects to get the final model. Figure 5.16 gives a clear picture of the operation and the completed model.

End of Example 5.2

5.3.4 Cellular Decomposition

A solid object can be represented by dividing its volume into smaller volumes or cells. Thus, cells need not be cubic or identical in shape. Cellular decomposition produces an approximate representation of the object because some cells will be partly in one object grid and others will be discarded. As a result, "empty spaces" are created.

This problem can be removed by using cell shapes of varying sizes so that they can conform to the object boundary. But further complications take place in describing complex sculptured cell shapes when computation becomes expensive. Depending on whether the cell is outside, entirely inside, or partially inside the object, it can be classified as empty, full, or partial.

There are various types of sides used in cellular decomposition. Two of the most common ones follow.

Simple Regular Grid. This type of grid is produced by dividing the given space into a number of regular cells. These cells generally are cubes in the 3D case and squares in the 2D case. Figure 5.17 gives a clear picture of this type of grid.

Regular-grid representation requires more storage. In order to improve the resolution of representation, the cell size has to be reduced. Thus, a storage problem is created, which, in turn, produces poor resolution.

Octree Adaptive Grid. The octree encoding recursively subdivides the cubic modeling space into eight octants until homogeneous cells are obtained. They can be subclassified as follows.

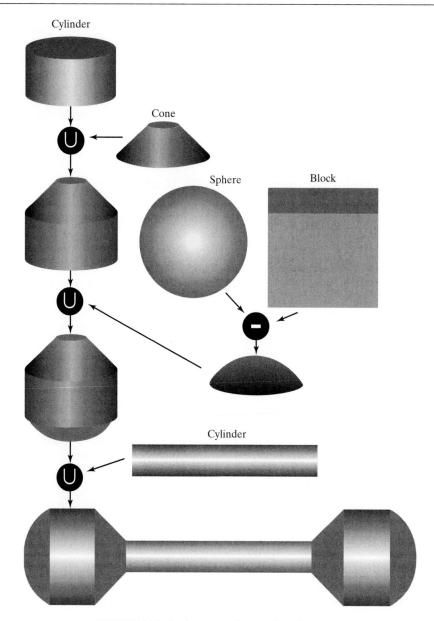

FIGURE 5.16 Boolean operations on the solid model.

Classical Octree Encoding.   The following recursive procedure is usually performed when the octree representation of a 3D object is described. We start with a cube that represents the whole modeling space. If the object contained in it is too complex, the cube is classified as a gray node and is divided into eight octants in the order shown in Figure 5.18. The procedure is repeated recursively until a white or black node

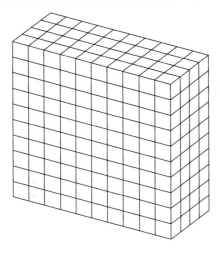

FIGURE 5.17 Regular grid.

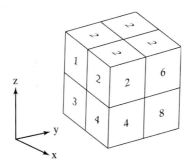

FIGURE 5.18 Classical octree representation.

is obtained or the minimal size of octants is reached. A white node is completely outside the object, whereas a black one is completely inside.

The octree can be stored as a classical tree with eight pointers per node, or by using the parenthesize linear notation, as shown in Figure 5.19. Every code of a gray node is followed by the codes of its eight sons.

When 3D objects are represented by means of octree, Boolean operations are also very simple. The two great advantages that prevent the use of classical octrees as a representative scheme in modeling systems are

1. Octree encoding of the solid yields minimum size nodes over the complete boundary, so the obtained octree is too large in most cases.
2. Once the Boolean operations have been performed, the algorithm for the computation of the boundaries from the octree becomes very complex.

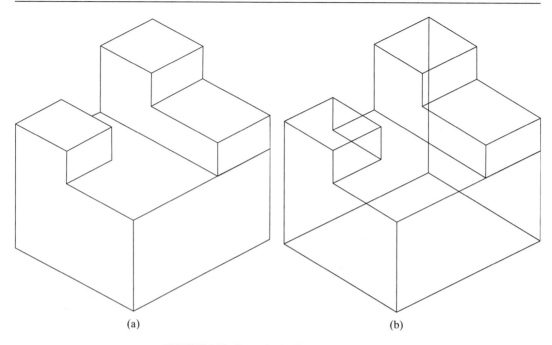

(a)   (b)

FIGURE 5.19 Parenthesize linear representation.

FIGURE 5.20 Octree encoding.

Exact Octree Encoding.   In this octree representation system, in addition to the classical node types—white, black, and gray—we have face, edge, and vertex nodes. Consider the polyhedral shown in Figure 5.20. The nodes are defined as follows.

Face node: The node that contains a piece of the polyhedral faces.
Edge node: The node formed at the intersection of two neighboring faces.
Vertex node: The node at the intersection of the face and edge of the object.

In the parenthesize linear representation of the octree, all nodes require only two or three digits for their representation. Table 5.1 describes such nodes.

TABLE 5.1 Description of Nodes.

Code	Description
00	White node
01	Black node
100	Gray node
101	Face node: In this case, following the code, there is a pointer to the corresponding equation.
110	Edge node: The code is followed by the two equation pointers and a bit indicating whether the edge is convex or not.
111	Vertex node

5.4   Applications of Solid Modeling

Solid models often resemble surface models or wireframe models with hidden lines removed. However, the major difference could be assessed in the severe limitations wireframes have when used as mathematical tool models to represent the parts needed. For instance, in modeling, parts need to exhibit certain properties that are essential to the design. Properties of part models are useful in predicting the weight, moment of inertia, and volume of finished products. Solid models represent a more accurate picture of the parts being designed. This is especially true for complex geometries.

A model created by surface elements can be clearly shown as a solid model by removing the hidden lines. However, these surface models do not represent the actual solid object because they contain no information on what lies in the interior of the part. Surface models when used in conjunction with engineering analysis programs such as the finite-element method, which requires properties such as weight, volume, and moment of inertia, usually need a secondary program to compute these properties. Solid models are recorded in the computer mathematically as volumes bounded by surfaces rather than as structures. Hence, it is possible to calculate the inertia properties of objects and visually display cross sections of parts to reveal the internal details that are often required for engineering analysis.

For example, consider a cube whose wireframe representation consists of points and lines (in contrast, the solid model of the cube is represented by a 3D object that contains a volume). If the volume of the wireframe model is to be calculated, then a formula for a cube is used. For complex shapes, it would be difficult to calculate volumes for each shape because the programmer would have to know the shape of the part in advance in order to use the appropriate formula. The advantage of using a solid model is that the volume of any complex shape can be calculated by dividing one face of the solid into a rectangular grid and tracing the rectangles back through the solid until they reach the back edge of the model.

Furthermore, solid modeling enables us to set up entire manufacturing process that can be simulated for real-time interference monitoring. Numerically controlled programs in combination with solid modeling can play a major role in optimizing the machining processes. This, in turn, increases the quality of products.

The finite-element method is applicable in several types of analyses. The most common is static analysis, which solves for deflections, strains, and stresses in a structure under a constant set of applied loads. Wireframe models were used for creating a geometry and carrying out analysis on it. Recent trends in finite-element analysis include a detailed stress analysis on a solid model rather than on a wireframe model. This new technology has been developed wherein the use of a solid model is done to carry out the analysis.

PROBLEMS

5.1. (a) Create drawings showing the effect of Boolean operations on the models given by Figures P5.1(a) (b).

(b) Using your computer workstation, recreate the sketches made in answering part (a).

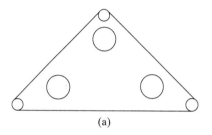

(a)

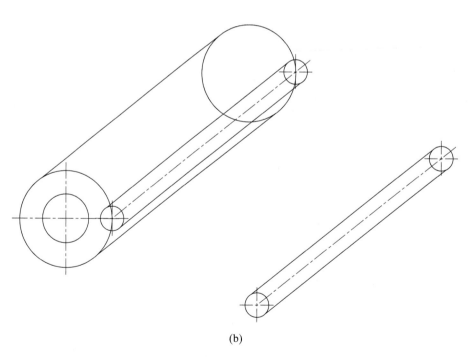

(b)

FIGURE P5.1   (a) Triangular model. (b) Cylindrical model.

5.2. (a) Following the procedures outlined in Section 5.2.2., show the effect of sweeping on the mechanical model shown in Figure P5.2 along the *x* and *y* directions.
   (b) Create the final part determined in the first half of this problem by using a CAD system.

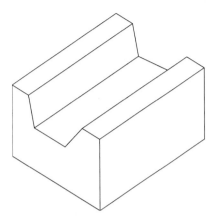

FIGURE P5.2 A solid model.

5.3. Making use of a graphical representation, show the effect of chambering a filleting on the model shown in Figure P5.2.

5.4. (a) Using boundary representation, construct the bevel gear assembly shown in Figure P5.3.
   (b) Given the bit brace shown in Figure P5.4, use boundary representation to create the part.
   (c) Make a 3D drawing of the gear assembly and brace using your CAD system.

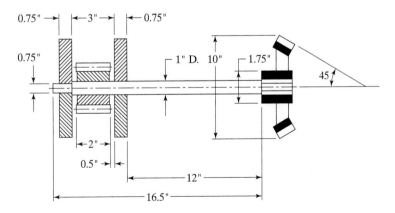

FIGURE P5.3 Bevel gear assembly.

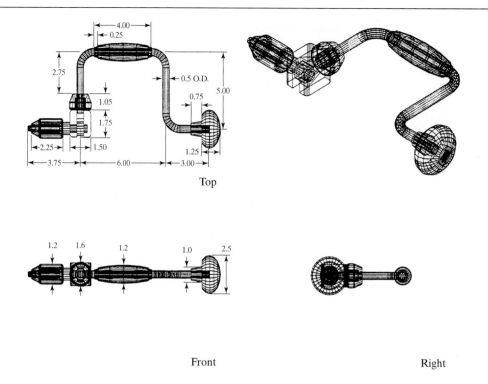

FIGURE P5.4 Bit brace.

5.5. (a) Figure P5.5 illustrates the shaft mounted on bearings A and D, with pulleys attached at points B and C. Construct this assembly using C-REP.

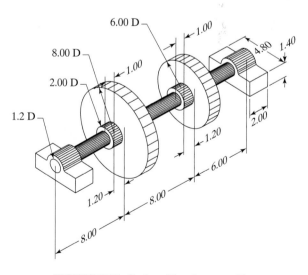

FIGURE P5.5 Shaft and bearing assembly.

(b) Figure P5.6 illustrates the crankshaft and flywheel assembly for a one-cylinder compressor. Using C-REP, create the system.

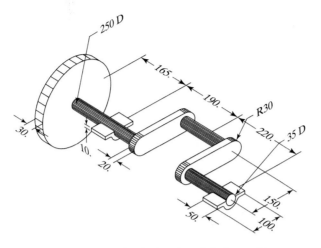

FIGURE P5.6 Flywheel and crankshaft assembly.

5.6. Figures P5.7, P5.8, P5.9, and P5.10 show solid model designs that need to be created using some of the features outlined in this chapter. Each example requires

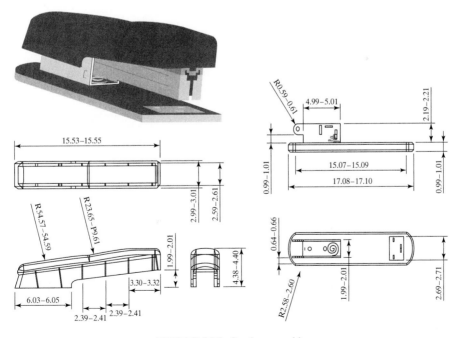

FIGURE P5.7 Stapler assembly.

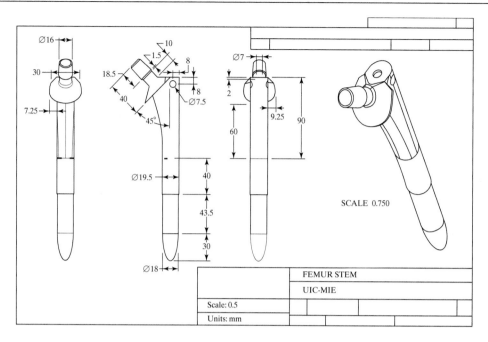

FIGURE P5.8 Total hip replacement implant assembly.

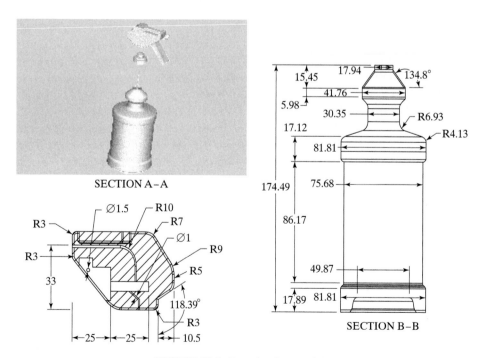

FIGURE P5.9 Spray bottle assembly.

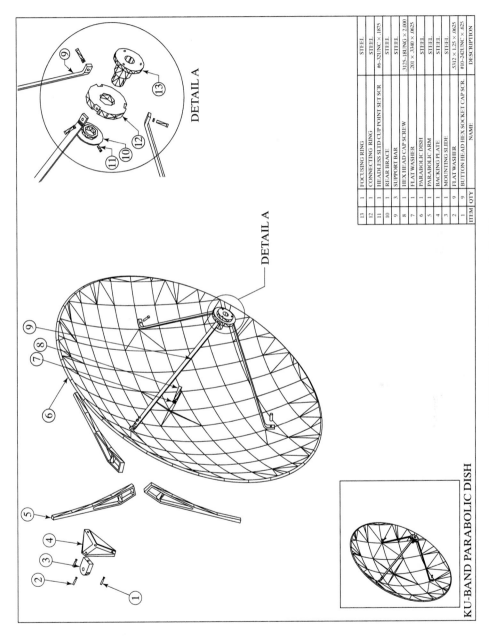

DETAIL A

DETAIL A

KU-BAND PARABOLIC DISH

ITEM	QTY	NAME	DESCRIPTION
13	1	FOCUSING RING	STEEL
12	1	CONNECTING RING	STEEL
11	1	HEADLESS SLIDE CUP POINT SET SCR	#6–32UNC × .1875
10	1	REAR BRACE	STEEL
9	3	SUPPORT BAR	STEEL
8	1	HEX HEAD CAP SCREW	.3125–18UNG × 2.000
7	1	FLAT WASHER	.201 × .3340 × .0625
6	1	PARABOLIC DISH	STEEL
5	1	PARABOLIC ARM	STEEL
4	1	BACKING PLATE	STEEL
3	1	MOUNTING SLIDE	STEEL
2	9	FLAT WASHER	.5312 × 1.25 × .0625
1	9	BUTTON HEAD HEX SOCKET CAP SCR.	#10–24ZUNC × .625

FIGURE P5.10A Ku-band parabolic dish.

199

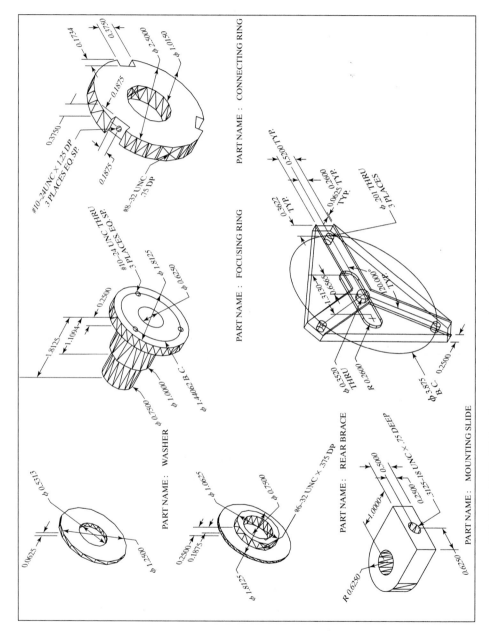

FIGURE P5.10B Washer, focusing ring, connecting ring, rear brace, mounting slide, and backing.

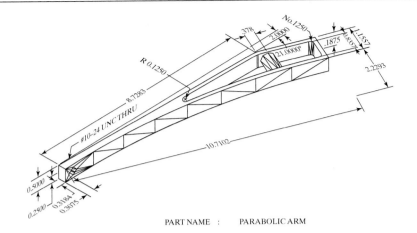

PART NAME : PARABOLIC ARM

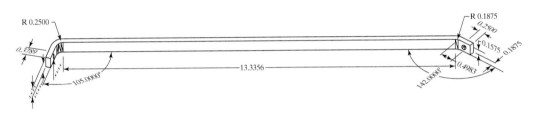

PART NAME : SUPPORT BAR

FIGURE P5.10C Parabolic arm and support bar.

additional dimensions and surface representations that need to be assumed by the student to complete the drawings. The objective is to have each drawing look as close as possible to the 3D design provided. Your final part should have the same dimensions of the views outlined as well as the shaded isometric view. These projects are intended to be made using existing CAD software codes such as AUTOCAD, PROE, and other modelers.

BIBLIOGRAPHY

Allen, G. (1982, November). An Introduction to Solid Modeling. *Computer Graphics World*, New York: pp. 32–36, 81–87.

Besant, C.B., & Lui, C.W.K. (1986). *Computer-Aided Design and Manufacture*. New York: Wiley.

Faun, I.D., & Pratt, M.J. (1979). *Computational Geometry for Design and Manufacture*. New York: Halstead.

Meagher, D.J. (1984, October). A New Mathematics for Solid Processing. *Computer Graphics World*, pp. 75–87.

Rooney, J., & Steadman, P. (1987). *Principles of Computer-Aided Design*. London: Pitman.

Sharpe, R.J., Thomas, P.J., and Thorne, R.W. (1982, October). Constructive Geometry in Three Dimensions for Computer-Aided Design. *Journal of Mechanical Design*, *104*, pp. 813–816.

Teicholz, E. (1985). *Computer-Aided Design and Manufacturing Handbook*, New York: McGraw-Hill.

CHAPTER 6

Optimization Techniques

6.1   Introduction

The conventional design process is based largely on the experience and intuition of the designer. Both of these characteristics contribute to the conceptual changes in the design and/or in introducing additional specifications to the design process. Hence, optimal designs are attained through a judgment call or simply by a trial-and-error approach. Therefore, the conventional design process can lead to uneconomical designs in terms of cost and time. Over the past two decades computers have changed our design process, providing high speed and accuracy to our optimization algorithms that were previously unattainable.

The optimal design function forces the designer to clearly identify a set of design variables and a cost function to be minimized subject to the constraints of the system. Typically, the designers create a general configuration for which numerical values of independent variables are not fixed. Then they establish an objective function that defines the value of the design in terms of the independent variables such as

$$G = G(x_1, x_2, \ldots, x_n)$$

where $x_i (i = 1, 2, \ldots, n)$ are the independent variables and G defines the objective function.

Objective functions could be cost, weight, or reliability. The objective function is subject to certain constraints that arise from certain limitations or compatibility conditions of the individual variables.

The solution methods to the optimal design problems can benefit greatly from the designer's experience and intuition. In addition, the role of computers is fundamental in the optimization process because each iteration cycle may require substantial calculations.

Computers can also be used to provide graphical representation of data and animation and simulate the working of the prototype before fabrication.

Design of mechanical systems requires a decision-making process based on selected models made under certain engineering assumptions. The models are then subjected to certain criteria involving cost, material, and performance etc., to obtain the desired model possible. This chapter provides the basic mathematical tools used in optimization and exposes the engineer to different methods and techniques focusing more on the application rather than on the theory. In addition, this chapter emphasizes the importance of modeling and assumptions used to arrive at the problem formulation. This in turn shows how the solution can be affected by the controlled variables. Essentially, optimization is being introduced as a means to find solutions when it is feasible.

6.2   System Modeling

System modeling requires a mathematical model that represents the system mathematical relations. Usually we denote the input by x and the output by y; therefore, the relationship between the two variables is

$$y = f(x) \tag{6.1}$$

The function f defines the relationship between x and y. This relationship could be as simple as a linear relationship such as $y = ax$, or it could be defined by a set of equations, which would require rigorous solutions. What follows are engineering functions that best illustrate the system model function.

6.2.1   Analysis and Design

Beams are used in a large number of engineering applications. Their use is generally accepted as a first approximation and in some cases their predictions are very accurate. The governing equations of beams are easily derived from the principle of mechanics and their analytical solution, also known as the "close form solution," provides the means by which we can investigate different boundary and loading conditions.

Consider a beam as shown in Figure 6.1 where the bending stress is known to be

$$\sigma = \frac{My}{I} \tag{6.2}$$

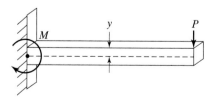

FIGURE 6.1   Simple beam.

M is the bending moment; y is the distance from the neutral axis, and σ defines the normal stress. The stress is related to the load P, by the relation P/A; furthermore, we can estimate the maximum deflection of the beam by

$$\delta = \frac{PL^3}{3EI} \tag{6.3}$$

The simple beam model provided in Figure 6.1, along with its mathematical functions in Equations (6.2) and (6.3) serve as a basis for analyzing problems, which can be modeled by a beam subjected to the same type of loading conditions.

Example 6.1

Consider a tree trunk, which can be modeled by a beam as shown in Figure 6.2. One can determine the wind speed or force that would cause the tree to break.

If the tree has a diameter equal to $2r$ then its polar moment of inertia is $I = \Pi r^4/4$. The maximum bending stress occurs at $y = r$ (distance from the neutral axis), and is given by

$$\sigma_{max} = \frac{4Fh}{\Pi r^3} \tag{6.4}$$

From this equation we can analyze the force F in relation to the maximum allowable stress that would cause the tree to break.

End of Example 6.1

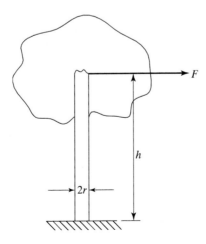

FIGURE 6.2 A tree subject to a lateral wind force F.

Example 6.2

A second example involves the modeling of an automobile wheel and tire (see Figure 6.3). The torsional shaft and a cylindrical mass represent this. We are interested in evaluating the natural frequency of the tire due the torsional effects of the tire; also, we need to know whether the frequency associated with braking is a concern. First, we need a model that represents the tire and shaft. This is done by assuming the tire to be a cylindrical mass and the shaft to be a beam with negligible mass.

Now the design problem is such that the relationship is governed by a set of differential equations of the form:

$$J\ddot{\theta} + K\theta = M_r \qquad (6.5)$$

Equation (6.5) defines the vibration characteristics of the tire/shaft, where K denotes the torsional stiffness of the beam, J is the polar moment of inertia of the tire/cylinder mass, and M defines an external excitation associated with the braking.

Let the torsional stiffness of the beam be given,

$$K = \frac{GI_p}{l} \qquad (6.6)$$

where I_p is the polar moment of inertia, l is the length, and d the diameter of the shaft and G defines the shear modulus of elasticity; furthermore, the polar moment of inertia is given by:

$$I_p = \frac{\Pi d^4}{32} \qquad (6.7)$$

For a typical shaft of 5 cm in diameter and a length of 2 m and assuming the shaft is made of steel, we compute the following constants.

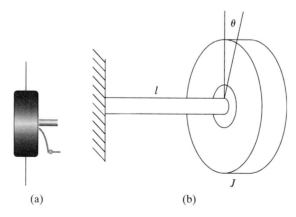

(a)   (b)

FIGURE 6.3   (a) Automobile wheel and tire. (b) Model representing the tire and shaft.

$$G = 80 \times 10^9 \, \text{N/m}^2$$

$$K = 2.455 \, \text{N} \cdot \text{m/rad}$$

$$I_p = 0.006136 \times 10^{-8} \, \text{m}^4$$

The natural frequency of the model is given by

$$\omega_n = \sqrt{\frac{K}{J}} \tag{6.8}$$

where ω_n defines the natural circular frequency, K the equivalent torsional stiffness, and J the mass moment of inertia. If the wheel makes 10 oscillations in 30.2 s then the frequency of excitation is 2.081 rad/s. Suppose we need to optimize the vehicle handling of the car by increasing the torsional stiffness value. We are concerned about the braking frequency, which is exciting the tire and is being applied through an external moment function

$$M = M_0 \sin(\omega t)$$

In this case the selection of K in Equation (6.7) must be done such that the external frequency is not equal to the natural frequency of the system tire mass, to avoid resonance. As the excitation frequency changes the torsional stiffness is optimized to provide comfort.

End of Example 6.2

6.3 Design Optimization

6.3.1 Formulation of an Optimal Design

As stated earlier, optimization is the process of maximizing a desired quality or minimizing an undesired one. Optimization theory is a body of mathematics that deals with the problem of maxima and minima and the process of finding the maxima and minima numerically. Any design process requires formulation of the objective in terms of a problem to which a solution is required. Formulation of an optimal design requires the conversion of the verbal description of the problem into an explicitly defined mathematical statement.

There are four steps to the formulation of an optimal design:

1. Identifying the design parameters.
2. Defining the design constraints.
3. Defining the objective functions.
4. Evaluating alternatives.

6.3.2   Design Parameters

The quantities or variables that define the mathematical model of a design are called "design variables" or "design parameters." In most solutions we are faced with the identification of those design variables. Furthermore, it is a challenging task to select only the variables we need to consider as the primary ones, which encompass the global optimization problem. It is desirable not to increase the number of variables because they complicate the convergence to a rapid solution. Usually, direct geometric quantities define the design variables. It is also important to have all design variables independent from each other.

6.3.3   Constraints

Constraints can be defined as the functions that relate the different variables and must be satisfied in order for a solution to exist. A functional design is one that satisfies all the constraints. For a constraint to be meaningful, it must be influenced by one or more variables. Constraints can be of many types. Constraint functions can be expressed either as equality or inequality constraints, depending on the type of design problem. Equality constraints are also called "functional constraints" or "constraining functions." They represent relations that must exist between the design variables. Let a constraint function be defined as:

$$\Phi(x_1, x_2, \ldots, x_n) = 0 \qquad (i = 1, m) \tag{6.9}$$

where m denotes the total number of constraints.

An example of a constraint function used in optimizing a volume of a cylindrical storage tank is defined by $V = \Pi x_1^2 x_2$. We write the constraint equation following the above Equation (6.9) as follows:

$$\phi(x_1, x_2) = \Pi x_1^2 x_2 - V = 0 \tag{6.10}$$

where x_1 and x_2 denote the radius and the height of the tank, respectively.

Inequality constraints arise because certain variables have practical limits on their values. The inequality constraints are called "regional constraints" or "limit equations." They are expressed as

$$\Psi_j(x_1, x_2, \ldots, x_n) < L_j \tag{6.11}$$

where $j = 1, p$, with p the total number of constraints. Constraint functions having only first-order terms in design variables are called "simple constraints." Linear programming problems have these types of constraints. In dynamics the latter are considered as position constraints.

6.3.4   Evaluation

A certain criterion is needed for comparison to decide which design of several alternatives is optimal. This evaluation criterion is based on the objective function and the constraints. In a situation where there are two or more cost functions, the most important criterion is taken as the cost function and the rest are treated as constraints.

There are a number of methods that could be used to solve the combined objective functions and the constraints. The solutions usually give either a unique solution or more than one solution.

A unique solution is rare and represents no alternative solution. However, when there is more than one solution, additional criteria are needed to select the most desirable solution. This is usually based on a company's needs, which could be labor cost and manpower, financial support, or functional or safety requirements.

Example 6.3

Consider a rectangular box used for storing important documents (see Figure 6.4). Define the objective function if C denotes the cost per unit area of the metal used for fabrication of the box. Define the constraint equations and the limits on their design variables.

Solution The length L, width W, and height H comprise one set of design variables for this problem. The cost function is the dollar cost of the sheet metal for the storage container. The total surface area of the sheet metal required for the container is

$$A = 2LH + 2HW + 2WL$$

If C is the dollar cost of the sheet metal per unit area, then the cost function for the problem is given by

$$T = C\,(2LH + 2HW + 2WL)$$

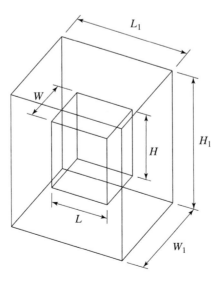

FIGURE 6.4 Rectangular box used for storing important documents.

Simply, V defines the volume of the box

$$V = LWH$$

Hence, the constraint function is

$$\phi = V - LWH = 0$$

The dimensions of the shelf limit all three design variables:

$$L < L_1 \quad W < W_1 \quad H < H_1$$

where L_1, W_1 and H_1 define the limits imposed by the shelf.

As shown in the example, the steps that generally follow in formulation of a design problem are

1. Identification of the design variables.
2. Selection of a cost function and developing an expression for it in terms of the design variables.
3. Identification of constraints and developing expressions for them in terms of design variables.

End of Example 6.3

6.4   Optimal Design Concept

Most engineering problems involve the task of minimizing a function subject to some constraint conditions. Most importantly one needs to identify the variables that define the function and make the right assumptions so a realistic solution is achievable. We can then ask the following questions.

How is each design described?
What are the criteria for best "design"?
What are the available means?

6.4.1   Design Optimization

1. Select a set of variables.
2. Select an objective function.
3. Determine a set of constraints.
4. Solutions will be based on finding the values for the variables that would minimize or maximize the objective function and satisfy the constraints at the same time.

Mathematically we express these steps in the following form:

$$X = (x_1, x_2, \ldots, x_n)$$

$$f(x) = \text{objective function}$$

$$h(x) = 0 \text{ equality of inequality constraints}$$

$$g(x) <= 0$$

Example 6.4

Consider a shaft as shown in Figure 6.5. Let the inner and outer diameter of the shaft be given by d_i and d_o, so t represents the thickness of the cylinder wall.

It is obvious from the given geometry that we can define a function that would relate d_o and d_i. Because

$$d_o = d_i + 2t$$

$$d_o - d_i - 2t = 0$$

Then we define

$$h(d_o, d_i, t) = d_o - d_i - 2t \qquad (6.12)$$

Let the maximum stress due to torsion be defined such that

$$\sigma_{max} \leq s \qquad (6.13)$$

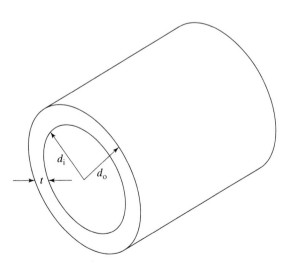

FIGURE 6.5 A hollow cylinder with thickness t.

where s is the maximum allowed stress in the design criteria. Neglecting bending, we can rewrite the stress as

$$\sigma_{max} = \tau_{max} = \frac{M_t(d_o/2)}{J} \tag{6.14}$$

where

M_t = torsional moment

J = polar moment of inertia

$$J = \left(\frac{\Pi}{32}\right)(d_0^4 - d_i^4)$$

Equation (6.13) can be expressed further as:

$$\sigma_{max} - s \le 0 \tag{6.15}$$

Substituting the value for s, we get

$$\sigma_{max} - M_t(d_o/2J) = 0 \tag{6.16}$$

Also, we know that

$$J - \left(\frac{\Pi}{32}\right)\left(d_0^4 - d_i^4\right) = 0 \tag{6.17}$$

The above equation reduces to

$$\frac{16 M_t d_0}{\Pi(d_0^4 - d_i^4)} - s \le 0 \tag{6.18}$$

Equation (6.17) defines a constraint equation that relates the design variables to a maximum allowed stress. If the design of the shaft requires that the stress criteria must be satisfied, then the equation comes in handy.

End of Example 6.4

6.5   Unconstrained Optimization

6.5.1   Single Variable Minimization

Unconstrained minimization applies to a function where the variable x is not bounded. To minimize a function $f(x)$ we will explore the possibilities of weak local minimum, strong local maximum and global minimum. If a function f is continuous, then the necessary condition for x^* to be local minimum is

$$f'(x^*) = 0 \tag{6.19}$$

where $f'(x)$ represents the derivative of the function $f(x)$ evaluated at $x = x^*$. If the function f is continuous, then the conditions sufficient for x^* to be a strong local minimum (Figure 6.6) are

$$f'(x^*) = 0$$

and

$$f''(x^*) > 0$$

Infection points are points where the slope is 0, neither minimum nor maximum.

Engineering problems defined by functions whose variables are not constrained define the unconstrained optimization. These problems are common when seeking minima describing the behavior of certain experimental data, understanding the fitting methods through polynomials and graphical solutions. Engineering principles usually yield functions with more than one variable; these variables are known as the generalized constraints, and they are conveniently chosen to describe the kinematics of the system. Kinetic energy, potential energy, impulse, momentum, and work are among the most used functions in engineering dynamics. They are expressed as

$$f = (q_1', q_2', \ldots, q_n', q_1, q_2, \ldots, q_n, t) \tag{6.20}$$

where $\{q\} = \{q_1, q_2, \ldots, q_n\}$ define the generalized coordinates, $\{q'\}$ represents their time derivatives, and t defines time. A function can then be minimized with respect to a particular variable.

Consider a function f where the independent variables are $\{x_1, x_2, \ldots, x_n\}$, the necessary and sufficient conditions for the function to be minimized is

1. The point $x^* = [x_1^*, x_2^*, \ldots, x_n^*]^T$ is a weak local minimum if there exists a $\delta > 0$ such that

$$f(x^*) \leq f(x) \qquad \text{for all } x \text{ such that } \|x - x^*\| < \delta$$

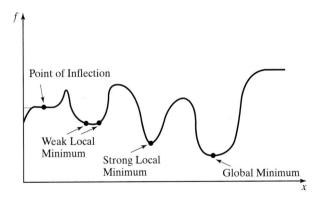

FIGURE 6.6 Function f showing weak local, global, and strong local minima.

2. x^* is a strong local minimum if $f(x^*) < f(x)$ for all x in the neighborhood of x^*.
3. x^* is a global minimum if $f(x^*) \leq f(x)$ for all $x \in R^n$.

The necessary condition for x^* to be a local minimum is

$$\nabla f(x^*) = 0 \quad \text{and} \quad \nabla^* f(x^*) \text{ is positive definite}$$

Example 6.5

Find whether the function $f = x^3$ has a minimum or maximum for $x \in [-1,1]$

Solution

$$f' = 3x^2$$
$$f' = 0 \Rightarrow x = 0$$
$$x \in [-1,1]$$
$$f''(x = 0) = 0$$

Hence, f has an inflection point at $x = 0$

End of Example 6.5

Example 6.6

Find the minimum cost associated with a tank used for storing natural gas (see Figure 6.7). The lids on both ends cost $20 per m^2, the cylindrical wall costs $10 per m^2, and it costs $20 per m^2 to maintain the tank over the life of its use. The volume of the tank is 120 m^3.

Solution   Let $x = 2r =$ diameter.

We define the objective function:

$$f = \left[2*\left(\frac{\Pi x^2}{4} \right) \right]*20 + 10(\Pi x^2) + 20\left(\frac{2\Pi x^2}{4} + \Pi x L \right) \tag{6.21}$$

$$f = 10\Pi x^2 + 10\Pi x L + 10\Pi x^2 + 20\Pi x L$$

Or

$$f = 20\Pi x^2 + 30\Pi x L \tag{6.22}$$

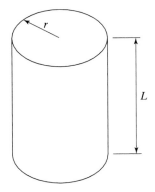

FIGURE 6.7   Tank used for storing gas.

The volume is defined by

$$\frac{\Pi x^2}{4} * L = 120 \tag{6.23}$$

We can deduce an expression for L:

$$L = \frac{480}{\Pi x^2} \tag{6.24}$$

Substituting L in the objective function we get,

$$f = 20\Pi x^2 + 30\Pi x \left(\frac{480}{\Pi x^2} \right) \tag{6.25}$$

which can be simplified further as

$$f = 20\Pi x^2 + \frac{14400}{x} \tag{6.26}$$

To minimize f, we evaluate $f'(x) = 0$

$$f'(x) = 40\Pi x - \frac{14400}{x^2} = 0$$

$$40\Pi x^3 = 14400$$

$$x^3 = 114.59 \tag{6.27}$$

$$x = 4.86 \text{ m}$$

End of Example 6.6

Example 6.7

In this example

x_i	y_i
1	6
3	10
6	2

$y = b + a/x$ is used to approximate the function that best represents the data. Determine a, b using the necessary and sufficient conditions.

Solution   The objective is to minimize the error between the estimated value through the function $y = b + a/x$ and the actual value of y_i from the data.

The problem of least squares is

$$\text{Minimize } f = \sum_{i=1}^{3} \left(b + \frac{a}{x_i} - y_i \right)^2 \tag{6.28}$$

Expanding Equation (6.51) we get the explicit form of f as:

$$f = 3b^2 + \frac{41}{36}a^2 + 3ab - \frac{58}{3}b - 36b + 140 \tag{6.29}$$

The necessary conditions require

$$\frac{\partial f}{\partial a} = 0 = 6b + 3a - 36 = 0$$

$$\frac{\partial f}{\partial b} = 0 = \frac{41}{18}a + 3b - \frac{58}{3} = 0 \tag{6.30}$$

which yields

$$a^* = 1.714, \quad b^* = 5.143 \tag{6.31}$$

and $f^* = 30.86$.

The linear equation is then expressed as

$$y = 1.714 + \frac{5.143}{x} \tag{6.32}$$

To check whether $(a*b*)$ is a minimum

$$\nabla^2 f = \begin{bmatrix} \dfrac{\partial^2 f}{\partial a^2} & \dfrac{\partial^2 f}{\partial a \partial b} \\[2mm] \dfrac{\partial^2 f}{\partial b \partial a} & \dfrac{\partial^2 f}{\partial b^2} \end{bmatrix} = \begin{bmatrix} \dfrac{41}{18} & 3 \\[2mm] 3 & 6 \end{bmatrix} \tag{6.33}$$

$6\left(\dfrac{41}{18}\right) - 3^2 > 0 \Rightarrow (a*, b*)$ is a strong local minimum.

End of Example 6.7

Example 6.8

In this example a conveyor is used to move sand from an area close to the beach (see Figure 6.8). The sand is being dumped into a truck at a speed V (m/s). Our goal is to select the most desirable motor and speed to fill the tank in the optimal time.

Consider the belt transport mechanism shown in Figure 6.8. The power is defined by

$$P = Qh + Q\frac{V^2}{g} = Q\left(h + \frac{V^2}{g}\right)\frac{\text{ft-lb}}{\text{sec}} \tag{6.34}$$

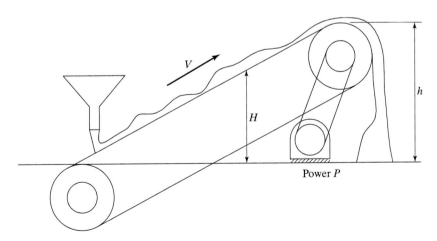

FIGURE 6.8 Belt transport mechanism.

where Q defines the sand mass density per unit volume, V is the speed, and g the gravity constant. The minimum of the function is then found

$$\frac{\partial P}{\partial V} = \frac{2VQ}{g}$$

(6.35)

End of Example 6.8

6.6   Constrained Optimization

Functional constraints are used to reduce the dimensions of the criterion function, where each constraint eliminates one variable. However, the elimination becomes difficult when the functional constraints are implicit functions of the design parameters. Lagrange multipliers provide a powerful method for finding the optima in multivariable problems involving functional constraints.

The function to be optimized is defined by augmenting the objective function by the constraints premultiplied by a variable called the Lagrange multiplier. This is given by

$$T = T_o + \sum_{j=1}^{m} \lambda_j \Psi_j$$

(6.36)

where T_o is the objective function, λ the undetermined multipliers, and Ψ the constraints.

The optimum is obtained by differentiating with respect to the independent variables and the undetermined multipliers and setting the derivatives to 0.

$$\frac{\partial T}{\partial x_i} = 0 \qquad \frac{\partial T}{\partial \lambda_j} = 0 \qquad (i = 1, n; \text{ and } j = 1, m)$$

(6.37)

Example 6.9

Solve for the optimal design problem of Example 6.6 by the method of Lagrange multipliers.

Solution   The objective function is

$$f = 20\pi x^2 + 30\pi xL$$

(6.38)

The function constraint is $\Psi(x, L) = \pi x^2/4L - 120 = 0$. Hence, the function to be optimized, which includes the undetermined multipliers and the constraints, becomes

$$F^* = 20\pi x^2 + 30\pi xL + \lambda\left(\frac{\pi x^2}{4}L - 120\right) = 0$$

(6.39)

Taking the partial derivatives of F^* with respect to x, L, and λ and setting them equal to 0 will yield three equations and three unknowns, solution of which gives the optimum values of x, L, and λ and of course F^*. The partial derivatives of F^* with respect to x, L, and λ are

$$\frac{\partial F^*}{\partial x} = 40\Pi x + 30\Pi L + \lambda\left(\frac{\pi x}{2}L\right) = 0 \tag{6.40}$$

$$\frac{\partial F^*}{\partial L} = 30\pi x + \frac{\lambda\pi x^2}{4} = 0 \tag{6.41}$$

$$\frac{\partial F^*}{\partial \lambda} = \frac{\pi x^2 L}{4} - 120 = 0 \tag{6.42}$$

Equation (6.35) gives a direct relationship between x and λ

$$\lambda = \frac{-120}{x} \tag{6.43}$$

Equation (6.36) reduces to

$$L = \frac{480}{\pi x^2} \tag{6.44}$$

Substituting Equations (6.37) and (6.38) into Equation (6.34), we can solve directly for x

$$x = 4.86 \text{ m}$$

The values of x and L are then obtained from Equations (6.36) and (6.37), respectively, and they are, as expected, exactly the same values obtained in Example 6.6. This example shows how we can search for the solution by adding the constraints equations premultiplied by the undetermined multipliers into the objective function. We then proceed with the derivations of the partial derivative functions with respect to each variable to obtain the algebraic equations needed to minimize the objective function.

End of Example 6.9

Example 6.10

Lagrange multipliers are a common practice in the solution of constrained dynamical systems. At the heart of these famous Langrange equations is an optimization problem, where a Lagrangian function, namely L, which is defined by

$$L = T - V \tag{6.45}$$

(where T is the kinetic energy and V the potential energy) is being minimized. Indeed, when the mechanical system is subject to constraints of the form

$$\phi_j(q, t) = 0 \qquad (j = 1, 2, \ldots, m) \tag{6.46}$$

We introduce a different form of the constraint by introducing the differential of ϕ, namely

$$d\phi_j = \frac{\partial \phi}{\partial q_1} dq_1 + \cdots + \frac{\partial \phi_j}{\partial q_n} dq_n + \frac{\partial q}{\partial t} dt = 0 \tag{6.47}$$

and noting that if we let

$$a_{ji} = \frac{\partial \phi_j}{\partial q_i} \quad \text{and} \quad \frac{\partial \phi_j}{\partial t} \tag{6.48}$$

then the constraint takes the following form:

$$\sum_{i=1}^{n} a_{ji} dq + a_{jt} dt = 0 \qquad (j = 1, 2, \ldots, m) \tag{6.49}$$

In accordance with the principle of virtual displacement, δt is 0 and the constraint forces perform no work. Therefore, if we let the generalized forces be given by C_i, then

$$\sum_{i=1}^{n} C_i \delta q = 0 \tag{6.50}$$

and

$$\sum a_{ji} \delta q_i = 0 \tag{6.51}$$

Premultiplying the above equation by a constant λ yields

$$\lambda_j \sum_{i=1}^{n} a_{ji} \delta q = 0 \qquad (j = 1, 2, \ldots, m) \tag{6.52}$$

which gives rise to

$$\sum_{i=1}^{n} \left(C_i - \sum_{j=1}^{m} \lambda_j a_{ji} \right) \delta q_i = 0 \tag{6.53}$$

So the λs have values defined by

$$C_i = \sum_{j=1}^{m} \lambda_j a_{ji} \tag{6.54}$$

By virtue of the minimization of the Lagrangian function we obtain the standard form of Lagrange differential equations given by

$$\sum_{i=1}^{3n} \left\{ \frac{d}{dt} \left(\frac{\partial T}{\partial q_i} \right) - \frac{\partial T}{\partial q} - Q_i + \sum_{j=1}^{2m} \lambda_j \frac{\partial \phi_j}{\partial q_i} \right\} \delta q_i = 0 \tag{6.55}$$

This equation defines all the differential equations, which governs the system dynamics. In reference to our optimization problem we can conclude that Equation (6.55) is the result of minimizing the function L subject to the constraints defined by Equation (6.49).

End of Example 6.10

Example 6.11

Mass m_2 slides relative to m_1, which in turn slides relative to a horizontal surface (Figure 6.9). Assuming all surfaces are frictionless derive the equations of motion of the system.

Solution   Let us introduce a coordinate X_3, which defines the relative motion of m_2 with respect to m_1. Obviously, we would like X_3 to be 0 or simply $X'_3 = 0$. This defines the constraint, which is in the form of Equation (6.46). From this we can define the coefficients

$$a_{11} = 0$$

$$a_{12} = 0$$

$$a_{13} = 1$$

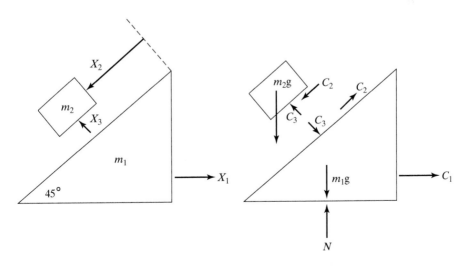

FIGURE 6.9   Mass m_2 sliding over horizontal surface.

Because there is only one constraint, we see the constraint forces to be

$$C_1 = 0$$
$$C_2 = 0$$
$$C_3 = \lambda$$

The total kinetic energy is

$$T = \frac{1}{2}m_1 x_1'^2 + \frac{1}{2}m_2\left[\left(x_1' - \frac{x_2' + x_3'}{\sqrt{2}}\right)^2 + \left(\frac{x_3' - x_2'}{\sqrt{2}}\right)^2\right]$$

$$= \frac{1}{2}(m_1 + m_2)x_1'^2 + \frac{1}{2}m_2\left[x_2'^2 + x_3'^2 - \sqrt{2}(x_2' + x_3')x_1'\right]$$

The potential energy is

$$V = \frac{m_2 g}{\sqrt{2}}(x_3 - x_2)$$

and therefore

$$L = \frac{1}{2}(m_1 + m_2)x_1'^2 + \frac{1}{2}m\left[x_2'^2 + x_3'^2 - \sqrt{2}(x_2' + x_3')x_1'\right] - \frac{m_2 g}{\sqrt{2}}(x_3 - x_2)$$

Next we evaluate the equations of motion based on Lagrange equations given by Equation (6.55). We obtain

$$(m_1 + m_2)x_1'' - \frac{m_2}{\sqrt{2}}x_2'' - \frac{m_2}{\sqrt{2}}x_3'' = 0$$

$$\frac{-m_2}{\sqrt{2}}x_1'' + m_2 x_2'' - \frac{m_2 g}{\sqrt{2}} = 0$$

$$\frac{-m_2}{\sqrt{2}}x_1'' + m_2 x_2'' + \frac{m_2 g}{\sqrt{2}} = \lambda$$

Noting that $x_3'' = 0$, we can solve for x_1'' and λ obtaining

$$x_1'' = \frac{m_2 g}{2m_1 + m_2}$$

and

$$\lambda = \frac{\sqrt{2}m_1 m_2 g}{2m_1 + m_2}$$

This example is a perfect illustration of how to make use of Lagrange multipliers in the context of dynamics.

End of Example 6.11

6.7 Fibonacci Method

This is a method used to find the interval that brackets the minimum of a function. This interval is known as the interval of uncertainty. Fibonacci is a genuine approach in determining the interval in less trial and making the minimum of the function converge to the desired value. What follows is a description of the Fibonacci algorithm.

6.7.1 Fibonacci Algorithm

Fibonacci used this method in the study of rabbits. Leonardo of Pisa developed the method in the reproduction of rabbits. His observation of the rabbit's multiplication at each mature period is shown in Figure 6.10. The new offspring denoted by ∘ matures into • and the mature rabbit • delivers ∘ and •. The progression translates into a sequential series of the form shown in Figure 6.10.

From Figure 6.10 we observe that the sequence of numbers is 1, 1, 2, 3, 5, 8, 13, 21,..., and we automatically deduce that starting from the third row the number is the sum of the preceding two. If we denote the Fibonacci numbers by $F_0, F_1, F_2, \ldots, F_n$ the sequence can be generated using

$$F_0 = 1 \qquad F_1 = 1 \tag{6.56}$$

$$F_i = F_{i-1} + F_{i-2} \quad i = 2, 3, \ldots, n \tag{6.57}$$

Now let us put Fibonacci numbers to practice by focusing on the reduction of the interval of uncertainty where the minimum of a function is to be found.

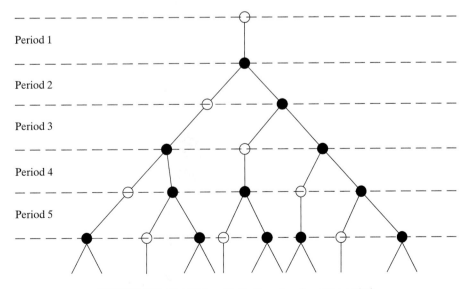

FIGURE 6.10 Rabbits' multiplication at each mature period.

Consider the starting interval of uncertainty to be between 1 and 4. We introduce points 2 and 3. Two cases arise.

Case 1: If $f_2 < f_3$ then 1–3 is the new interval.
Case 2: If $f_2 > f_3$ then 2–4 is the new interval.

Because the two cases are equally likely to occur, it is desirable that points 2 and 3 be placed symmetrically with respect to the center of the interval. If case 1 occurs, let us rename points 1 and 3 as 4 and 1. If case 2 occurs let us rename points 2 and 3 as 1 and 2 (see Figure 6.11).

The interval relations follow from

$$I_1 = I_2 + I_3 \tag{6.58}$$

$$I_2 = I_3 + I_4 \tag{6.59}$$

$$I_{n-2} = I_{n-1} + I_n \tag{6.60}$$

$$I_{n-1} = 2I_n \tag{6.61}$$

By proceeding in reverse order and expressing each interval in terms of I_n, we get

$$I_{n-1} = 2I_n \tag{6.62}$$

$$I_{n-2} = I_{n-1} + I_n = 3I_n \tag{6.63}$$

$$I_{n-3} = I_{n-2} + I_{n-1} = 5I_n \tag{6.64}$$

$$I_{n-4} = I_{n-3} + I_{n-2} = 8I_n \tag{6.65}$$

The coefficients $2, 3, 5, 8, \ldots$ are the Fibonacci numbers. Hence, we deduce the following relation.

$$I_{n-j} = F_{j+1}I_n \qquad j = 1, 2, 3, \ldots, n - 1 \tag{6.66}$$

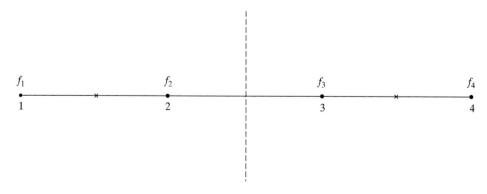

FIGURE 6.11 Initial setup of the uncertainty interval.

For $j = n - 1$ and $n - 2$

$$I_1 = F_n I_n \tag{6.67}$$

$$I_2 = F_{n-1} I_n \tag{6.68}$$

$$I_n = \frac{I_1}{F_n} \tag{6.69}$$

$$I_n = \frac{I_2}{F_{n-1}} \tag{6.70}$$

$$\Rightarrow I_2 = \frac{F_{n-1}}{F_n} I_1 \tag{6.71}$$

For a given interval I_1, I_2 is calculated from Equation (6.36).

Example 6.12

A typical problem in the physics of projectiles is proposed to illustrate how the Fibonacci series can be used in obtaining the minimum of a function. A projectile released from a height h with an initial velocity V making an angle θ with the horizontal axis, and subject to a gravitational field g, as shown in Figure 6.12, travels a distance D when it hits the ground. D is given by the distance along x where the mass falls.

If $h = 50$ m, $V = 90$ m/s, and $g = 9.81$ m/s^2, determine the angle θ in degrees for which the distance D is a maximum. Also calculate the maximum distance D in meters. Use the range for θ of $0°$ to $80°$ and compare the results for $n = 7$ and $n = 19$ for Fibonacci interval reductions.

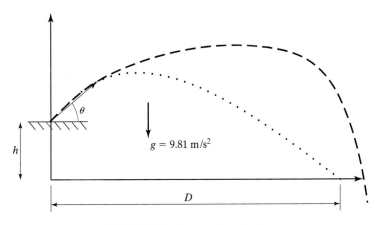

FIGURE 6.12 Physics of projectiles.

Solution   Note that the acceleration components in a uniform gravitational field are

$$a_x = 0$$
$$a_y = -g$$

Noting that the motion along x and y proceed independently, we obtain the velocities

$$v_x = v_0 \cos \theta$$
$$v_y = v_0 \sin \theta - gt$$

Similarly, the displacement components are obtained

$$x = v_0 t \cos \theta$$
$$y = v_0 \sin \theta - \frac{1}{2} g t^2$$

Solving for t from x, we obtain the trajectory

$$y = x \tan \theta - \frac{gx}{2v_0^2 \cos^2 \theta}$$

Using the initial conditions at $t = 0$, $y = h$, and letting D represent the distance when it hits the ground we obtain

$$D = \left(\frac{V \sin \theta}{g} + \sqrt{\frac{2h}{g} + \left(\frac{V \sin \theta}{g} \right)^2} \right) V \cos \theta$$

We need to minimize D, $F = -D$
  Let $\theta = x$, then

$$x = [0, 80]$$

seven interval reductions $\Rightarrow n = 8$

First iteration

$$a_1 = 0 \quad b_1 = 80 \quad L_1 = 0$$

$$\Delta_2 = L_1 \frac{F_6}{F_8} = 80 \times \frac{13}{34} = 30.5882$$

$$x_1 = a_1 + \Delta_2 = 0 + 30.5882 = 30.5882 \qquad F(x_1) = -442.8605 \text{ m}$$

$$x_2 = b_1 - \Delta_2 = 80 - 30.5882 = 49.4118 \qquad F(x_2) = -455.7228 \text{ m}$$

$F(x_2) < F(x_1)$, so discard the interval 0–30.5882
New interval $[30.5882, 80]$

Second iteration

$$a_2 = 30.5882 \quad b_2 = 80 \quad L_2 = 49.4118$$

$$\Delta_3 = L_2 \frac{F_5}{F_7} = 49.4118 \times \frac{8}{21} = 18.8235$$

$$x_1 = a_2 + \Delta_2 = 30.5882 + 18.8235 = 49.4118 \quad F(x_1) = -455.7228 \text{ m}$$

$$x_2 = b_2 - \Delta_3 = 80 - 18.8235 = 61.1765$$

$F(x_2) > F(x_1)$, so discard the interval 61.1765–80

New interval [30.5882,61.1765]

Sixth iteration

$$a_6 = 37.6471 \quad b_6 = 44.7059 \quad L_6 = 7.0588$$

$$\Delta_7 = L_6 \frac{F_1}{F_3} = 7.0588 \times \frac{1}{3} = 2.3529$$

$$x_1 = a_2 + \Delta_2 = 37.6471 + 2.3529 = 40 \qquad F(x_1) = -468.2327 \text{ m}$$

$$x_2 = b_6 - \Delta_7 = 44.7059 - 2.3529 = 42.3529 \quad F(x_2) = -468.8715 \text{ m}$$

$F(x_2) < F(x_1)$, so discard the interval 37.6471–40

New interval [40,44.7059]

Seventh iteration

$$a_7 = 40 \quad b_7 = 44.7059 \quad L_7 = 4.7059$$

$$\Delta_8 = L_7 \frac{F_1}{F_3} = 4.7059 \times \frac{1}{2} = 2.3529$$

$$x_1 = a_7 + \Delta_8 = 40 + 2.3529 = 42.3529 \qquad F(x_1) = -468.8715 \text{ m}$$

$$x_2 = b_7 - \Delta_8 = 44.7059 - 2.3529 = 42.3529 \quad F(x_2) = -468.8715 \text{ m}$$

So for the maximum results, the angle is $x = \theta = 42.3529$ and $D = -F = 468.8715$ m

Note: A MATLAB program is written to generate the above iterations. The MATLAB program is listed below. Copy the program in the MATLAB editor and save and run the program. Be sure you set the path of the file you saved to the working folder.

```
F=[1 1 2 3 5 8 13 21 34]
PI=3.14159;
G=9.81;
```

```
V=90;
H=50;
a=0
b=80
for i = 1:7
  i
  L= b-a
  delta = L * F(8-i)/F(10-i)
  F1=F(8-i)
  F2=F(10-i)
  x1 = a + delta
  x2 = b - delta
  Y1=PI*x1/180;
  sin(Y1);
  Fx1=-(V*sin(Y1)/G + sqrt(2*H/G + (V*sin(Y1)/G)^2)*V*cos(Y1))
  Y2=PI*x2/180;
  sin(Y2);
  Fx2=-(V*sin(Y2)/G + sqrt(2*H/G + (V*sin(Y2)/G)^2)*V*cos(Y2))
  if Fx1 < Fx2
    b = b-delta
    a
      else
        a = a + delta
        b
  end
end
```

19 interval reductions $\Rightarrow n = 20$ we get the following results

First iteration

$$a_1 = 0 \quad b_1 = 80 \quad L_1 = 80$$

$$\Delta_2 = L_1 \frac{F_{18}}{F_{20}} = 80 \times \frac{4181}{10946} = 30.5573$$

$$x_1 = a_1 + \Delta_2 = 0 + 30.5573 = 30.5573 \quad F(x_1) = -442.7232 \text{ m}$$

$$x_2 = b_2 - \Delta_2 = 80 - 30.5573 = 49.4427 \quad F(x_2) = -455.6145 \text{ m}$$

$F(x_2) < F(x_1)$, So discard the interval $0 - 30.5573$

New interval $[0, 30.5573]$

Second iteration

$$a_2 = 30.5573 \quad b_2 = 80 \quad L_2 = 49.4427$$

$$\Delta_3 = L_2 \frac{F_{17}}{F_{19}} = 49.4427 \times \frac{2584}{6765} = 18.8854$$

$$x_1 = a_2 + \Delta_3 = 30.5573 + 18.8854 = 49.4427 \quad F(x_1) = -455.6145 \text{ m}$$

$$x_2 = b_2 - \Delta_2 = 80 - 18.8854 = 61.1146 \qquad F(x_2) = -383.8412 \text{ m}$$

$F(x_2) > F(x_1)$, so discard the interval 61.1146–80

New interval $[30.5573, 61.1146]$

Seventh iteration

$$a_7 = 40.5262 \quad b_7 = 44.9845 \quad L_7 = 4.4582$$

$$\Delta_8 = L_7 \frac{F_{13}}{F_{15}} = 4.4582 \times \frac{233}{610} = 1.7029$$

$$x_1 = a_7 + \Delta_8 = 40.5262 + 1.7029 = 42.2291 \quad F(x_1) = -468.8992 \text{ m}$$

$$x_2 = b_7 - \Delta_8 = 44.9845 - 1.7029 = 43.2816 \quad F(x_2) = -468.4445 \text{ m}$$

$F(x_2) > F(x_1)$, so discard the interval 43.2816–44.9845

New interval $[40.5262, 43.2816]$

Eighth iteration

$$a_8 = 40.5262 \quad b_8 = 43.2816 \quad L_8 = 2.7553$$

$$\Delta_9 = L_8 \frac{F_{12}}{F_{14}} = 2.7553 \times \frac{144}{377} = 1.0524$$

$$x_1 = a_8 + \Delta_9 = 40.5262 + 1.0524 = 41.5787 \quad F(x_1) = -468.9318 \text{ m}$$

$$x_2 = b_8 - \Delta_9 = 43.2816 - 1.0524 = 42.2291 \quad F(x_2) = -468.8992 \text{ m}$$

$F(x_2) > F(x_1)$, so discard the interval 42.2291–43.2816

New interval $[40.5262, 42.2291]$

Nineteenth iteration

$$a_{19} = 41.7833 \quad b_{19} = 41.7979 \quad L_{19} = 0.0146$$

$$\Delta_{20} = L_{19} \frac{F_0}{F_2} = 0.0146 \times \frac{1}{2} = 0.0073$$

$$x_1 = a_{19} + \Delta_{20} = 41.7833 + 0.0146 = 41.7906 \quad F(x_1) = -468.9419 \text{ m}$$

$$x_2 = b_{19} - \Delta_{20} = 41.7979 - 0.0146 = 41.7906 \quad F(x_2) = -468.9419 \text{ m}$$

So for maximum results,

$$x = 41.7906 \text{ and } D = -F = 468.9419 \text{ m}$$

Note: The MATLAB program to generate the above iterations is listed below. Copy the program in the MATLAB editor, save, and run the program. Be sure you set the path of the file you saved to the working folder.

```
F=[1 1 2 3 5 8 13 21 34 55 89 144 233 377 610 987 1597 2584 4181 6765 10946]
PI=3.14159;
G=9.81;
V=90;
H=50;
a=0
b=80
for i = 1:19
  i
  L= b-a
  delta = L * F(20-i)/F(22-i)
  F1=F(20-i)
  F2=F(22-i)
  x1 = a + delta
  x2 = b - delta
  Y1=PI*x1/180;
  sin(Y1);
  Fx1=-(V*sin(Y1)/G + sqrt(2*H/G + (V*sin(Y1)/G)^2)*V*cos(Y1))
  Y2=PI*x2/180;
  sin(Y2);
  Fx2=-(V*sin(Y2)/G + sqrt(2*H/G + (V*sin(Y2)/G)^2)*V*cos(Y2))
  if Fx1 < Fx2
    b= b-delta
    a
      else
        a = a + delta
        b
  end
end
```

End of Example 6.12

6.8   Newton's Method

A most common method in finding the root of a function is defined as Newton's method. The objective is to find x for a given function f is 0. This technique makes use of the slope of the function and the interval points that form the enclosure that forces f to be 0. It works as follows:

$$x_{k+1} = x_k - \frac{f_k}{f'_k} \tag{6.72}$$

Start at x_k and evaluate f_k and f'_k. The next point is obtained through Equation (6.72). x_{k+1} is the next approximation to the zero of the function $f(x)$ (see Figure 6.13).

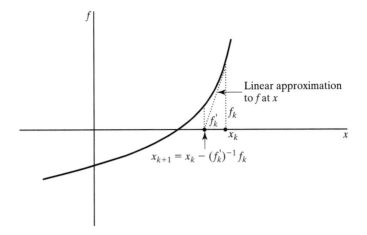

FIGURE 6.13 Newton's method.

Example 6.13

Imagine a brick wall of thickness 0.05 m. The inner wall temperature of the wall, T_0, is 625 K, but the outer surface temperature, T_1, is unknown. The heat loss from the outer surface is due to convection as well as radiation. The temperature T_1 is determined by the equation

$$f(T_1) \equiv \frac{k}{\Delta x}(T_1 - T_0) + \varepsilon\sigma(T_1^4 - T_\infty^4) + h(T_1 - T_f) = 0 \qquad (6.73)$$

where

k: Thermal conductivity of the wall, 1.2 W/mK

ε: Emissivity, 0.8

T_0: Inner wall temperature, 625

T_1: Outer wall temperature (unknown), K

T_∞: Temperature of the surrounding environment, 298 K

T_f: Temperature of the air, 298 K

h: Heat transfer coefficient, 20 W/m^2 K

σ: Stefan-Boltzmann constant, 5.67×10^{-8} W/m^2 K^4

Δx: Thickness of the wall, 0.05 m

Determine T_1 by Newton iteration.

Solution   A MATLAB program was written to try several iterations of the method and check at what point the solution converges.

```
k = 1.2; e = 0.8; Tf = 298;Tinf=298; h=20;
n= 1
T1=400
```

```
        T1_new=0;T0=625;
        sig = 5.678E-8; wall_thick = 0.05;
        f = k/wall_thick * (T1-T0) + e * sig * ( T1^4-Tinf^4) + h*(T1-Tf)
        fd = k/wall_thick + e * sig * 4* T1^3 + h;
        T1_new = T1 - f/fd;
    while abs(T1-T1_new)>0.000001
      n=n+1
      T1=T1_new
      f = k/wall_thick * (T1-T0) + e * sig * ( T1^4-Tinf^4) + h * (T1-Tf)
      fd = k/wall_thick + e * sig * 4* T1^3 + h;
      T1_new = T1 - f/fd;
    end
```

The result is:

$$n = 1 \quad T_1 = 400 \qquad f = -2.5554e + 003$$
$$n = 2 \quad T_1 = 445.9362 \quad f = 99.2640$$
$$n = 3 \quad T_1 = 444.2849 \quad f = 0.1474$$
$$n = 4 \quad T_1 = 444.2825 \quad f = 3.2549e - 007$$
$$\text{ans} = 444.2825$$

The final answer is $T_1 = 444.3$ K.

End of Example 6.13

6.9   Linear Programming

There are times when the general equations of optimization take a characteristic linear form. In this case, the formulation and solution of the design problem is done by the method of linear programming.

The linear programming method deals with objective functions of the form

$$T = \sum_i k_i x_i \tag{6.74}$$

to be maximized or minimized subject to some constraints that are also linear in x.

$$\begin{aligned}
\psi_1 &= a_{11}x_1 + a_{12}x_2 + \cdots + a_{1n}x_n \geq l_1 \\
\psi_2 &= a_{21}x_1 + a_{22}x_2 + \cdots + a_{2n}x_n \geq l_2 \\
&\quad\cdot \qquad\quad \cdot \qquad\quad \cdot \qquad\qquad\quad \cdot \\
&\quad\cdot \qquad\quad \cdot \qquad\quad \cdot \qquad\qquad\quad \cdot \\
\psi_n &= a_{n1}x_1 + a_{n2}x_2 + \cdots + a_{nn}x_n \geq l_n
\end{aligned} \tag{6.75}$$

The general linear programming consists of m linear equations involving n variables. The nonnegative values of the variables that satisfy the constraint equations and maximize or minimize the linear objective function are to be found.

The linear programming approach is illustrated in the following example using two variables.

Example 6.14

An objective function is given by

$$T = 4x_1 + x_2$$

Subject to the following constraints:

$$2x_1 + x_2 > 2$$
$$4x_1 - 3x_2 > -3$$
$$2x_1 + 3x_2 < 21$$
$$4x_1 - x_2 < 16$$

In addition,

$$x_1 > 0 \quad \text{and} \quad x_2 > 0 \quad \text{(nonnegativity requirements)}$$

Find the optimal point for the objective function (CT) using the linear programming method.

Solution   This problem can be solved graphically, as shown in Figure 6.14. The limiting equations are satisfied by any solution inside the shaded area. The optimization can be written as

$$x_2 = T - 4x_1$$

The slashed lines represent this equation for different values of T. It is apparent that the point D is the optimal solution with $T = 23.43$, $x_1 = 4.93$, and $x_2 = 3.71$.

The procedure in linear programming is to start at any one corner of the shaded polygon and jump to an adjacent corner having a higher value of T until no adjacent corner exists with a higher value.

End of Example 6.14

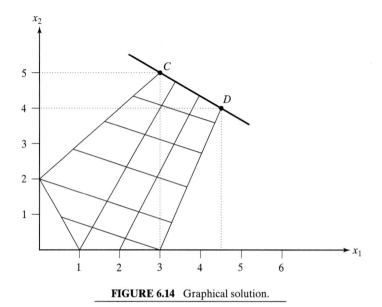

FIGURE 6.14 Graphical solution.

6.10 Geometric Programming

Geometric programming is a nonlinear optimization technique using polynomial programming developed by Duffin, Peterson, and Zener (1967).

An example of the objective function used in geometric programming is given by

$$T = x_1 + 2x_1^1 x_2 + \frac{3}{\sqrt{5}}\sqrt{x_1 x_2} + x_3^3 \tag{6.76}$$

These objective functions take the following form:

$$T = u_1 + u_2 + \cdots + u_p \tag{6.77}$$

Next, a function G is defined such that

$$G = \left(\frac{u_1}{s_1}\right)^{s_1}\left(\frac{u_2}{s_2}\right)^{s_2}\cdots\left(\frac{u_p}{s_p}\right)^{s_p} \tag{6.78}$$

where the s_p s are chosen properly to minimize T.

The method uses a concept of duality similar to that used for linear programming. The dual problem is simpler to solve than the primal problem. The method is quite complex but works well on a computer and has the advantage of providing a global optimum.

6.11 Other Optimization Techniques

There are many other methods to solve an optimization problem. Some of the common solution techniques are

Search methods:
  Exhaustive search
  Grid search
  Random search
  Simplex search

Gradient methods:
  Steepest descent
  Conjugate gradients

Second-derivative methods
Nonlinear programming:
  Johnson's method
  Powell's method for unconstrained situations.

In addition, there are other methods that could be applied to special problems.

These numerical methods can be used to solve the design problem once it is formulated. The methods are iterative and generate a sequence of design points before converging to an optimal solution. Hence, these are best suited for computer implementation to exploit computer speed for beginning repetitive calculations. The software used for design optimization should have interactive facilities to enable the designer to alter the course of the design process if necessary. The software should also be able to interrupt the iterative process to inform the designer about the status of the design. There are many computer algorithms available, most of which have been written in FORTRAN.

PROBLEMS

6.1. Find the dimensions of an oil storage tank (Figure P6.1) resulting in a minimum cost using optimal conditions (method by differentiation). The following data is provided. Cost of the lids is 10 per m^2, the lifelong maintenance of its surface is 80 per m^2 and the main body tank surface cost is 8 per m^2. The overall volume is fixed at 60 m^3.

6.2. Determine the dimensions of a storage box that is constructed from an aluminum sheet 220 mm $\times$ 300 mm by cutting four squares of side (l) from the corners and folding and gluing the edges as shown in Figure P6.2.

6.3. A projectile is landed with an initial velocity of $v = 70$ m/s (Figure P6.3). Determine the angle θ so the projectile lands on a height $h = 30$ m from the ground, when the distance traveled in the horizontal direction is minimum.

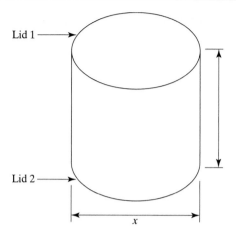

FIGURE P6.1   Oil storage tank.

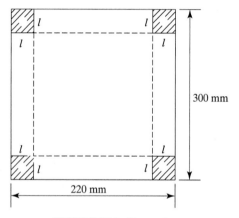

FIGURE P6.2   Storage box.

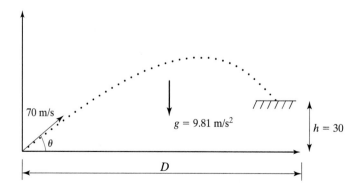

FIGURE P6.3   Projectile.

6.4. For the projectile problem described in Example 6.12, what is the initial slope θ for which the height is maximum. What is the corresponding D when h is maximum?

6.5. Rework the problem in Example 6.11 considering the case where Coulomb friction exists between the blocks.

6.6. An endless V-belt with a pitch diameter of 500 mm is tightly wrapped around pulleys of pitch radii 60 mm and 40 mm, as shown in Figure P6.4. Determine the center distance of the pulleys. Now consider the problem when only two parameters (i.e., pitch diameter of the V-belt and radius of one of the pulleys) are known. Find the relationship to optimize the distance between the centers of the pulleys.

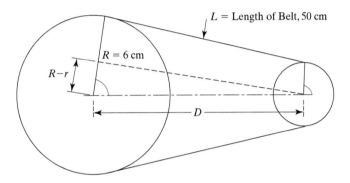

FIGURE P6.4 Endless V-belt.

6.7. Find an optimal solution using the graphical method for the problem constraints given by

$$-2x_1 + 6x_2 < 20$$
$$2x_1 + 2x_2 < 12$$
$$2x_1 - 2x_2 < 4$$
$$2x_1 + 6x_2 > 12$$

and

$$x_1 > 0 \quad \text{and} \quad x_2 > 0$$

and the objective function

$$U = 2x_1 + 4x_2 = \text{maximum}.$$

6.8. Design an artificial leg for a person who has lost a leg above the knee. The artificial leg should capture as many normal movements as possible. Consider a mechanism with two links connected with the knee joint and optimize the knee movement.

6.9. Formulate a design optimization problem for a cylindrical can that has a volume of 475 cm^3. The height-to-diameter ratio for the can is limited between 1.5 and 3.5. The cost of the material is estimated at $3 per cm^2.

6.10. Solve the design problem given in problem 9 using the Lagrange multipliers optimization method.

6.11. Figure P6.5 shows a two-arm robotic arm manipulator. The lengths of the arms are 5 and 7 m. Determine the range of motion of the end effector placed at the end point of link 2 so that the motion starts at $x = 12$ m and ends at $y = 12$ m following the circular path and avoiding the block. (Assume a clearance between the tip of link 2 and the block to be 0.1 m.)

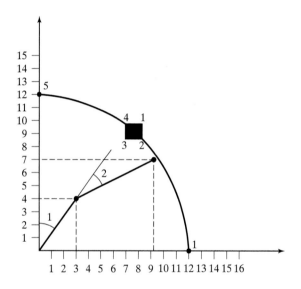

FIGURE P6.5   Two-arm robotic arm manipulator.

6.12 A one-cylinder hand pump has the dimensions shown in Figure P6.6. Derive a set of equations that can be used to design the handle and the fixed joint for pumping the maximum amount of fluid with minimum hand force.

BIBLIOGRAPHY

Arora, J. (1989). *Introduction to Optimum Design*. New York: McGraw-Hill.

Brent, Richard P. (1973). *Algorithms of Minimization without Derivatives*. Englewood Cliffs, NJ: Prentice Hall, pp. 47–60.

Cauchy, A. (1947, 25). "Methode generale pour la resolution des systems d'equations simultanes." *Copmt. Rend.*, pp. 536–538.

Chandrupatla, T.R. (1998, 152). "An Efficient Quadratic Fit-Sectioning Algorithm for Minimization without Derivatives," *Computer Methods in Applied Mechanics and Engineering*, pp. 211–217.

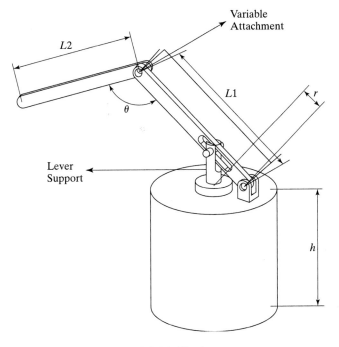

FIGURE P6.6 Hand pump.

Chandrupatla, T.R. (1997, 28). "A New Hybrid Quadratic/Bisection Algorithm for Finding the Zero of a Nonlinear Function without Using Derivatives," *Advances in Engineering Software*, pp. 145–149.

Courant, R., (1943, 49). "Variational Methods for the Solution of Problems of Equilibrium and Vibrations." *Bull. Am. Math. Soc.*, pp. 1–23.

Dantzig, G.B., (1951). "Maximization of a Linear Function of Variables Subject to Linear Inequalities" in T.C. Koopmans (Ed.), *Activity Analysis of Production and Allocation*. New York: Wiley. Reading, MA: Addison Wesley.

Duffin, R.J., Peterson, E.L., and Zener, C. (1967). *Geometric Programming*. New York: Wiley.

Forsythe George E., Malcom, M.A., and Moler, C.B. (1977). *Computer Methods for Mathematical Computations*. Englewood Cliffs, NJ: Prentice Hall.

Fox, R.L. (1971). *Optimization Methods for Engineering Design*.

Haftka, R.T. (1992). *Elements of Structural Optimization*, 3rd ed. Kluwer Academic Publishers.

Haug, E.J. and Arora, J.S. (1979). *Applied Optimal Design*. New York: Wiley.

Johnson, R.C. (1961). Optimum Design of Mechanical Elements. New York: Wiley.

Press, William H., Teukolsky, S.A., Vetterling, W.T., and Flannery, B.P. (1992). *Numerical Recipes*. New York: Cambridge University Press.

Sidall, J. (1982). *Optimal Engineering Design*. New York: Marcel Dekker.

Zener, C. (1971). *Engineering Design by Geometric Programming*. New York: Wiley.

Zener, C., *A Mathematical Aid in Optimizing Engineering Design*.

CHAPTER 7

Introduction to the Finite-Element Method

7.1   Introduction

The finite-element method (FEM), praised by many engineers as the best thing to happen since computers, is essentially a technique that discretizes a given physical or mathematical problem into smaller fundamental parts, called "elements". Then an analysis of the element is conducted using the required mathematics. Finally, the solution to the problem as a whole is obtained through an assembly procedure of the individual solutions of the elements. Hence, complex problems can be tackled by dividing the problem into smaller and simpler problems that can be solved by using existing mathematical tools. These finite-element techniques have been used in many fields of engineering and science. General-purpose codes have been developed, many of which are quite interactive and user-friendly to those who need not necessarily know the in-depth details of FEM. Engineering students and practicing engineers mostly use these codes.

Intricate geometries of mechanical components need huge amounts of data to describe completely the discretized finite-element model. Accuracy of data is also of prime importance because the main processing errors would otherwise go undetected. The role of a CAD workstation is to provide the means of graphically displaying the huge amount of data for visual inspection and quick review of the analysis. Finite-element programs have two types of data: the input required to run the program and the generated output that describes the behavior of the system under the assumed conditions. To further enhance communication between the user and the machine in which a particular finite-element program resides, many vendors of CAD software are developing preprocessors and postprocessors that allow the user to graphically visualize their input and

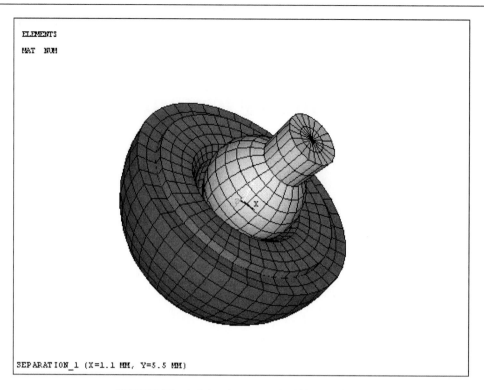

ELEMENTS

MAT NUM

SEPARATION_1 (X=1.1 MM, Y=5.5 MM)

FIGURE 7.1   A finite-element mesh of hip prosthesis.

output (Figures 7.1 and 7.2). Therefore, CAD workstations equipped with such software assist the user to interact with finite-element programs, thus minimizing the time required to learn how to use the FEM program. Most importantly, the graphics capability of CAD workstations provides the user the means to visually display huge amounts of outputs, making the interpretation faster and more convenient.

This chapter introduces the basics of the finite-element method. Step-by-step examples are provided to guide the reader through problem solving.

7.2   Basic Concepts in the Finite-Element Method

The basic steps in FEA (finite-element analysis) consist of three phases:

a) Preprocessing phase

1. Creates and discretizes the solution domain into finite elements, that is, subdivides the problem into nodes and elements.
2. Assumes a shape function to represent the physical behavior of an element, that is, an approximate continuous function is assumed to represent the solution of an element.

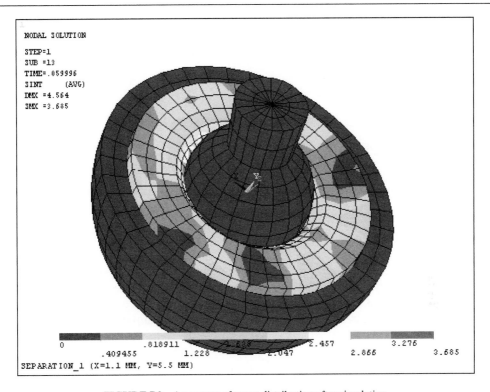

0   .818911   2.457   3.276
    .409455   1.228   2.866   3.685
SEPARATION_1 (X=1.1 MM, Y=5.5 MM)

FIGURE 7.2   An output of stress distribution after simulation.

3. Develops equations for an element.
4. Assembles elements to present the entire problem. Constructs the global stiffness matrix.
5. Applies boundary conditions, initial conditions, and loading.

b) Solution phase: Solves a set of linear or nonlinear algebraic equations in elasto-dynamic problems to obtain nodal results, such as displacement values at different nodes or temperature values at different nodes in a heat transfer problem.

c) Postprocessor phase: Obtains other important information. At this point, you may be interested in values of principles stresses, heat fluxes, etc.

In the preprocessing phase the FEM takes the object to be analyzed and performs a discretization of the body into a finite number of elements. There is usually a selection of the elements used that is most suitable for the problem solution. Based on the equation for a single element, the entire problem is formulated by an assembly of these element equations. Before a solution is adapted the boundary conditions, initial conditions, and loading conditions are introduced. At this stage the solution phase is adapted in solving a set of linear or nonlinear equations simultaneously. The solution yields values such as displacements, or temperature at nodes. The final phase of the

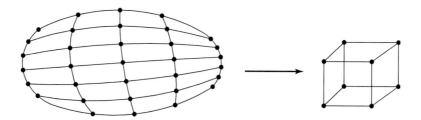

FIGURE 7.3   A general discretization of a body into finite elements.

FEM is the postprocessor, where one chooses the type of output to be displayed. The latter might require additional steps in analysis to extract the information needed.

Consider an element of a continuum as shown in Figure 7.3. Let the element be represented by a small cube. The nodal points are defined as the endpoints of the edges of the cube, which are eight in this case.

All the elements are connected through the nodal points. Any deformation of the body caused by external loads or temperatures induces certain displacements at the nodes. In general, the displacements are the unknowns and are related to the external loads or temperatures through a mathematical relationship of the form

$$f^{\Lambda e} = k^e u^e + f^{\Lambda e}_{\text{add}} \tag{7.1}$$

where k^e (e being the element) is the local element stiffness matrix, $f^{\Lambda e}$ is the external forces applied at each element, u^e represents the nodal displacements for the element, and $f^{\Lambda e}_{\text{add}}$ represents the additional forces. These additional forces could be a result of surface traction or of the material being initially under stress. For the moment, we will assume them to be 0. Hence, Equation (7.1) reduces to

$$f^{\Lambda e} = k^e u^e \tag{7.2}$$

It is important at times to express this equation using the relationship between stresses and strains:

$$\sigma^e = s^e u^e \tag{7.3}$$

where σ^e is the element stress matrix, and s^e is the constitutive relationship connecting u^e and σ^e. From Equation (7.2), we can see that if $f^{\Lambda e}$ and k^e are known, u^e can be evaluated. Similarly, if u^e and k^e are known, we can compute $f^{\Lambda e}$.

The FEM's most basic function is to automatically generate the local stiffness matrix knowing the element type and the properties of the material of the element. Several types of elements that are available in the finite-element library are given in Figure 7.4. The well-known general-purpose FEM packages provide an element library. These codes and others can select any of these elements with the proper number of nodes. Also, the nodal loads can be specified at various nodes based on the boundary conditions. By using the options of the preprocessor and postprocessor offered by the FEM code, a CAD workstation with graphical capabilities can visualize the graphical display of the discretized components before executing the main FEM process. Thus, it is

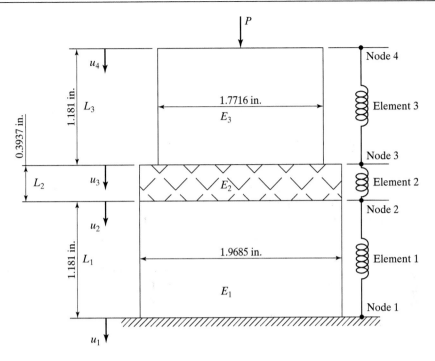

FIGURE 7.4 A variable cross-sectional bar subject to a compressive load.

important at this stage to understand the basic mathematics involved in finite-element formulations.

Example 7.1

In the study of structures, we need to analyze the stress conditions on columns used to support a given load.

A load of $P = 180$ lb acts on the variable cross-sectional bar in which one end is fixed and a compressive load acts at the other end. Dimensions of the bar are shown in the Figure 7.4. Calculate the deflection at various points along its length. Calculate the reaction force at the fixed end and compute stresses in each element.

Solution From Figure 7.4 we compute the cross-sectional areas, and assign the values of the young modulus of elasticity to each of the segment bars.

$$A_1 = 2.3248 \text{ in}^2 \quad E_1 = 669400.12 \text{ lb/in}^2$$
$$A_2 = 0.7750 \text{ in}^2 \quad E_2 = 458 \text{ lb/in}^2$$
$$A_3 = 2.0922 \text{ in}^2 \quad E_3 = 669400.12 \text{ lb/in}^2$$
$$P = 180 \text{ lb}$$

The stiffness of each bar segment is derived from Hooke's law where

$$k_1 = \frac{A_1 E_1}{L_1} = 1317714.986 \text{ lb/in.} \tag{7.4}$$

$$k_2 = \frac{A_2 E_2}{L_2} = 901.575 \text{ lb/in.} \tag{7.5}$$

$$k_3 = \frac{A_3 E_3}{L_3} = 1185909.253 \text{ lb/in.} \tag{7.6}$$

Using the spring representation of the bar segments as shown in Figure 7.4 we can draw a free-body diagram of the forces at each node (Figure 7.5) and apply the first law of mechanics where $\Sigma F = 0$, then at each node we have the following

At node 1

$$R_1 - k_1(u_2 - u_1) = 0 \tag{7.7}$$

At node 2

$$k_1(u_2 - u_1) - k_2(u_3 - u_2) = 0 \tag{7.8}$$

At node 3

$$k_2(u_3 - u_2) - k_3(u_4 - u_3) = 0 \tag{7.9}$$

At node 4

$$k_3(u_4 - u_3) - P = 0 \tag{7.10}$$

The above equations can be written in a matrix form as

$$\begin{bmatrix} k_1 & -k_1 & 0 & 0 \\ -k_1 & k_1 + k_2 & -k_2 & 0 \\ 0 & -k_2 & k_2 + k_3 & -k_3 \\ 0 & 0 & -k_3 & k_3 \end{bmatrix} \begin{bmatrix} u_1 \\ u_2 \\ u_3 \\ u_4 \end{bmatrix} = \begin{bmatrix} -R_1 \\ 0 \\ 0 \\ P \end{bmatrix} \tag{7.11}$$

Because $u_1 = 0$, this is equivalent to eliminating row 1 and column 4 of the stiffness matrix.

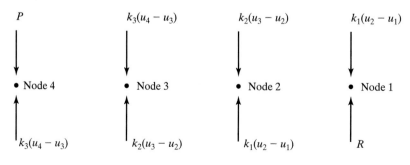

FIGURE 7.5   Free-body diagram of the forces.

Hence, matrix Equation (7.11) reduces to

$$
\begin{bmatrix}
k_1 + k_2 & -k_2 & 0 \\
-k_2 & k_2 + k_3 & -k_3 \\
0 & -k_3 & k_3
\end{bmatrix}
\begin{bmatrix}
u_2 \\
u_3 \\
u_4
\end{bmatrix}
=
\begin{bmatrix}
0 \\
0 \\
P
\end{bmatrix}
\tag{7.12}
$$

Plugging in the values for all the Ks and substituting the value for P, we obtain

$$
\begin{bmatrix}
1318616.556 & -901.57 & 0 \\
-901.57 & 1186810.823 & -1185909.253 \\
0 & -1185909.253 & 1185909.253
\end{bmatrix}
\begin{bmatrix}
u_2 \\
u_3 \\
u_4
\end{bmatrix}
=
\begin{bmatrix}
0 \\
0 \\
180
\end{bmatrix}
\tag{7.13}
$$

The solution of Equation (7.13) can be completed through some of the methods outlined in the Appendix (Cramer's rule), which yield

$$u_2 = 0.0001366 \text{ in.}$$

$$u_3 = 0.199788 \text{ in.}$$

$$u_4 = 0.199940 \text{ in.}$$

Putting $u_1 = 0$ in Equation (7.7), we obtain

$$-k_1 u_2 = -R_1$$

from which we compute the reaction force R_1

$$R_1 = 180 \text{ lb}$$

Stresses are obtained using the stress–strain relationship for each segment of the bar, that is

$$\sigma^{(1)} = E_1 \frac{(u_2 - u_1)}{L_1} = 77.4259 \text{ lb/in}^2$$

$$\sigma^{(2)} = E_2 \frac{(u_3 - u_2)}{L_2} = 232.2589 \text{ lb/in}^2$$

$$\sigma^{(3)} = E_3 \frac{(u_4 - u_3)}{L_3} = 113.351 \text{ lb/in}^2$$

End of Example 7.1

Example 7.2

This is similar to Example 7.1, however, element z is replaced with two identical supports, which form elements 2 and 3.

A load of $P = 180$ lb acts on the variable cross-sectional bar in which one end is fixed and a compressive load acts at the other end. Dimensions of the bar are indicated in Figure 7.6. Calculate the deflection at various points along its length. Calculate the reaction force at the fixed end and the corresponding stresses in each element.

Solution   The cross-sectional areas are found to be

$$A_1 = 3.04 \text{ in}^2$$

$$A_2 = A_3 = .2739 \text{ in}^2$$

$$A_4 = 2.456 \text{ in}^2$$

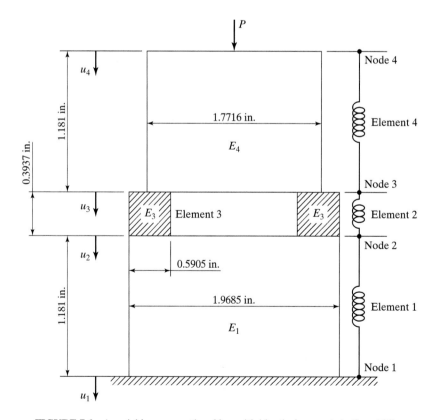

FIGURE 7.6   A variable cross-sectional bar with identical supports in the middle.

the load P is

$$P = 180 \text{ lb}$$

the young's modulus of elasticity for each segment is given by

$$E_1 = 669400.12 \text{ lb/in}^2$$

$$E_2 = E_3 = 458 \text{ lb/in}^2$$

$$E_4 = 669400.12 \text{ lb/in}^2$$

The element stiffness is found in a similar fashion as Example 7.1, where

$$k_1 = \frac{A_1 E_1}{L_1} = 1724887.221 \text{ lb/in.}$$

both elements 2 and 3 are

$$k_2 = k_3 = \frac{A_2 E_2}{L_2} = 318.64 \text{ lb/in.}$$

and element 4 stiffness is

$$k_4 = \frac{A_4 E_4}{L_4} = 1397158.65 \text{ lb/in.}$$

At node 1

$$R_1 - k_1(u_2 - u_1) = 0 \tag{7.14}$$

At node 2

$$k_1(u_2 - u_1) - (k_2 + k_3)(u_3 - u_2) = 0 \tag{7.15}$$

At node 3

$$(k_2 + k_3)(u_3 - u_2) - k_4(u_4 - u_3) = 0 \tag{7.16}$$

At node 4

$$k_3(u_4 - u_3) - P = 0 \tag{7.17}$$

The above equation can be written in a matrix form as

$$\begin{bmatrix} k_1 & -k_1 & 0 & 0 \\ -k_1 & k_1 + k_2 + k_3 & -(k_2 + k_3) & 0 \\ 0 & -(k_2 + k_3) & k_2 + k_3 + k_4 & -k_4 \\ 0 & 0 & -k_4 & k_4 \end{bmatrix} \begin{bmatrix} u_1 \\ u_2 \\ u_3 \\ u_4 \end{bmatrix} = \begin{bmatrix} -R_1 \\ 0 \\ 0 \\ P \end{bmatrix}. \tag{7.18}$$

Because $u_1 = 0$, Equation (7.18) can then be reduced to

$$\begin{bmatrix} k_1 + k_2 + k_4 & -(k_2 + k_3) & 0 \\ -(k_2 + k_3) & k_2 + k_3 + k_4 & -k_4 \\ 0 & -k_4 & k_4 \end{bmatrix} \begin{bmatrix} u_2 \\ u_3 \\ u_4 \end{bmatrix} = \begin{bmatrix} 0 \\ 0 \\ P \end{bmatrix} \tag{7.19}$$

Substituting all the known values of Ks and P we obtain

$$\begin{bmatrix} 1725524.507 & -637.2856 & 0 \\ -637.2856 & 1397795.936 & -1397158.65 \\ 0 & -1397158.65 & 1397158.65 \end{bmatrix} \begin{bmatrix} u_2 \\ u_3 \\ u_4 \end{bmatrix} = \begin{bmatrix} 0 \\ 0 \\ 180 \end{bmatrix}$$

The solution of which is found to be

$$u_2 = 0.0001 \text{ in.}$$

$$u_3 = 0.2826 \text{ in.}$$

$$u_4 = 0.2827 \text{ in.}$$

u_2, u_3, and u_4 correspond to the displacement of the nodes and provide us with the deformation of the variable bar under the loading of P. The reaction force at node 1 is obtained from Equation (7.18), where the first equation is

$$-k_1 u_2 = -R_1$$

Therefore,

$$R_1 = 172.3 \text{ lb}$$

Stresses for each element are obtained using the stress–strain relationship, where

$$\sigma^{(1)} = E_1 \frac{(u_2 - u_1)}{l_1} = 56.675 \text{ lb/in}^2$$

$$\sigma^{(2)} = E_2 \frac{(u_3 - u_2)}{l_2} = 328.63 \text{ lb/in}^2$$

$$\sigma^{(4)} = E_4 \frac{(u_4 - u_3)}{l_3} = 56.675 \text{ lb/in}^2$$

End of Example 7.2

Example 7.3

A tapering round bar is fixed at one end and a tensile load $P = 180$ lb is applied at the other end (Figure 7.7). The maximum and minimum radius of the bar is 20 in. and 10 in., respectively. The bar's modulus of elasticity $E = 669400.12$ lb/in^2. Consider the bar as a set of four elements of equal length and uniformly increasing diameter. Find the global stiffness matrix and displacements at each node and reaction force.

Solution   Let the tapered round bar be represented by a four-element model as shown in Figure 7.8.

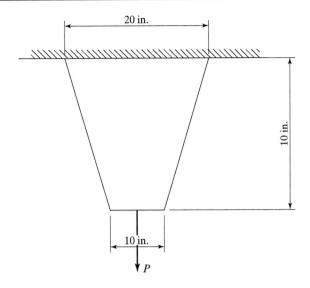

FIGURE 7.7 A tapered round bar subject to a tensile load P.

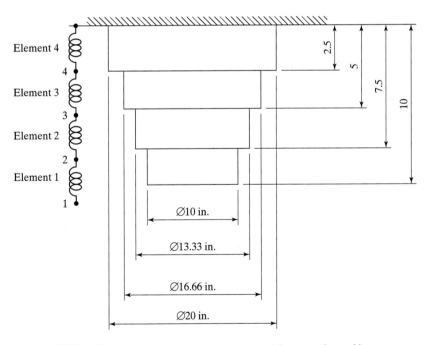

FIGURE 7.8 A four-element representation of the tapered round bar.

The geometrical data and stiffness properties for each element are:

$$A_1 = 78.5398 \text{ in}^2 \quad A_2 = 139.626 \text{ in}^2 \quad A_3 = 218.166 \text{ in}^2 \quad A_4 = 314.159 \text{ in}^2$$

$$k_1 = 21029825 \quad k_2 = 37386355.52 \quad k_3 = 58416180.5 \quad k_4 = 784119300$$

Following the equilibrium equation of $\Sigma F = 0$ at each node, we write the following:

At node 1

$$k_1(u_2 - u_1) - P = 0 \tag{7.20}$$

At node 2

$$k_2(u_3 - u_2) - k_1(u_2 - u_1) = 0 \tag{7.21}$$

At node 3

$$k_3(u_4 - u_3) - k_2(u_3 - u_2) = 0 \tag{7.22}$$

At node 4

$$k_4(u_5 - u_4) - k_3(u_4 - u_3) = 0 \tag{7.23}$$

At node 5

$$R - k_4(u_5 - u_4) = 0 \tag{7.24}$$

The above equations can be written in a compact form as

$$
\begin{bmatrix}
k_1 & -k_1 & 0 & 0 & 0 \\
-k_1 & k_1 + k_2 & k_2 & 0 & 0 \\
0 & -k_2 & k_2 + k_3 & -k_3 & 0 \\
0 & 0 & -k_3 & k_3 + k_4 & -k_4 \\
0 & 0 & 0 & -k_4 & k_4
\end{bmatrix}
\begin{Bmatrix}
u_1 \\ u_2 \\ u_3 \\ u_4 \\ u_5
\end{Bmatrix}
=
\begin{Bmatrix}
P \\ 0 \\ 0 \\ 0 \\ -R
\end{Bmatrix}
\tag{7.25}
$$

Applying boundary conditions, that is $u_5 = 0$, we reduce the above to four equations:

Therefore, the matrix equation becomes

$$
\begin{bmatrix}
k_1 & -k_1 & 0 & 0 \\
-k_1 & k_1 + k_2 & -k_2 & 0 \\
0 & -k_2 & k_2 + k_3 & -k_3 \\
0 & 0 & -k_3 & k_3 + k_4
\end{bmatrix}
\begin{Bmatrix}
u_1 \\ u_2 \\ u_3 \\ u_4
\end{Bmatrix}
=
\begin{Bmatrix}
P \\ 0 \\ 0 \\ 0
\end{Bmatrix}
\tag{7.26}
$$

A solution of which is found to be

$$u_1 = 0.1860 \times 10^{-4} \text{ in.}$$

$$u_2 = 0.1004 \times 10^{-4} \text{ in.}$$

$$u_3 = 0.0522 \times 10^{-4} \text{ in.}$$

$$u_4 = 0.0214 \times 10^{-4} \text{ in.} \tag{7.27}$$

The reaction force is obtained by writing the fifth equation form, Equation (7.25), where

$$R = k_4(u_5 - u_4) \tag{7.28}$$

Substituting the values of the u_5 and u_4 and k_4, we obtain

$$R = 180.01 \text{ lb} \tag{7.29}$$

End of Example 7.3

7.3 Potential-Energy Formulation

The finite-element method is based on the minimization of the total potential-energy formulation. When a closed form solution is not possible, approximation methods such as finite element are the most commonly used in solid mechanics. To illustrate how finite element is formulated, we will consider an elastic body such as the one shown in Figure 7.9, where the body is subjected to a loading force, which causes it to deform.

From Hooke's law, we write

$$F = \frac{AE}{L}\delta \tag{7.30}$$

where F represents the compressive force

A represents area of the elastic body

E represents the young's modulus of elasticity

δ represents the displacement in the y direction

L is the length of the segment.

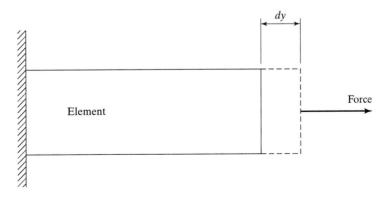

FIGURE 7.9   Elastic body.

From Hooke's law the force–displacement relationship is

$$F = ky$$

The work performed by the compressive force F is stored in the material in a form of a strain energy. FEA discretizes bodies into elements, hence if we can compute the strain energy associated with each element we can then evaluate the total strain energy associated with all external forces applied to the body.

Consider Figure 7.9. Let the element deformation be noted as dy. The strain energy is given by the work of F over the deformed length. The stored energy is

$$d\Lambda = \int_0^{y_1} F dy = \int_0^{y_1} ky \, dy = \frac{1}{2}ky_1^2 \tag{7.31}$$

where Λ represents the energy.

The normal stress and strain are directly related to the stored energy if we make the following substitutions

$$\frac{F}{A} = \sigma_y \Rightarrow F = \sigma_y \, dx dz \tag{7.32}$$

where σ_y is the stress in the y direction and ϵ is the strain. Hence we can express the energy equation in terms of the stress-strain as follows.

$$d\Lambda = \frac{1}{2}\sigma \epsilon \, dV \tag{7.33}$$

where $d\Lambda$ represents the element strain energy and the volume of the element is

$$dV = dx dy dz \tag{7.34}$$

We can then write the strain energy for an element introducing the superscript e, where

$$\Lambda^e = \int d\Lambda = \int \frac{\sigma \epsilon}{2} dV \tag{7.35}$$

The stress can be substituted for by

$$\sigma^{(e)} = E \epsilon \tag{7.36}$$

Using the above relation in Equation (7.32), we obtain

$$\Lambda^e = \int \frac{E \epsilon^2}{2} dV \tag{7.37}$$

The total energy, which consists of the strain energy due to deformation of the body and the work performed by the external forces, can be expressed as function of the combined energy as

$$\Pi = \sum_{e=1}^{n} \Lambda^e - \sum_{i=1}^{n} F_i u_i \tag{7.38}$$

where u_i denotes displacement along the force direction F_i. Note that F_i represents the extreme force applied to each element.

It follows that a stable system requires that the potential energy be minimum at equilibrium

$$\frac{\partial \Pi}{\partial u_i} = \frac{\partial}{\partial u_i}\left[\sum \Lambda^{(e)} - \sum F_i u_i\right] = 0 \tag{7.39}$$

We know that the strain is defined making use of the relative displacement between adjacent elements

$$\in = \frac{(u_{i+1} - u_i)}{l} \tag{7.40}$$

Equation (7.39) has two components. Let us find an expression for the first term, then

$$\frac{\partial \Lambda^e}{\partial u_i} = \frac{A_{\text{avg}}E}{l}(u_i - u_{i+1}) \tag{7.41}$$

and

$$\frac{\partial \Lambda^e}{\partial u_{i+1}} = \frac{A_{\text{avg}}E}{l}(u_{i+1} - u_i) \tag{7.42}$$

The above equations can be expressed in a matrix form as follows

$$\left\{\begin{array}{c} \dfrac{\partial \Lambda^{(e)}}{\partial u_i} \\[2mm] \dfrac{\partial \Lambda^{(e)}}{\partial u_{i+1}} \end{array}\right\} = k_{\text{eq}}\begin{bmatrix} 1 & -1 \\ -1 & 1 \end{bmatrix}\left\{\begin{array}{c} u_i \\ u_{i+1} \end{array}\right\} \tag{7.43}$$

where

$$k_{\text{eq}} = \frac{(A_{\text{avg}}E)}{l}$$

Similarly, we take the second in Equation (7.39) and obtain

$$\frac{\partial}{\partial u_i}(F_i u_i) = F_i \tag{7.44}$$

and

$$\frac{\partial}{\partial u_{i+1}}(F_{i+1}u_{i+1}) = F_{i+1} \tag{7.45}$$

Combining Equations (7.43), (7.44) and (7.45) leads to the elemental force–displacement relation

$$F^{(e)} = k^{(e)}u^{(e)} \tag{7.46}$$

or

$$k_{eq} \begin{bmatrix} 1 & -1 \\ -1 & 1 \end{bmatrix} \begin{Bmatrix} u_i \\ u_{i+1} \end{Bmatrix} = \begin{Bmatrix} F_i \\ F_{i+1} \end{Bmatrix} \tag{7.47}$$

where $k^{(e)}$ is the element stiffness matrix, $u^{(e)}$ the element displacement associated with node i or $i + 1$, and $F^{(e)}$ the external forces acting at the nodes.

In summary, we see that the minimization of the concept of potential energy leads to an equation similar to the discrete method adapted in the early development of this chapter.

Other popular methods in finite element are presented for the reader to see how these methods lead to results similar to the minimization of potential energy.

7.4   Closed-Form Solution

The closed-form solution is used when all the variables have explicit mathematical forms that can be dealt with in terms of extracting a solution. Consider a continuous body subject to a compressive load P (Figure 7.10). The objective is to determine the displacement or deformation at any point. Let the continuous body have a variable cross-sectional area. The equilibrium equation at any cross-sectional area can be written as

$$P - \sigma_{avg}(A(y)) = 0, \tag{7.48}$$

where

$$\sigma_{avg} = E \in \tag{7.49}$$

Substituting the above equation into Equation (7.48) we get

$$P - E \in A(y) = 0 \tag{7.50}$$

Recall that the strain is defined as

$$\in = \frac{du}{dy} \tag{7.51}$$

Thus,

$$P - EA(y)\frac{du}{dy} = 0 \tag{7.52}$$

which implies that

$$du = \frac{Pdy}{EA(y)} \tag{7.53}$$

Integrating the above equation will lead to exact solution to the displacement.

$$u = \int_0^u du = \int_0^l \frac{Pdy}{EA(y)} \tag{7.54}$$

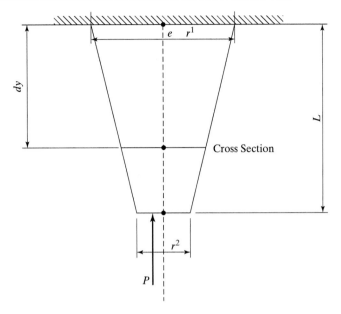

FIGURE 7.10   A nonuniform bar subjected to compressive load P.

if we assume the load is constant and that

$$A(y) = \left(\frac{r_2 - r_1}{L}\right)y + r_1 \tag{7.55}$$

Equation (7.48) becomes

$$u = \int_0^L \frac{Pdy}{E\left[\left(\frac{r_2 - r_1}{L}\right)y + r_1\right]} \tag{7.56}$$

or

$$u = \frac{P}{E}\int_0^L \frac{dy}{(ay + r_1)} \tag{7.57}$$

where

$$a = \frac{r_2 - r_1}{L} = const. \tag{7.58}$$

Let $z = ay + r_1 \Rightarrow dz = ady$. Hence,

$$u = \frac{P}{Ea}\int \frac{dz}{z} = \frac{P}{Ea}[\ln(z)] + c \tag{7.59}$$

Let $u(0) = 0$, then $C = -\dfrac{P}{Ea} \ln \tau_1$

$$u = \frac{P}{Ea}[\ln(ay + r_1) - \ln(r_1)] \tag{7.60}$$

or

$$u = \frac{P}{Ea}\left[\ln\left(\frac{ay + r_1}{r_1}\right)\right] \tag{7.61}$$

The above solution can be used to find displacement at various points along the length. Note that from Equation (7.58) if $y = L$, we have

$$aL + r_1 = r_2$$

and the displacement is

$$u = \frac{P}{Ea}[\ln r_2 - \ln r_1] \tag{7.62}$$

Thus, the solution depends on r_1 and r_2, which we should know first-hand.

We can compare the exact solution to the one obtained in Example 7.3 where the geometry of the nodal is equivalent to the one in Example 7.2. As a matter of fact, the solution in the example is an approximation by means of element and assembly procedure. In Example 7.3 the method used leads to a discretization of the bar from which a solution is derived. The solution had to be reformulated depending on the number of elements. The more elements used the closer the solution is to the exact solution given by Equation (7.61).

7.5   Weighted-Residual Method

The weighted residual method (WRM) assumes an approximate solution to the governing differential equations. The solution criterion is one where the boundary conditions and initial conditions of the problems are satisfied. It is evident that the approximate solution leads to some marginal errors. If we require that the errors vanish over a given interval or at some given points then we will force the approximate solution to converge to an accurate solution.

Consider the differential equation discussed in previous example where

$$\begin{cases} A(y)E\dfrac{du}{dy} - P = 0 \\ \qquad \text{with} \\ \quad u(0) = 0. \end{cases} \tag{7.63}$$

Let us choose a displacement field u to approximate the solution, that is let

$$u(y) = C_0 + C_1 y + C_2 y^2 \tag{7.64}$$

where C_0, C_1, and C_2 are unknown coefficients.

If we substitute $u(y)$ and $A(y)$ into the differential equation we get

$$\left[\left(\frac{r_2 - r_1}{L} \right) y + r_1 \right] E(C_1 + 2C_2 y) - P = \varepsilon \tag{7.65}$$

where ε stands for residual.

The equation above has two constants C_1 and C_2. If we require that ε vanishes at two points we will get two equations that can be used to solve for C_1 and C_2.

Solving Equation (7.66) for these conditions, we get

$$\varepsilon\big|_{y=\frac{L}{2}} = 0 \quad \text{and} \quad \varepsilon\big|_{y=L} = 0$$

$$C_1 = +\frac{P}{E} \frac{(3r_2 - r_1)}{r_2(r_2 + r_1)}$$

$$C_2 = -\frac{P}{EL} \frac{(r_2 - r_1)}{r_2(r_2 + r_1)} \tag{7.66}$$

and $C_0 = 0$ for $u(0) = 0$

The final solution for the displacement field is

$$u(y) = \frac{P}{E \, r_2(r_2 + r_1)} \left[(3r_2 - r_1)y - \frac{r_2 - r_1}{L} y^2 \right] \tag{7.67}$$

The solution can be used to compare it to the exact solution derived in the previous section.

7.6 Galerkin Method

The Galerkin method requires the integer of the error function over some selected interval to be forced to 0 and that the error be orthogonal to some weighting functions ϕ_i, according to the integral

$$\int_\Omega \phi_i \, \varepsilon \, dy = 0, \tag{7.68}$$

where $\Omega = [0, L]$ for $i = 1, \ldots, n$.

These are selected as part of the approximate solution. This is simply done by assigning the ϕ functions to the terms that multiply the coefficients.

Because we assume $u(y)$ to be $u(y) = C_0 + C_1 y + C_2 y^2$ as defined in Equation (7.63) then $\phi_1 = y$ and $\phi_2 = y^2$.

TABLE 7.1   Comparison of displacement values by different methods.

Location of the point along the length of the object (in inches)	Results from the approximation method (Example 7.3) ($\times 10^{-4}$)	Results from the exact solution method ($\times 10^{-4}$)	Results from weighted residual methods ($\times 10^{-4}$)	Results from Galerkin method ($\times 10^{-4}$)
$y = 0$	0	0	0	0
$y = 2.5$	0.0214	0.6000	0.532	0.547
$y = 5$	0.0522	1.090	1.008	1.032
$y = 7.5$	0.1004	1.504	1.428	1.454
$y = 10$	0.1860	1.863	1.792	1.814

Now we use Equation (7.67) and substitute $\phi_1 = y$ and the residual ε from Equation (7.65). Furthermore let the values of r_1 and r_2 be given from Example 7.3, then we obtain

$$\int_0^L y \left[(10 + y)(C_1 + 2C_2 y) - \frac{P}{E} \right] dy = 0 \tag{7.69}$$

$$\int_0^L y^2 \left[(10 + y)(C_1 + 2C_2 y) - \frac{P}{E} \right] dy = 0 \tag{7.70}$$

From Example 7.3 the load P is 180 lb.

Integrating the above two equations leads to two linear equations in terms of C_1 and C_2. Solving the two equations we get $C_1 = .2314 \times 10^{-4}$ and $C_2 = -0.50 \times 10^{-6}$. The solution is then approximated by

$$u(y) = (C_1 + C_2 y^2) \tag{7.71}$$

Table 7.1 shows the comparison between the results obtained from the approximation method, exact solution method, WRM, and the Galerkin method. The results are all in good approximation with one another. These methods become a very powerful tool in the finite-element method when used to approximate the solutions to a given problem.

PROBLEMS

7.1. Use the method of discrete elements as described in Examples 7.1 and 7.2 to find the displacement at nodes 2 and 1 in Figure P7.1. Find the reaction force due to the compressive load $P = 150$ lb.

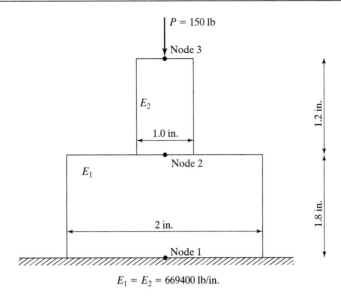

$$E_1 = E_2 = 669400 \text{ lb/in.}$$

FIGURE P7.1   Block subject to compromise load.

7.2. Repeat Problem 7.1, and find the displacement at midpoint of node 1 and node 2.

7.3. A block composed of three distinct segments is used to support loading $P = 150$ lbs from a hammer (Figure P7.2). Segments 1 and 2 are identical and are made of steel. ($E = 3 \times 10^6$ psi). Find the stress in each segment.

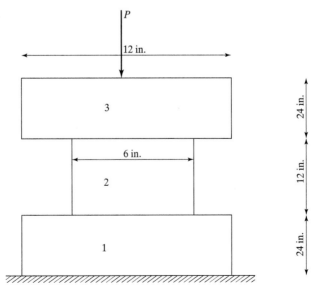

FIGURE P7.2   Block composed of three distinct segments.

7.4. Consider the steel plate shown in Figure P7.3. Use 3 elements to formulate the following

(a) Develop the stiffness matrix K using the node force equilibrium equation.
(b) Determine the stresses in each element.

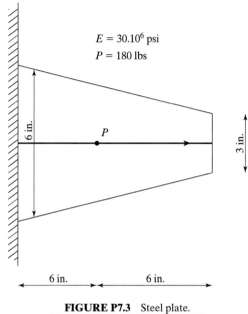

$E = 30.10^6$ psi
$P = 180$ lbs

6 in.

P

3 in.

6 in.   6 in.

FIGURE P7.3   Steel plate.

7.5. Consider the differential equations:

$$A(y)E\frac{du}{dy} - P = 0$$

$$u(0) = 0$$

$$u(L) = 0$$

Assume a displacement field

$$u(y) = C_0 + C_1 y + C_2 y^2 + C_3 y^3$$

and a cross-sectional area, r_1, and r are constants.

$$A(y) = r_1 + ry^2$$

Use the Galerkin method to find the displacement response.

7.6. Repeat Example 7.3 using the WRM if the residual ε conditions are sum

$$\varepsilon|_{y=\frac{L}{2}} = 0 \quad \text{and} \quad \varepsilon|_{y=0} = 0$$

BIBLIOGRAPHY

Akin, J. (ed.) (1986). *Finite Element Analysis for Undergraduates*. Orlando, Florida: Academic Press.

ANSYS Engineering Analysis System. (1983). Houston, PA: Swanson Analysis Systems, Inc.

Burnett, D.S. (1987). *Finite Element Analysis: From Concepts to Applications*. Reading, MA: Addison-Wesley.

Engineering Mechanics Research Corp. (1991). Software products pamphlets on finite elements. Troy, MI.

Engineering Mechanics Research Corp. (1991). SHAPE NISOPT publication. Troy, MI.

Huston, R.L, and Passerello, C.E. (1984). *Finite Element Methods: An Introduction*. New York: Marcel Dekker.

Kenneth, H. (1975). *Finite Element Methods for Engineers*. New York: Wiley.

Martin H.C., and Carey, G.F. (1973). *Introduction to Finite Element Analysis Theory and Applications*. New York: McGraw-Hill.

Reddy, J.N. (1984). *An Introduction to Finite Element Method*. New York: McGraw-Hill.

Rockey, K.C. (1975). *The Finite Element Method: A Basic Introduction*. New York: Wiley.

Stasa, F.L. (1985). *Applied Finite Element Analysis for Engineers. HRW Series in Mechanical Engineering*. New York: CBS College Publishing.

Timoshenko, S.D., and Goodier, J.N. (1970). *Theory of Elasticity*. New York: McGraw-Hill.

Zienkiewcz, O.C., and Taylor, R.L. (1989). *The Finite Element Method*. New York: McGraw-Hill.

CHAPTER 8

Trusses—A Finite-Element Approach

8.1   Introduction to Truss Analysis

Trusses are used in many engineering applications, including bridges, buildings, and towers and support structures. A truss is a structure in which the displacements, translations, or compressions of any truss member vary linearly with the applied forces. That is, any increment in displacement is proportional to the force causing it to deform. All deformations are assumed small, so that the resulting displacements do not significantly affect the geometry of the structure and hence do not alter the forces in the members. In this case Hooke's law is preserved and the theory of elasticity is used to search for solutions of the truss. Most often, the truss design requires that its member be tested for tension, compression, stress, and strain relations. The applied loads are then tested against the possible yield stress to determine their evaluated limits and the overall stability of the truss.

For large and complicated truss structures, manual computation is often impractical to analyze the static equilibrium conditions; therefore, a digital computer has to be used to accommodate the required computations. Over the past two decades, finite-element method (FEM) codes have been developed to take a large number of engineering applications, as trusses have always been a favorite topic for which FEM is needed to demonstrate its usefulness. What we have proposed in this chapter is a method by which FEM can be introduced in the solution of trusses. In the analysis that follows, it is assumed that the members are connected by smooth pins or by a ball-and-socket joint in 3D truss. Planar trusses (2D) are emphasized and the solution provided can be extended to 3D without difficulties.

8.2   Finite-Element Formulation

Trusses are typical structures in which the finite-element method can be best illustrated. We know that FEM relies on (a) discretizing the finite element of the system; (b) developing the mathematical relationships between the forces and displacements, stresses and strains, etc., for a given element; and (c) formulating the general problem through an assembly procedure of all the elements to solve the given problem.

Consider an element of an arbitrary truss, as shown in Figure 8.1. It is subjected to either tension or compression, as is the case for all the truss elements. Let us label the element's ends 1 and 2, and, consequently, call the corresponding forces F_1 and F_2 (Figure 8.2).

We also know from static analysis that for the element to be in a state of equilibrium, we need the following equation to be true

$$F_1 + F_2 = 0 \qquad (8.1)$$

which simply says that the forces at both ends are equal and opposite in direction. This is true for both tension and compression of the element. Using Hooke's law, we can write the force displacement relation as

$$U = F_{1,2}\frac{L}{AE} \qquad (8.2)$$

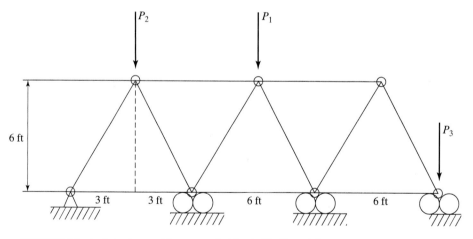

FIGURE 8.1 A planar truss subject to vertical loads (P_1, P_2, and P_3 represent arbitrary points).

or

$$F_{1,2} = kU \qquad (8.3)$$

where $k = AE/L$ is the stiffness constant when the element is under tension or compression. Note that $F_{1,2}$ denotes either F_1 or F_2. The relative displacement between the nodal points of this truss element can be written as

$$U = U_2 - U_1 \qquad (8.4)$$

FIGURE 8.2 A typical truss element.

where U_1 and U_2 are the displacements at ends 1 and 2, respectively. We also refer to ends 1 and 2 as nodes 1 and 2 of the truss element.

Using Equation (8.3), we can write

$$F_1 = kU_1 - kU_2 \tag{8.5}$$

and

$$F_2 = -kU_1 + kU_2 \tag{8.6}$$

Using matrix notation, we write Equations (8.5) and (8.6) in combined form as

$$\begin{bmatrix} F_1 \\ F_2 \end{bmatrix} = \begin{bmatrix} k & -k \\ -k & k \end{bmatrix} \begin{bmatrix} U_1 \\ U_2 \end{bmatrix} \tag{8.7}$$

or simply

$$\{F\} = [k]\{U\} \tag{8.8}$$

where

$$\{F\} = \begin{Bmatrix} F_1 \\ F_2 \end{Bmatrix} = \text{the nodal force vector for the element}$$

$$\{U\} = \begin{Bmatrix} U_1 \\ U_2 \end{Bmatrix} = \text{the nodal displacement vector}$$

and

$$[k] = k \begin{bmatrix} 1 & -1 \\ -1 & 1 \end{bmatrix} = \text{the element stiffness matrix}$$

Thus, Equation (8.8) shows that the nodal displacements and nodal forces are related by the element (local) stiffness matrix. As the orientation and loading of various elements in the structure (a truss in this case) vary from each other, we need to develop the local stiffness that will apply to any element orientation.

In the sequel, a more general 2D local stiffness will be developed. A uniform system for symbol notation will be adopted that is crucial for easy reading and understanding and subsequent computer implementation.

Let us consider an orientation of a truss element, as shown in Figure 8.3. For $\theta = 0$, we developed a relationship between the forces and the displacements given by Equation (8.7); let e_i be a unit vector along the line of action of the forces.

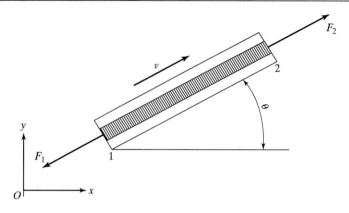

FIGURE 8.3 A truss element making an angle θ with the x-axis.

Because we have to express all forces (tension or compression) in the global axes (x, y) given by the fixed inertial frame, we define the element force components as follows:

$$F_{1x} = F_1 \cos \theta,$$
$$F_{1y} = F_1 \sin \theta,$$

(8.9)

$$F_{2x} = F_2 \cos \theta,$$
$$F_{2y} = F_2 \sin \theta.$$

(8.10)

Given that the relative displacement u is along the unit vector v, then

$$U = (U_2 - U_1)E$$

(8.11)

where

$$E = (\cos \theta)\bar{i} + (\sin \theta)\bar{j}$$

(8.12)

and

$$U_1 = U_{1x}\bar{i} + U_{1y}\bar{j}$$
$$U_2 = U_{2x}\bar{i} + U_{2y}\bar{j}$$

(8.13)

then by substitution of Equations (8.13) and (8.12) into Equation (8.11) and making use of Equations (8.3), (8.9), and (8.10), we obtain an expression for each nodal force in terms of the local displacement, the orientation θ, and the element stiffness k.

$$F_{1x} = (k \cos^2 \theta)U_{1x} + (k \sin \theta \cos \theta)U_{1y} - (k \cos^2 \theta)U_{2x} - (k \sin \theta \cos \theta)U_{2y}$$

(8.14)

$$F_{1y} = (k \sin \theta \cos \theta)U_{1x} + (k \sin^2 \theta)U_{1y} - (k \sin \theta \cos \theta)U_{2x} - (k \sin^2 \theta)U_{2y}$$

(8.15)

$$F_{2x} = (-k \cos^2 \theta)U_{1x} - (k \sin \theta \cos \theta)U_{1y} + (k \cos^2 \theta)U_{2x} + (k \sin \theta \cos \theta)U_{2y}$$

$$(8.16)$$

$$F_{2y} = (k \sin \theta \cos \theta)U_{2x} - (k \sin^2 \theta)U_{2y} + (k \sin \theta \cos \theta)U_{2x} + (k \sin^2 \theta)U_{2y}$$

$$(8.17)$$

Writing Equations (8.14) through (8.17) in matrix form yields

$$\begin{bmatrix} F_{1x} \\ F_{1y} \\ F_{2x} \\ F_{2y} \end{bmatrix} = k \begin{bmatrix} c^2 & sc & -c^2 & -sc \\ sc & s^2 & -sc & -s^2 \\ -c^2 & -sc & c^2 & sc \\ -sc & -s^2 & sc & s^2 \end{bmatrix} \begin{bmatrix} U_{1x} \\ U_{1y} \\ U_{2x} \\ U_{2y} \end{bmatrix} \qquad (8.18)$$

where s and c are abbreviations for $\sin \theta$ and $\cos \theta$, respectively, and k is the stiffness constant. We can write Equation (8.18) in more compact form as

$$[F] = [k][U] \qquad (8.19)$$

where the local forces, local displacement, and local stiffness are defined as follows:

$$[F] = \begin{bmatrix} F_{1x} \\ F_{1y} \\ F_{2x} \\ F_{2y} \end{bmatrix} \qquad [U] = \begin{bmatrix} U_{1x} \\ U_{1y} \\ U_{2x} \\ U_{2y} \end{bmatrix} \qquad (8.20)$$

and

$$[k] = \frac{AE}{L} \begin{bmatrix} c^2 & sc & -c^2 & -sc \\ sc & s^2 & -sc & -s^2 \\ -c^2 & -sc & c^2 & sc \\ -sc & -s^2 & sc & s^2 \end{bmatrix} \qquad (8.21)$$

For $\theta = 0$, the local stiffness matrix is simply

$$[k] = \frac{AE}{L} \begin{bmatrix} 1 & 0 & -1 & 0 \\ 0 & 0 & 0 & 0 \\ -1 & 0 & 1 & 0 \\ 0 & 0 & 0 & 0 \end{bmatrix} \qquad (8.22)$$

which checks with Equation (8.8). Note how the 0 rows and columns are simply used to expand the local stiffness matrix given by Equation (8.8) to account for the 0 forces and displacements along the y-axis.

8.3   Properties of the Local Stiffness Matrix

First, we observe that the local stiffness matrix is symmetric and that its coefficients are functions of $\cos\theta$ and $\sin\theta$. In addition, let the local stiffness be partitioned as follows:

$$[k] = \begin{bmatrix} c^2 & sc & -c^2 & -sc \\ sc & s^2 & -sc & -s^2 \\ -c^2 & -sc & c^2 & sc \\ -sc & -s^2 & sc & s^2 \end{bmatrix} = \begin{bmatrix} A & B \\ C & D \end{bmatrix} \tag{8.23}$$

where we can see that the partitioned matrices $A, B, C,$ and D are such that

$$A = D$$
$$B = C \tag{8.24}$$
$$A = -B$$

It is evident from the partition and the relationship stated above that we can deduce the following criteria to build the local stiffness: we only need to know submatrix A, and then submatrix B is obtained by premultiplying A by $-A$; C and D are then obtained from A and B, respectively.

8.4   Global Stiffness Matrix

The global stiffness matrix relates the global forces (external forces) and the global displacements (displacements associated with each joint). We developed the local stiffness matrix for an arbitrary element of the truss—what remains is to assemble all the local stiffness matrices associated with the truss elements. Later, it will be apparent in our analysis that the efficiency of the computer program is greatly dependent on the technique developed to formulate the global stiffness matrix.

The classical approach for a truss is to take a free-body diagram of each joint and, using the equilibrium equations, group all the equations together and isolate the global stiffness matrix. This approach is tedious and requires a large computational effort from the computer. The method that is illustrated in what follows to obtain the global stiffness matrix is one that Huston and Passerelo have developed. It shows how the building of the global stiffness matrix can be done by a simple strategy in which connectivity tables are used to identify the truss elements and their joints. The method is as follows.

Step 1: Consider an arbitrary truss, as shown in Figure 8.4. First, label the truss elements and joints in an arbitrary fashion, as shown in Figure 8.4. There are five joints (1, 2, ..., 5) and seven elements ([1], [2], ..., [7]).

Step 2: We proceed to develop three tables that basically store geometrical information about the truss. Table 8.1 has the truss–joint/matrix–column matching, where pairs starting from 1 develop the column numbers, 2.

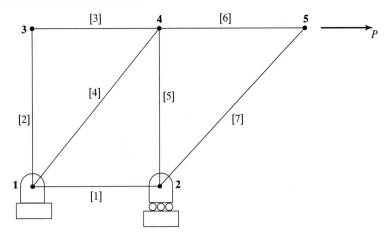

FIGURE 8.4 A two-dimensional truss.

Table 8.2 identifies the connection joints to all the elements of the truss.

Using Tables 8.1 and 8.2, we construct Table 8.3, which will be used to assemble the global matrix.

To show how Table 8.3 is constructed, consider truss element 1. From Table 8.2, we read the connecting joints to element 1, which are 1 and 2; with these joint numbers, we use Table 8.1 to extract the corresponding column numbers, which are 1, 2 and 3, 4. Therefore, in Table 8.3 number 1 (referring to the element number), we insert the

TABLE 8.1 Truss–Joint/Matrix–Column Matrix.

Joint	Column	Numbers
1	1	2
2	3	4
3	5	6
4	7	8
5	9	10

TABLE 8.2 Elements vs Joint Numbers.

Truss element e	N_1	N_2
1	1	2
2	1	3
3	3	4
4	1	4
5	2	4
6	4	5
7	2	5

TABLE 8.3 Truss Elements vs $k_{ij}{}^e$

i,j from $k_{ij}{}^e$	1	2	Truss 3	Elements E 4	5	6	7
1	1	1	5	1	3	7	3
2	2	2	6	2	4	8	4
3	3	5	7	7	7	9	9
4	4	6	8	8	8	10	10

values 1, 2, 3, and 4, as shown. We repeat the procedure for the remaining elements 2 to 7. Table 8.3 plays an important role in identifying the location where the local stiffness matrix terms will be inserted in the global matrix.

For the whole truss system, we write the equation relating the global forces and displacements:

$$\{F\} = [K]\{U\} \tag{8.25}$$

where

$$\{F\} = \begin{bmatrix} F_{1x} \\ F_{1y} \\ F_{2x} \\ F_{2y} \\ F_{3x} \\ F_{3y} \\ F_{4x} \\ F_{4y} \\ F_{5x} \\ F_{5y} \end{bmatrix} \quad \text{and} \quad \{U\} = \begin{bmatrix} U_{1x} \\ U_{1y} \\ U_{2x} \\ U_{2y} \\ U_{3x} \\ U_{3y} \\ U_{4x} \\ U_{4y} \\ U_{5x} \\ U_{5y} \end{bmatrix} \tag{8.26}$$

And

$$[K] = \begin{bmatrix} K_{1,1} & K_{1,2} & K_{1,3} & \cdots & K_{1,10} \\ K_{2,1} & K_{2,2} & K_{2,3} & \cdots & K_{2,10} \\ \vdots & \vdots & \vdots & \ddots & \vdots \\ K_{10,1} & K_{10,2} & K_{10,3} & \cdots & K_{10,10} \end{bmatrix} \tag{8.27}$$

Note that the size of the global stiffness matrix $[K]$ is 10 by 10. This is equal to the number of nodal points (joints in this case) in the truss multiplied by the degrees of freedom permitted at each node (2 for the planar truss shown).

Thus, the $[K]$ in Equation (8.27) is the assembled global stiffness matrix obtained from the assembly of individual element stiffness matrices, that is,

$$f_i^e = k_{ij}^e u_j \quad (e = 1, \ldots, N; i, j = 1, \ldots, 4) \tag{8.28}$$

where k^e_{ij} is the local element stiffness matrix and is given by Equation (8.23), and N denotes the number of elements

For $\theta = 0$, k^1_{ij} is given by Equation (8.24), and for $\theta = 90$, k^2_{ij} is

$$k^2_{ij} = \frac{AE}{L} \begin{bmatrix} 0 & 0 & 0 & 0 \\ 0 & 1 & 0 & -1 \\ 0 & 0 & 0 & 0 \\ 0 & -1 & 0 & 1 \end{bmatrix} \tag{8.29}$$

In order to construct the global stiffness matrix, first evaluate all the local element stiffness matrices. Then Table 8.3 is used to transfer the terms from the local stiffness matrices to the locations in the global stiffness matrix.

For example, consider element 1 from Table 8.3. The element column identifies the location in the global stiffness matrix of its local stiffness. The variation by pair of the column numbers identifies the i, j entries of the local stiffness matrix in the global stiffness matrix K_{ij}. For example, the column numbers for element 1 basically correspond to the local stiffness matrix for element 1. When transferred to the location in the assembled global stiffness matrix looks like

$$K^1 = \begin{bmatrix} K^1_{11} & K^1_{12} & K^1_{13} & K^1_{14} & 0 & 0 & 0 & 0 & 0 & 0 \\ K^1_{21} & K^1_{22} & K^1_{23} & K^1_{24} & 0 & 0 & 0 & 0 & 0 & 0 \\ K^1_{31} & K^1_{32} & K^1_{33} & K^1_{34} & 0 & 0 & 0 & 0 & 0 & 0 \\ K^1_{41} & K^1_{42} & K^1_{43} & K^1_{44} & 0 & 0 & 0 & 0 & 0 & 0 \\ 0 & 0 & 0 & 0 & 0 & 0 & 0 & 0 & 0 & 0 \\ 0 & 0 & 0 & 0 & 0 & 0 & 0 & 0 & 0 & 0 \\ 0 & 0 & 0 & 0 & 0 & 0 & 0 & 0 & 0 & 0 \\ 0 & 0 & 0 & 0 & 0 & 0 & 0 & 0 & 0 & 0 \\ 0 & 0 & 0 & 0 & 0 & 0 & 0 & 0 & 0 & 0 \\ 0 & 0 & 0 & 0 & 0 & 0 & 0 & 0 & 0 & 0 \end{bmatrix} \tag{8.30}$$

For element 2, we read the row and column entries, which are 1, 2, 5, and 6, from Table 8.3. Hence, its contribution to the global stiffness is given by

$$K^2 = \begin{bmatrix} K^2_{11} & K^2_{12} & 0 & 0 & K^2_{13} & K^2_{14} & 0 & 0 & 0 & 0 \\ K^2_{21} & K^2_{22} & 0 & 0 & K^2_{23} & K^2_{24} & 0 & 0 & 0 & 0 \\ 0 & 0 & 0 & 0 & 0 & 0 & 0 & 0 & 0 & 0 \\ 0 & 0 & 0 & 0 & 0 & 0 & 0 & 0 & 0 & 0 \\ K^2_{31} & K^2_{32} & 0 & 0 & K^2_{33} & K^2_{34} & 0 & 0 & 0 & 0 \\ K^2_{41} & K^2_{42} & 0 & 0 & K^2_{43} & K^2_{44} & 0 & 0 & 0 & 0 \\ 0 & 0 & 0 & 0 & 0 & 0 & 0 & 0 & 0 & 0 \\ 0 & 0 & 0 & 0 & 0 & 0 & 0 & 0 & 0 & 0 \\ 0 & 0 & 0 & 0 & 0 & 0 & 0 & 0 & 0 & 0 \\ 0 & 0 & 0 & 0 & 0 & 0 & 0 & 0 & 0 & 0 \end{bmatrix} \tag{8.31}$$

For element 5, we get

$$
K^5 = \begin{bmatrix}
0 & 0 & 0 & 0 & 0 & 0 & 0 & 0 & 0 & 0 \\
0 & 0 & 0 & 0 & 0 & 0 & 0 & 0 & 0 & 0 \\
0 & 0 & K^5_{11} & K^5_{12} & 0 & 0 & K^5_{13} & K^5_{14} & 0 & 0 \\
0 & 0 & K^5_{21} & K^5_{22} & 0 & 0 & K^5_{23} & K^5_{24} & 0 & 0 \\
0 & 0 & 0 & 0 & 0 & 0 & 0 & 0 & 0 & 0 \\
0 & 0 & 0 & 0 & 0 & 0 & 0 & 0 & 0 & 0 \\
0 & 0 & K^5_{31} & K^5_{32} & 0 & 0 & K^5_{33} & K^5_{34} & 0 & 0 \\
0 & 0 & K^5_{41} & K^5_{42} & 0 & 0 & K^5_{43} & K^5_{44} & 0 & 0 \\
0 & 0 & 0 & 0 & 0 & 0 & 0 & 0 & 0 & 0 \\
0 & 0 & 0 & 0 & 0 & 0 & 0 & 0 & 0 & 0
\end{bmatrix}
\tag{8.32}
$$

Once all the elements are completed and their local stiffness matrices are inserted into the global stiffness matrix K, the general global matrix of the system is obtained by adding all the entries in different locations if they are more than one.

$$
K_{ij} = K^1_{ij} + K^2_{ij} + K^3_{ij} + \cdots + K^7_{ij}
\tag{8.33}
$$

The global stiffness is found to be

$$
\begin{bmatrix}
k^1_{11}+k^2_{11}+k^4_{11} & k^1_{12}+k^2_{12}+k^4_{12} & k^1_{13} & k^1_{14} & k^2_{13} & k^2_{14} & k^3_{13} & k^3_{14} & 0 & 0 \\
k^1_{21}+k^2_{21}+k^4_{21} & k^1_{22}+k^2_{22}+k^4_{22} & k^1_{23} & k^1_{24} & k^2_{23} & k^2_{24} & k^3_{23} & k^3_{24} & 0 & 0 \\
k^1_{31} & k^1_{32} & k^1_{33}+k^5_{11}+k^7_{11} & k^1_{34}+k^5_{12}+k^7_{12} & 0 & 0 & k^5_{13} & k^5_{14} & k^7_{13} & k^7_{14} \\
k^1_{41} & k^1_{42} & k^1_{43}+k^5_{21}+k^7_{21} & k^1_{44}+k^5_{22}+k^7_{22} & 0 & 0 & k^5_{23} & k^5_{24} & k^7_{23} & k^7_{24} \\
k^2_{31} & k^2_{32} & 0 & 0 & k^2_{33}+k^3_{11} & k^2_{34}+k^3_{12} & k^3_{13} & k^3_{14} & 0 & 0 \\
k^2_{41} & k^2_{42} & 0 & 0 & k^2_{43}+k^3_{21} & k^2_{44}+k^3_{22} & k^3_{23} & k^3_{24} & 0 & 0 \\
k^4_{31} & k^4_{32} & k^5_{31} & k^5_{32} & k^3_{31} & k^3_{32} & k^3_{33}+k^3_{33}+k^6_{11} & k^3_{34}+k^4_{34}+k^6_{12} & k^6_{13} & k^6_{24} \\
k^4_{41} & k^4_{42} & k^5_{41} & k^5_{42} & k^3_{41} & k^3_{42} & k^3_{43}+k^4_{43}+k^6_{21}+k^5_{43} & k^3_{44}+k^4_{44}+k^6_{22}+k^5_{44} & k^6_{13} & k^6_{24} \\
0 & 0 & k^7_{31} & k^7_{32} & 0 & 0 & k^6_{31} & k^6_{32} & k^7_{33}+k^6_{33} & k^7_{34}+k^6_{34} \\
0 & 0 & k^7_{41} & k^7_{42} & 0 & 0 & k^6_{41} & k^6_{42} & k^7_{43}+k^6_{43} & k^7_{44}+k^6_{44}
\end{bmatrix}
$$

The above outlined procedure for developing the global stiffness matrix could be automated using computer coding.

8.5   Solution of the Truss Problem

The global force and displacement vectors are related through the global stiffness matrix:

$$[F] = [K][U] \tag{8.34}$$

After the development of $[K]$, the global stiffness matrix, the identification of the boundary forces and displacements is important. These are to be substituted into the $[F]$ and $[U]$ vectors.

For the truss shown in Figure 8.4, the reaction forces at joint 1 in the x and y directions are the reaction forces R_{1x} and R_{1y}, respectively. The reaction at joint 2 is only in the y direction as it is the roller joint, that is, R_{2y}. Also, force P acts as an external force in the x direction at joint 5.

Thus,

$$F_{1x} = R_{1x}$$

$$F_{1y} = R_{1y}$$

$$F_{2y} = R_{2y} \tag{8.35}$$

$$F_{5x} = P$$

Except for these, all other forces are equal to 0.

Substituting these values into force vector $[F]$, we get

$$[F] = \begin{bmatrix} R_{1x} \\ R_{1y} \\ 0 \\ R_{2y} \\ 0 \\ 0 \\ 0 \\ 0 \\ P \\ 0 \end{bmatrix} \tag{8.36}$$

Similarly, the displacement boundary condition can be identified, where for joints 1 and 2 we have

$$U_{1x} = 0$$

$$U_{1y} = 0 \tag{8.37}$$

$$U_{2y} = 0$$

All others are nonzero. Substituting these zero displacements into the displacement vector $[U]$, we get

$$[U] = \begin{bmatrix} 0 \\ 0 \\ U_{2x} \\ 0 \\ U_{3x} \\ U_{3y} \\ U_{4x} \\ U_{4y} \\ U_{5x} \\ U_{5y} \end{bmatrix} \tag{8.38}$$

Substituting $[F]$ and $[U]$ from Equations (8.36) and (8.38) into Equation (8.25), we obtain the general equations governing the truss force/displacement equilibrium conditions.

$$\begin{bmatrix} R_{1x} \\ R_{1y} \\ 0 \\ R_{2y} \\ 0 \\ 0 \\ 0 \\ 0 \\ P \\ 0 \end{bmatrix} = \begin{bmatrix} K_{11} & K_{12} & \cdots & K_{1,10} \\ K_{21} & K_{22} & \cdots & K_{2,10} \\ \vdots & \vdots & & \\ \vdots & \vdots & & \\ \vdots & \vdots & & \\ \vdots & \vdots & & \\ \vdots & \vdots & & \\ \vdots & \vdots & & \\ \vdots & \vdots & & \\ K_{10,1} & K_{10,2} & \cdots & K_{10,10} \end{bmatrix} \begin{bmatrix} 0 \\ 0 \\ U_{2x} \\ 0 \\ U_{3x} \\ U_{3y} \\ U_{4x} \\ U_{4y} \\ U_{5x} \\ U_{5y} \end{bmatrix} \tag{8.39}$$

Note how in Equation (8.39) the unknowns are in the global force array as well as in the joint displacement vector. A typical strategy to solve a problem in which the unknowns are on both sides of the equation is to solve for the U's first by partitioning the matrices such that the force vector is completely in terms of the known forces. Eliminating the reaction forces does the partitioning. The resulting equation is

$$\begin{bmatrix} 0 \\ 0 \\ 0 \\ 0 \\ 0 \\ P \\ 0 \end{bmatrix} = [K'] \begin{bmatrix} U_{2x} \\ U_{3x} \\ U_{3y} \\ U_{4x} \\ U_{4y} \\ U_{5x} \\ U_{5y} \end{bmatrix} \tag{8.40}$$

where $[K']$ is the new stiffness matrix resulting from the global stiffness after eliminating the rows and columns corresponding to the zero displacements. Equation (8.40) constitutes a set of seven equations and seven unknowns, which can be solved using the Gaussian elimination method, Cramer's rule (see Appendix A), or simply the inverse of $[K']$ as

$$\begin{bmatrix} U_{2x} \\ U_{3x} \\ U_{3y} \\ U_{4x} \\ U_{4y} \\ U_{5x} \\ U_{5y} \end{bmatrix} = [K']^{-1} \begin{bmatrix} 0 \\ 0 \\ 0 \\ 0 \\ 0 \\ P \\ 0 \end{bmatrix} \tag{8.41}$$

Once the equations are solved for the displacements, reactions R_{1x}, R_{1y}, and R_{2y} can be evaluated by premultiplying the corresponding terms of $[K]$ and $[U]$ in Equation (8.39). The solutions are found to be

$$R_{1x} = -P$$

$$R_{1y} = -\frac{Pb}{a} \tag{8.42}$$

$$R_{2y} = \frac{Pb}{a}$$

The answers obtained from the FEM analysis as described before can be checked by simply taking the free-body diagram for the truss as shown in Figure 8.5.

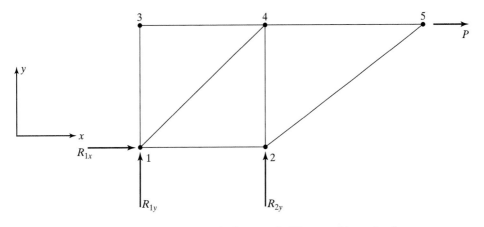

FIGURE 8.5 A simple free-body diagram of a 2D truss subject to loading.

Writing the equilibrium equations

$$\sum F_x = 0 \quad \sum F_y = 0 \quad \sum M = 0 \tag{8.43}$$

We get

$$\sum F_x = R_{1x} + P = 0 \Rightarrow R_{1x} = -P$$

$$\sum F_y = R_{1y} + P_{2y} = 0 \Rightarrow R_{1y} = -R_{2y} \tag{8.44}$$

$$\sum M_1 = R_{2y}a - Pb = 0 \Rightarrow R_{2y} = \frac{Pb}{a}$$

which checks with the FEM solution.

8.6 Evaluation of the Local Forces

The internal forces are those that are either compressing or causing the truss elements in tension. To find the components of the forces acting at each end, we use the previously computed global displacements and local stiffness matrix.

From Equation (8.21), we write the element force–displacement relation as

$$\begin{bmatrix} F_{1x}^e \\ F_{1y}^e \\ F_{2x}^e \\ F_{2y}^e \end{bmatrix} = \frac{AE}{l} \begin{bmatrix} c_e^2 & s_e c_e & -c_e^2 & -s_e c_e \\ s_e c_e & s_e^2 & -s_e c_e & -s_e^2 \\ -c_e^2 & -s_e c_e & c_e^2 & s_e c_e \\ -s_e c_e & -s_e^2 & s_e c_e & s_e^2 \end{bmatrix} \begin{bmatrix} u_{1x}^e \\ u_{1y}^e \\ u_{2x}^e \\ u_{2y}^e \end{bmatrix} \tag{8.45}$$

The stiffness matrix in this equation (for the particular element at hand) is known since it was used to form the global stiffness matrix. The nodal displacements are also known from the global displacement vector. The relationship between the global and local displacements is explained below.

Let the local displacement be written as u^e_{ij}, where e is the element number of the truss, i denotes either end 1 or end 2 of the element, and j assigns the direction x or y to the end displacements. Assuming that all elements of the truss undergo the same displacements at each joint, we then write the following:

For joint 1:

$$U_{1x} = u_{1x}^1 = u_{1x}^2 = u_{1x}^4$$

$$U_{1y} = u_{1y}^1 = u_{1y}^2 = u_{1y}^4 \tag{8.46}$$

For joint 2:

$$U_{2x} = u_{2x}^1 = u_{1x}^5 = u_{1x}^7$$
$$U_{2y} = u_{2y}^1 = u_{1y}^5 = u_{1y}^7 \tag{8.47}$$

For joint 3:

$$U_{3x} = u_{2x}^2 = u_{1x}^3$$
$$U_{3y} = u_{2y}^2 = u_{1y}^3 \tag{8.48}$$

For joint 4:

$$U_{4x} = u_{2x}^3 = u_{2x}^4 = u_{1x}^6 = u_{2x}^5$$
$$U_{4y} = u_{2y}^3 = u_{2y}^4 = u_{1y}^6 = u_{2x}^5 \tag{8.49}$$

For joint 5

$$U_{5x} = u_{2x}^7 = u_{2x}^6$$
$$U_{5y} = u_{2y}^7 = u_{2y}^6 \tag{8.50}$$

The nodal displacements for any particular element can be found from the relationships between the global displacements and the local displacement by using Equations (8.46) to (8.50). Subsequent substitution of these values for a particular element in Equation (8.45) and multiplying by the corresponding stiffness matrix terms yield the nodal forces. The signs of these forces indicate whether the member is in tension or compression.

A complete program based on the previously outlined finite-element procedure for 2D trusses is given in Appendix B. The reader is urged to use it to analyze a variety of trusses. The program is written to highlight the simplicity of the method discussed in solving 2D finite-element trusses. Therefore, it is limited to determined trusses, with concentrated forces acting at the joints. Indeed, it can easily be extended to handle concentrated loads and inclined supports. These could serve as projects to readers with advance knowledge of truss analysis.

Example 8.1   Analysis of a Three-Element Truss

Use the finite-element method to solve for the truss in Figure 8.6. (a) Find the global stiffness matrix. (b) Solve for the reaction forces. (c) Solve for the member forces and determine whether a truss element is in tension or compression.

Solution   The first step in our analysis is to label the truss for the joint numbers and link numbers as shown in the figure. The second step is to compute the local stiffness matrices for each member using Equation (8.21), which gives all element stiffness matrices.

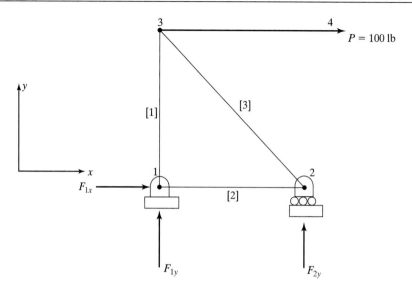

FIGURE 8.6 A three-element truss subject to loading.

The element stiffness matrices are

$$[K_{ij}^1] = \frac{A_1 E}{l} \begin{bmatrix} 0 & 0 & 0 & 0 \\ 0 & 1 & 0 & -1 \\ 0 & 0 & 0 & 0 \\ 0 & -1 & 0 & 1 \end{bmatrix}$$

$$[K_{ij}^2] = \frac{A_2 E}{l\sqrt{3}} \begin{bmatrix} 1 & 0 & -1 & 0 \\ 0 & 0 & 0 & 0 \\ -1 & 0 & 1 & 0 \\ 0 & 0 & 0 & 0 \end{bmatrix}$$

$$[K_{ij}^3] = \frac{A_3 E}{8l} \begin{bmatrix} 3 & -\sqrt{3} & -3 & \sqrt{3} \\ -\sqrt{3} & 1 & \sqrt{3} & -1 \\ -3 & \sqrt{3} & 3 & -\sqrt{3} \\ \sqrt{3} & -1 & -\sqrt{3} & 1 \end{bmatrix}$$

Where A_1, A_2, A_3, and L_1, L_2, L_3 are the areas of cross section and lengths of the members of the truss, respectively, and E is Young's modulus of elasticity.

$$A_1 = A_2 = A_3 = A$$

And $L_1 = 1$, such that

$$L_2 = l\sqrt{3}$$
$$L_3 = 2l$$

TABLE 8.4

Joint Number	Column	Number
1	1	2
2	3	4
3	5	6

TABLE 8.5

Elements	Joint	Number
1	1	3
2	1	2
3	2	3

TABLE 8.6

K_{ij}	1	2	3
1	1	1	3
2	2	2	4
3	5	3	5
4	6	4	6

Now let us construct Tables 8.4, 8.5, and 8.6 (see earlier Tables 8.1, 8.2, and 8.3), which help in arriving at the global stiffness matrix K.

Using the local stiffness matrices and transferring the entries with the help of Table 8.6, we can arrive at the global stiffness matrix:

$$
\frac{AE}{l}
\begin{bmatrix}
\frac{1}{\sqrt{3}} & 0 & -\frac{1}{\sqrt{3}} & 0 & 0 & 0 \\
0 & 1 & 0 & 0 & 0 & -1 \\
-\frac{1}{\sqrt{3}} & 0 & \frac{8+3\sqrt{3}}{8\sqrt{3}} & -\frac{\sqrt{3}}{8} & -\frac{3}{8} & \frac{\sqrt{3}}{8} \\
0 & 0 & -\frac{\sqrt{3}}{8} & \frac{1}{8} & \frac{\sqrt{3}}{8} & -\frac{1}{8} \\
0 & 0 & -\frac{3}{8} & \frac{\sqrt{3}}{8} & \frac{3}{8} & -\frac{\sqrt{3}}{8} \\
0 & -1 & \frac{\sqrt{3}}{8} & -\frac{1}{8} & -\frac{\sqrt{3}}{8} & \frac{9}{8}
\end{bmatrix}
\begin{bmatrix}
U_{1x} \\ U_{1y} \\ U_{2x} \\ U_{2y} \\ U_{3x} \\ U_{3y}
\end{bmatrix}
=
\begin{bmatrix}
F_{1x} \\ F_{1y} \\ 0 \\ F_{2y} \\ P \\ 0
\end{bmatrix}
$$

Zeros in the force vector indicate that the forces in the x and y directions at joints 2 and 3 are zeroes because of the roller and free joint, respectively.

Applying the displacement boundary conditions, $U_{1x} = 0, U_{1y} = 0, U_{2y} = 0$, and eliminating the corresponding rows and columns, we get

$$
\begin{bmatrix}
0.952 & -0.375 & 0.2165 \\
-0.375 & 0.375 & -0.2165 \\
0.2165 & -0.2165 & 1.125
\end{bmatrix}
\begin{bmatrix} U_{2x} \\ U_{3x} \\ U_{3y} \end{bmatrix}
=
\begin{bmatrix} 0 \\ 100 \\ 0 \end{bmatrix}
$$

Solving for the unknowns, we obtain

$$
U_{2x} = 173.31 \frac{l}{AE}
$$

$$
U_{3x} = 473.13 \frac{l}{AE}
$$

$$
U_{3y} = 57.57 \frac{l}{AE}
$$

The reaction forces can be computed using Equation (8.43) as

$$
F_{1x} = \left(\frac{1}{\sqrt{3}} U_{1x} - \frac{1}{\sqrt{3}} U_{2x} \right) \frac{AE}{l} = -100.0 \text{ lb}
$$

$$
F_{1y} = \left(1.U_{1y} - 1.U_{3y} \right) \frac{AE}{l} = -57.57 \text{ lb}
$$

$$
F_{2y} = \left(-\frac{\sqrt{3}}{8} U_{2x} + \frac{\sqrt{3}}{8} U_{3y} - \frac{1}{8} U_{3y} \right) = -57.71 \text{ lb}
$$

These results can be verified using the free-body diagram of the truss (Figure 8.5)

$$
\sum F_x = 0 \quad \sum F_y = 0 \quad \text{and} \quad \sum M = 0
$$

$$
\sum F_x = 0 \text{ gives } F_{1x} + 100.0 = 0, \text{ that is, } F_{1x} = -100.0 \text{ lb}
$$

$$
\sum F_y = 0 \text{ gives } F_{1y} + F_{2y} = 0, \text{ that is, } F_{1y} = -F_{2y}
$$

$$
\sum M = 0 \text{ gives } pl - F_{2y}\sqrt{3}l = 0.0, \text{ that is, } F_{2y} = \begin{cases} +57.73 \\ -F_{1y} \end{cases}
$$

Therefore, members 1 and 3 are in tension, whereas member 2 is in compression.

The member forces are obtained from the local element force–displacement relationship:

$$
\begin{Bmatrix} F^e_{1x} \\ F^e_{1y} \\ F^e_{2x} \\ F^e_{2y} \end{Bmatrix}
=
\frac{AE}{l}
\begin{bmatrix}
c^2 & sc & -c^2 & -sc \\
sc & s^2 & -sc & -s^2 \\
-c^2 & -sc & c^2 & sc \\
-sc & -s^2 & sc & s^2
\end{bmatrix}
\begin{Bmatrix} u^e_{1x} \\ u^e_{1y} \\ u^e_{2x} \\ u^e_{2y} \end{Bmatrix}
$$

The global and local displacement at each joint are related as follows

$$U_{1x} = u_{1x}^0 = 0$$

$$U_{1y} = u_{1y}^1 = 0$$

$$U_{3x} = u_{2x}^1$$

$$U_{3y} = u_{2y}^1$$

Using the local stiffness already computed and given by Equations (8.51) to (8.53), we obtain the element:

$$
\begin{Bmatrix} F_{1x}^1 \\ F_{1y}^1 \\ F_{2x}^1 \\ F_{2y}^1 \end{Bmatrix} = \frac{AE}{l} \begin{bmatrix} 0 & 0 & 0 & 0 \\ 0 & 1 & 0 & -1 \\ 0 & 0 & 0 & 0 \\ 0 & -1 & 0 & 1 \end{bmatrix} \begin{Bmatrix} 0 \\ 0 \\ U_{3x} \\ U_{3y} \end{Bmatrix}
$$

$$\Rightarrow F_{1y}^1 = -\left(\frac{AE}{l}\right)U_{3x} = -\left(\frac{AE}{l}\right)473.3\frac{l}{AE} = -473.3 \text{ lb}$$

$$F_{2y}^1 = \left(\frac{AE}{l}\right)U_{3y} = 473.3 \text{ lb}$$

The forces acting on element 1 clearly show that it is in tension as predicted. Similarly, we can obtain the magnitude of the forces and directions for elements 2 and 3.

End of Example 8.1

8.7   Stress Analysis

In the analysis of a truss the main objective is to decide whether the truss elements are designed to sustain the load they support. For that, we need to evaluate the stress or average stress in each element. The latter is an indication as to whether the tension or compression can be sustained.

Let the element stress be given by

$$\sigma^{(e)} = E \in {}^{(e)} \tag{8.51}$$

$$\sigma^{(e)} = E^{(e)}\frac{(u_2^{(e)} - u_1^{(e)})}{l} \tag{8.52}$$

Now we can compute the stress for each element of the truss in the previous example, Equation 8.4. For each element we can write

$$\sigma^{(1)} = E^{(1)}\frac{(u_2^{(1)} - u_1^{(1)})}{l} = E^{(1)}\frac{(U_{3y} - U_{1y})}{l}$$

$$\sigma^{(2)} = E^{(2)}\frac{(u_2^{(2)} - u_1^{(2)})}{l} = E^{(2)}\frac{(U_{2x} - U_{1x})}{\sqrt{3}l}$$

$$\sigma^{(3)} = E^{(3)}\frac{(u_2^{(3)} - u_1^{(3)})}{l} = E^{(3)}\frac{(U_{3x} - U_{2x})}{2l}$$

and the results are

$$\sigma^{(1)} = E\frac{U_{3y}}{l} = \frac{E}{l}\left(57.57\frac{l}{AE}\right)$$

$$\sigma^{(2)} = E\frac{U_{2x}}{l\sqrt{3}} = \frac{E}{l\sqrt{3}}\left(173.31\frac{l}{AE}\right)$$

$$\sigma^{(1)} = E\frac{U_{2x} - U_{3x}}{2l} = \frac{E}{2l}\left(115.74\frac{l}{AE}\right)$$

8.8   Force and Displacement Incidence Matrices

The global forces and local forces as well their corresponding global and local displacements can be shown to have special relationships that can be found by means of incidence matrices. These matrices are derived by examining the global and local displacement relation at the nodes and joints of the truss. It turns out that the incidence matrices can be built strictly based on the information provided by Table 8.3 (element local stiffness connectivity matrix). We will explore this idea further, but first examine the global displacements and the local displacements at joint 1 of the truss shown in Figure 8.1.

$$U_{1x} = u_{1x}^{(1)} = u_{1x}^{(2)}$$
$$U_{1y} = u_{1y}^{(1)} = u_{1y}^{(2)}$$

Similarly the global or local displacement relation for joint 2 and 3 can be expressed as

$$U_{2x} = u_{2x}^{(2)} = u_{1x}^{(3)} \qquad U_{3x} = u_{2x}^{(1)} = u_{2x}^{(3)}$$
$$U_{2y} = u_{2y}^{(2)} = u_{1y}^{(3)} \qquad U_{3y} = u_{2y}^{(1)} = u_{2y}^{(3)}$$

Writing the above relations in a matrix form yields

$$[U] = [\Lambda]^{(e)}[u]^{(e)}$$

where

$$U = \begin{bmatrix} U_{1x} \\ U_{1y} \\ U_{2x} \\ U_{2y} \\ U_{3x} \\ U_{3y} \end{bmatrix}$$

Element 1: The global displacement can be written as a function of the local displacement following the displacement relation shown above:

$$[U] = \begin{bmatrix} 1 & 0 & 0 & 0 \\ 0 & 1 & 0 & 0 \\ 0 & 0 & 0 & 0 \\ 0 & 0 & 0 & 0 \\ 0 & 0 & 1 & 0 \\ 0 & 0 & 0 & 1 \end{bmatrix} \begin{bmatrix} u_{1x}^{(1)} \\ u_{1y}^{(1)} \\ u_{2x}^{(1)} \\ u_{2y}^{(1)} \end{bmatrix}$$

Element 2:

$$[U] = \begin{bmatrix} 1 & 0 & 0 & 0 \\ 0 & 1 & 0 & 0 \\ 0 & 0 & 1 & 0 \\ 0 & 0 & 0 & 1 \\ 0 & 0 & 0 & 0 \\ 0 & 0 & 0 & 0 \end{bmatrix} \begin{bmatrix} u_{1x}^{(2)} \\ u_{1y}^{(2)} \\ u_{2x}^{(2)} \\ u_{2y}^{(2)} \end{bmatrix}$$

Element 3: Following the above procedure or using the relation between the global displacement and the local displacement of element 3 we get

$$[U] = \begin{bmatrix} 0 & 0 & 0 & 0 \\ 0 & 0 & 0 & 0 \\ 1 & 0 & 0 & 0 \\ 0 & 1 & 0 & 0 \\ 0 & 0 & 1 & 0 \\ 0 & 0 & 0 & 1 \end{bmatrix} \begin{bmatrix} u_{1x}^{(3)} \\ u_{1y}^{(3)} \\ u_{2x}^{(3)} \\ u_{2y}^{(3)} \end{bmatrix}$$

$\Lambda^{(e)}$ denotes the incidence matrix for element e. Writing the above relations in a matrix form yields

$$U = \Lambda u \tag{8.53}$$

If we examine Table 8.6, we see that the entries of the nonzero elements correspond to the element column numbers from the table. Hence, we can build the incidence matrices for all elements once the element–joint table is completed. Once the global displacements are solved for in the FEM of a truss we automatically can solve for the local displacements by means of the incidence matrices. Furthermore, we can develop a relationship between the global forces and the local forces and therefore be in a position to evaluate the internal forces acting on each truss element. This information is vital in the stress analysis of the truss members and in evaluation of the stress conditions on the element. In the case of the 2D truss, the local forces put the element truss member under tension or compression, as they are axial loading forces used to determine the strength of the elements in supporting loads. We can develop a relationship between the global forces and the local forces by noting that

$$[U] = [\Lambda]^{(e)}[u]^{(e)} \tag{8.54}$$

And from the global force–displacement relation

$$[F] = [K][U] \tag{8.55}$$

We rewrite $[F]$ as function of the local displacement by substituting Equation (8.54) into the above equation

$$[F]^{(e)} = [K][\Lambda]^{(e)}[u]^{(e)} \tag{8.56}$$

The above global force represents the contribution of element e to the global force vector $[F]$. Hence, the total force vector is obtained by summing the contribution of all the elements such that

$$[F] = \sum [K][\Lambda^{(e)}]\{u^e\} \tag{8.57}$$

From the local force–displacement

$$\{f\}^{(e)} = [k^e]\{u\}^e \tag{8.58}$$

we rewrite the global force equation as

$$[F] = [K][\Lambda^e][k^{(e)}]^{-1}\{f\}^{(e)} \tag{8.59}$$

Substituting the local displacements as a function of the incidence matrix and local forces we obtain

$$[F] = [K][\Lambda^e][k^e]^T\{f\}^e \tag{8.60}$$

where $[k]^{-1} = [k]^T$. Let us define

$$[\Lambda^*] = [K][\Lambda^e][k^e]^T \tag{8.61}$$

Then we write the relationship between the local forces and global forces as

$$[\Lambda^*]^T = [k^e][\Lambda^e]^T[K]^T \tag{8.62}$$

$$\{f\}^e = [\Lambda^*]^T[F] \tag{8.63}$$

For each element we can derive the corresponding local forces from the existing information on $[F]$ used in the global formulation of the *FE* problems. This is done quite interactively if large codes are needed.

8.9   Analysis of 3D Trusses

The analysis of 3D trusses is similar to the 2D case except the element stiffness must be developed for an arbitrary element in space. Consider such an element as shown in Figure 8.7. The direction cosines with respect to each axis are given by

$$\cos \alpha = \frac{x_j - x_i}{L} \tag{8.64}$$

$$\cos \beta = \frac{y_j - y_i}{L} \tag{8.65}$$

$$\cos \gamma = \frac{z_j - z_i}{L} \tag{8.66}$$

where L is the length of the member and is given by

$$L = \sqrt{(x_j - x_i)^2 + (y_j - y_i)^2 + (z_j - z_i)^2} \tag{8.67}$$

x_i, y_i, z_i or x_j, y_j, z_j denote the coordinate of node i or j, respectively.

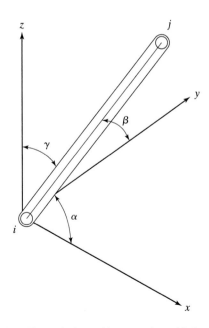

FIGURE 8.7   The angle formed by a member with the x, y, z-axis.

For a local element the force–displacement relation is given by

$$f^{(e)} = k^{(e)}u^{(e)} \tag{8.68}$$

where the local stiffness is defined by

$$[K]^{(e)} = k \begin{bmatrix}
\cos^2\alpha & \cos\alpha\,\cos\beta & \cos\alpha\,\cos\gamma & -\cos^2\alpha & -\cos\alpha\,\cos\beta & -\cos\alpha\,\cos\gamma \\
\cos\alpha\,\cos\beta & \cos^2\beta & \cos\beta\,\cos\gamma & -\cos\alpha\,\cos\gamma & -\cos^2\beta & -\cos\beta\,\cos\gamma \\
\cos\alpha\,\cos\gamma & \cos\beta\,\cos\gamma & \cos^2\gamma & -\cos\alpha\,\cos\gamma & -\cos\beta\,\cos\gamma & -\cos^2\gamma \\
-\cos^2\alpha & -\cos\alpha\,\cos\beta & -\cos\alpha\,\cos\gamma & \cos^2\alpha & \cos\alpha\,\cos\beta & \cos\alpha\,\cos\gamma \\
-\cos\alpha\,\cos\beta & -\cos^2\beta & -\cos\beta\,\cos\gamma & \cos\alpha\,\cos\beta & \cos^2\beta & \cos\beta\,\cos\gamma \\
-\cos\alpha\,\cos\gamma & -\cos\beta\,\cos\gamma & -\cos^2\gamma & \cos\alpha\,\cos\beta & \cos\beta\,\cos\gamma & \cos^2\gamma
\end{bmatrix}$$

The local forces and displacement are given by

$$\{F^{(e)}\} = \begin{Bmatrix} F_{1x}^{(e)} \\ F_{1y}^{(e)} \\ F_{1z}^{(e)} \\ F_{2x}^{(e)} \\ F_{2y}^{(e)} \\ F_{2z}^{(e)} \end{Bmatrix} \quad \text{and} \quad \{u^{(e)}\} = \begin{Bmatrix} u_{1x}^{(e)} \\ u_{1y}^{(e)} \\ u_{1z}^{(e)} \\ u_{2x}^{(e)} \\ u_{2y}^{(e)} \\ u_{2z}^{(e)} \end{Bmatrix} \tag{8.69}$$

Note how the nodes are represented by the subscripts 1 and 2 and the superscript denotes the element number.

PROBLEMS

8.1. For the plane truss shown in Figure P8.1, derive the global stiffness matrix knowing that the joint is a roller, joint 2 is fixed, and each bar has the same material properties E and A. Define the boundary conditions for each joint and

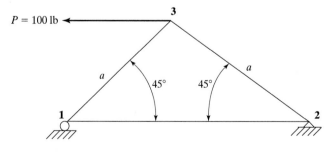

FIGURE P8.1 Plane truss.

solve for the nodal displacement and reaction forces. (Assume $A = 1 \times 1 \text{ in}^2$, $a = 6 \text{ ft}$, $E = 30 \times 10^6 \text{ psi}$)

8.2. (a) Write a truss finite-element program to check the answers to Problem 8.1.
(b) Find the axial forces in the three bars and determine whether each bar is in tension or compression.

(Assume $E = 30 \times 10^6 \text{ psi}$ and $A = 1 \times 1 \text{ in}^2$ for all truss elements.)

8.3. Find the incidence matrices relating the global displacement and the local displacement for elements 1, 2, and 3 in Problem 8.1 [use Equation (8.38)]

$$
\begin{bmatrix} U_{1x} \\ U_{1y} \\ \vdots \\ U_{nx} \\ U_{ny} \end{bmatrix} = [\Lambda^e] \begin{bmatrix} u^e_{1x} \\ u^e_{1y} \\ u^e_{2x} \\ u^e_{2y} \end{bmatrix}
$$

where n is the number of joints.

8.4. Use the incidence matrices approach developed in Problem 8.3 to write an equation relating the local forces of element 2 to the global forces of the truss in Problem 8.1.

8.5. Use a finite element program to solve for the trusses in Figure P8.2 and Figure P8.3. Find the reaction forces and element forces, and state whether they are in tension or compression.

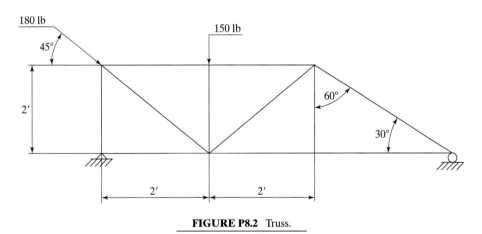

FIGURE P8.2 Truss.

8.6. a. Find the deformation of each truss member in Figure P8.4.
b. State whether the truss elements are in tension or compression.
c. What are the stresses in each element of the truss?

$$E = 29.5 \times 10^5 \text{ psi}$$
$$A = 1.0 \text{ in}^2.$$

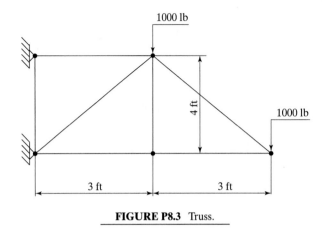

FIGURE P8.3 Truss.

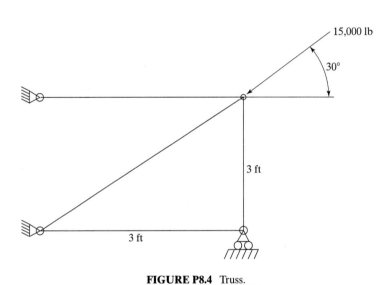

FIGURE P8.4 Truss.

8.7. Check the results of Problem 8.6 for the last two member (elements) of the truss using the standard equilibrium equation of the joints.

8.8. For the truss shown in Figure P8.5 given that all elements have the material properties E and cross-section area

$$E = 29.5 \times 10^5 \text{ psi}, \quad A = 1.0 \text{ in}^2$$

a. Label the truss.
b. Derive all the joint/elements tables.
c. Derive the incident matrices for all elements.

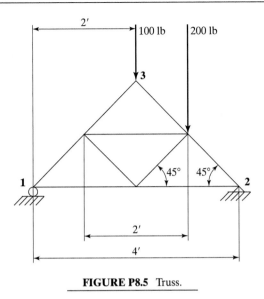

FIGURE P8.5 Truss.

8.9. a. Solve for the reaction force, and element deformation in Problem 8.8.
   b. Solve for the stresses in all element members.

8.10. Find the forces in all the members of the truss shown in Figure P8.6. Assume
   EA/l to be the same for all members. Use any FE code at your disposal.

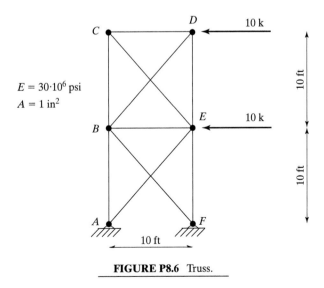

$E = 30 \cdot 10^6$ psi
$A = 1$ in^2

FIGURE P8.6 Truss.

BIBLIOGRAPHY

Akin, J., Ed (1986). *Finite Element Analysis for Undergraduates*. Orlando, FL: Academic Press.

ANSYS Engineering Analysis System. (1983). Houston, PA: Swanson Analysis Systems, Inc.

Burnett, D.S. (1987). *Finite Element Analysis: From Concepts to Applications*. Reading, MA: Addison-Wesley.

Huston, R.L, and Passerello, C.E. (1984). *Finite Element Methods: An Introduction*. New York: Marcel Dekker.

Kenneth, H. (1978) *Finite Element Methods for Engineers*. New York: John Wiley.

Martin, H.C., and Carey, G.F. (1973). *Introduction to Finite Element Analysis: Theory and Applications*. New York: McGraw Hill.

Reddy, J.N. (1984). *An Introduction to Finite Element Method*. New York: McGraw-Hill.

Rockey, K.C. (1975). *The Finite Element Method: A Basic Introduction*. New York: John Wiley.

Stasa, F.L. (1985) *Applied Finite Element Analysis for Engineers, HRW Series in Mechanical Engineering*. New York: CBS College Publishing.

Timoshenko, S.D., and Goodier, S. (1967). *Theory of Elasticity*. New York: McGraw-Hill.

Zienkiewcz, O.C., and Taylor, R.L. (1989). *The Finite Element Method*. New York: McGraw-Hill.

Engineering Mechanics Research Corp., *Software Products pamphlets on Finite Elements*. (1991). Troy, MI.

SHAPE NISOPT Publication EMRC. (1991). Troy, MI.

CHAPTER 9

Heat-Conduction Analysis and the Finite-Element Method

9.1   Introduction

In most instances, the important problems of engineering involving an exchange of energy by the flow of heat are those in which there is a transfer of internal energy between two systems. In general the internal energy transfer is called "heat transfer." When such exchanges of internal energy or heat take place, the first law of thermodynamics requires that the heat given up by one body must equal that taken up by the other. The second law of thermodynamics demands that the transfer of heat take place from the hotter system to the colder system. It is customary to categorize the various heat transfer processes into three basic types or modes, although it is certainly a rare instance when one encounters a problem of practical importance that does not involve at least two, and sometimes all three, of these modes occurring simultaneously. The three modes are conduction, convection, and radiation. Heat conduction will be the focus of this chapter. *Heat conduction* is the term applied to the mechanism of internal energy exchange from one body to another, or from one part of a body to another part, by the exchange of kinetic energy.

When the relationship between force and displacement can be approximated by a linear function, the problem reduces to a one-dimensional analysis. This is seen in the study of trusses, where the element deformation is expressed as a linear function in terms of the element force. A number of engineering problems, and heat conduction in particular, can be solved using one-dimensional element, and linear functions are used to approximate the solution. In this chapter, we will extend the one-dimensional solution to heat-conduction problems, and define the concept of shape functions for one- and two-dimensions in the finite-element method (FEM).

9.2   One-Dimensional Elements

Now we apply the FEM to the solution of heat flow in some simple one-dimensional steady-state heat-conduction systems. Several physical shapes fall into the one-dimensional analysis, such as spherical and cylindrical systems, in which the temperature of the body is a function only of radial distance. Consider the straight bar of Figure 9.1, where the heat flows across the end surfaces. Heat is also assumed to be generated internally by a heat source at a rate f per unit volume. The temperature varies only along the axial direction x, and we want to formulate a finite-element technique that would yield the temperature $T = T(x)$ along the position x in the steady-state condition.

In steady-state conditions, the net rate of heat flow into any differential element is 0. We know that for heat conduction analysis, the Fourier heat conduction equation is

$$q = -\kappa \frac{dT}{dx} \tag{9.1}$$

This equation states that the heat flux q in direction x is proportional to the gradient of temperature in direction x. The conductivity constant is defined by κ. The negative sign indicates that heat flows from the high temperature to the low temperature point.

From the differential element in Figure 9.1, we can write the heat flux balance:

$$qA + fAdx - [qA + d(Aq)] = 0 \tag{9.2a}$$

Taking the differentiation of q, the heat flux equation becomes

$$qA + fAdx - \left[qA + \frac{dq}{dx}dxA \right] = 0 \tag{9.2b}$$

where A = uniform cross-sectional area

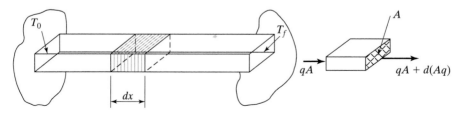

FIGURE 9.1   A typical bar with temperature T_0 and T_f at each end.

This reduces to a first-order differential equation of the form

$$\frac{dq}{dx} = f \tag{9.3}$$

A = cross sectional area

f = heat source/unit volume

q = heat flux

T = temperature

Substituting Equation (9.1) into Equation (9.3), we get the governing differential equation for the temperature:

$$\kappa \frac{d^2T}{dx^2} = -f \tag{9.4}$$

The boundary conditions for the physical problem described in Figure 9.1 are

$$T = T_0 \quad \text{at} \quad x = 0 \quad \text{and} \quad T = T_f \quad \text{at} \quad x = L$$

Integrating Equation (9.4) we get an explicit solution for the temperature at any point along the bar.

$$T(x) = \frac{fL}{2\kappa}\left(x - \frac{x^2}{L}\right) + \left(\frac{T_f - T_0}{L}\right)x + T_0 \tag{9.5}$$

where f is a constant heat source.

For a one-dimensional problem the temperature at any point x can be found using Equation 9.5. Finite-element analysis is tailored for engineering problems where the closed form solution cannot be evaluated and the numerical approximation is required. There are a number of scenarios that can make the governing heat equation nonlinear and the closed form unattainable. What follow are the initial steps in applying the FEM to heat-conduction problems. First, we develop the solution to one-dimensional heat conduction problems and compare that to the solution given by Equation 9.5.

9.3   Finite-Element Formulation

We must use either the principle of virtual work or energy to derive the necessary governing equations in the FEM. The method as shown in the previous two chapters leads to the formulation of the element stiffness and stiffness matrix.

We first develop the following energy equation as

$$I = \int_0^L \left[\kappa A \frac{d^2T}{dx^2} + fA\right] dx \tag{9.6}$$

which yields Equation (9.4) for $dI = 0$ using the standard manipulation of calculus of variations. Equation (9.6) could be expressed further in two parts, I_1 and I_2 as

$$I = \underbrace{\int_0^L \frac{d}{dx}\left[A\kappa\frac{dT}{dx}\right]T\,dx}_{I_1} + \underbrace{\int_0^L fAT\,dx}_{I_2} \qquad (9.7)$$

Integrating the function I_1 by parts, we get

$$I_1 = TA\kappa\frac{dT}{dx}\Big|_0^L - \int_0^L \frac{dT}{dx}A\kappa\frac{dT}{dx}dx \qquad (9.8)$$

The first term defines the boundary conditions' contributions, which if we assume that the boundary conditions are such that

$$T_{(x=0)} = T_L$$

and

$$q|_{x=L} = h(T_L - T_\infty),$$

where

    T_∞ = ambient temperature

    h = convection coefficent

Then the functional I becomes

$$I = -\int_0^L \frac{dT}{dx}Ak\frac{dT}{dx}dx - \int fAT\,dx + \frac{1}{2}h(T_L - T_\infty)^2 \qquad (9.8a)$$

We have an expression for I ready to use if the temperature $T = T(x)$ has an explicit form in x that can be substituted into the equation so that we can carry on the integration. Next, consider the functional $I^{(e)}$ for an element rather than for the total system:

$$I^{(e)} = -\int_{x_1}^{x_2} \frac{dT}{dx}A\kappa\frac{dT}{dx}dx + TA\kappa\frac{dT}{dx}\Big|_{x_1}^{x_2} + \int_{x_1}^{x_2} fAT\,dx \qquad (9.9)$$

$$I^{(e)} = I_1^{(e)} + I_2^{(e)} + I_3^{(e)}, \qquad (9.10)$$

where $I_1^{(e)}$, $I_2^{(e)}$, and $I_3^{(e)}$ correspond to the three terms of element $I^{(e)}$, respectively. To develop all the $I_1^{(e)}$ terms we need to find an expression for the temperature T. Assume a linear interpolation for the temperature between x_1 and x_2 because the distance between these two points is assumed small. A representation of the temperature is shown in Figure 9.2, where the temperature varies linearly as

$$T = ax + b \qquad (9.11)$$

where a and b are constants.

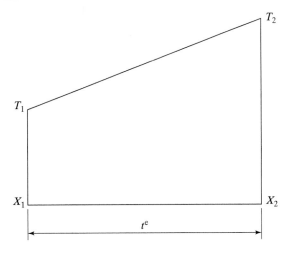

FIGURE 9.2 Linear interpolation of the temperature.

At each node, the temperature is assumed to be T_1 and T_2, respectively, and we can write the temperature equation for each node as

$$T_1 = ax_1 + b$$
$$T_2 = ax_2 + b \tag{9.12}$$

From which we can solve for a and b:

$$a = \frac{T_2 - T_1}{L_e} \quad \text{and} \quad b = T_1 - \frac{T_2 - T_1}{L_e}x_1$$

where L_e denotes the length of the element $(x_2 - x_1)$. Substituting the values of a and b into Equation (9.11), we get an expression for T that is written by introducing shape functions as

$$T = T_1N_1 + T_2N_2 \tag{9.13}$$

where

$$N_1 = \frac{x_2 - x}{L_e} \quad \text{and} \quad N_2 = \frac{x - x_1}{L_e} \tag{9.14}$$

The latter are known as shape functions. These functions are linear in x and represent the characteristic of the function assumed in representing the temperature between x_1 and x_2.

In matrix form, the temperature from Equation (9.13) can be expressed as

$$T = \begin{bmatrix} T_1 & T_2 \end{bmatrix} \begin{bmatrix} N_1 \\ N_2 \end{bmatrix} \tag{9.15}$$

We note in Equation (9.9) that the derivative of $T(x)$ is also required; hence, the derivative of T as given by Equation (9.15) takes the following form:

$$\frac{dT}{dx} = [T_1 \quad T_2] \begin{bmatrix} \dfrac{dN_1}{dx} \\ \dfrac{dN_2}{dx} \end{bmatrix} \tag{9.16}$$

with

$$\frac{dN_1}{dx} = -\frac{1}{L_e} \quad \text{and} \quad \frac{dN_2}{dx} = \frac{1}{L_e} \tag{9.17}$$

The functional $I^{(e)}$ then becomes
   The properties of these shape functions are:

1. At node 1, $N_1 = 1$ and $N_2 = 0$
2. At node 2, $N_1 = 0$ and $N_2 = 1$
3. The sum of shape functions is $N_1 + N_2 = 1$

$$I^{(e)} = \int_{x_1}^{x_2} [T_1 \quad T_2] \begin{bmatrix} \dfrac{dN_1}{dx} \\ \dfrac{dN_2}{dx} \end{bmatrix} A\kappa \begin{bmatrix} \dfrac{dN_1}{dx} & \dfrac{dN_2}{dx} \end{bmatrix} \begin{bmatrix} T_1 \\ T_2 \end{bmatrix} dx - \int_{x_1}^{x_2} f A [T_1 \quad T_2] \begin{bmatrix} N_1 \\ N_2 \end{bmatrix} dx$$

$$+ \frac{1}{2} h(T_L - T_\infty) \tag{9.18}$$

Here the boundary conditions at both ends are defined by the last term in the above equation.
   Let the first term I_1^e be defined by

$$I_1^{(e)} = A\kappa \int_{x_1}^{x_2} [T_1 \quad T_2] \begin{bmatrix} \left(\dfrac{dN_1}{dx}\right)^2 & \dfrac{dN_1}{dx}\dfrac{dN_2}{dx} \\ \dfrac{dN_2}{dx}\dfrac{dN_1}{dx} & \left(\dfrac{dN_2}{dx}\right)^2 \end{bmatrix} \begin{bmatrix} T_1 \\ T_2 \end{bmatrix} dx \tag{9.19}$$

Substituting Equation (9.17) derivatives into Equation (9.19) and integrating yield

$$I_1^{(e)} = A\kappa [T_1 \quad T_2] \begin{bmatrix} \dfrac{1}{L_e} & -\dfrac{1}{L_e} \\ -\dfrac{1}{L_e} & \dfrac{1}{L_e} \end{bmatrix} \begin{bmatrix} T_1 \\ T_2 \end{bmatrix} \tag{9.20}$$

Similarly, let $I^{(e)}_2$ denote the term defined in Equation (9.18). Evaluating this term we obtain the term which involves the contribution of the heat source f.

$$I_2^{(e)} = \int_{x_1}^{x_2} fA[T_1 \quad T_2]\begin{bmatrix} N_1 \\ N_2 \end{bmatrix} dx = \frac{fAL_e}{2}[T_1 \quad T_2]\begin{bmatrix} 1 \\ 1 \end{bmatrix}$$

$$N_1 = \frac{x_2 - x}{L_e} \Rightarrow \int_{x_1}^{x_2} N_1 \, dx = -\frac{(x_2 - x)^2}{2L_e}\Big|_{x_1}^{x_2} \Rightarrow \frac{(x_2 - x_1)^2}{2L_e} = \frac{L_e^2}{2L_e} = \frac{L_e}{2} \tag{9.21}$$

Next, writing the steady-state condition for an element we get

$$\left\{ \frac{\partial I_1^{(e)}}{\partial T_e} \right\} = \{0\} \tag{9.22}$$

which yields

$$k^e = \frac{\kappa A}{L_e}\begin{bmatrix} 1 & -1 \\ -1 & 1 \end{bmatrix} \tag{9.23}$$

and the element loading vector from the second term $I_2^{(e)}$ yields

$$f_Q = \frac{fAL_e}{2}\begin{bmatrix} 1 \\ 1 \end{bmatrix} \tag{9.24}$$

Combining the last equations we obtain the first step in the finite-element formulation, where

$$[k^e]\{T_{Xout}\} = f_e \tag{9.25}$$

Note how $[k^e]$ is analogous to a local stiffness matrix (we refer to it as the conductivity matrix), how $\{T\}$ is analogous to nodal displacements, and how $\{f_e\}$ is analogous to nodal forces. With this in mind, we can use a table analogous to Table 9.3 in the analysis of trusses to develop the connectivity relations between elements. The latter will assist us in the formulation of the global stiffness matrix and the heat-source array. The global problem can be stated as

$$[K]\{T\} = \{F\}, \tag{9.26}$$

where $[K]$ is the global conductivity matrix (equivalent to the global stiffness) assembled from the element conductivity matrix k^e, $\{T\}$ the nodal temperatures, and $\{F\}$ the heat-source contribution.

9.3.1 Boundary Condition Contribution

The term in the functional I in Equation (9.9) which deals with the convection can be written further as

$$\frac{1}{2}T_L h T_L - (h T_\infty)T_L + \frac{1}{2}h T_\infty^2,$$

where we see the last term drops out from the variational $\partial I/\partial T$.

We see that hT_L term will be added to the K matrix at the (L, L) location and hT_∞ will be added to the F vector at the Lth location. The way the K and F will be formulated is shown below

$$\begin{bmatrix} K_{11} & \cdots & \cdots & K_{1L} \\ K_{21} & \cdots & \cdots & K_{2L} \\ \vdots & & & \vdots \\ K_{L1} & & & K_{LL} + hT_L \end{bmatrix} \begin{Bmatrix} T_1 \\ T_2 \\ \vdots \\ T_L \end{Bmatrix} = \begin{Bmatrix} F_1 \\ F_2 \\ \vdots \\ F_L + hT_\infty \end{Bmatrix} \tag{9.27}$$

9.3.2   Handling of Additional Constraints

The handling of specified temperature boundary conditions such as $T_L = T_0$ can be accompanied by either the elimination or the penalty approach. The procedure for elimination is demonstrated below.

Elimination Approach   This technique works through the elimination of rows and columns of the corresponding temperature and then modifying the force vector to include the boundary. The force–displacement relation is as described in the finite-element solution of trusses. In general, we write we the global problem as

$$KU = F \tag{9.28}$$

Consider the constraint where the displacement is defined by

$$U_1 = C_1$$

The global displacement vector is array of order $n \times 1$ so that u^T is of order $1 \times n$.

$$U = [U_1 \quad U_2 \quad U_3 \quad \cdots \quad U_n]^T$$

and similarly the global force vector is

$$F = [F_1 \quad F_2 \quad F_3 \quad \cdots \quad F_n]^T$$

We first start by defining the potential energy π as a function of elastic energy and the work associated with F.

$$\pi = \frac{1}{2} U^T K U - U^T F \tag{9.29}$$

This is one way of obtaining the balance equation of force–displacement as stated previously. The energy-explicit matrix form is further shown to be expressed as

$$\pi = \frac{1}{2} \begin{pmatrix} U_1 K_{11} U_1 + U_1 K_{12} U_2 + \cdots + U_2 K_{1N} U_N \\ U_2 K_{21} U_1 + U_2 K_{22} U_2 + \cdots + U_2 K_{2N} U_N \\ \vdots \\ \vdots \\ +U_N K_{N1} U_1 + U_N K_{N2} U_2 + \cdots + U_N K_{NN} U_N \end{pmatrix}$$
$$- (U_1 F_1 + U_2 F_2 + \cdots + U_N F_N) \tag{9.30}$$

Let us substitute the boundary condition $U_1 = C_1$. Then we get

$$\pi = \frac{1}{2} \begin{pmatrix} C_1 K_{11} C_1 + C_1 K_{12} U_2 + \cdots + C_1 K_{1N} U_N \\ U_2 K_{21} C_1 + U_2 K_{22} U_2 + \cdots + U_2 K_{2N} U_N \\ \vdots \\ \vdots \\ +U_N K_{N1} C_1 + U_N K_{N2} U_2 + \cdots + U_N K_{NN} U_N \end{pmatrix}$$
$$- (C_1 F_1 + U_2 F_2 + \cdots + U_N F_N). \tag{9.31}$$

To yield the problem at hand we need to minimize π, hence

$$\frac{\partial \pi}{\partial U_i} = 0 \quad \text{for} \quad i = 1, 2, 3, \ldots, N$$

But for $I = 1$, we have $u_1 = c_1$ (fixed), which yields

$$\begin{bmatrix} K_{22} & K_{23} & \cdots & K_{2N} \\ K_{32} & K_{33} & \cdots & K_{3N} \\ \vdots & & & \\ K_{N2} & K_{N3} & & K_{NN} \end{bmatrix} \begin{Bmatrix} U_2 \\ U_3 \\ \vdots \\ U_N \end{Bmatrix} = \begin{Bmatrix} F_2 - K_{21} C_1 \\ F_3 - K_{31} C_1 \\ \vdots \\ F_N - K_{N1} C_1 \end{Bmatrix}. \tag{9.32}$$

The above matrix equation represents a set of $(N - 1) \times (N - 1)$ equations, with the original K matrix being reduced by eliminating the first row and first column as well as the first element of the vector F. We see that the boundary conditions are subtracted from the force vector array by premultiplying it with the elements of the first row of K. This technique will be used in the solutions of heat-transfer problems.

Penalty Approach An alternative to the elimination approach is the penalty approach. In handling constraints this might be easier to implement and works well for multiple constraints. The methods are designed to handle the boundary conditions once the global problem has been formulated. Once more, let the boundary condition be given by the displacement at node 1 such that

$$U_1 = C_1$$

The total potential energy is then defined by adding an extra term to account for the additional boundary condition or simply to account for the additional energy contribution from the boundary conditions.

$$\pi = \frac{1}{2} U^T K U - U^T F + \frac{1}{2} Q(U_1 - C_1)^2 \tag{9.33}$$

So, the energy term $1/2 Q(U_1 - C_1)^2$ is significant only if the value of Q is large enough to emphasize the contribution of $(U_1 - C_1)$.

Minimization of π results into

$$
\begin{bmatrix}
K_{11} + Q & K_{12} & \cdots & K_{1N} \\
K_{21} & K_{22} & \cdots & K_{2N} \\
\vdots & \vdots & \vdots & \vdots \\
K_{N1} & K_{N2} & & K_{NN}
\end{bmatrix}
\begin{Bmatrix}
U_1 \\
U_2 \\
\vdots \\
U_N
\end{Bmatrix}
=
\begin{Bmatrix}
F_1 + QC_1 \\
F_2 \\
\vdots \\
F_N
\end{Bmatrix}
\tag{9.34}
$$

Here we have used the symmetry condition as well; i.e., $K_{12} = K_{21}, \ldots, K_{N1} = K_{1N}$, otherwise we cannot derive Equation (9.32).

Examining Equation (9.34), it is apparent that Q is added to K_{11} in the global K matrix and QC_1 is added to the element force vector F_1. We can view Q as a stiffness value whose numerical values can be defined or selected by noting the first equation so that

$$
(K_{11} + Q)U_1 + K_{12}U_2 + K_{13}U_3 + \cdots + K_{1N}U_N = F_1 + QC_1 \tag{9.35}
$$

If we divide by Q we obtain

$$
\left(\frac{K_{11}}{Q} + 1 \right) U_1 + \frac{K_{12}}{Q} U_2 + \cdots + \frac{K_{1N}}{Q} U_N = \frac{F_1}{Q} + C_1 \tag{9.36}
$$

Observe how if Q is chosen to be a large volume then the equation reduces to

$$
U_1 = C_1 \tag{9.37}
$$

which is the desired boundary condition. We also see further that Q is large in comparison to $K_{11}, K_{12}, \ldots, K_{1N}$, hence we need to select Q large enough to satisfy the condition of the above equation. A suggested value by previous work has been found to be

$$
Q = \max|K_{ij}| \times 10^4 \tag{9.38}
$$

Example 9.1

Determine the temperature distribution in the composite wall used to isolate the outside. Convection heat transfer on the inner surface of the wall is given by $T_\infty = 500°C$ and $h = 25$ W/m^2°C. The following conductivity constants for each wall are $\kappa_1 = 20$ W/m°C, $\kappa_2 = 30$ W/m°C, and $\kappa_3 = 40$ W/m°C respectively. Let the cross-sectional area $A = 1$ m^2 and $L_1 = 0.4$ m, $L_2 = 0.3$ m, $L_3 = 0.1$ m, as shown in Figure 9.3.

This example is used to demonstrate not only how to build the conductivity stiffness matrices and the loading vector F but how to implement the technique that describes how the boundary conditions are employed.

Solution Let the temperature at each wall be denoted by T and let the width of the wall represent the length of each element. We need to compute the local conductivity stiffness for each element. Because the conductivity constant is given per unit length, we write

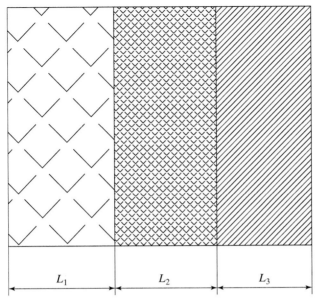

$T_\infty = 500\,°C$

$h = 25\,W/m\,°C$

L_1 L_2 L_3

FIGURE 9.3 Composite wall.

$$K^{(1)} = \frac{\kappa_1}{L_1}\begin{bmatrix} 1 & -1 \\ -1 & 1 \end{bmatrix}$$

$$K^{(2)} = \frac{\kappa_2}{L_2}\begin{bmatrix} 1 & -1 \\ -1 & 1 \end{bmatrix}$$

$$K^{(3)} = \frac{\kappa_3}{L_3}\begin{bmatrix} 1 & -1 \\ -1 & 1 \end{bmatrix} \tag{9.39}$$

The global K is found by assembling $K^{(1)}$, $K^{(2)}$, and $K^{(3)}$, which results in

$$K = 50\begin{bmatrix} 1 & -1 & 0 & 0 \\ -1 & 3 & -2 & 0 \\ 0 & -2 & 10 & -8 \\ 0 & 0 & -8 & 8 \end{bmatrix} \tag{9.40}$$

Because convection occurs at node 1, we add $h = 25$ to $(1,1)$ location in K, which results in

$$K = 50\begin{bmatrix} 1.5 & -1 & 0 & 0 \\ -1 & 3 & -2 & 0 \\ 0 & -2 & 10 & -8 \\ 0 & 0 & -8 & 8 \end{bmatrix} \tag{9.41}$$

We have no heat generation or source occurring in the problem, then the F vector consists only of hT_∞:

$$\{F\} = [25 \times 500, 0, 0, 0] \tag{9.42}$$

Applying the boundary conditions $T_4 = 10°C$, can be handled by the penalty approach. Let us choose a value for Q from the previously proposed procedure, where

$$Q = \max|K_{ij}| \times 10^4$$

$$= 50 \times 10 \times 10^4 \tag{9.43}$$

As stated in the penalty function we add the Q value to the K matrix in the (4×4) location and in the $(1,1)$ location, Qc_1 to the $(1,4)$ location of the F vector, and QT_4 to the (1×4) location of the F vector, resulting in

$$K = 50 \begin{bmatrix} 1.5 & -1 & 0 & 0 \\ -1 & 3 & -2 & 0 \\ 0 & -2 & 10 & -8 \\ 0 & 0 & -8 & 100,008 \end{bmatrix} \begin{Bmatrix} T_1 \\ T_2 \\ T_3 \\ T_4 \end{Bmatrix} = \begin{Bmatrix} 25 \times 500 \\ 0 \\ 0 \\ 5 \times 10^7 \end{Bmatrix} \tag{9.44}$$

the solution of which is found to be

$$T = [229.6559 \quad 94.4839 \quad 26.8979 \quad 10.0014]°C \tag{9.45}$$

End of Example 9.1

9.3.3   Finite-Difference Approach

Finite difference is discussed briefly through the following example for the purpose of validating the one-dimensional solution we have derived.

Example 9.2

A special design for a construction-building wall is made of three studs containing the materials siding, sheathing, and insulation batting. The inside room temperature is maintained at 85°F and the outside air temperature is measured at 15°F. The area of the wall exposed to air is 180 ft². Determine the temperature distribution through the wall.

TABLE 9.1   Characteristics of the wall

Items	Resistance (hr · ft² · F/Btu)	U-factor (Btu/hr · ft² · F)
Outside film resistance	0.17	5.88
Siding	0.81	1.23
Sheathing	1.32	0.76
Insulation	11.0	0.091
Inside film resistance	0.68	1.47

The steady-state condition of this system can be explained through Fourier's law.

$$q_x = -kA\frac{\partial T}{\partial X} \tag{9.46}$$

We can express the gradient of temperature by $(T_{i+1} - T_i)/l$, and the heat-transfer rate becomes

$$q = \frac{kA(T_{i+1} - T_i)}{l} \tag{9.47}$$

or

$$q = UA(T_{i+1} - T_i) \tag{9.48}$$

where U is defined by k/l.

The heat transfer between the surface and fluid is due to convection. Newton's law of cooling governs the heat-transfer rate between the fluid and the surface

$$q = hA(T_s - T_f) \tag{9.49}$$

where h is the convection coefficient, T_s is the temperature of the surface and T_f is the temperature of fluid.

The heat loss through the wall due to conduction must be equal to the heat loss to the surrounding cold air by convection. That is

$$-kA\frac{\partial T}{\partial X} = hA(T_s - T_f) \tag{9.50}$$

Expanding the above equation on the temperature distribution at the edge of each wall leads to the following equations:

$$U_2A(T_3 - T_2) = U_1A(T_2 - T_1)$$

$$U_3A(T_4 - T_3) = U_2A(T_3 - T_2)$$

$$U_4A(T_5 - T_4) = U_3A(T_4 - T_3)$$

$$U_5A(T_6 - T_5) = U_4A(T_5 - T_4) \tag{9.51}$$

Expressing the above in a matrix form we get

$$A\begin{bmatrix} U_1 + U_2 & -U_2 & 0 & 0 \\ -U_2 & U_2 + U_3 & -U_3 & 0 \\ 0 & -U_3 & U_3 + U_4 & -U_4 \\ 0 & 0 & -U_4 & U_4 + U_5 \end{bmatrix}\begin{bmatrix} T_2 \\ T_3 \\ T_4 \\ T_5 \end{bmatrix} = \begin{bmatrix} U_1AT_1 \\ 0 \\ 0 \\ U_5AT_6 \end{bmatrix} \tag{9.52}$$

For the numerical values given we define the four equations or four unknowns as

$$180\begin{bmatrix} 7.11 & -1.23 & 0 & 0 \\ -1.23 & 1.99 & -.76 & 0 \\ 0 & -0.76 & 0.851 & -0.091 \\ 0 & 0 & -0.091 & 1.561 \end{bmatrix}\begin{bmatrix} T_2 \\ T_3 \\ T_4 \\ T_5 \end{bmatrix} = \begin{bmatrix} 15876 \\ 0 \\ 0 \\ 22491 \end{bmatrix} \tag{9.53}$$

The solution is found to be

$$[T_2 \quad T_3 \quad T_4 \quad T_5] = [15.8523 \quad 19.9266 \quad 26.5205 \quad 81.5909]F \tag{9.54}$$

End of Example 9.2

9.4   Heat Conduction Analysis of a Two-Element Rod

Let us divide our system into elements with three nodes, as shown in Figure 9.4. In the development of the connectivity Table 9.2, we list the node numbers under each element.

First, we note that the global connectivity matrix K is a 3-by-3 matrix. The contribution of the conductivity matrices for elements 1 and 2 is

$$[K_{ij}^1] = \frac{\kappa A}{L_e}\begin{bmatrix} 1 & -1 & 0 \\ -1 & 1 & 0 \\ 0 & 0 & 0 \end{bmatrix} \tag{9.55}$$

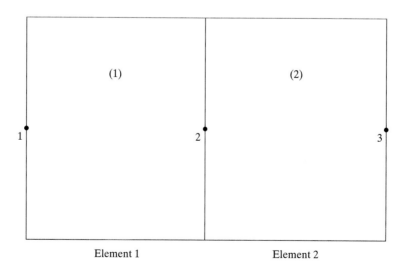

FIGURE 9.4   Elements with three nodes.

TABLE 9.2

K_{ij}	Elements	
	1	2
1	1	2
2	2	3

Note how in these local conductivity matrices, the 0 row and column correspond to the node that is not part of the element in question. The global conductivity matrix is then obtained by summation:

$$K = [K_{ij}^1] + [K_{ij}^2] \tag{9.56}$$

$$K = \frac{kA}{L_e} \begin{bmatrix} 1 & -1 & 0 \\ -1 & 2 & -1 \\ 0 & -1 & 1 \end{bmatrix} \tag{9.57}$$

Similarly, the global heat-source force vector is obtained by adding the two local force vectors:

$$[F] = \frac{fAL_e}{2} \begin{Bmatrix} 1 \\ 1 \\ 0 \end{Bmatrix} + \frac{fAL_e}{2} \begin{Bmatrix} 0 \\ 1 \\ 1 \end{Bmatrix} = \frac{fAL_e}{2} \begin{Bmatrix} 1 \\ 2 \\ 1 \end{Bmatrix} \tag{9.58}$$

Thus, combining and writing in the form of Equation (9.26), we obtain

$$\frac{kA}{L_e} \begin{bmatrix} 1 & -1 & 0 \\ -1 & 2 & -1 \\ 0 & -1 & 1 \end{bmatrix} \begin{bmatrix} T_1 \\ T_2 \\ T_3 \end{bmatrix} = \frac{fAL_e}{2} \begin{bmatrix} 1 \\ 2 \\ 1 \end{bmatrix} \tag{9.59}$$

Applying the boundary conditions

$$T_1(x = 0) = 0 \quad \text{and} \quad T_3(x = L) = 0$$

we solve for T_2, which results in

$$\frac{kA}{L_e} \begin{bmatrix} 1 & -1 & 0 \\ -1 & 2 & -1 \\ 0 & -1 & 1 \end{bmatrix} \begin{bmatrix} 0 \\ T_2 \\ 0 \end{bmatrix} = \begin{bmatrix} \dfrac{fAL_e}{2} \\ fAL_e \\ \dfrac{fAL_e}{2} \end{bmatrix} \tag{9.60}$$

which reduces to

$$T_2 = \frac{1}{2}\frac{fL_e^2}{k} = \frac{1}{8}\frac{fL^2}{k} \quad \left(L_e = \frac{L}{2} \Rightarrow L_e^2 = \frac{L^2}{4}\right) \tag{9.61}$$

For simplicity, let

$$f = \frac{1\,\Omega}{\mathrm{m}^3} \quad \kappa = \frac{1\,\Omega}{\mathrm{m}^\kappa} \quad L = 1\ \mathrm{m}$$

then the temperature at node 2 becomes

$$T_2 = \frac{1}{8} = 0.125°\mathrm{F} \tag{9.62}$$

For the boundary conditions such that $T_f = 0$, then we get an explicit solution of the temperature distribution for the assumed boundary conditions from simple integrating as stated in Equation (9.5)

$$T(x) = \frac{fL}{2k}\left(x - \frac{x^2}{L}\right) \tag{9.63}$$

where we can see that $T(x = 1/2) = 0.125°\mathrm{F}$ checks exactly with our finite-element solution given by the above equation.

9.5 Formulation of Global Stiffness Matrix for N Elements

The concept of a global conductivity matrix $[K]$ in the above example is exactly the same as the global stiffness matrix that was discussed in Chapter 8. $\{T\}$ and $\{F\}$ now represent the nodal temperature vector and the heat-source-contribution vector, respectively, instead of the nodal displacement and the nodal force vectors as described in Chapter 7 and 8. Table 9.1 is simply used as a guide to help in the formulation of the global conductivity matrix.

Consider a body discredited into n one-dimensional elements, as shown in Figure 9.5. Let the boundary conditions be such that

$$T_1 = T_{N+1} = 0 \tag{9.64}$$

The connectivity table (Table 9.3) shows that the global conductivity matrix is of the order $(n + 1) \times (n + 1)$. The ascending order of elements helps the global K to have a predictable bandwidth.

FIGURE 9.5   Discretization of a heat-conduction rod into n elements.

TABLE 9.3 Connectivity matrix for the n elements

ij			Elements, e, i, j	from k_{ij}^e
	1	2	3...	n
1	1	2	3...	n
2	2	3	4...	$n+1$

By following the steps discussed in previous section and using the table information for inserting the local stiffness terms to the global matrix from Table 9.3, the global problem takes the following form:

$$n \begin{bmatrix} 1 & -1 & 0 & & & 0 \\ -1 & 1+1 & -1 & & & \\ 0 & -1 & 1+1 & -1 & \cdots & 0 \\ \vdots & \vdots & \vdots & \vdots & \ddots & \vdots \\ & & & -1 & 1+1 & -1 \\ 0 & & & 0 & -1 & 1 \end{bmatrix} \begin{bmatrix} T_1 \\ T_2 \\ T_3 \\ \vdots \\ T_{n+1} \end{bmatrix} = \begin{bmatrix} \dfrac{1}{2n} \\ \dfrac{1}{2n} + \dfrac{1}{2n} \\ \dfrac{1}{2n} + \dfrac{1}{2n} \\ \vdots \\ \dfrac{1}{2n} \end{bmatrix} \quad (9.65)$$

where f is assumed to be 1 for simplicity. By applying the boundary conditions, the problem reduces to

$$\begin{bmatrix} 2 & -1 & 0 & & & 0 \\ -1 & 2 & -1 & & & \\ 0 & -1 & 2 & -1 & \cdots & 0 \\ \vdots & \vdots & \vdots & \vdots & \ddots & \vdots \\ & & & -1 & 2 & -1 \\ & & & 0 & -1 & 2 \end{bmatrix} \begin{bmatrix} T_2 \\ T_3 \\ \vdots \\ T_{n-1} \\ T_n \end{bmatrix} = \dfrac{1}{n^2} \begin{bmatrix} 1 \\ 1 \\ 1 \\ \vdots \\ 1 \\ 1 \end{bmatrix} \quad (9.66)$$

Example 9.3

For the one-dimensional heat transfer problem given by

$$\dfrac{d^2T}{dx^2} = -10 \quad \text{where } A = 1 \quad (0 \le x \le 1 \text{ with } T(0) = 0)$$

find the temperature at $x = 0.2, 0.4, 0.6, 0.8,$ and 1.0 m (Figure 9.6).

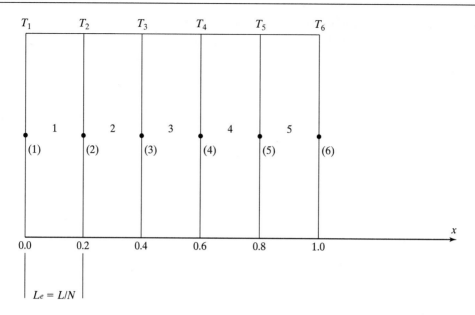

FIGURE 9.6   One-dimensional heat transfer.

Solution   The connectivity table is

TABLE 9.4   Connectivity table

K_{ij}	1	2	3	4	5
1	1	2	3	4	5
2	2	3	4	5	6

Each element has an element conductivity matrix K^e of the form:

$$K^e = \frac{kA}{L_e}\begin{bmatrix} 1 & -1 \\ -1 & 1 \end{bmatrix} \tag{9.67}$$

Substituting

$$A = 1\ \text{m}^2 \quad L_e = \frac{L}{N} = \frac{1}{5} = 0.2\ \text{m}$$

and assuming the conductivity constant to be $k = 1$, then we evaluate the element conductivity matrix:

$$K^e = 5\begin{bmatrix} 1 & -1 \\ -1 & 1 \end{bmatrix} \tag{9.68}$$

Using the connectivity table, we expand the local matrices K^e to an order of 5×5, and the global matrix $[K]$ is obtained by summation:

$$[K] = 5 \begin{bmatrix} 1 & -1 & 0 & 0 & 0 & 0 \\ -1 & 2 & -1 & 0 & 0 & 0 \\ 0 & -1 & 2 & -1 & 0 & 0 \\ 0 & 0 & -1 & 2 & -1 & 0 \\ 0 & 0 & 0 & -1 & 2 & -1 \\ 0 & 0 & 0 & 0 & -1 & 1 \end{bmatrix} \tag{9.69}$$

By applying the boundary conditions, the global temperature vector becomes

$$\{T\} = \begin{bmatrix} 0 \\ T_2 \\ T_3 \\ T_4 \\ T_5 \\ T_6 \end{bmatrix} \tag{9.70}$$

The forcing vector for an element is shown to be

$$F^e = \frac{f A L_e}{2} \begin{bmatrix} 1 \\ 1 \end{bmatrix} \tag{9.71}$$

where f is the heat generation per unit volume and is obtained from the relation

$$\kappa \frac{d^2 T}{dx^2} = -f \tag{9.72}$$

Substituting $\kappa = 1$ and $d^2 T / dx^2 = -10$ yields $f = 10$. Substituting those into F^e values, we get

$$F^e = \begin{bmatrix} 1 \\ 1 \end{bmatrix} \tag{9.73}$$

Assembling the global force vector using the connectivity table yields

$$F = \begin{bmatrix} 1 \\ 1+1 \\ 1+1 \\ 1+1 \\ 1+1 \\ 1 \end{bmatrix} = \begin{bmatrix} 1 \\ 2 \\ 2 \\ 2 \\ 2 \\ 1 \end{bmatrix} \tag{9.74}$$

Using the relation $[K]\{T\} = \{F\}$, we write

$$5\begin{bmatrix} 1 & -1 & 0 & 0 & 0 & 0 \\ -1 & 2 & -1 & 0 & 0 & 0 \\ 0 & -1 & 2 & -1 & 0 & 0 \\ 0 & 0 & -1 & 2 & -1 & 0 \\ 0 & 0 & 0 & -1 & 2 & -1 \\ 0 & 0 & 0 & 0 & -1 & 1 \end{bmatrix}\begin{bmatrix} T_1 \\ T_2 \\ T_3 \\ T_4 \\ T_5 \\ T_6 \end{bmatrix} = \begin{bmatrix} 1 \\ 2 \\ 2 \\ 2 \\ 2 \\ 1 \end{bmatrix} \qquad (9.75)$$

By deleting the first and last rows together with their corresponding columns, and modifying the force vector we obtain

$$\begin{bmatrix} 2 & -1 & 0 & 0 \\ -1 & 2 & -1 & 0 \\ 0 & -1 & 2 & -1 \\ 0 & 0 & -1 & 2 \end{bmatrix}\begin{bmatrix} T_2 \\ T_3 \\ T_4 \\ T_5 \end{bmatrix} = \begin{bmatrix} 0.4 \\ 0.4 \\ 0.4 \\ 0.4 \end{bmatrix} \qquad (9.76)$$

Note that $T_2 = T_5$ and $T_3 = T_4$. From symmetry, we can solve the equation very easily. The solutions are as follows:

$$\begin{bmatrix} T_1 \\ T_2 \\ T_3 \\ T_4 \\ T_5 \\ T_6 \end{bmatrix} = \begin{bmatrix} 0 \\ 0.8 \\ 1.2 \\ 1.2 \\ 0.8 \\ 0 \end{bmatrix} \,°C \qquad (9.77)$$

End of Example 9.3

9.6   2D Heat-Conduction Analysis

In a fashion similar to the one-dimensional analysis, the finite-element method can be used to analyze 2D and 3D heat conduction problems. Let us examine the 2D case and bear in mind that, first, we need to develop the element temperature relationship and then expand it to the global problem.

The heat-conduction problem is formulated by a variational boundary value problem as

$$\delta I = 0 \qquad (9.78)$$

where

$$I = \frac{1}{2} \int_{\Omega} [k(\nabla T)^2 + 2fT] \, d\Omega \tag{9.79}$$

and where k = thermal conductivity, which we assume is constant

$\quad f$ = heat source

$\quad \nabla T$ = temperature gradient

$\quad (\nabla T)^2 = \nabla T \cdot \nabla T$, "." denotes the dot product

$\quad \Omega$ = domain of interest

Note that the heat convection part is neglected. If domain Ω is divided into N elements, as shown in Figure 9.5, then

$$I = \sum_{e=1}^{N} I^e \tag{9.80}$$

where

$$I^e = \frac{1}{2} \int_{\Omega_e} [k(\nabla T^e)^2 + 2f^e T^e] \, d\Omega \tag{9.81}$$

Let us consider the triangular element shown in Figure 9.7. The local representation of the temperature can be expressed as

$$T(x, y) = T_1 N_1^e + T_2 N_2^e + T_3 N_3^e \tag{9.82}$$

where $N_i^e(x, y)(i = 1, 2, 3)$ are the shape functions given by

$$N_i^e = a_i^e + b_i^e x + c_i^e y \tag{9.83}$$

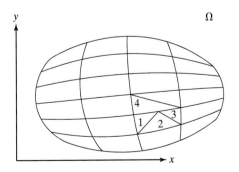
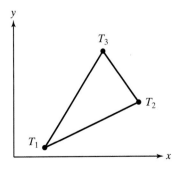

FIGURE 9.7   Triangular element.

The shape functions must satisfy the following conditions:

1. Also $\sum_{i=1}^{3} N_i^e = 1$
2. $N^e_{\,i}(x, y)$ are linear in both x and y.
3. $N^e_{\,i}(x, y)$ have the value 1 at node i and 0 at other nodes.
4. $N^e_{\,i}(x, y)$ are 0 at all points in Ω, except those of $N^e_{\,i}(x, y)$, which can be written as

$$N_i^e(x, y) = [a_i^e \quad b_i^e \quad c_i^e] \begin{bmatrix} 1 \\ x \\ y \end{bmatrix} \tag{9.84}$$

and for the three nodes of the triangular element, we can write

$$\begin{bmatrix} N_1^e \\ N_2^e \\ N_3^e \end{bmatrix} = \begin{bmatrix} a_1^e & b_1^e & c_1^e \\ a_2^e & b_2^e & c_2^e \\ a_3^e & b_3^e & c_3^e \end{bmatrix} \begin{bmatrix} 1 \\ x \\ y \end{bmatrix} \tag{9.85}$$

For node 1, following condition 1, Equation (9.85) yields

$$N_1^e = 1 = a_1^e + b_1^e x_1 + c_1^e y_1$$

$$N_2^e = 0 = a_1^e + b_1^e x_2 + c_1^e y_2$$

$$N_3^e = 0 = a_1^e + b_1^e x_3 + c_1^e y_3 \tag{9.86}$$

which can be written in matrix form as

$$\begin{bmatrix} 1 \\ 0 \\ 0 \end{bmatrix} = [A] \begin{bmatrix} a_1^e \\ b_1^e \\ c_1^e \end{bmatrix} \tag{9.87}$$

where

$$[A] = \begin{bmatrix} 1 & x_1 & y_1 \\ 1 & x_2 & y_2 \\ 1 & x_3 & y_3 \end{bmatrix} \tag{9.88}$$

Solving for coefficients a, b, and c, we get

$$\begin{bmatrix} a_1^e \\ b_1^e \\ c_1^e \end{bmatrix} = \begin{bmatrix} 1 & x_1 & y_1 \\ 1 & x_2 & y_2 \\ 1 & x_3 & y_3 \end{bmatrix}^{-1} \begin{bmatrix} 1 \\ 0 \\ 0 \end{bmatrix} = [A]^{-1} \begin{bmatrix} 1 \\ 0 \\ 0 \end{bmatrix} \tag{9.89}$$

Similarly, for the interpolation functions N_2 and N_3, we get

$$\begin{bmatrix} a_2^e \\ b_2^e \\ c_2^e \end{bmatrix} = [A]^{-1} \begin{bmatrix} 0 \\ 1 \\ 0 \end{bmatrix} \quad \text{and} \quad \begin{bmatrix} a_3^e \\ b_3^e \\ c_3^e \end{bmatrix} = [A]^{-1} \begin{bmatrix} 0 \\ 0 \\ 1 \end{bmatrix} \tag{9.90}$$

The inverse of matrix A is

$$[A]^{-1} = \frac{1}{2a} \begin{bmatrix} (x_2 y_3 - x_3 y_2) & (y_2 - y_3) & (x_3 - x_2) \\ (x_3 y_1 - x_1 y_3) & (y_3 - y_1) & (x_1 - x_3) \\ (x_1 y_2 - x_2 y_1) & (y_1 - y_2) & (x_2 - x_1) \end{bmatrix} \tag{9.91}$$

where a is the area of the triangle. By combining Equations (9.89) and (9.90), the inverse of A is

$$[A]^{-1} = \begin{bmatrix} a_1^e & b_1^e & c_1^e \\ a_2^e & b_2^e & c_2^e \\ a_3^e & b_3^e & c_3^e \end{bmatrix} \tag{9.92}$$

Then the triangle element functions can be written in a more general form:

$$\{N^e\} = \begin{bmatrix} N_1^e \\ N_2^e \\ N_3^e \end{bmatrix} = [A]^{-1} \begin{bmatrix} 1 \\ x \\ y \end{bmatrix} \tag{9.93}$$

where

$$N_1^e = \frac{1}{2a}[(x_2 y_3 - x_3 y_2) + x(y_2 - y_3) + y(x_3 - x_2)]$$

$$N_2^e = \frac{1}{2a}[(x_3 y_1 - x_1 y_3) + x(y_3 - y_1) + y(x_1 - x_3)]$$

$$N_3^e = \frac{1}{2a}[(x_1 y_2 - x_2 y_1) + x(y_1 - y_2) + y(x_2 - x_1)] \tag{9.94}$$

Now that we have defined the shape function, we can proceed in the evaluation of the conductivity matrix of individual elements.

9.7   Element-Conductivity Matrix

From Equation (9.81), we write the variational equation in terms of elements. This defines the element equation as

$$I^e = \frac{1}{2} \int_{\Omega_e} [k^e (\nabla T)^2 + f^e T^e] \, d\Omega. \tag{9.95}$$

The temperature at the nodes of the triangle element is expressed following the triangular element assumption developed in the previous section where

$$T(x, y) = T_1 N_1^e + T_2 N_2^e + T_3 N_3^e \qquad (9.96)$$

From Equation (9.94), we define the partial derivatives $w, r, t, x,$ and y as

$$\frac{\partial N_i^e}{\partial x} = b_i^e \quad \text{and} \quad \frac{\partial N_i^e}{\partial y} = c_i^e \qquad (9.97)$$

Hence, we can write the gradient of the temperature as follows

$$\nabla T = \begin{bmatrix} \dfrac{\partial T}{\partial x} \\ \dfrac{\partial T}{\partial y} \end{bmatrix} = \begin{bmatrix} \dfrac{\partial N_1}{\partial x} & \dfrac{\partial N_2}{\partial x} & \dfrac{\partial N_3}{\partial x} \\ \dfrac{\partial N_1}{\partial y} & \dfrac{\partial N_2}{\partial y} & \dfrac{\partial N_3}{\partial y} \end{bmatrix} \begin{bmatrix} T_1 \\ T_2 \\ T_3 \end{bmatrix} \qquad (9.98)$$

which, expressed in compact form, yields

$$\nabla T = BT$$

where

$$B = \begin{bmatrix} b_1^e & b_2^e & b_3^e \\ c_1^e & c_2^e & c_3^e \end{bmatrix} \quad \text{and} \quad T = \begin{bmatrix} T_1 \\ T_2 \\ T_3 \end{bmatrix} \qquad (9.99)$$

Note how the coefficients of B are obtained from the partial derivatives of the shape functions given by Equation (9.97).

Now we can define $(\nabla T)^2$ needed in Equation (9.96)

$$(\nabla T)^2 = \begin{bmatrix} \dfrac{\partial T}{\partial x} & \dfrac{\partial T}{\partial y} \end{bmatrix} \begin{bmatrix} \dfrac{\partial T}{\partial x} \\ \dfrac{\partial T}{\partial y} \end{bmatrix} \qquad (9.100)$$

For a given element, this equation can be expressed as

$$[\nabla T^e]^2 = \{T^e\}^T [B^e]^T [B^e] \{T^e\}. \qquad (9.101)$$

This yields

$$I_1^e = \frac{1}{2} k \int_{\Omega_e} \{T^e\}^T [B^e]^T [B^e] \{T^e\} \, d\Omega \qquad (9.102)$$

Because $[B]$ and $[T]$ are constant matrices, Equation (9.102) reduces to

$$I_1^e = \frac{1}{2} k \{T^e\}^T [B^e]^T [B^e] \{T^e\} \int_{\Omega_e} d\Omega \qquad (9.103)$$

or simply

$$I_1^e = \frac{1}{2}\{T^e\}^T[k^e]\{T^e\} \tag{9.104}$$

where $[k^e]$ denotes the element-conductivity matrix:

$$[K^e] = ka[B^e]^T[B^e] \tag{9.105}$$

which takes the final form

$$[K^e] = ka \begin{bmatrix} (b_1^2 + c_1^2) & (b_1b_2 + c_1c_2) & (b_1b_3 + c_1c_3) \\ (b_2b_1 + c_2c_1) & (b_2^2 + c_2^2) & (b_2b_3 + c_2c_3) \\ (b_3b_1 + c_3c_1) & (b_3b_2 + c_3c_2) & (b_3^2 + c_3^2) \end{bmatrix}, \tag{9.106}$$

and a is the area of the triangular element.

9.8   Element-Forcing Function

To complete the integration of Equation (9.95), we need to evaluate the second term, $I^e{}_2$

$$I_2^e = \int_{\Omega_e} f^e T^e \, d\Omega \tag{9.107}$$

As we have done with temperature, the heat source f can be expressed in a similar fashion:

$$f = f_1^e N_1^e + f_2^e N_2^e + f_3^e N_3^e = [f_1^e \quad f_2^e \quad f_3^e] \begin{bmatrix} N_1^e \\ N_2^e \\ N_3^e \end{bmatrix} \tag{9.108}$$

For an arbitrary element, this equation can be written in compact matrix form:

$$f^e = \{f^e\}\{N^e\} \tag{9.109}$$

Recall that

$$T^e = T_1^e N_1^e + T_2^e N_2^e + T_3^e N_3^e = [N_1^e \quad N_2^e \quad N_3^e] \begin{bmatrix} T_1^e \\ T_2^e \\ T_3^e \end{bmatrix} \tag{9.110}$$

or

$$T^e = \{N^e\}^T\{T^e\} \tag{9.111}$$

Therefore, $I^e{}_2$ after substitution becomes

$$I_2^e = \int_{\Omega_e} \{f^e\}\{N^e\}\{N^e\}^T\{T^e\} \, d\Omega = \{g^e\}\{T^e\} \tag{9.112}$$

where

$$\{g^e\}^T = \{f^e\}^T \int_{\Omega_e} \{N^e\}\{N^e\}^T \, d\Omega \tag{9.113}$$

The integrand $\{N^e\}\{N^e\}^T$ yields

$$\{N^e\}\{N^e\}^T = [A]^{-1} \begin{bmatrix} 1 \\ x \\ y \end{bmatrix} \begin{bmatrix} 1 & x & y \end{bmatrix} [A^T]^{-1} = [A]^{-1} \begin{bmatrix} 1 & x & y \\ x & x^2 & xy \\ y & xy & y^2 \end{bmatrix} [A^T]^{-1} \qquad (9.114)$$

Note that $[A]$, given by Equation (9.88), is a constant matrix. Therefore, the integral of $\{g\}$ depends only on the matrix with variables x and y. Integrating each element of the matrix is rather tedious and long. An alternative is to use a method developed by Eisenberg and Malvern.

From this method, we have the following statement of the integral:

$$\int_{\Omega_e} N_1^m N_2^n N_3^p \, d\Omega = \frac{m!n!p!}{(m + n + p + 2)!} 2a \qquad (9.115)$$

$$\{g^e\} = \left[\int_{\Omega_e} \{N^e\}\{N^e\}^T \, d\Omega \right] \{f^e\} \qquad (9.116)$$

Hence,

$$\{g^e\} = \left\{ \int_{\Omega_e} \begin{bmatrix} N_1^2 & N_1N_2 & N_1N_3 \\ N_2N_1 & N_2^2 & N_2N_3 \\ N_3N_1 & N_3N_2 & N_3^2 \end{bmatrix} d\Omega \right\} \{f^e\}, \qquad (9.117)$$

which yields

$$\{g^e\} = \frac{a}{12} \begin{bmatrix} 2 & 1 & 1 \\ 1 & 2 & 1 \\ 1 & 1 & 2 \end{bmatrix} \{f^e\} \qquad (9.118)$$

The element integral of the variational formulation is broken into two parts:

$$I^e = I_1^e + I_2^e \qquad (9.119)$$

which simplifies to

$$I^e = \frac{1}{2}\{T^e\}^T[K^e]\{T^e\} + \{g^e\}^T\{T^e\} \qquad (9.120)$$

The "global integral" over the domain Ω of the entire body becomes

$$I = \sum_{e=1}^{N} I^e = \sum \left\{ \frac{1}{2}\{T^e\}^T[K^e]\{T^e\} + \{g^e\}^T\{T^e\} \right\} \qquad (9.121)$$

or

$$I = \frac{1}{2}\{T\}^T \left[\sum_{e=1}^{N} [K^e] \right] \{T\} - \left[\sum_{e=1}^{N} \{F^e\}^T \right] \{T\} \qquad (9.122)$$

where

$$\{F^e\}^T = -\{g^e\}^T$$

and

$$\{T\} = [T_1 T_2 \ldots T_n]^T$$

Hence,

$$I = \frac{1}{2}\{T\}^T[K]\{T\} - \{F\}^T\{T\} \tag{9.123}$$

where the global conductivity matrix is defined by

$$[K] = \sum_{e=1}^{N}[K^e] \tag{9.124}$$

and the global function (equivalent to the global force in the analysis of a truss) is

$$\{F\} = \sum_{e=1}^{N}\{F^e\} \tag{9.125}$$

The variation $\delta I = 0$ is equivalent to

$$\frac{\partial I}{\partial T_i} = 0 \qquad (i = 1, \ldots, n) \tag{9.126}$$

Applying Equation (9.76) to Equation (9.73) gives the global equation governing the temperature distribution and the heat source:

$$[K]\{T\} = \{F\} \tag{9.127}$$

This equation is similar to our FEM application to the truss and the one-dimensional heat flow problems.

The analysis of 2D heat-conduction problems can be done by using the FEM procedures developed herein. One proceeds by identifying the element shape functions and then evaluating the local conductivity (stiffness) matrices. The global $[K]$ is then assembled using Equation (9.125). The element forcing function is computed using Equation (9.113) and then the global array $\{F\}$ is assembled according to Equation (9.124).

Example 9.4   Temperature Distribution on a Square Plate

For the square plate shown in Figure 9.8, find element matrices $[B_e]$ and $[K_e]$ and solve for all the element-conductivity matrices. Find the temperature distribution at all of the nodes shown for the boundary conditions given.

Solution   There are four types of elements, as shown in Figure 9.8. The area of each triangular element is $a = 1/8$.

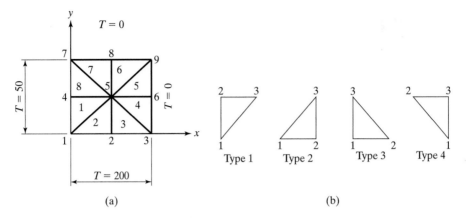

(a)   (b)

FIGURE 9.8   (a) Element discretization of the plate. (b) All possible element types.

Figure 9.9 shows the temperature distribution along the x- and y-axes for the plate. Matrices $[B_e]$ for each type of element are obtained from

$$[B^e] = \frac{1}{2a}\begin{bmatrix} (y_2 - y_3) & (y_3 - y_1) & (y_1 - y_2) \\ (x_3 - x_2) & (x_1 - x_3) & (x_2 - x_1) \end{bmatrix}$$

from which we can compute the contribution of each element. This is simply done by evaluating the B_e matrix by identifying the (x, y) coordinate of each node. The element corresponding B_e matrices are found to be:

$$[B^1] = \begin{bmatrix} 0 & 2 & -2 \\ 2 & -2 & 0 \end{bmatrix}$$

$$[B^2] = \begin{bmatrix} -2 & 2 & 0 \\ 0 & -2 & 2 \end{bmatrix}$$

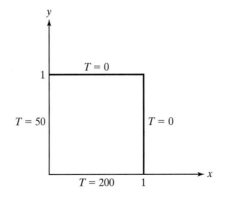

FIGURE 9.9   Temperature distribution.

$$[B^3] = \begin{bmatrix} -2 & 2 & 0 \\ -2 & 0 & 2 \end{bmatrix}$$

$$[B^4] = \begin{bmatrix} 0 & 2 & -2 \\ 2 & 0 & -2 \end{bmatrix}$$

The element conductivity matrices are then obtained from

$$[k^e] = ka[B^e]^T[B^e]$$

which results in

$$[k^1] = [k^2] = \frac{k}{8}\begin{bmatrix} 4 & -4 & 0 \\ -4 & 8 & -4 \\ 0 & -4 & 4 \end{bmatrix}$$

$$[k^3] = \frac{k}{8}\begin{bmatrix} 8 & -4 & -4 \\ -4 & 4 & 0 \\ -4 & 0 & 4 \end{bmatrix}$$

$$[k^4] = \frac{k}{8}\begin{bmatrix} 4 & 0 & -4 \\ 0 & 4 & -4 \\ -4 & -4 & 8 \end{bmatrix}$$

The relationship between elements and nodes is described by Table 9.5. From the boundary conditions, we get

$$\{T\} = \begin{bmatrix} T_1 \\ T_2 \\ T_3 \\ T_4 \\ T_5 \\ T_6 \\ T_7 \\ T_8 \\ T_9 \end{bmatrix} = \begin{bmatrix} 125 \\ 200 \\ 100 \\ 50 \\ T_5 \\ 0 \\ 25 \\ 0 \\ 0 \end{bmatrix}$$

TABLE 9.5   Element conductivity stiffness matrix

	Elements							
Nodes	1	2	3	4	5	6	7	8
1	1	1	2	3	4	5	5	5
2	4	2	3	5	5	7	8	6
3	5	5	5	6	7	8	9	9

where T_5 is the only unknown. Hence, from the global equation $[k][T] = [F]$, the equation becomes

$$\sum_{i=1}^{9} k_{5i}T_i = F_5$$

Because there is no heat source, F_5 is simply given by adding to 0 the contribution from the penalty function or $F_5 = 0 + \ldots$. From the relationship between $[K^e]$ and the triangles, we can easily deduce the following contribution from each element for the element conductivity stiffness matrix.

$$[K_{ij}^e] = \frac{k}{8} \begin{cases} (4 + 4) & \text{for } i = j \text{ and } \angle i = 90° \\ 4 & \text{for } i \neq j \text{ and } \angle i = 90° \\ -4 & \text{for } i \neq j \text{ and nonhypotenuse} \\ 0 & \text{for } i \neq j \text{ and hypotenuse} \end{cases}$$

From this equation, k_{5i} is then extracted and found to be

$$k_{5i} = \frac{k}{8} \begin{bmatrix} 0 \\ -8 \\ 0 \\ -8 \\ 32 \\ -8 \\ 0 \\ -8 \\ 0 \end{bmatrix}$$

Solving for T_5 we obtain

$$T_5 = 62.5°C$$

End of Example 9.4

Example 9.5   Steady-State Heat Conduction

Find the temperature distribution for steady-state heat transfer conduction in a square domain, as shown in Figure 9.10, with

$$T(0, y) = 10 \quad \text{and} \quad T(1, y) = T(x, 0) = T(x, 1) = 0$$

$$(0 \leq x \leq 1; 0 \leq y \leq 1)$$

The boundary value for this problem is given by

$$\frac{\partial^2 T}{\partial x^2} + \frac{\partial^2 T}{\partial y^2} = 0$$

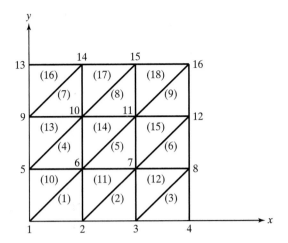

FIGURE 9.10 Square domain with triangular elements.

Solution This solution differs from the previous example in two respects: (1) there are only two types of elements used and (2) we doubled the number of elements to learn more about the temperature inside the plate. As shown in Figure 9.10, we divide this domain into 18 elements. There are two different types of triangles in the model (Figure 9.11). The method of numbering the elements and nodes is arbitrary. However, one has to do it systematically so as to obtain matrices that require less storage space. Once the global conductivity matrix $[K]$ is formulated, its bandwidth will be checked to see whether its final form is mathematically sound. Let us proceed in the solution of this problem by identifying the element types and computing their corresponding $[B]$ and $[K]$ matrices.

The area of the two triangles is given by

$$a = \left(\frac{1}{2}\right)\left(\frac{1}{3}\right)\left(\frac{1}{3}\right) = \frac{1}{18}$$

For an arbitrary triangular element, we have

$$[B^e] = \frac{1}{2a}\begin{bmatrix} (y_2 - y_3) & (y_3 - y_1) & (y_1 - y_2) \\ (x_3 - x_2) & (x_1 - x_3) & (x_2 - x_1) \end{bmatrix}$$

and the coordinates are

$$(x_1, y_1) = (0, 0)$$

$$(x_2, y_2) = \left(\frac{1}{3}, 0\right)$$

$$(x_3, y_3) = \left(0, \frac{1}{3}\right)$$

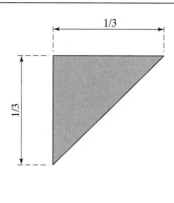

FIGURE 9.11   Element types for the finite-element model.

For a type 1 element $[B_1]$ becomes

$$B^1 = 9 \begin{bmatrix} -\dfrac{1}{3} & \dfrac{1}{3} & 0 \\ 0 & -\dfrac{1}{3} & \dfrac{1}{3} \end{bmatrix} = \begin{bmatrix} -3 & 3 & 0 \\ 0 & -3 & 3 \end{bmatrix}$$

$$[B^e] = 9 \begin{bmatrix} 0 & \dfrac{1}{3} & -\dfrac{1}{3} \\ -\dfrac{1}{3} & 0 & \dfrac{1}{3} \end{bmatrix} = \begin{bmatrix} 0 & 3 & -3 \\ -3 & 0 & 3 \end{bmatrix}$$

The conductivity matrix is given by

$$[k^e] = ka[B^e]^T[B^e]$$

For a type 1 element,

$$[k^e] = \frac{k}{18} \begin{bmatrix} 9 & -9 & 0 \\ -9 & 18 & -9 \\ 0 & -9 & 9 \end{bmatrix}$$

For a type 2 element,

$$[k^e] = \frac{k}{18} \begin{bmatrix} 9 & 0 & -9 \\ 0 & 9 & -9 \\ -9 & -9 & 18 \end{bmatrix}$$

The relationship between elements and nodes is given in Table 9.6

Assembling the element-conductivity matrices yields the global conductivity matrix:

$$K = [k^1] + [k^2] + [k^3] + \cdots + [k^{18}]$$

As in Example 9.4 we can deduce the element conductivity relations:

$$[k_{ij}^e] = \frac{k}{18} \begin{cases} (9+9) & \text{for } i = j \text{ and } \angle i = 90° \\ 9 & \text{for } i = j \text{ and } \angle i \neq 90° \\ -9 & \text{for } i \neq j \text{ and nonhypotenuse} \\ 0 & \text{for } i \neq j \text{ and hypotenuse} \end{cases}$$

Then Equation (9.23) takes the following form

$$K = k \begin{bmatrix} 1 \\ -\frac{1}{2} & 2 \\ 0 & -\frac{1}{2} & 2 \\ 0 & 0 & -\frac{1}{2} & 1 \\ -\frac{1}{2} & 0 & 0 & 0 & 2 \\ & -1 & 0 & 0 & -1 & 4 \\ & & -1 & 0 & 0 & -1 & 4 \\ & & & -\frac{1}{2} & 0 & 0 & -1 & 2 \\ & & & & -\frac{1}{2} & 0 & 0 & 0 & 2 \\ & & & & & -1 & 0 & 0 & -1 & 4 \\ & & & & & & -1 & 0 & 0 & -1 & 4 \\ & & & & & & & -\frac{1}{2} & 0 & 0 & -1 & 2 \\ & & & & & & & & -\frac{1}{2} & 0 & 0 & 0 & 1 \\ & & & & & & & & & -1 & 0 & 0 & -\frac{1}{2} & 2 \\ & & & & & & & & & & -1 & 0 & 0 & -\frac{1}{2} & 2 \\ & & & & & & & & & & & -\frac{1}{2} & 0 & 0 & -\frac{1}{2} & 1 \end{bmatrix}$$

End of Example 9.5

TABLE 9.6   Connectivity relations of elements and nodes

Nodes				Elements		
	1	2	3	4	...	18
1	1	2	3	5	...	11
2	2	3	4	6	...	15
3	6	7	8	10	...	16

9.8.3   Boundary Conditions

$$T_1 = T_{13} = 1/2(10 + 0) = 5°C \quad \text{and} \quad T_5 = T_9 = 10°C$$

and

$$T_2 = T_3 = T_4 = T_8 = T_{12} = T_{14} = T_{15} = T_{16} = 0$$

Therefore, the unknown nodal temperatures are T_6, T_7, T_{10}, and T_{11}. Note that the heat source f is 0; thus, the system of equation becomes

$$[K]\{T\} = 0 \tag{9.128}$$

where

$$\{T\} = [5 \quad 0 \quad 0 \quad 0 \quad 10 \quad T_6 \quad T_7 \quad 0 \quad 10 \quad T_{10} \quad T_{11} \quad 0 \quad 5 \quad 0 \quad 0 \quad 0]$$

Using the boundary conditions on the global system, we obtain the equations for the unknown nodal temperatures

$$\begin{align}
4T_6 - T_7 - T_{10} &= 10 \\
-T_6 + 4T_7 - T_{11} &= 0 \\
-T_7 - T_{10} + 4T_{11} &= 0 \\
-T_6 + 4T_{10} - T_{11} &= 10
\end{align} \tag{9.129}$$

From the property of symmetry of the system, we know $T_6 = T_{10}$ and $T_7 = T_{11}$. The solution is as follows:

$$T_6 = T_{10} = \frac{15}{4} = 3.75 \tag{9.130}$$

and

$$T_7 = T_{11} = \frac{5}{4} = 1.25$$

9.9   FEM and Optimization

In order to survive in today's competitive industrial/scientific world, products must have the following characteristic features:

1. Low cost
2. High built-in reliability of performance
3. Limited time frame for design/manufacture

The first factor is usually achieved by minimizing the volume/mass/weight of the structure component, whereas the second factor would need the various constraints defined in the problem statement to be satisfied in the process of design. The third factor emphasizes the reduction of the overall time for bringing the product into the market by using proper computational tools/manufacturing techniques, which will complete the process at higher speeds.

In recent times, state-of-the-art structural optimization algorithms and design sensitivity analysis methods have come into existence, which cover the first two points mentioned above to a considerable extent. The third point could be brought into control by using a combination of hardware and software. The concepts of inherent vector and concurrent processing made possible by recent advances in computer architecture would assist in the design and analysis stage as well as in the numerical control machines, Group Technology, and CIM architectures discussed in the latter chapters. This technology will definitely be a key to the speed of the manufacturing process.

The structural optimization process deals with a systematic procedure of manipulating the design variables that describe the structural system while simultaneously satisfying prescribed limits on the structural response.

The design variables for a component could include volume or mass or weight; minimizing these would reduce the cost. These design variables can be grouped and linked in many ways and can be fixed in certain regions of the structural system. This is needed for uniformity of structure and in creating a symmetrical design under unsymmetrical loading conditions. Prescribed limits on the response of the structure may refer to nodal displacements and element stresses under static loading as well as eigenvalues for free vibration (natural frequencies) and/or for stability (buckling load factors).

Finite-element discretization is a powerful tool used for the optimization of design of machine components. This method of analysis breaks up the complex geometry of the structure into a large number of "finite elements" whose response to applied stresses and constraints can be well approximated with simple functions. The accuracy of results in this type of analysis is a strong function of the manner in which the structure is subdivided into finite elements. Hence, it is seen that there are three major operations integrated into the procedure of structural optimization.

These are:

1. Finite-element analysis
2. Design sensitivity analysis
3. Optimization algorithm

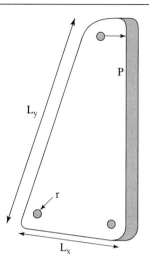

FIGURE 9.12   Bracket used in a universal joint.

A number of powerful and versatile programs have been developed that can treat large-scale structural design problems.

Let us discuss an example of design optimization applied to the solid cantilever structure shown in Figure 9.12. A software package called SHAPE developed by EMRC was used for this purpose. The cantilever is loaded at midheight at the right end. Because of the symmetry and antisymmetry conditions, only one quarter was modeled with 7680 tetrahedron and 2244 nodes (6732 degrees of freedom). Using consistent units, the constraints for the problem are $L_x = L_y = 16, L_z = 3, E = 3.0 \times 10^4, u = 0.3, p = 2 (7p = 14)$, and Von-Mises stress <10 (all elements).

One layer of the displacement elements was frozen at the fixed end, which means the node displacements of the elements on that side were 0 because they are subject to no change in the process. The package adopts an iterative procedure to arrive at the final optimized design. At the end of each iteration, the design variables are compared with the prescribed limits (constraints). Based on the need/requirement subsequent to this comparison, new boundaries may be created as appropriate by removal of the material from inside the system. The finite-element mesh of the structure is sufficient to model the boundaries by parametric curves.

The changes in the shape and the stress at various stages during shape optimization are shown in Figures 9.13–9.15. The final material volume is 140.4, compared to the initial design material volume of 768.0, indicating a savings of nearly 82% in terms of material, as reported in the description to the software SHAPES a NISA II product of EMRC. The combination of the finite-element method, optimization techniques, and graphics enables the designer/engineer to obtain optimal design in real time, releasing him or her from the exhaustive time one spends in arriving at such a conclusion. Once completed, this is a perfect example of how CAD and engineers can be blended together to form the ultimate CAD system, drawing from the best capabilities of each.

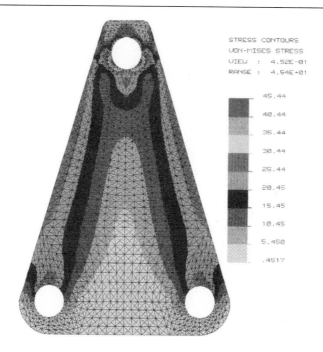

FIGURE 9.13 Initial shape (courtesy of EMRC, Troy, Michigan).

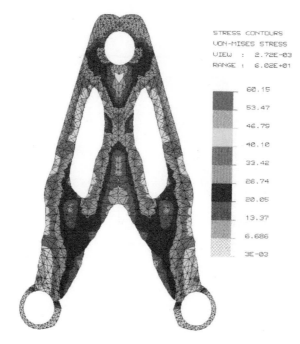

FIGURE 9.14 Iteration 14 (courtesy of EMRC, Troy, Michigan).

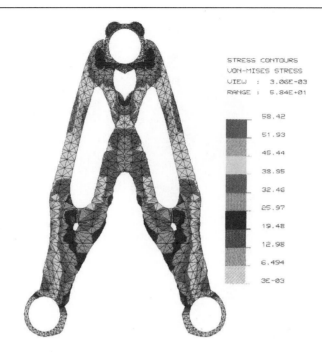

FIGURE 9.15   Iteration 40 (courtesy of EMRC, Troy, Michigan).

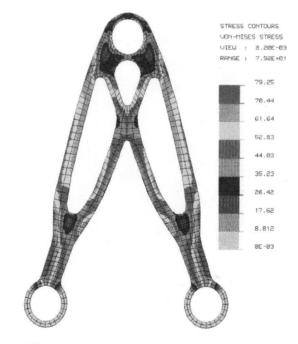

FIGURE 9.16   Final shape (courtesy of EMRC, Troy, Michigan).

Let us consider another design optimization example taken again from EMRC using the finite-element discretization procedure.

The design of a bracket used in an automotive universal joint is to be optimized. The brackets shown in Figure 9.12 are loaded by a force P applied toward the right at the middle of the top bolt hole. The periphery of the bottom two bolt holes is restricted against translation in the x and y directions.

For the process of design optimization, only half of the system needs to be modeled because of the condition of antisymmetry. The modeled half was 1619 elements and 881 nodes (1762 nodes). One layer of elements around each bolt hole is frozen because of the support and load conditions. The width of material beyond this layer is arbitrarily assigned for the initial design. Using consistent units, the constants for the problem are $L_x = 10$, $L_y = 15$, $t = 0.3$, $r = 1.0$, $E = 2.074 \times 10^4$, $D = 0.3$, $P = 15$, and Von-Mises stress <80 (all elements).

Figures 9.14 through 9.16 illustrate the changes in shape and stress during the shape optimization process. The final design (Figure 9.16) is about 68% lighter than the original design based on the material volume of 48.07.

PROBLEMS

9.1. Determine the temperature distribution in the wall shown in Figure P9.1. The outside temperature T_o at the wall surface is 32°C and the material properties of the two sections of the walls have constants K_1 and K_2 of 50 W/m°C and 100 W/m°C, respectively.

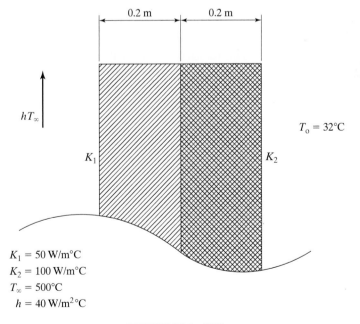

$K_1 = 50$ W/m°C
$K_2 = 100$ W/m°C
$T_\infty = 500$°C
$h = 40$ W/m²°C

FIGURE P9.1   Wall.

9.2. A plate of constant cross-sectional area is subject to different temperature conditions as shown in Figure P9.2. Its thermal conductivity is 1.0 W/m°C and $T_\infty = 40°C$. Find the temperature at the nodes of elements 3 and 6 using the discretized elements as shown in Figures P9.2a and P9.2b respectively.

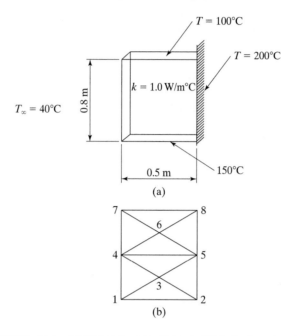

(a)

(b)

FIGURE P9.2   Plate. (a) Right triangular elements. (b) Left triangular elements.

9.3. For the one-dimensional rod in Figure P9.3 assume the length to be 10 in., T_o to be 110°F, and the conductivity constant $k = 25$ BTU/(h · ft°F). Use a four-element nodal to determine the temperature at the midpoint. The ambient temperature is assumed to be 80° F and $h' = 5$ BTU/(h · ft²°F).

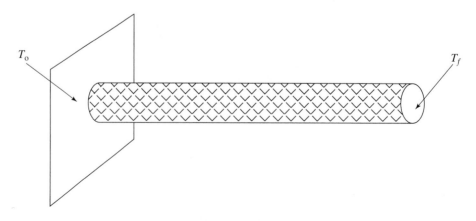

FIGURE P9.3   One-dimensional rod.

9.4. For the following heat-conduction problem

$$\frac{1}{3}\frac{d^2T}{dx^2} = -4$$

and the given boundary conditions at

$$T_{(x=0)} = T_0$$
$$T_{(x=L)} = T_f$$

find the temperature at $x = 2$ in. and 4 in. if the total length is $x = 6$ in., $A = 1$ in^2.

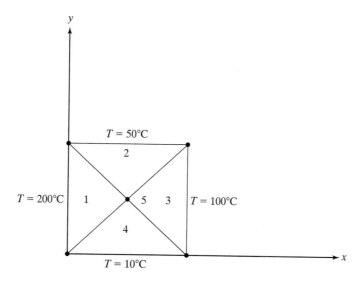

FIGURE P9.4   Metallic plate.

9.5. A thin rod 100 cm long with a 1 cm^2 cross-sectional area has a temperature distribution given by

$$\frac{d^2T}{dx^2} = -10.0 \qquad (0 \le x \le 100.0)$$

with boundary conditions

$$T(0) = 10°C \quad \text{and} \quad T(100) = 0°C$$

Using one-dimensional finite elements, compute the temperature at the middle point of the rod ($x = 50$ cm) when the rod is discretized (a) using two elements and (b) using four elements.

Compare the finite-element solution with the one obtained by integrating the governing differential equation.

9.6. A thin metallic plate 100 cm by 100 cm by 1 cm is discretized using three-noded 2D triangular elements, as shown in Figure P9.4. The boundary conditions at the various edges of the plate are also shown in the figure. Find the following:

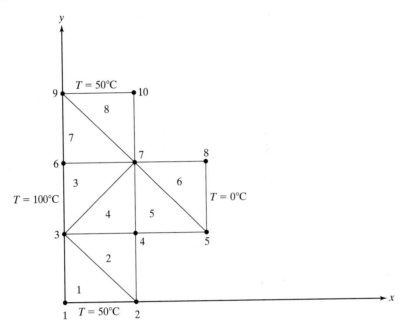

FIGURE P9.5   Boundary conditions and discretization of a plate.

    a. The local conductivity matrix for each element.
    b. The contribution to the global conductivity matrix from all local conductivity matrices of elements 1, 2, 3, and 4.
    c. The temperature at the midnode, node 5.

9.7. The boundary conditions and discretization of a plate are shown in Figure P9.5.

    a. Write the various tables needed for the solution process.
    b. Find the incidence matrix relating the local and global nodal temperatures.
    c. Write the local and global heat-source-contribution vectors.
    d. Assemble the global nodal temperature matrix.
    e. Write the final equations after imposing the boundary conditions.

9.8. A building wall is made of three layers. The outermost layer is 4 in. thick and the properties are $k = 0.76$ Btu/hr-ft-°F; $T = 10$°F. The middle layer is 6 in. and the material properties are $k = 0.40$ Btu/hr-ft-°F . The inner layer is made of 0.5-in. material with properties $k = 0.28$ Btu/hr-ft-°F and $T = 200$°C. The coefficient of outside air is given by 5.5 Btu/hr-ft²-°F and for the inner air the coefficient is 1.4 Btu/hr-ft²-°F. What will be the temperature of the surface of the wall?

9.9. A wall is made of three layers

    1. 8 in. of fire-clay brick, $k = 0.75$ Btu/hr-ft-°F
    2. 6 in. of fired diatomaceous earth brick, $k = 0.3$ Btu/hr-ft-°F
    3. 4-in. layer of common brick, $k = 0.4$ Btu/hr-ft-°F

The outside surface temperature is held at 300°F and the inside surface temperature is 1900°F.

a. Find the temperature between different walls.
b. If the inside space is filled with gases of hot temperature 2100°F and the outside air film temperature is 100°F, find the temperature between two surfaces. The conductivity constants for gases are $k = 0.12, k_2 = 0.08$, $k_3 = 0.1$ Btu/hr-ft-°F, respectively.

9.10. An iron rod of diameter 0.5 in. and 12 in. long is heated to 230°F at one end and exposed to a convective fluid, which is at 70°F, the film coefficient $h = 1.6$ Btu/hr-ft^2-°F, and insulated at the free end. Use two elements to determine the temperature at midpoint.

BIBLIOGRAPHY

ANSYS Engineering Analysis System (1983). Houston, PA: Swanson Analysis Systems, Inc.

Burnett, D. S. (1987). *Finite Element Analysis: From Concepts to Applications.* Reading, MA: Addison-Wesley.

Huston, R. L, and Passerello, C. E. (1984). *Finite Element Methods: An Introduction* New York: Marcel Dekker.

Kenneth, H. (1975). *Finite Element Methods for Engineers*, New York: John Wiley.

Martin, H. C. and Carey, G. F. (1973). *Introduction to Finite Element Analysis: theory and applications.* New York: McGraw Hill.

Reddy, J. N. (1989). *An Introduction to Finite Element Method.* New York: McGraw-Hill.

Rockey, K. C. (1975). *The Finite Element Method: A Basic Introduction.* New York: John Wiley.

Stasa F. L. (1985). *Applied Finite Element Analysis for Engineers, HRW Series in Mechanical Engineering.* New York: CBS College Publishing.

Timoshenko, S. D., and Goodier, S. (1970). *Theory of Elasticity.* New York: McGraw-Hill.

Zienkiewcz, O. C., and Taylor, R. L. (1989). *The Finite Element Method.* New York: McGraw-Hill.

CHAPTER 10

Dynamic Analysis— A Finite-Element Approach

10.1 Introduction

In the preceding chapters we examined the area of finite element associated with the first law of mechanics. The structure's response to time variant loads needs to be captured by using differential equations that govern the motion. Applying Newton's Second Law or Lagrange equations usually does this. Up to this point we have discussed only cases in which the load on the structure is static and therefore the response is also static and proportional to the structural stiffness and applied loads. It is apparent that the response of a structure will be different if we account for the inertia forces and the time variant effects due to the kinematics and forces applied to the system. This chapter will be used to show how we can use finite-element method (FEM) to formulate and solve for dynamic problems. The FEM was used successfully to determine element stiffness matrices in the study of trusses. The method is extended to derive the mass element matrices and their corresponding global mass matrix for the structure. In most cases the differential equations for a structure assuming small deformation take the form

$$[M]\{\ddot{u}\} + [C]\{\dot{u}\} + [K]\{u\} = \{F\} \tag{10.1}$$

The inertia product is given by the product of mass times acceleration, the damping forces are given by the product of the damping coefficient C times the velocity, and the stiffness force is given by the product of the stiffness by the displacement. The right-hand side is usually devoted to external forces applied on the structure. When discretizing a structure into a large number of elements we automatically increase the number of differential equations needed to represent the structure. A solution of these equations will require memory and CPU time that can vary from seconds to minutes, hours, and even more. Depending on the size of the problem we can foresee hundreds and thousands of second-order differential equations. In most engineering problems we reduce the dynamic analysis to the solution of an eigenvalue problem. The eigenvalue problem is one that involves the extraction of the natural frequencies of the system or structure at hand. This information is crucial when designing a product or device. If we assume a solution of the form

$$\{u\} = A \sin \omega t \tag{10.2}$$

then the dynamic analysis of structures takes the form

$$([K] - \omega^2[M])\{u\} = \{F\} \tag{10.3}$$

where $[K]$ is the global stiffness matrix, $[M]$ is the global mass, ω^2 denotes the natural frequency, $\{u\}$ the global displacement array and $\{F\}$ the external excitation force vector.

One of the finite element's most popular approaches in vibration is the computation of the natural frequencies of a mechanical system. Because both $[K]$ and $[M]$ can be calculated directly from FEM provided that the geometric properties and the boundary conditions of the problem are known, we can evaluate $[\omega^2]$ making use of numerical procedures readily available in most of the engineering numerical analysis books. In this chapter we will focus on the analysis of the eigenvalue problem and in the formulation of the mass matrix in particular and the corresponding stiffness by showing how both the stiffness and mass can be calculated and develop the necessary steps to compute $[\omega^2]$.

10.2   Element Stiffness and Mass Matrices

Once more let us examine a beam under a compressive load, where the compressive force is not constant but rather a force that is harmonically exciting the beam as a function of time. That is the external force of

$$F = F_0 \sin \omega t \tag{10.4}$$

Let F be applied at the end of the beam as shown in Figure 10.1

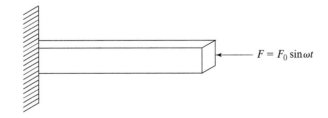

FIGURE 10.1   A beam excited longitudinally by a harmonic force F.

FIGURE 10.2   A beam element with nodes 1 and 2 under compressive load.

In previous chapters we developed the element stiffness matrix when a beam is discretized into N elements. Essentially, each element acts as a spring with a stiffness value k equal to

$$k^{(e)} = \frac{AE}{l}$$

Again observe the element shown in Figure 10.2, which is subjected to axial forces at each end (node); the actual displacement of the element can be written as function of the node displacements u_1 and u_2. The stiffness matrix can be obtained from the energy function minimization on the basis of equilibrium. This is derived by first developing the potential and kinetic energy due to axial deformation under the load F.

First we write the beam displacement in terms of u_1 and u_2 as follows:

$$u(x, t) = \left(1 - \frac{x}{l}\right)u_1(t) + \frac{x}{l}u_2(t) \tag{10.5}$$

Note how the displacement at $x = 0$ is u_1 and at $x = l$ it is u_2. This is consistent with our assumed displacement function. Now we can compute the energy terms needed for our finite-element formulation.

The strain energy of the bar is given by the integral

$$V(t) = \frac{1}{2}\int_0^l EA\left[\frac{\partial u(x, t)}{\partial t}\right]^2 dx \tag{10.6}$$

The kinetic energy of the element can be computed from the integral

$$T(t) = \frac{1}{2}\int_0^l A\rho(x)\left[\frac{\partial u(x, t)}{\partial x}\right]^2 dx \tag{10.7}$$

where $\rho(x)$ is the density of the bar.

Differentiating the displacement field $u(x,t)$ with respect to x in Equation (10.5) and substituting it into Equation (10.6) yield an explicit expression for the potential energy of the form

$$V(t) = EA(u_1^2 - 2u_1u_2 + u_2^2)/2l \tag{10.8}$$

The velocity equation is given by

$$\frac{\partial u(x, t)}{\partial t} = \left(1 - \frac{x}{l}\right)\dot{u}_1(t) + \frac{x}{l}\dot{u}_2(t) \tag{10.9}$$

Substituting Equation (10.9) into Equation (10.7), we obtain the kinetic energy equation in terms of $\dot{u}(t) = [\dot{u}_1(t) \quad \dot{u}_2(t)]$ which can be written as

$$T(t) = 1/2 \, \dot{u}^T M \, \dot{u} \tag{10.10}$$

where M is defined by

$$M = \frac{\rho A l}{6} \begin{bmatrix} 2 & 1 \\ 1 & 2 \end{bmatrix} \tag{10.11}$$

Expressing the potential energy due to axial deformation in a matrix form from Equation (10.8) results in

$$V(t) = \frac{1}{2}[u_1 u_2][b]\begin{bmatrix} u_1 \\ u_2 \end{bmatrix} = \frac{1}{2} u^T k u$$

where

$$k = \frac{EA}{l} \begin{bmatrix} 1 & -1 \\ -1 & 1 \end{bmatrix} \tag{10.12}$$

This stiffness was derived in the study of trusses and can be functionally derived from the energy equation as shown above.

10.3   Axial Deformation

10.3.1 One-Element Equation of Motion

The equations of vibration can be obtained from the preceding expressions for the kinetic energy $T(t)$ and strain energy $V(t)$ by using the variational or Lagrangian approach. The equation of motion can be calculated from energy in the structure from

$$\frac{\partial}{\partial t}\left(\frac{\partial T}{\partial \dot{u}_i}\right) - \frac{\partial T}{\partial u_i} + \frac{\partial V}{\partial u_i} = f_i(t) \qquad i = 1, 2, \ldots, n \tag{10.13}$$

where u_i is the coordinate of the system, which is assumed to have n degrees of freedom, and where f_i is the external force applied at coordinates u_i. Here the energies T and V are the total kinetic energy and strain energy, respectively, in the structure.

Consider a cantilever beam of length l as shown in Figure 10.1. Analysis of the boundary conditions indicates that the time response at the clamped end must be 0. Hence, the total kinetic energy becomes

$$T(t) = \frac{1}{2}\frac{\rho A l}{3}(\dot{u}_2^2) \tag{10.14}$$

and the total strain energy is

$$V(t) = \frac{1}{2}\frac{EA}{l}u_2^2 \tag{10.15}$$

Substitution of these two energy expressions into Lagrange equation (10.13) we get

$$\frac{\rho A l}{3} \ddot{u}_2(t) + \frac{EA}{l} u_2(t) = 0 \tag{10.16}$$

which constitutes a simple finite-element model of the cantilever *bar using only one element*.

This finite-element model of the bar can now be solved, given a set of initial conditions, for the nodal displacement $u_2(t)$. The solution to the equation is

$$u_2(t) = \sqrt{u_0^2 + \left(\frac{\dot{u}_0}{\omega_n}\right)^2} \sin\left(\omega_n t + \tan^{-1}\frac{\omega_n u_0}{\dot{u}_o}\right) \tag{10.17}$$

10.3.2 Three-Element Equation of Motion

The total strain energy is the sum of the strain energy associated with each element, that is,

$$V(t) = V_1(t) + V_2(t) + V_3(t)$$

$$= \frac{3EA}{2l}\left\{\begin{bmatrix} 0 \\ u_2 \end{bmatrix}\begin{bmatrix} 1 & -1 \\ -1 & 1 \end{bmatrix}\begin{bmatrix} 0 \\ u_2 \end{bmatrix} + \begin{bmatrix} u_2 \\ u_3 \end{bmatrix}^T\begin{bmatrix} 1 & -1 \\ -1 & 1 \end{bmatrix}\begin{bmatrix} u_2 \\ u_3 \end{bmatrix} + \begin{bmatrix} u_3 \\ u_4 \end{bmatrix}^T\begin{bmatrix} 1 & -1 \\ -1 & 1 \end{bmatrix}\begin{bmatrix} u_3 \\ u_4 \end{bmatrix}\right\}$$

$$= \frac{3EA}{2l}(2u_2^2 - 2u_2u_3 + 2u_3^2 - 2u_3u_4 + u_4^2) \tag{10.18}$$

The vector of derivatives of this total strain energy given in the Lagrangian equation is found to be

$$\begin{bmatrix} \dfrac{\partial T}{\partial u_2} \\[2mm] \dfrac{\partial T}{\partial \dot{u}} \\[2mm] \dfrac{\partial T}{\partial \dot{u}_4} \end{bmatrix} = \frac{\rho A l}{18}\begin{bmatrix} 4 & 1 & 0 \\ 1 & 4 & 1 \\ 0 & 1 & 2 \end{bmatrix}\begin{bmatrix} \ddot{u}_2(t) \\ \ddot{u}_3(t) \\ \ddot{u}_4(t) \end{bmatrix} \tag{10.19}$$

In a similar fashion, the total kinetic energy can be expressed by adding the contribution of the kinetic energy from all three elements, where we write

$$T(t) = \frac{\rho A l}{36}\left\{\begin{bmatrix} 0 \\ \dot{u}_2 \end{bmatrix}^T\begin{bmatrix} 2 & 1 \\ 1 & 2 \end{bmatrix}\begin{bmatrix} 0 \\ \dot{u}_2 \end{bmatrix} + \begin{bmatrix} \dot{u}_2 \\ \dot{u}_3 \end{bmatrix}^T\begin{bmatrix} 2 & 1 \\ 1 & 2 \end{bmatrix}\begin{bmatrix} \dot{u}_2 \\ \dot{u}_3 \end{bmatrix} + \begin{bmatrix} \dot{u}_3 \\ \dot{u}_4 \end{bmatrix}^T\begin{bmatrix} 2 & 1 \\ 1 & 2 \end{bmatrix}\begin{bmatrix} \dot{u}_3 \\ \dot{u}_4 \end{bmatrix}\right\}$$

$$\tag{10.20}$$

The first term in the Lagrangian equation, which is responsible for the mass matrix, then becomes

$$\frac{d}{dt}\begin{bmatrix} \dfrac{\partial T}{\partial \dot{u}_2} \\ \dfrac{\partial T}{\partial \dot{u}_3} \\ \dfrac{\partial T}{\partial \dot{u}_4} \end{bmatrix} = \frac{\rho A l}{18}\begin{bmatrix} 4 & 1 & 0 \\ 1 & 4 & 1 \\ 0 & 1 & 2 \end{bmatrix}\begin{bmatrix} \ddot{u}_2(t) \\ \ddot{u}_3(t) \\ \ddot{u}_4(t) \end{bmatrix} \tag{10.21}$$

Combining all the Lagrangian terms, the equations of motion take the form

$$M\ddot{u}(t) + Ku(t) = 0 \tag{10.22}$$

where $u(t) = [u_2\, u_3\, u_4]^T$ is the vector of nodal displacements. Here the matrix

$$M = \frac{\rho A l}{18}\begin{bmatrix} 4 & 1 & 0 \\ 1 & 4 & 1 \\ 0 & 1 & 2 \end{bmatrix} \tag{10.23}$$

is the global mass matrix and the corresponding

$$K = \frac{3EA}{l}\begin{bmatrix} 2 & -1 & 0 \\ -1 & 2 & -1 \\ 0 & -1 & 1 \end{bmatrix} \tag{10.24}$$

is the global stiffness matrix.

The FEM allows us to derive both the mass and stiffness of a structure by means of the energy method. It is obvious that the size of these matrices can expand rapidly if we choose a large number of elements. When solving a linear problem we are mostly interested in the vibration characteristics of the problem and not necessarily its time response. Hence, we reduce the problem to a so-called eigenvalue problem by first assuming a solution to equations of the form given by Equation (10.22) that is given by

$$u(x, t) = X(x)e^{j\omega t} \tag{10.25}$$

We have essentially reduced the problem to a free-vibration, where the right-hand side of the governing equations is set to 0. Substitution of Equation (10.25) into Equation (10.22) yields

$$\{[k] - w^2[M]\}\{X\} = \{0\} \tag{10.26}$$

We can solve for w^2 by setting the following determinant equal to 0.

$$|[k] - w^2[M]| = 0 \tag{10.27}$$

Equation (10.26) represents the generalized eigenvalue problem. We will revisit the solution of Equation (10.27) later in this chapter, when we introduce methods that will help us determine the values of the eigenvalues.

10.4 Bending or Transverse Deformation of a Beam

Let us consider a beam subject to transverse loading, which causes it to bend, as shown in Figure 10.3. The deflection of the neutral axis at any location x is represented by the variable y; for small deflections we have the flexure formula, which defines the stress, the moment, and the vertical displacement measured from the neutral axis as

$$\sigma = -\frac{My}{I} \tag{10.28}$$

or

$$EI\frac{d^2v}{dx^2} = M(x), \tag{10.29}$$

where I is the second moment of inertia. From the standard strength of materials the above equation can be expressed further as

$$EI\frac{d^4v}{dx^4} = \frac{dV(x)}{dx} = \varphi(\mathrm{n}) \tag{10.30}$$

where we can see that Equation (10.30) is obtained by the differentiation of Equation (10.29) and recognizing that the rate of change of the shear force V with respect to x is given by the rate of change of the applied moment due to the load, where $V(x)$ is the transverse shear, $w(x)$ the load per unit length, and γ the deflection of the neutral axis. Once again we need to apply the beam theory in the context of finite element for the purpose of deriving the mass and stiffness matrices corresponding to an element. Ultimately, we will derive the dynamic equations governing the deflection of the beam (Bernoulli) under certain loading conditions.

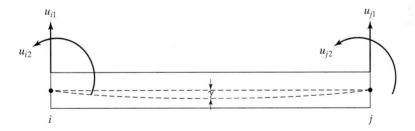

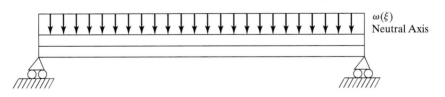

FIGURE 10.3 Simply supported beam.

The total potential energy of the beam equals the strain energy less the potential energy due to the external loads. Let us represent the energy equation by

$$\pi = u - V \tag{10.31}$$

The strain energy contribution is obtained from the following integral, where we can assume that the energy for a differential element will also have the same equation except the limits on the integral will be those associated with the element. If we ignore the contribution of the energy due to the external forces, the energy equation reduces to

$$\pi = \int \frac{EI}{2} \left[\frac{d^2v}{dx^2} \right]^2 dx \tag{10.31}$$

In the above equation we neglected the shear strain. We will be back to its contribution in the next section, when we discuss the effects of both axial and bending on the formulation problem.

The displacement u at each node is expressed in terms of vertical and longitudinal components as shown in Figure 10.3, hence the deflection can be expressed as a fourth-order polynomial

$$v = a_1 + b_1 x + c x^2 + d x^3 \tag{10.32}$$

which defines a cubic spline. The coefficients can be found by making use of boundary conditions at both ends. The equation above becomes

$$u = N_1 u_1 + N_2 u_2 + N_3 u_3 + N_4 u_4 \tag{10.33}$$

Note how we have substituted u for v in the above equation. We can write Equation (10.33) in a matrix form where we can isolate the shape function and the displacement vector and express u as

$$u(x) = [N_1 \quad N_2 \quad N_3 \quad N_4] \begin{Bmatrix} u_1 \\ u_2 \\ u_3 \\ u_4 \end{Bmatrix} \tag{10.34}$$

where the shape functions are

$$N_1 = 1 - \frac{3x^2}{L^2} + \frac{2x^3}{L^3}$$

$$N_2 = x - \frac{2x^2}{L} + \frac{x^3}{L^2}$$

$$N_3 = \frac{3x^2}{L} - \frac{2x^3}{L^3} \tag{10.35}$$

$$N_4 = -\frac{x^2}{L} + \frac{x^3}{L^2}$$

By substituting Equation (10.34) into the strain energy equation we obtain

$$
\pi = \frac{1}{2}[u_1 \quad u_2 \quad u_3 \quad u_4] \int_0^L EI \begin{bmatrix} N_1'' \\ N_2'' \\ N_3'' \\ N_4'' \end{bmatrix} [N_1'' \quad N_2'' \quad N_3'' \quad N_4''] \begin{bmatrix} u_1 \\ u_2 \\ u_3 \\ u_4 \end{bmatrix} \tag{10.36}
$$

By taking the second derivatives of the shape functions we get

$$
N_1'' = -\frac{6}{L^2} + \frac{12x}{L^3}
$$

$$
N_2'' = -\frac{4}{L} + \frac{6x}{L^2}
$$

$$
N_3'' = \frac{6}{L^2} - \frac{12x}{L^3} \tag{10.37}
$$

$$
N_4'' = -\frac{2}{L} + \frac{6x}{L^2}
$$

By substitution of the above equation into π and recalling that the displacement at the equilibrium position occurs such that the value of the system total energy is minimum, we get

$$
\frac{\partial \pi}{\partial u} = 0 \tag{10.38}
$$

which leads to

$$
\frac{EI}{L^3} \begin{bmatrix} 12 & 6L & -12 & 6L \\ 6L & 4l^2 & -6L & 2L^2 \\ -12 & -6L & 12 & -6L \\ 6L & 2L^2 & -6L & 4L^2 \end{bmatrix} \begin{Bmatrix} u_1 \\ u_2 \\ u_3 \\ u_4 \end{Bmatrix} \tag{10.39}
$$

Hence, the stiffness matrix for a beam element due to deflection (bending) is

$$
[k^e] = \frac{EI}{L^3} \begin{bmatrix} 12 & 6L & -12 & 6L \\ 6L & 4L^3 & -6L & 2L^2 \\ -12 & -6L & 12 & -6L \\ 6L & 2L^2 & -6L & 4L^2 \end{bmatrix} \tag{10.40}
$$

Once again we have denoted by $[k^e]$ the element stiffness matrix to be consistent with our formulation of the FEM. Now we can tackle the formulation of the mass matrix.

Consider the uniform bar shown later in the chapter in Figure 10.5. The element has a velocity $\dot{u}$ in the x direction. If we discretize the bar into N elements, we evaluate the kinetic energy of the bar by integrating over the total length of the bar. To obtain the kinetic energy of the element we first define the kinetic energy equation as follows

$$T = \frac{1}{2} \int_0^L \dot{u} \, dm \tag{10.41}$$

or

$$T = \frac{1}{2} \int \dot{u} \, \rho A dx \tag{10.42}$$

where $dm = \rho A dx$.

The displacement field can be expressed as a function of basis function or shape functions such that

$$u(x, t) = \sum_{i=1}^N \phi_i(x) q_i(t) \tag{10.43}$$

where $q(t)$ defines the generalized coordinates.

Substituting Equation (10.43) into the kinetic energy of the bar yields

$$T = \frac{1}{2} \int_0^L \left(\sum_{i=1}^N \phi_i \dot{q} \right) \left(\sum_{i=1}^N \phi_i \dot{q} \right) \rho A dx \tag{10.44}$$

which leads to

$$T = \frac{1}{2} \int_0^L \sum_{i=1}^N \sum_{j=1}^N M_{ij} \, \dot{q}_i \, \dot{q}_j \tag{10.45}$$

The mass matrix M_{ij} is then defined by the following expression

$$M_{ij} = \int_0^L \rho(x) A(x) \phi_i(x) \phi_j(x) \, dx \tag{10.46}$$

or simply

$$M_{ij} = \int_0^L \rho(x) A(x) N_i(x) N_j(x) \, dx \tag{10.47}$$

where N_i and N_j are the shape functions used in determining the element stiffness $k^{(e)}$ matrix, while ϕ_i and ϕ_j are interpolating functions with the following property: when ϕ is equal to N, M_{ij} is referred as the consistent mass matrix. For the sake of simplicity the shape functions N are used for the evaluation of the mass matrix.

For a uniform beam subject to bending the mass matrix is found to be

$$[M] = \frac{mL}{420} \begin{bmatrix} 156 & 54 & 22L & -13L \\ 54 & 156 & 13L & -22L \\ 22L & 13L & 4L^2 & -3L^2 \\ -13L & -22L & -3L^2 & 4L^2 \end{bmatrix} \qquad (10.48)$$

where m is the total mass of the beam or element and is defined by

$m = \rho A$,

ρ = Mass/unit volume,

A = Cross-sectional area,

L = Length of the beam.

Example 10.1

Find the coefficients M_{11} and M_{12} of the mass matrix using the shape function defined in the evaluation of the element stiffness matrix given by Equation (10.35).

Solution Using Equation (10.47) and substituting both subscripts i and j with 1 we obtain:

$$M_{11} = \int_0^L \rho A N_1 N_1 \, dx$$

Factorizing the constants ρ and A we get

$$M_{11} = \rho A \int [N_1][N_1]^T \, dx$$

Note that

$$N_1 = 1 - 3\left(\frac{x}{L}\right)^2 + 2\left(\frac{x}{L}\right)^3$$

The above integral becomes

$$M_{11} = \rho A \int_0^L \left[1 - 3\left(\frac{x}{L}\right)^2 + 2\left(\frac{x}{L}\right)^3\right]^2 dx$$

$$= \rho A \int \left\{\left[1 - 3\left(\frac{x}{L}\right)^2\right]^2 + 4\left[1 - 3\left(\frac{x}{L}\right)^2\right]\left[2\left(\frac{x}{L}\right)^3\right] + 4\left[\frac{x}{L}\right]^6\right\} dx$$

$$= \rho A \int_L \left\{1 - \frac{6}{L^2}x^2 + \frac{4}{L^3}x^3 + \frac{9}{L^4}x^4 - \frac{12}{L^5}x^5 + \frac{4}{L^6}x^6\right\} dx$$

$$= L\left(1 - \frac{6}{3} + 1 + \frac{9}{5} - 2 + \frac{4}{7}\right) = \frac{156L}{420}$$

In a similar fashion we derive the element M_{44}

$$M_{44} = \rho A \int_0^L N_4^2 \, dx$$

$$N_4 N_4 \Rightarrow \left(-\frac{x^2}{L} + \frac{x^3}{L^2} \right)\left(-\frac{x^2}{L} + \frac{x^3}{L^2} \right) = \frac{x^4}{L^2} - \frac{x^5}{L^3} - \frac{x^5}{L^3} + \frac{x^6}{L^4}$$

$$M_{44} = \int_0^L \left(\frac{x^4}{L^2} - 2\frac{x^5}{L^3} + \frac{x^6}{L^4} \right) dx = \frac{1}{5}\frac{x^5}{L^2} - \frac{2}{6}\frac{x^6}{L^3} + \frac{1}{7}\frac{x^7}{L^4}$$

$$= \frac{L^3}{5} - \frac{1}{3}L^3 + \frac{1}{7}L^3 = \frac{4}{420}L^3$$

Hence,

$$M_{44} = \frac{4}{420}L^3$$

End of Example 10.1

10.5 Bernoulli Beam

Consider a beam element whose nodal deformations are described by the displacements and a rotation at each end as shown in Figure 10.5. We note that the node displacements are along the longitudinal and normal axis. Essentially, we have two translations at each node plus one rotation. A beam with both axial and bending deformation is referred as a Bernoulli Beam, which bears the name of one of the greatest scientists in beam theory.

Each joint depicts a longititudinal and lateral deformation and a rotation. Hence, the element is subject to axial and bending deformation. The transverse shear is neglected. We write the total strain energy as a combination of both the longitudinal deformation and the bending deformation. Therefore, the energy due to the strain deformation can be calculated from

$$U = \int_0^L \left\{ \left[\frac{EA}{2} \right]\left[\frac{du}{dx} \right]^2 + \frac{EI}{2}\left[\frac{d^2v}{dx^2} \right]^2 \right\} dx \tag{10.49}$$

Combining the results obtained in Equation (10.12) and Equation (10.40), we obtain the elastic stiffness matrix of the beam as

$$[k^e] = \begin{bmatrix} \dfrac{EI}{L} & 0 & 0 & -\dfrac{EA}{L} & 0 & 0 \\[2ex] 0 & 12\dfrac{EI}{L^3} & 6\dfrac{EI}{L^2} & 0 & -12\dfrac{EI}{L^3} & 6\dfrac{EI}{L^3} \\[2ex] 0 & \dfrac{6EI}{L^2} & 4\dfrac{EI}{L} & 0 & -6\dfrac{EI}{L^3} & 2\dfrac{EI}{L} \\[2ex] -\dfrac{EA}{L} & 0 & 0 & \dfrac{EA}{L} & 0 & 0 \\[2ex] 0 & -12\dfrac{EI}{L^3} & -6\dfrac{EI}{L^3} & 0 & 12\dfrac{EI}{L^3} & -6\dfrac{EI}{L^2} \\[2ex] 0 & 6\dfrac{EI}{L^3} & 2\dfrac{EI}{L} & 0 & -6\dfrac{EI}{L^2} & 4\dfrac{EI}{L} \end{bmatrix} \qquad (10.50)$$

In a similar fashion we obtain the mass element matrix for the beam using Equations (10.11) and (10.48) as follows

$$[M^e] = \rho AL \begin{bmatrix} \dfrac{1}{3} & 0 & 0 & \dfrac{1}{6} & 0 & 0 \\[2ex] 0 & \dfrac{13}{35} & \dfrac{11L}{210} & 0 & \dfrac{9}{70} & -\dfrac{13}{420} \\[2ex] 0 & \dfrac{11L}{210} & \dfrac{L^2}{105} & 0 & \dfrac{13}{420}L & -\dfrac{1}{140}L^2 \\[2ex] \dfrac{1}{6} & 0 & 0 & \dfrac{1}{3} & 0 & 0 \\[2ex] 0 & \dfrac{9}{70} & \dfrac{13}{40}L & 0 & \dfrac{13}{35} & -\dfrac{11}{210}L \\[2ex] 0 & -\dfrac{13L}{420} & -\dfrac{L^2}{140} & 0 & -\dfrac{11}{210}L & \dfrac{L^2}{105} \end{bmatrix} \qquad (10.51)$$

So we have established a procedure by which a mass and a stiffness element can be computed. In a similar way we will explore how the load vector is computed so we can complete the governing dynamic equations. The load vector represents the contribution of the external forces and moments applied to the beam.

10.6 Force Vector

When the load is distributed over the beam we need to find the generalized force vector that represents the contribution of the distributed force at the degrees of freedom used to denote the beam deformation. In this case the load will affect the longitudinal direction that is normal to the beam axis and will ultimately affect the bending moments at the nodes. The contribution in the axial direction along the beam neutral axis will be zero. If we let the load $F(x,t)$ be w, the generalized force vector can be expressed as

$$F_i = \int_0^L F(x, t) N_i(x) \, dx \tag{10.52}$$

For the case of a beam subjected to bending at the endpoints we have a displacement and a rotation, resulting in both a reaction force and a moment. If we substitute, for the shape function N, the one used in the derivation of the mass and stiffness element in the Bernoulli beam then we obtain

$$\{F\} = \begin{bmatrix} 0 \\ wL/12 \\ wL^2/2 \\ 0 \\ wL/2 \\ -wL^2/12 \end{bmatrix} \tag{10.53}$$

Example 10.2

Two distinct uniform beams with different boundary conditions are being evaluated (Figure 10.4). They are both of length L, have a cross-sectional area A, and a modulus

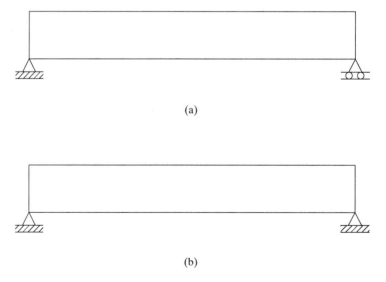

(a)

(b)

FIGURE 10.4 Two beams. (a) Simply supported at the right and fixed at the left end. (b) Fixed at both ends.

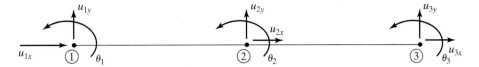

FIGURE 10.5 Bernoulli beam.

of elasticity E. The boundary conditions are such that the first beam is simply supported with a pin and roller at one end and fixed at the other, while the second beam has both ends fixed. Derive the mass and stiffness matrix for a two-element model for both cases and explain how the boundary conditions alter the global matrices K and M.

Solution Let the beam be discretized as shown above in Figure 10.5, where the displacement and rotation at each node are represented by u_{ix}, u_{iy}, and θ_i ($i = 1$, number of nodes).

Let $\{u\}$ denote the global displacement array, and then we can determine the size of the array by simply examining that at each node we have 3 degrees of freedom; hence, the global displacement vector $\{u\}$ should be of size 9.

$$\{u\} = \begin{Bmatrix} u_1 \\ u_2 \\ \vdots \\ \vdots \\ u_a \end{Bmatrix}$$

The global K matrix is defined by summing the stiffness of elements.

$$[K] = [K^{(1)}] + [K^{(2)}]$$

where

$$[k^e] = \begin{bmatrix} \dfrac{EI}{L} & 0 & 0 & -\dfrac{EA}{L} & 0 & 0 \\[2ex] 0 & 12\dfrac{EI}{L^3} & 6\dfrac{EI}{L^2} & 0 & -12\dfrac{EI}{L^3} & 6\dfrac{EI}{L^3} \\[2ex] 0 & \dfrac{6EI}{L^2} & 4\dfrac{EI}{L} & 0 & -6\dfrac{EI}{L^3} & 2\dfrac{EI}{L} \\[2ex] -\dfrac{EA}{L} & 0 & 0 & \dfrac{EA}{L} & 0 & 0 \\[2ex] 0 & -12\dfrac{EI}{L^3} & -6\dfrac{EI}{L^3} & 0 & 12\dfrac{EI}{L^3} & -6\dfrac{EI}{L^2} \\[2ex] 0 & 6\dfrac{EI}{L^3} & 2\dfrac{EI}{L} & 0 & -6\dfrac{EI}{L^2} & 4\dfrac{EI}{L} \end{bmatrix}$$

This element stiffness for a beam undergoing two translations and one rotation at each joint is given by Equation (10.50).

10.7 Boundary Conditions

From the beam end supports we deduce the following criteria for

(a) The case where the beam is fixed at one end and simply supported at the other

$$u_{1X} = u_{1Y} = 0$$

$$u_{3y} = 0$$

(b) The case with fixed-fixed conditions at both ends of the beam

$$u_{1x} = u_{1y} = 0$$

$$u_{3x} = u_{3y} = 0$$

Furthermore let the axial deformation u_{2x} be negligible, then the global stiffness matrix reduces for case (a) to

$$
K_{5x5} = \frac{EI}{L^3}
\begin{bmatrix}
4L^2 & -6L & 2L^2 & 0 & 6 \\
-6L & 24 & 0 & 6L & 0 \\
2L^2 & 0 & 8L^2 & 2L^2 & 0 \\
0 & 6L & 2L^2 & 4L^2 & 0 \\
0 & 0 & 0 & 0 & \dfrac{AL^2}{I}
\end{bmatrix}.
$$

Following the outlined procedure above, we develop the global mass matrix by first noting that for a uniform beam the element mass is

$$
[M^e] = \rho AL
\begin{bmatrix}
\dfrac{1}{3} & 0 & 0 & \dfrac{1}{6} & 0 & 0 \\
0 & \dfrac{13}{35} & \dfrac{11}{210}L & 0 & \dfrac{9}{70} & -\dfrac{13}{420}L \\
0 & \dfrac{11}{210}L & \dfrac{1}{105}L^2 & 0 & \dfrac{13}{420}L & -\dfrac{L^2}{140} \\
\dfrac{1}{6} & 0 & 0 & \dfrac{1}{3} & 0 & 0 \\
0 & \dfrac{9}{10} & \dfrac{13}{420}L & 0 & \dfrac{13}{35} & -\dfrac{11}{210}L \\
0 & -\dfrac{13}{420}L & -\dfrac{1}{140}L^2 & 0 & -\dfrac{11}{210}L & \dfrac{1}{105}L
\end{bmatrix}
$$

We obtain the global matrix by adding the element mass matrix for each element

$$[M] = [M^{(1)}] + [M^{(2)}]$$

Applying the boundary conditions for case (a) the mass matrix reduces to

$$[M] = \frac{\rho AL}{420} \begin{bmatrix} 4L^2 & 13L & -3L^2 & 0 & 0 \\ 13L & 312 & 0 & -13L & 0 \\ -3L & 0 & 8L^2 & -3L^2 & 0 \\ 0 & -13L & -3L^2 & 4L^2 & 0 \\ 0 & 0 & 0 & 0 & \dfrac{1}{3} \end{bmatrix}$$

Combining $[M]$ and $[K]$, and following the assumed solution outlined in Equation (10.25), we can express the characteristic equation for the eigenvalue problem as the determinant of the following equation:

$$\|[K] - w^2[M]\| = 0$$

the eigenvalues of which can be computed by determining the determinant of the matrix and setting it equal to 0. This will result in the natural frequencies of the assumed beam with the boundary conditions outlined in case (a). In a similar fashion we can build the mass and stiffness matrices for case (b). We note that for case (b) the boundary conditions result in five displacements to be 0, hence reducing the size of the global matrices by five. We should then expect five eigenvalues for case (a) and four eigenvalues for case (b).

End of Example 10.2

10.8   Planar Beam Structure

Planar structures are common in engineering because their analysis is vital to design, longevity, and safety (Figure 10.6). In the previous section we derived the element stiffness or mass matrix of a beam, but we assumed the beam neutral axis to be horizontal, coinciding with the x-axis of the coordinates x, y. Obviously, if a beam is positioned in space and we have several of them whose inclinations with respect to the global frame xy are different, then their mass and stiffness element matrices will contribute differently to the global stiffness and mass matrices. What follows is a derivation of element $[M^{(e)}]$ or $[K^{(e)}]$ when it is subjected to such orientation in space (Figure 10.7).

   We have previously defined the element stiffness or mass for a uniform beam when the beam is in a longitudinal position. Let $[u_{1x}, u_{1y}, \theta_1, u_{2x}, u_{2y}, \theta_2]$ represent the displacement at each node with respect to a local coordinate system of the beam with x

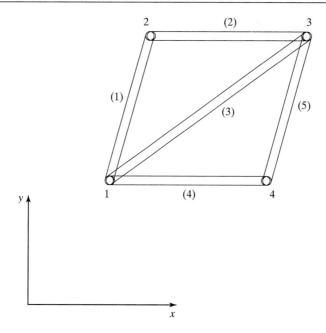

FIGURE 10.6   A planar beam structure in space.

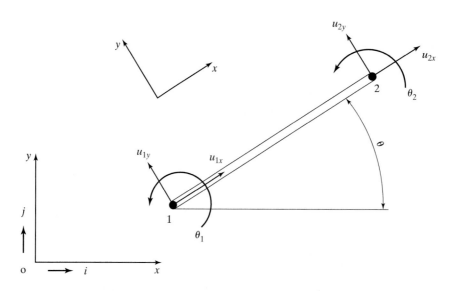

FIGURE 10.7   A simple beam with an orientation θ in a 2D space.

along the neutral axis of the beam. Then we can transform the local coordinates to global ones along xy by using a transformation matrix R such that

$$\begin{Bmatrix} u_{1x} \\ u_{1y} \\ \theta_1 \\ u_{2x} \\ u_{2y} \\ \theta_2 \end{Bmatrix} = \begin{bmatrix} \cos\theta & -\sin\theta & 0 & 0 & 0 & 0 \\ -\sin\theta & \cos\theta & 0 & 0 & 0 & 0 \\ 0 & 0 & 1 & 0 & 0 & 0 \\ 0 & 0 & 0 & \cos\theta & -\sin\theta & 0 \\ 0 & 0 & 0 & \sin\theta & \cos\theta & 0 \\ 0 & 0 & 0 & 0 & 0 & 1 \end{bmatrix} \begin{Bmatrix} u_{1x} \\ u_{1y} \\ \theta_1 \\ u_{2x} \\ u_{2y} \\ \theta_2 \end{Bmatrix} \tag{10.54}$$

or simply

$$\{U\} = \{R^{(e)}\}\{u\}. \tag{10.55}$$

The new element mass and stiffness matrices become

$$[M^e] = [R^{(e)}]^T[M^e][R^e] \tag{10.56}$$

$$[K^e] = [R^{(e)}]^T[K^e][R^e] \tag{10.57}$$

Note that the element mass and stiffness matrices on the right-hand side of Equations (10.56) and (10.57) are those associated with zero orientation, or simply the matrices developed for the element coinciding with the horizontal (x-axis). This orientation is justified for the measurement of the orientation angle commencing from the horizontal line to the neutral axis of the beam element (CCW).

10.9 Eigenvalue Problem

Once the dynamic equations are formulated we need to solve for the eigenvalues and eigenvectors of the system. What follows are some common methods used in the solution of such problems. The actual solution procedure used to solve the eigenvalue problem is discussed, and some considerations are outlined for further study.

A very common eigenvalue problem is encountered in vibration analysis. Examining Equation (10.26) we can generalize the solution of the problem to the following form

$$k\phi = \lambda M\phi \tag{10.58}$$

The solution for the n eigenvectors and corresponding eigenvalues can be written as

$$k\phi = M\phi \Lambda \tag{10.59}$$

where the column of ϕ represents the eigenvectors whereas the eigenvalues are stored in the matrix Λ, which is a diagonal matrix listing the eigenvalues.

The eigenvalues are the roots of the characteristic polynomial,

$$p(\lambda) = \det(K - \lambda M) \tag{10.60}$$

This is easily shown in the solution of free-vibration problems, where the equations of motion are represented in a matrix as

$$M\ddot{X} + KX = 0 \tag{10.61}$$

Assuming a solution of the form

$$x = X \sin wt \tag{10.62}$$

we get

$$(-M\omega^2 + K)X = 0 \tag{10.63}$$

or simply

$$(K - \lambda_i M)X_i = 0 \tag{10.64}$$

where $\lambda = \omega^2$ and X is analogous to ϕ in Equation (10.58).

Example 10.3

Consider a linear system composed of two masses and springs interconnected to form an oscillatory system used to characterize the dynamics of a train-car model. We are interested in the solution of this problem from the point of view of learning about the frequency response and the system modes of vibration (Figure 10.8.).

The equations of motion can easily be derived using Newton's law, where we denote by x_1 and x_2 the displacements of mass 1 and 2, respectively.

$$M\ddot{x} + Kx = 0 \tag{10.65}$$

where

$$K = \begin{bmatrix} k_1 + k_2 & -k_2 \\ -k_2 & k_2 \end{bmatrix} \quad \text{and} \quad M = \begin{bmatrix} m_1 & 0 \\ 0 & m_2 \end{bmatrix}$$

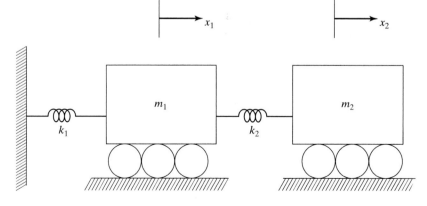

FIGURE 10.8   A two-degree of freedom mass-spring system.

Find:

    a. the eigenvalues

    b. the corresponding eigenvectors

The physical parameters have the following values: $m_1 = 9$ kg, $m_2 = 1$ kg, $k_1 = 72$ N/m, and $k_2 = 4.5$ N/m.

Solution For these values the characteristic equation

$$\det|-\omega^2 M + K| = 0$$
$$\Rightarrow m_1 m_2 \omega^4 - (m_1 k_2 + m_2 k_1 + m_2 k_2)\omega^2 + k_1 k_2 = 0$$
$$\Rightarrow \omega^4 - 13\omega^2 + 36 = (\omega^2 - 9)(\omega^2 - 4) = 0$$

so that $\omega_1{}^2 = 9$ and $\omega_2{}^2 = 4$. There are two roots, and each corresponds to two values of the constant ω in the assumed form of the solution:

$$\omega_1 = \pm 3 \text{ rad/s} \qquad \omega_2 = \pm 2 \text{ rad/s}$$

Now we need to solve for the eigenvectors corresponding to each eigenvalue. We proceed by noticing that the equations of motion reduce to

$$(-\omega_1^2 M + K)u_1 = 0$$

where u_1 denotes the vector associated with the first eigenvalue ω_1. Let such a vector u_1 be expressed in terms of its components, so we get

$$\begin{bmatrix} -\omega_1^2 m_1 + k_1 + k_2 & -k_2 \\ -k_2 & -\omega_1^2 m_2 + k_2 \end{bmatrix} \begin{bmatrix} u_{11} \\ u_{12} \end{bmatrix} = 0$$

and for ω_2 the vector u_2 satisfies

$$(-\omega_2^2 M + K)u_2 = 0$$

Similarly, the two equations and two unknowns are found from the simple relation we have derived from the assumed solution such as

$$\begin{bmatrix} -\omega_2^2 m_1 + k_1 + k_2 & -k_2 \\ -k_2 & -\omega_2^2 m_2 + k_2 \end{bmatrix} \begin{bmatrix} u_{21} \\ u_{22} \end{bmatrix} = 0$$

These expressions can be solved for the vectors u_1 and u_2, where we can see after substitution of the assumed values the above equations become:

$$\begin{bmatrix} -4.5 & -4.5 \\ -4.5 & -4.5 \end{bmatrix} \begin{bmatrix} u_{11} \\ u_{12} \end{bmatrix} = 0$$

$$\begin{bmatrix} 40.5 & -4.5 \\ -4.5 & +0.5 \end{bmatrix} \begin{bmatrix} u_{21} \\ u_{22} \end{bmatrix} = 0$$

The solution for the first mode shape vector u_1 is as follows:

$$-4.5u_{11} = 4.5u_{12} \Rightarrow \frac{u_{11}}{u_{12}} = -1$$

$$u_{11} = -1$$

$$u_{12} = 1$$

or

$$u_1 = \begin{bmatrix} -1 \\ 1 \end{bmatrix}$$

We find the second in a similar fashion to be

$$40.5u_{21} = -4.5u_{22} \Rightarrow \frac{u_{21}}{u_{22}} = \frac{1}{9},$$

Hence,

$$u_{21} = \frac{1}{9}$$

$$u_{22} = 1$$

and

$$u_2 = \begin{bmatrix} 1 \\ 1/9 \end{bmatrix}$$

End of Example 10.3

Example 10.4

Calculate the displacements of the two masses–two springs system in the previous problem for the given initial conditions $x_{10} = 1$ mm, $x_{20} = 0$, and $\dot{x}_{10} = \dot{x}_{20} = 0$.

Solution   The solution of the free vibration problem at hand can be expressed in a matrix form as follows:

$$\begin{bmatrix} x_1(t) \\ x_2(t) \end{bmatrix} = \begin{bmatrix} u_{11} & u_{21} \\ u_{12} & u_{22} \end{bmatrix} \begin{bmatrix} A_1 \sin(\omega_1 t + \phi_1) \\ A_2 \sin(\omega_2 t + \phi_2) \end{bmatrix}$$

$$= \begin{bmatrix} -A_1 \sin(3t + \phi_1) + \dfrac{1}{9} A_2 \sin(2t + \phi_2) \\ A_1 \sin(3t + \phi_1) + A_2 \sin(2t + \phi_2) \end{bmatrix}$$

At $t = 0$ this yields

$$\begin{bmatrix} 1 \\ 0 \end{bmatrix} = \begin{bmatrix} -A_1 \sin \phi_1 + \dfrac{1}{9} A_2 \sin \phi_2 \\ A_1 \sin \phi_1 + A_2 \sin \phi_2 \end{bmatrix}$$

$$1 = -A_1 \sin \phi_1 + \dfrac{1}{9} A_2 \sin \phi_2$$

$$0 = A_1 \sin \phi_1 + A_2 \sin \phi_2$$

Differentiating the above equations and evaluating them at $t = 0$ yields

$$\begin{bmatrix} \dot{x}_1(0) \\ \dot{x}_2(0) \end{bmatrix} = \begin{bmatrix} 0 \\ 0 \end{bmatrix} = \begin{bmatrix} -3A_1 \cos \phi_1 + \dfrac{2}{9} A_2 \cos \phi_2 \\ 3A_1 \cos \phi_1 + 2A_2 \cos \phi_2 \end{bmatrix}$$

$$0 = -3A_1 \cos \phi_1 + \dfrac{2}{9} A_2 \cos \phi_2$$

$$0 = 3A_1 \cos \phi_1 + 2A_2 \cos \phi_2$$

Adding the above two equations yields

$$\frac{20}{9} \cos \phi_2 = 0$$

so that $\phi_2 = \pi/2$. Because $\phi_2 = \pi/2$ the velocity equation reduces to

$$3A_1 \cos \phi_1 = 0$$

Substituting $\phi_1 = \pi/2$ in the above two equations gives

$$1 = -A_1 + \frac{1}{9} A_2 \quad \text{and} \quad 0 = A_1 + A_2$$

which has a solution of

$$A_1 = -9/10 \text{ mm}, \ A_2 = 9/10 \text{ mm}$$

Thus,

$$x_1(t) = +\frac{9}{10} \sin\left(3t + \frac{\pi}{2} \right) + \frac{1}{10} \sin\left(2t + \frac{\pi}{2} \right) = 0.9 \cos 3t + 0.1 \cos 2t \text{ mm}$$

$$x_2(t) = -\frac{9}{10} \sin\left(3t + \frac{\pi}{2} \right) + \frac{9}{10} \sin\left(2t + \frac{\pi}{2} \right) = -0.9(\cos 3t - \cos 2t) \text{ mm}$$

Above is a classic example of a two degrees-of-freedom vibration problem, where students can evaluate the mode shapes and frequencies and deduce the transient solution resulting from the solution of the free-vibration problem. We should also note how the mode shapes and frequencies contribute to the dynamic solution of lumped-mass systems, where the magnitude of vibration is dependent both on the initial conditions and the mode shapes or eigenvectors.

End of Example 10.4

10.10 Modal Analysis

Computing the eigenvalues and eigenvectors of a mechanical system can become strenuous and cumbersome if the number of degrees of freedom increases. When a system possesses a large number of degrees of freedom, the determinant of a matrix that results in the characteristic of the equations can lead to polynomial to the power $2*N$. Keep in mind that the roots of such a polynomial need to be found and the solution of N equations and N unknowns for each eigenvalue need to be resolved. To avoid such a long route a number of other methods have been developed. What follows is a modal analysis approach in extracting the eigenvalues and eigenvectors once the generalized mass and stiffness matrix are found.

Let the general equation of a free vibration system be given by

$$M\ddot{x} + Kx = 0 \tag{10.66}$$

and let the initial conditions imposed on the system be such that

$$x(0) = x_0 \quad \dot{x}(0) = \dot{x}_0$$

The steps involved in calculating the eigenvalues and eigenvectors require that we make the mass matrix an identity matrix. This is simply obtained by premultiplying the equations of motion above by the inverse matrix of M. Let us assume that our mass matrix is an identity matrix; then it is easy to calculate as a first step.

1. Calculate the $M^{-1/2}$.
    Then we proceed by computing the normalized stiffness matrix.
2. Compute the $\overline{K} = M^{-1/2}KM^{-1/2}$ mass normalized stiffness matrix.
    Now we can make use of newly formulated stiffness and mass to proceed to the next step of computing the eigenvalues and eigenvectors. Let v denote the eigenvectors, then
3. Calculate the symmetric eigenvalue problem for $\widetilde{K}$ to get ω^2_i and $\mathbf{v}_i$.
    From the above step we note that the eigenvectors need to be normalized. So we proceed by performing the following task
4. Normalize $\mathbf{v}_i$ and form the matrix of eigenvectors $P = [\mathbf{v}_1 \quad \mathbf{v}_2]$.
    The mode shapes are then found making use of the mass matrix.
5. Calculate the matrix of mode shapes $S = M^{-1/2}P$ and $S^{-1} = P^T M^{1/2}$. At this point the eigenvalues and eigenvectors are completely extracted and the only thing

remaining is to develop a general solution to the free-vibration problem making use of the initial conditions.

6. Calculate the modal initial conditions: $\mathbf{r}(0) = S^{-1}\mathbf{x}_0$, $\dot{\mathbf{r}}(0) = S^{-1}\dot{\mathbf{x}}_0$
7. Substitute the components of $\mathbf{r}(0)$ and $\dot{\mathbf{r}}(0)$ into equations of solution of modal equations to get the solutions in the modal coordinates.
8. Obtain the final solution by $\mathbf{x}(t) = S\,\mathbf{r}(t)$, where S is the transformation from the modal coordinate to the generalized coordinates of the system.

To illustrate the above steps, follow Example 10.5.

Example 10.5

Calculate the solution of the n-degree-of-freedom system shown in Figure 10.9 for $n = 3$ by modal analysis. Use the values $m_1 = m_2 = m_3 = 1$ kg and $k_1 = k_2 = k_3 = 1$ N/m,

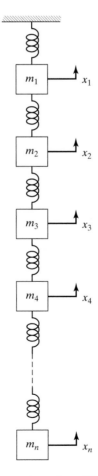

FIGURE 10.9 A mass–spring system of N degrees of freedom.

and the initial condition $x_1(0) = 1$ m with all other initial displacements and velocities zero.

Solution   The mass and stiffness matrices for $n = 3$ for the given values become

$$M\ddot{x} + Kx = 0$$

where

$$M = \begin{bmatrix} m_1 & 0 & 0 & \cdots & 0 \\ 0 & m_2 & 0 & \cdots & 0 \\ 0 & 0 & m_3 & \cdots & 0 \\ \vdots & & & \ddots & \\ 0 & 0 & 0 & \cdots & m_n \end{bmatrix}$$

$$K = \begin{bmatrix} k_1 + k_2 & -k_2 & 0 & \cdots & 0 \\ -k_2 & k_2 + k_3 & -k_3 & \cdots & 0 \\ 0 & -k_3 & k_3 + k_4 & \cdots & 0 \\ \vdots & & & \ddots & -k_{n-1} \\ 0 & 0 & 0 & -k_{n-1} & k_n \end{bmatrix}$$

$$M = I \qquad K = \begin{bmatrix} 2 & -1 & 0 \\ -1 & 2 & -1 \\ 0 & -1 & 1 \end{bmatrix}$$

Following the steps outlined in the modal analysis procedure we get

1. $M^{-\frac{1}{2}} = I$

2. $\overline{K} = M^{-\frac{1}{2}} K M^{-\frac{1}{2}} = I \begin{bmatrix} 2 & -1 & 0 \\ -1 & 2 & -1 \\ 0 & -1 & 1 \end{bmatrix} I = \begin{bmatrix} 2 & -1 & 0 \\ -1 & 2 & -1 \\ 0 & -1 & 1 \end{bmatrix}$

3. $\det(\lambda I - \overline{K}) = \det\left(\begin{bmatrix} \lambda - 2 & 1 & 0 \\ 1 & \lambda - 2 & 1 \\ 0 & 1 & \lambda - 1 \end{bmatrix} \right)$

    $= (\lambda - 2)\det\left(\begin{bmatrix} \lambda - 2 & 1 \\ 1 & \lambda - 1 \end{bmatrix} \right)$

    $-1 \det\left(\begin{bmatrix} 1 & 1 \\ 0 & \lambda - 1 \end{bmatrix} \right) + 0 \det\left(\begin{bmatrix} 1 & \lambda - 2 \\ 0 & 1 \end{bmatrix} \right)$

    $= (\lambda - 2)[(\lambda - 2)(\lambda - 1) - 1] - 1[\lambda - 1 - 0]$

    $= (\lambda - 1)(\lambda - 2)^2 - (\lambda - 2) - \lambda + 1$

    $= \lambda^3 - 5\lambda^2 + 6\lambda - 1 = 0$

The roots of this cubic equation are

$$\lambda_1 = 0.1981 \quad \lambda_2 = 1.5550 \quad \lambda_3 = 3.2470$$

Thus, the system's natural frequencies are

$$\omega_1 = 0.445 \quad \omega_2 = 1.247 \quad \omega_3 = 1.8019$$

To calculate the first eigenvector, substitute $\lambda_1 = 0.1981$ into $(\overline{K} - \lambda I)v_1 = 0$ and solve for the vector $v_1 = [v_1 \quad v_2 \quad v_3]^T$. This yields

$$\begin{bmatrix} 2 - 0.1981 & -1 & 0 \\ -1 & 2 - 0.1981 & -1 \\ 0 & -1 & 1 - 0.1981 \end{bmatrix} \begin{bmatrix} v_{11} \\ v_{21} \\ v_{31} \end{bmatrix} = \begin{bmatrix} 0 \\ 0 \\ 0 \end{bmatrix}$$

Multiplying out this last expression yields three equations, only two of which are independent:

$$(1.8019)v_{11} - v_{21} = 0$$
$$-v_{11} + (1.8019)v_{21} - v_{31} = 0$$
$$-v_{21} + (0.8019)v_{31} = 0$$

Solving the first and third equations yields

$$v_{11} = 0.4450v_{31} \quad \text{and} \quad v_{21} = 0.8019v_{31}$$

The second equation is dependent and does not yield any new information. Substituting these values into the vector v_1 yields

$$v_1 = v_{31} \begin{bmatrix} 0.445 \\ 0.8019 \\ 1 \end{bmatrix}$$

4. Normalizing the vector yields

$$v_1^T v_1 = v_{31}^2 [(0.4450)^2 + (0.8019)^2 + 1^2] = 1$$

Solving for v_{31} and substituting back into the expression for v_1 yields the normalized version of the eigenvector v_1 as

$$v_1 = \begin{bmatrix} 0.3280 \\ 0.5910 \\ 0.7370 \end{bmatrix}$$

Similarly, v_2 and v_3 can be calculated and normalized to be

$$v_2 = \begin{bmatrix} -0.7370 \\ -0.3280 \\ 0.5910 \end{bmatrix} \quad v_3 = \begin{bmatrix} -0.5910 \\ 0.7370 \\ -0.3280 \end{bmatrix}$$

The matrix P is then given by

$$P = \begin{bmatrix} 0.3280 & -0.7370 & -0.10 \\ 0.5910 & -0.3280 & 0.7370 \\ 0.7370 & 0.5910 & -0.3280 \end{bmatrix}$$

5. The matrix $S = M^{-\frac{1}{2}}P = \dfrac{1}{2}IP$ or

$$S = \begin{bmatrix} 0.1640 & -0.3685 & -0.2955 \\ 0.2955 & -0.1640 & 0.3685 \\ 0.3685 & 0.2955 & -0.1640 \end{bmatrix}$$

and

$$S^{-1} = P^{T}M^{\frac{1}{2}} = 2P^{T}I = \begin{bmatrix} 0.6560 & 1.1820 & 1.4740 \\ -1.4740 & -0.6560 & 1.1820 \\ -1.1820 & 1.4740 & -0.6560 \end{bmatrix}.$$

6. The initial conditions in modal coordinates become

$$r(0) = S^{1}x_0 = S^{-1}0 = 0$$

and

$$r(0) = S^{-1}x_0 = \begin{bmatrix} 0.6560 & 1.1820 & 1.4740 \\ -1.4740 & -0.6560 & 1.1820 \\ -1.1820 & 1.4740 & -0.6560 \end{bmatrix}\begin{bmatrix} 1 \\ 0 \\ 0 \end{bmatrix} = \begin{bmatrix} 0.6560 \\ -1.4740 \\ -1.1820 \end{bmatrix}$$

7. The modal solutions are each of the form given by

$$r_1(t) = (0.6560)\sin\left(0.4450t + \frac{\pi}{2}\right) = 0.6560\cos(0.4450t)$$

$$r_2(t) = (-1.4740)\sin\left(1.247t + \frac{\pi}{2}\right) = -1.4740\cos(1.2470t)$$

$$r_3(t) = (-1.1820)\sin\left(1.8019t + \frac{\pi}{2}\right) = -1.1820\cos(1.8019t)$$

End of Example 10.5

PROBLEMS

10.1. Consider a uniform beam of cross section area A and length l be subject to an axial loading force of 100N.

   a. Find the axial deformation at midpoint.
   b. If the force is changed to a sinusoidal force 100Sin2t, what is the axial deformation at the midpoint of the beam?

10.2. Develop the general mass matrix for N elements for cantilever beam with cross-section area A and length l.

10.3. For Example 10.1, find the coefficients of the mass matrix M_{22}, M_{33}.

10.4. The displacement field can be expressed as a function of shape functions such as

$$u(x, t) = \sum_{i=1}^{w} N(x)q(t)$$

In the case of a bending beam fixed at one end and free at the other,

   a. Find the corresponding shape functions.
   b. Derive the mass matrix for element M_{11} and M_{12}.
   c. How does answer to question (b) differ from that of Example 10.1?

10.5. Find the natural frequencies of the L4-L5 segment of the spine in the axial dissection if the vertebrae are represented by 2D rectangular plates as shown in Figure P10.1.

$E = 10^6$ kPa $m = 0.25$ kg

$E_1 = 4500$ kPa $\rho = 0.1$ kg

$A = A_1 = 176.7$ mm^2 $l = 50$ mm

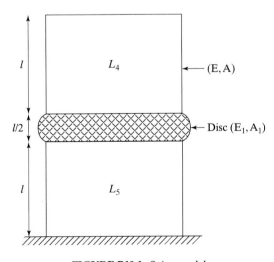

FIGURE P10.1 Spine model.

10.6. Consider the support on which the spine rests to be a continuous stiffness and damper to a platform of negligible mass (Figure P10.2). The support excitation is a harmonic function.

  a. Develop the equations of motion in the axial direction for the spinal model.
  b. Solve for the maximum displacement of the spine.

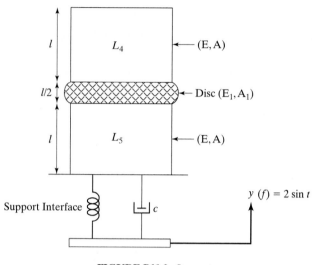

FIGURE P10.2 Support.

10.7. Let the spinal column be represented by a lumped mass model as shown in Figure P10.3.

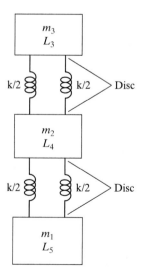

FIGURE P10.3 Spinal column represented by a lumped mass.

   a. Find the mass matrix.
   b. Find the global stiffness matrix for the boundary condition shown.
   c. Extract the natural frequencies due to axial deformation.

10.8. Rework problem 10.7 considering 5 elements, two discs and three vertebras.

10.9. For the clamped-clamped beam shown in Figure P10.4:

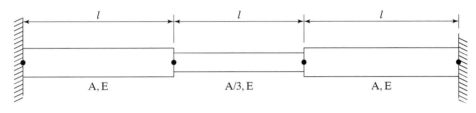

   l   *l*   *l*

   A, E   A/3, E   A, E

FIGURE P10.4 Beam.

   a. Find the mass matrix of the beam under flexion using finite element method.
   b. Build the stiffness matrix.
   c. Use the method of nodal analysis described in Example 10.5 to compute the natural frequency due to bending.

10.10. Determine the frequency equation for the two span beams (Figure P10.5) fixed at both ends and simply supported at midspan using finite element method.

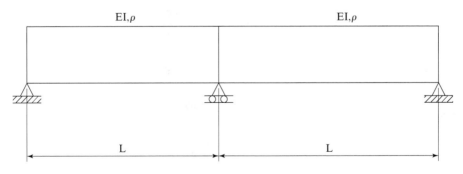

   EI,ρ EI,ρ

        L   L

FIGURE P10.5 Two span beams.

10.11. A cantilever beam carries a mass m at the free end as shown in Figure P10.6. Derive the mass and stiffness matrix for 2 and 3 elements. How does m affect the computation of the natural frequencies?

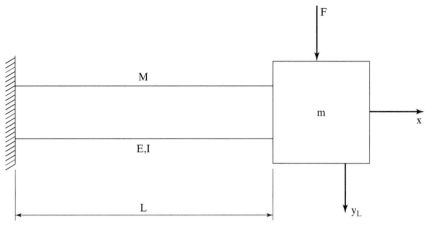

FIGURE P10.6 A cantilever beam.

BIBLIOGRAPHY

Argyris, J. H. (1955). "Energy Theorems in Structural Analysis," *Aircraft Engineering*. Vol. 27.

Argyris, J. H., and Kelsey, S. (1960). *Energy Theorems in Structural Analysis*. London, England: Butterworth.

Bathe, K.J. (1982). *Finite Element Procedures in Engineering Analysis*. Englewood Cliffs, NJ: Prentice-Hall.

Cook, R.D. (1981). *Concepts and Applications of Finite Element Analysis*. New York: John Wiley.

Courant R. (1943). "Variational Method for the Solution of Problems of Equilibrium and Vibrations," *Bulletin of the American Mathematical Society*. Vol. 49.

Craig, R. (1981). *Structural Dynamics—An Introduction to Computer Methods*. New York: John Wiley.

Fertis, D.G. (1984). *Dynamics and Vibration of Structures* (rev. ed.). Malabar, FL: Robert E. Krieger Publishing Co.

Fertis, D.G. (1988). *Nonlinear Mechanics*. Boca Raton FL: CRC Press.

Hurty, W. (1965). "Dynamic Analysis of Structural Systems Using Component Modes," *AIAA Journal*. Vol. 3: No. 4.

James, M.L., Smith, G.M., Wolford, J.C., and Whaley, P.W. (1989). *Vibration of Mechanical and Structural Systems with Microcomputer Applications*. New York: Harper & Row.

Martin, H.C., and Carey, G.F. (1973). *Introduction to Finite Element Analysis Theory and Application*. New York: McGraw-Hill.

Pestel, C.C., and Leckie, F.A. (1963). *Matrix Methods in Elastomechanics*. New York: McGraw-Hill.

Timoshenko S., and Woinosky-Krieger, S. (1959). *Theory of Plates and Shells* (2nd ed.). New York: McGraw-Hill.

Turner M.J., Clough R.W., Martin H.L., and Top L.J. (1956). "Stiffness and Deflection Analysis of Complex Structures," *Journal of Aeronautical Sciences*. Vol. 23: No. 9.

Weaver, W., and Johnson, P.R. (1987). *Structural Dynamics by Finite Elements*. Englewood Cliffs, NJ: Prentice Hall.

Yang, T.Y. (1986). *Finite Element Structural Analysis*. Englewood Cliffs, NJ: Prentice Hall.

CHAPTER 11

Industrial Robotics

A robot is a reprogrammable, multifunctional manipulator designed to move material, parts, tools or specialized devices through variable programmed motions for the performance of a variety of tasks.

The Robot Institute of America

11.1 Introduction

In today's highly competitive markets, more and more companies are pressed to deliver quality products at low prices. To meet such a challenge, a number of companies are turning to computer-based automation and computer-integrated manufacturing. The high costs associated with conventional manufacturing techniques and their task limitations have opened the door for the use of robots.

Historically, robots have fascinated many of us because of their capabilities to emulate human beings. Although our perceptions of robots are still far from being realistic, we are beginning to feel their impact on industrial technology, especially in the field of space exploration.

The concept of a robot can be traced back to ancient Egypt, but its industrial utility began in the 1950s when teleoperators were developed to handle radioactive materials. These were the so-called master–slave manipulators, in which an operator used the master and, through a window, saw how the slave manipulator duplicated the task.

It was not until the early 1960s that the first industrial robot was built in the United States. The initial use of robots was hampered by economics and hardware. The operational cost for robots was in the range of $9 an hour, compared to the average hourly wage of a worker at that time of about $5 an hour. In addition, the technology was limited to a few applications.

In the mid-1970s, robots were used in a wider range of applications. This was due in particular to the development of microprocessors. Increasingly, robots began to be used in manufacturing operations. Furthermore, there was an increased awareness that for well-defined repetitive operations, robots could outperform human operators.

In the 1980s, workers' hourly wages increased to about $20 an hour, whereas the hourly wages of operating robots didn't change much (Figure 11.1).

Robots became more sophisticated and reliable, factors that have driven a number of industrial sectors to implement them in their manufacturing operations. The automotive industry accounts for about 55% of the robots in operation in the United States. They are used on the assembly line and perform a variety of tasks usually done by skilled operators. The tasks range from pick and place, welding, and pointing to the placement of engine blocks in cars. Today's manufacturing cells are designed around the capabilities of robot speed and reach and they are becoming an essential element of manufacturing processes. The benefits robots offer are numerous and include:

- Increased productivity
- Reduced labor costs
- Effective equipment utilization
- Utilization in hazardous environments
- Improved quality
- Handsome returns on investment
- Improved flexibility
- Short lead times
- Improved competitive positions

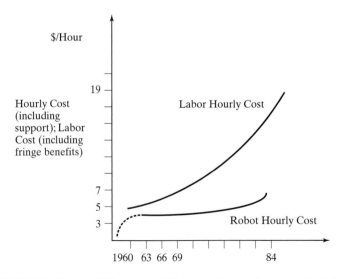

FIGURE 11.1 History of labor cost and Unimate robot cost in automotive industry.

The primary applications for industrial robots in the United States are in manufacturing areas for automobiles and electrical machinery, where welding and material handling are the primary tasks. In addition, robots are increasingly being used for die casting, investment casting, forging, press work, spray painting and surface treatment, foundries, plastic molding, and loading and unloading of machine tools.

In this chapter, the basic concepts of different robot configurations are presented, together with the programs, features, and different options they possess.

11.2 Configuration of a Robot

The basic components of a robot are the manipulator, the controller, and the power supply. Today's robots come with additional options such as minicomputers or microcomputers as storage and control devices and external sensors such as digital vision, force sensors, transducers, tactile sensors, and effectors.

11.2.1 The Manipulator

The manipulator consists of "arm" and "wrist," both of which are mounted on a support stand. The workspace, or volume of the robot, is the volume in which the arm and wrist subassembly unit can travel at any point. Mechanically, robot manipulators can be classified into the following types.

Rectangular or Cartesian Robots. For these robots, all motions are done in translation along three linear orthogonal axes (Figure 11.2). This type of robot is referred to as the "pick and place" robot. The base axis of the Cartesian system can be extended to enlarge the working volume of the robot.

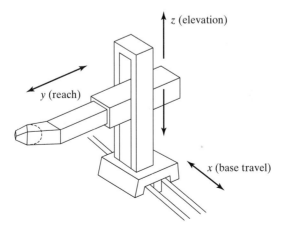

FIGURE 11.2 Robot in a Cartesian coordinate system.

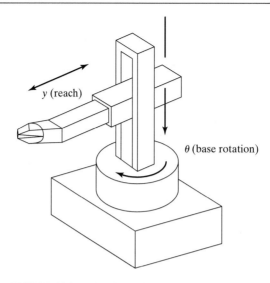

FIGURE 11.3 Robot in a cylindrical coordinate system.

Cylindrical Robots.   These robots consist of two linear orthogonal translations and a base rotation (Figure 11.3). The base rotary motion can provide rapid positioning. The maximum and minimum reach of the horizontal axis determine the maximum and minimum workspace of the robot.

Spherical Robots.   Spherical robots have two rotations and one translation (Figure 11.4). They have the lowest weight and shortest joint travel for most robots. The linear axis forms the radius of the workspace (sphere).

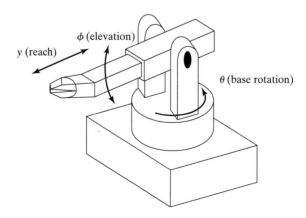

FIGURE 11.4 Robot in a spherical coordinate system.

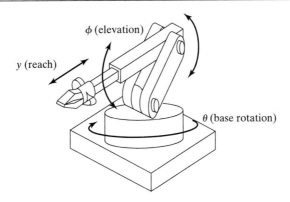

FIGURE 11.5   Robot with revolute joints.

Revolute or Articulated Robots.   These robots use a series of rotary motions similar to those performed by human arms (Figure 11.5). They have the flexibility to reach under or over an object.

11.2.2 The Controller

The control unit is the "brains of the robot." The basic function of the controller is to direct the motion of the end effector in terms of position and orientation. It works in a fashion similar to the control unit in numerically controlled (NC) machine. Thus, robots can also be classified by their method of control.

The control unit is equipped with different controllers to perform point-to-point operations or continuous path motion. The most common controllers found in industrial robotic systems are as follows.

Point-to-Point (PTP) Robots.   Also known as nonservo robots, these are used mostly in pick-and-place operations. The controller sends signals to the manipulator's actuators and controls, which in turn articulate the manipulator's arms to perform the desired task. The control unit's functions include the conversion of secondary programs into machine language to generate the appropriate pulses to drive the motors. PTP robots have fewer than six degrees of freedom and are capable of stopping at several different programmed positions, although their path between the programmed points cannot be specified. The advantages of these robots include speed of operation, accuracy, and reliability. The drawback is the limited tasks they can perform.

Continuous-Path Controlled Robots.   Also known as "walk-through" continuous-path robots, these emulate a human operator in performing operations such as painting and welding. The controlled path is achieved by the human operator's hand leading the end effector through the desired path, which is stored as digitized information in the computer.

When played back the generated program gives the same motion. Hence, in programming the operator's hand motion, the path and the speed of execution are essentially defined. One last note on the walk-through method and why the end effector must be manually driven to create the desired path of motion: Essentially, tasks like welding vary from one application to another and programming them efficiently is expensive. Hence, duplicating an experienced welder is faster and more economical.

The point-to-point motion controller is based on an open loop and the controlled robot uses the closed loop type of feedback controller. The latter requires more tooling and hence is the most expensive option a robot can have.

Controlled-Path Robots. These robots have the most sophisticated level of motion control. Given a few intermediate points, a smooth path is generated by the computer using mathematical tools such as cubic splines. They generally have six degrees of freedom and are capable of straight-line and arc interpolated motion and continuous paths.

11.2.3 The Power Supply

There are three types of power sources: electric, pneumatic, and hydraulic. The characteristics of each are discussed here.

Electric Drives. Direct-current (dc) servo and stepper motors are the two main types of electric drives used in robotic applications. These dc motors can provide high torques in small volumes and they are precise, clean, and reliable. The torque produced is proportional to the magnitude and direction of current flow in the rotating armature. The electrical energy is converted to mechanical energy.

As costs decrease and technological improvements take place, dc servo motors will be the principal drives for robotic applications.

The dc stepper motors are driven by a sequence of electric pulses and the number of pulses directly controls the portion of the motor in an open-loop fashion. These motors are used for less sophisticated robotic applications. They are larger than servo motors and have limited performance capabilities.

The advantages of electric drives include

- low cost
- reduced floor space
- high accuracy and repeatability
- easy maintenance

Pneumatic Drives. These are the simplest to design and cost less than other drives. However, they are used in less sophisticated robotic applications like pick-and-place and quick-assembly operations. Because air is easily compressible, these robots are difficult to position and control. Hence, they have low accuracy and poor repeatability.

The advantages of pneumatic drives include

- low operating cost
- low maintenance
- quick assembly

Hydraulic Drives. These were the primary sources of power in earlier robots. They have the greatest strength because they produce the greatest power in the smallest volume. However, they are very noisy, take up a large space, and have high maintenance costs.

The advantages of hydraulic drives include

- high speed
- highest power-to-weight ratio
- design simplicity
- good physical strength

11.3   Programming Robots

The controller is the part of the robot that initiates and terminates the motion of the manipulator. It stores position and sequence data in memory and communicates with the outside world.

There are two ways of programming the controller to accomplish these functions: online programming and offline programming.

11.3.1 Online Programming

The process of programming the controller by online programming is known as "teaching" the robot. The process of teaching involves reaching, editing, and replaying the desired path. In the teaching mode, the robot is manually led through a desired sequence of motions by the operator. The movement information and other necessary data are recorded by the controller as the robot is guided through the desired sequence. Online programming can be carried out by two techniques: manual teaching and lead-through programming.

Manual Teaching. This is normally done by means of a portable hand-held programming unit that contains a number of buttons and joysticks used to direct the controller in moving the robot to different locations. Subsequently, every move is saved in memory so that a file of motion is created that can be replayed by the robot (Figure 11.6). Manual teaching is used to program nonservo robots.

Lead-Through Programming. In this technique, the operator grasps the manipulator and leads it through the tasks or motions, simultaneously recording the positions (Figure 11.7). Lead-through programming is used for operations such as spray painting, arc welding, and other complex motion trajectories.

Lead-through programming is the most widely used method to program a robot. It is the most natural way of programming the controller to make the robot perform required tasks. During the programming, the speed of the robot can be controlled, enabling the programming to be carried out safely. At the same time, the operator can coordinate the robot's motion with other equipment with which the robot has to interact. This type

FIGURE 11.6 Use of a teach box in manual programming of the PUMA robot. (Courtesy of Staubli & Unimation, Inc., Duncan, SC.)

of programming does not require special skills and can be performed with ease and speed. Repetitive program sequences can be stored in memory for future recall. The only disadvantage is the loss of valuable production time while programming is being carried out. Lead-through programming is used with point-to-point servo robots.

11.3.2 Offline Programming

Programming a robot by programming languages does not require the robot's participation. The major benefit of explicit programming languages is that external data such as sensor feedback can easily be used. Programming languages reduce robot downtime and make the interface with other machines simpler.

Currently, considerable research is going on in offline programming methods and their implementation. The increased sophistication in controllers, sensors, and other hardware makes offline programming even more feasible. Unlike online programming, the offline method requires the programmer to have some knowledge of programming and of the design of the robotic sensor-based motion strategies. It is apparent that

FIGURE 11.7 Lead-through programming. (Courtesy of ESAB Automation, Hanover, PA)

some difficulties arise when developing a generalized programming system adaptable to all robotic systems.

Some offline programming systems currently in use are VAL, SIGLA, GEOMAP, ROBEX, RAPT, CATIA, AL, ANIMATE/PLACE, GRASP, and AUTO PASS.

11.4 Programming Languages

The programming of NC machines led to a higher-level programming language used for robot motive controls. The first robot-level programming language was developed at the Massachusetts Institute of Technology (MIT) by Heinrich A. Ernst in 1961 and was called the "Mechanical Hand Interpreter," or MHI. It is modeled around guarded moves; that is, the hand moves until a sensor detects a particular situation. A program contains commands like "move" to indicate direction and speed, "until" to test a sensor, "if continue" to continue the program if desired conditions are met, and "of goto" to indicate logical branching.

In 1973, Silver developed the nest program called MINI at MIT. This language was an extension of LISP; however, the major limitation of this language was its inability to control robotic joints dependently.

WAVE was another general-purpose programming language developed by R.F. Paul in 1977 at the Stanford Artificial Intelligence Laboratory (Paul, 1981). It was modeled using the assembly language POP-10 and it had the ability to specify the robotic joint and hand compliance.

Further research in software for robotic control resulted in languages such as VAL, developed by B.E. Shimano and Unimation Inc. in 1980 and 1983, and EMILY, ML, and AML developed at IBM in 1979. Recently, AMML/E was developed, which is based on AML and is for IBM PCs or compatibles.

All the robotic programming languages can be classified under a five-level classification scheme based on the abilities of their problem-solving methodologies. Table 11.1 illustrates such classification levels of robotic programming languages. The functions of a Level 4 structured programming language are shown in Figure 11.9.

The heart of a structured programming language is its logic in the form of program control (Figure 11.8). The impression of robot intelligence is created by the combination of program control with various functions. In the Level 4 language, the user provides each robot task with a control algorithm executed by the robot controller.

Level 5 is the ideal level because it virtually eliminates all the tedious programming steps concerned with the details of a particular task. This level of programming relies on vision sensors and built-in artificial-intelligence functions. It is still at the research level, and robots equipped with such programs are not commercially available.

The major difference among these programming languages is their level of sophistication in detecting and using external sensor information. The more sophisticated languages can interface with a variety of external sensors and are capable of updating the position of stored precision points based on various sensory inputs. Thus, more sophisticated languages allow continual robot performance in the presence of uncertainty and environmental changes.

TABLE 11.1   Human Intelligence Levels of Robotic Programming Languages

Level 5 Task-oriented level	AUTOPASS, LAMA
Level 4 Structured programming level	AL, AML, HELP, RAPT, RAIL, PAL ROBEX, MCL, MAPEX
Level 3 Primitive-motion level	AML/E, EMILY, RCL, RPL, PRBE, SIGLE, VAL,
Level 2 Point-to-point level	ANORAD
Level 1 Microcomputer level	T3, FUNKY

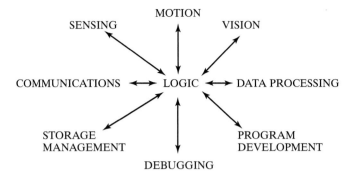

FIGURE 11.8 Program control using logic.

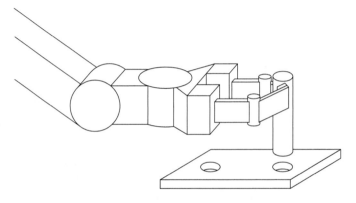

FIGURE 11.9 Insertion of a peg in a hole by a robot.

Let us illustrate a typical robot operation that has been programmed in VAL, a well-known commercial language. VAL closely resembles the BASIC computer language; it is a user-friendly interpreted language that can handle most of today's robotic applications.

Example 11.1   VAL Program to Move Objects

The following program, called PALLET, is used to sequentially move nine objects from a three-row, three-column pallet to a location called MACH. The program is composed of two points, the main program and a subroutine SUB. As with any program, all variables must be defined prior to execution.

```
PROGRAM PALLET
I.  SET HOLE= CORNER
2. SETI COL = 0
100 SETI ROW = 0
```

```
200 GOSUB PALLET.SUB
5. SHIFT HOLE BY 50.00, 0.00,0.00
6. SET I ROW = ROW + 1
7. IF ROW LT 3 THEN 200
8. SHIFT HOLE BY = 150.00, 50.00, 0.00
9. SET I COL = COL + 1
10. IF COL LT 3 THEN 100
.END
PROGRAM PALLET.SUB
1. OPEN I 0.00
2. APPROS HOLE, 100.00
3. MOVES HOLE,
4. CLOSEI0.00
5. DEPART 50.00
6. APPROS MACH,50.00
7. MOVES MACH,
8. OPENI 0.00
9. DEPART 50.00 10. RETURN 0
END
```

In this program, the specific corner and MACH locations represent two precise points that can be identified by a lead-through operation prior to task execution. The numerical distances are specified in millimeters and the I associated with SETI, OPENI, and CLOSEI commands denotes an immediate operation. APPROS denotes a straight-line approach to position the gripper 100 mm directly above each object prior to a straight-line move to the object (MOVES HOLE). Subsequently, the grasp function is defined by CLOSEI 0.00. The implementation of this program on a PUMA 560 robot takes less than 1 min to complete, depending on the distance between MACH and CORNER and the selected speed.

End of Example 11.1

Example 11.2   A Peg-in-Hole Insertion Program in AML

To illustrate the procedure of programming a robot, a program written in AML language for peg insertion in a hole is given below.

```
PICKUP: SUBR(PART
DATA,TRIES);
        MOVE(GRIPPER
DIAMETER(PART2DATA)+0.2);
        MOVE(<1,2,3>,XYZ-POSITION(PAKT-DATA) +<0,0,1>);
        TRY
```

```
                    PICKUP(PART
                    DATA,TRIES);
                    END;
                 TRY-PICKUP:SUBR(PART-DATA,TRIES);
                        IF TRIES LT I THEN RETURN('NO PART');
                        DMOVE(3,=1.0);
                        IF GRASP(DIAMETER(PART-DATA)='NO PART'
                        THEN TRY-PICKUP(PART-DATA,TRIES-1);
                        END;
                 GRASP:SUBR(DIAMETER,F);
                        FMONS:NEW APPLY ($MONITOR, PINCH-FORCE(F));
                        MOVE (GRIPPER,O,FMONS)
                        RETURN (IF QPOSITION-(GRIPPER)LE DIAMETER/2
                        THEN 'NO PART'
                        ELSE 'PART');
                        END;
                 INSERT: SUBR(PART-DATA,HOLE);
                        FMONS: NEW APPLY (SMONITOR, TIP-FORCE(LANDINGFORCE));
                        MOVE(<1,2,3>,HOLE + <0,0,25>);
                        DMOVE(3,= I .0. FMONS);
                        IF QMONITOR(FMONS) = 1
                        THEN RETURN ('NO HOLE');
                        MOVE(3HOLE(3) + PART-LENGTH(PART-DATA));
                        END;
                 PART-IN-HOLE:SUBR(PART-DATA,HOLE);
                        PICKUP (PART-DATA,2.);
                        INSERT (PART-DATA,HOLE); END;
```

This program was written for an IBM 7565 robotic manipulator just for testing the six degrees-of-freedom motion as well as the grip-motion and speed sensors. It moves the robot to seven different kinematic attitudes and sets the distance between the jaws of the gripper and its speed (Figure 11.9).

AML allows the user to specify motion in the joint variable space and to specify motion in Cartesian space. The MOVE command indicates the destination frame to which the arm should move. In AML, the aggregates of the form (speed, acceleration, deceleration) are added to the MOVE statement to specify speed, acceleration, and deceleration, respectively, of the robot. The predefined variable GRIPPER indicates the gripper that can be programmed to move to a certain opening. The primitive MONITOR is specified in the motion commands to detect asychronous events. The programmer specifies the sensors to monitor and specifies when they are to be triggered and motion halted. The syntax for MONITOR is MONITOR (sensors, test type, limit 1, limit2).

End of Example 11.2

11.5   Sensory System of a Robot

Sensors are for the most part used to add a degree of intelligence to robots. Without sensors, robots are unable to respond to any change in their working environment. For example, with a sensor, a robot used in a pick-and-place operation always tends to pick the desired object even if the object is moved to a different location. Serious collision problems can occur if an obstacle appears in the path of the robot gripper. These are some of the concerns of programming a robot to perform a certain task.

Robots equipped with an array of sensors possess a certain degree of artificial intelligence that allows them to operate in a changing environment by making real-time decisions that can change their course of action. The real-time decisions are based on information received from the sensors. Such robots are called "intelligent robots."

The sensory system of the robot monitors and interprets the events in the working environment. The feedback received from the environment enables the robot to react in an orderly fashion so as to comply with its objectives. A data-acquisition system uses data from the sensors to feed back into the robot-control algorithm, which in turn activates the actuators to drive the robot. Monitoring joint positions, velocities, acceleration, and gripper force is carried out by the interval measurement devices and sensors through special algorithms. A robotic gripper with built-in sensors is shown in Figure 11.10.

11.5.1   Classification of Robotic Sensors

Robotic sensors can be broadly classified into two groups: internal and external sensors.

Internal Sensors.   Internal sensors establish their configuration in their own set of coordinate axes. They measure movement, speed, acceleration, and stress. Movement sensors are of different types, either rectilinear (translational) or angular (rotational).

External Sensors.   External sensors allow the robot to position itself relative to its environment. They are classified as contact and noncontact sensors. Contact sensors can be further divided into tactile and force–torque sensors. A simple tactile sensor is a microswitch that senses the presence of barriers, obstacles, and surfaces beyond which the robot is not permitted to move. Thus, tactile sensors can be used to avoid collisions, to signal the robot system that a target was reached, or to measure object dimensions during inspection. External sensors are used for approximation, touch, geometry, vision, and safety. They usually consist of the following sensors:

- Tactile (touch) sensors
- Proximity detectors
- Force feedback devices
- Vision sensors

Tactile sensors can also be subclassified into stress sensors and touch sensors. Stress tactile sensors produce a signal indicating the magnitude and distribution of

FIGURE 11.10 A robotic gripper with built-in sensor. (Courtesy of Center for Engineering Design, University of Utah Salt Lake City, UT).

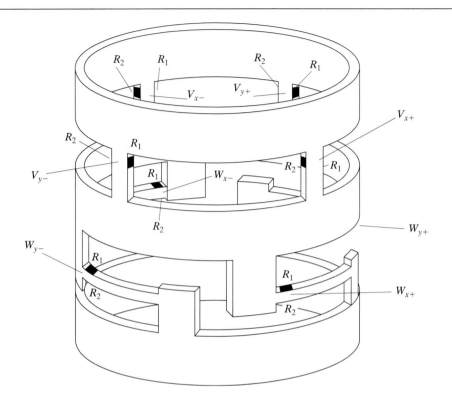

FIGURE 11.11   A six-axis sensor based on a design by SRI International (Menlo Park, CA).

contact forces; touch sensors produce a binary output signal. However, tactile sensors do not indicate the presence of objects until they come in contact with the object.

Force and torque sensors are located between the end effector and the last joint of the wrist; they measure the force and torque components by sensing deflections of the sensing element.

Force sensors generally consist of piezoelectric transducers or strain gages mounted on the compliant sections of the manipulator's end effector. They measure three components of force and three components of torque acting between the gripper and the object being held. A six-axis wrist sensor is shown in Figure 11.11. It consists of strain gages mounted on elastic beams. Strain gages are low-cost and high-resolution and have a high degree of reliability. The SRI sensor has eight elastic beams of which four are parallel to the z-axis and are labeled V_{x+}, $V_{y+}V_{x-}$, and V_{y-}. The other four beams are perpendicular to the z-axis and are labeled W_{x+}, W_{y+}, W_{x-}, and W_{y-}. Two foil strain gages, R_1, and R_2, are mounted on each of the eight beams to respond to the compressive or tensile strains generated along the axis of the beam. On beams V_{x+} and V_{x-}, gages are placed on the two faces perpendicular to the y direction. On beams V_{y+} and V_{y-}, gages are placed on the face perpendicular to the x direction. On beams

W_{x+}, W_{y+}, and W_{y-}, the gages are placed perpendicular to the z direction. The two strain groups, R_1 and R_2, are connected to a potentiometer circuit, whose output voltage is given by the name of its beam. When a peg-hole insertion task is applied, the voltages proportional to three force and three torque components acting on the wrist are given by the following linear combinations:

$$F_x = V_{y+} + V_{y-} \tag{11.1}$$

$$F_y = V_{x+} + V_{x-} \tag{11.2}$$

$$F_z = W_{x+} + W_{x-} + W_{y+} + W_{y-} \tag{11.3}$$

$$M_x = W_{y+} - W_{y-} \tag{11.4}$$

$$M_y = -W_{x+} + W_{x-} \tag{11.5}$$

$$M_z = V_{x+} - V_{x-} + V_{y+} + V_{y-} \tag{11.6}$$

Now, these six components of the force and torque are sent to the computer for processing. The computer then generates six correction signals that are sent as references to the six corresponding joints. The manipulator then moves the peg based on these signals toward the center of the hole in order to insert the peg into the hole. It is essential to have a certain degree of compliance between the grasped peg (object) and the end of the robot's wrist. When passive devices are employed, such as a remote center compliance device (RCC), the compliance is provided by the device itself. With active devices, the mechanical flexibility of the wrist plays the same role.

11.5.2 Vision Systems

Vision systems typically use a number of video cameras linked to vision processors that are capable of digitizing and processing the acquired digital information. The vision processor analyzes the image and defines the object. The major applications of vision systems are in assembly processes, quality control, part classification, and inspection. These systems are capable of screening parts that do not meet specifications; they can also detect the presence or absence of a part.

A typical robotic vision system has a video camera that is interfaced with the vision computer through a video buffer, called a "frame grabber," and a visual information preprocessor (Figure 11.12). The video signal is sent to a TV monitor and is displayed continuously for analysis. The preprocessor stores the useful information and hence reduces processing time. Upon instruction, a frozen frame from the camera is scanned row by row and the corresponding output signal is stored in the frame grabber in digital form. This digitized image is transferred to the vision computer in parallel bytes for image processing. Some of the cameras available today are the Image Orthicon Tube, Vicicon Tube, Plumbicon Tube, Charge-Coupled Device (CCD), and the Image Dissector Tube.

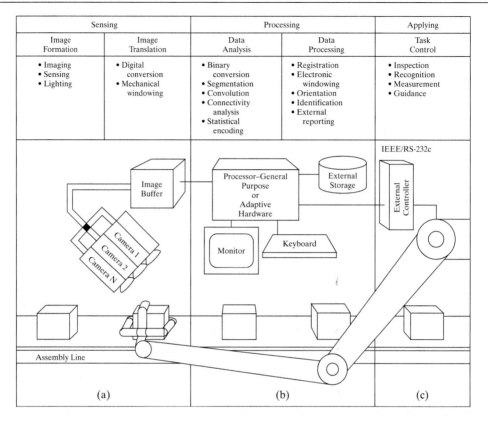

Sensing		Processing		Applying
Image Formation	Image Translation	Data Analysis	Data Processing	Task Control
• Imaging • Sensing • Lighting	• Digital conversion • Mechanical windowing	• Binary conversion • Segmentation • Convolution • Connectivity analysis • Statistical encoding	• Registration • Electronic windowing • Orientation • Identification • External reporting	• Inspection • Recognition • Measurement • Guidance

FIGURE 11.12 Three parts of the machine vision process. For an assembly-line robot, for example, there is (a) sensor consisting of a camera and translator, (b) an image-data processor to perform both analysis and processing, and (c) an external controller for application development. (Courtesy of Pattern Processing Technologies Inc.).

11.5.3 Other Sensors

A range sensor/detector can provide precise measurement of the distance between the object and the sensor itself. A range detector measures the distance from a reference point, on the sensor itself, and a point on the object using the principle of beam triangulation. The distance is measured by measuring the time taken for the last beam to travel to the object and back again. The triangular principle that is used is shown in Figure 11.13.

The sensor consists of a light source and an array of light-sensitive elements. These photosensors are scanned to detect the one that has the maximum output signal. If X is the distance of the ith light detector, then by using the two similar triangles, it can be shown that

$$Y = \frac{ZH}{X_i - Z}$$

where Y is the distance of the object from the range detector.

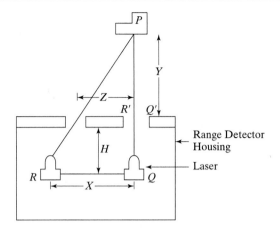

FIGURE 11.13   Principle of beam triangulation.

11.6   Fundamentals of Gripper Design

The end effector of a robotic manipulator is connected to the end link through the wrist. In most gripper designs, the wrist is equipped with three possible rotations. These motions along the rotary axis are called roll, pitch, and yaw. A wrist with the three rotary motions is shown in Figure 11.14. Roll is rotation in a plane perpendicular to the end of the arm, pitch is rotation in the vertical plane, and yaw is rotation in the horizontal plane.

Various parameters have to be considered to design a wrist. The design requirements also depend greatly on the application of the robot.

A wrist is usually designed as a low-power, high-torque type of device. Because the wrist does not move far and fast, its power requirements are low. However, forces and moments transmitted through the wrist can be nearly as large as those transmitted through the robotic arm. Physical control, which can be electronic, pneumatic, hydraulic, or mechanical, is also an important aspect in designing grippers and manipulators. Pneumatics was the major method of physical control for powering manipulators and

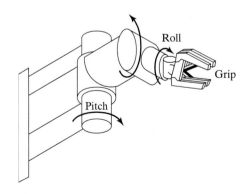

FIGURE 11.14   Details of robotic wrist articulation.

grippers in early robots. Now, with advances in microprocessor technology, electronic control has become more feasible and affordable. Mathematical algorithms were developed in parallel to predict and finally generate the optimal control mechanism for driving the manipulators and grippers. The ability of a gripper to grasp parts in a stable manner in space and to provide feedback on the amount of force that is being applied on the object is a major consideration for certain robot tasks. Feedback is provided through sensors.

The most common robot applications are pick and place, welding, and spray painting. These applications usually do not require great emphasis on the interaction between the objects and the robot end effectors, or grippers. Therefore, sensing is limited to simple feedback measuring the end-effector position with the loop of operation. A primary concern in the design and control of grippers for complex tasks is the constant monitoring of the force stimuli during the course of a particular motion. Therefore, the ability of a robotic manipulator to react to contact forces and tactile stimuli defines its so-called compliance. As technology evolves, more-complex manufacturing processes will be done by robotic manipulators equipped with sensors that allow a certain controllability of its compliance to account for external contact forces that are unaccounted for. Generally, compliance is either passive or programmed into the robot control system. The passive one is inherent from the robot's structure such as its material properties.

It is essential to determine the mechanism responsible for compliant motion. Compliant motion is attained by deriving the proper mathematical relationships between the forces interacting between the robot and its contacting environment. Once these contact forces are established, predictions of the robot's response can be analyzed. Usually, it is assumed that contact forces cause local deformation at the points of contact; hence, relationships between forces and displacements can be established.

If we assume that the deformation is denoted by u, then

$$f = ku$$

represents the linear relationship between the contact forces f and displacements u through the stiffness matrix k. The inverse of k is the mechanical compliance matrix, say, c. Hence,

$$u = cf$$

Using sensors, we can determine f, and knowing the mechanical compliance c, we can compute u, which in turn can be used to read just the position of the gripper (end effector).

The versatility of the human hand is unattainable in the robot gripper design. The precision by which the hand can perform certain tasks like inserting a pen into a hollow and the handling of fragile objects is one that we would like to achieve in gripper design. Those tasks that qualify as simple and require minimum effort by humans are more complicated and require much more sophisticated motion control from robots.

Precision and flexibility of the gripper can become conflicting requirements, although both are desirable. Multijointed fingers of a mechanical hand give it an enormous flexibility for manipulating objects. However, controlling the motion of such a system has yet to be fully exploited.

Most of the active hands built to date have anthropomorphic designs with several jointed fingers. However, fingers sometimes are not required to manipulate grasped

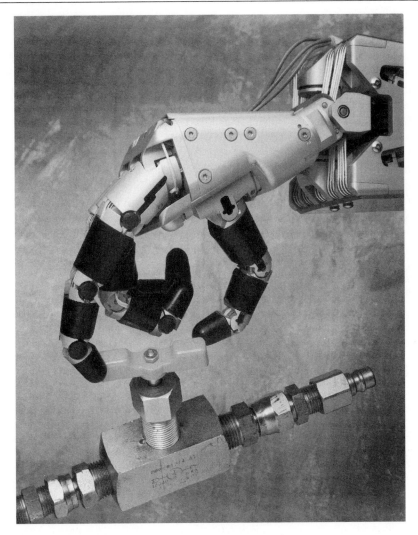

FIGURE 11.15 Utah MIT hand. (Courtesy of Center for Engineering Design, University of Utah, Salt Lake City, UT.)

objects. Nonanthropomorphic mechanical hands (grippers) can manipulate objects in up to five degrees of freedom using rotating belts. The advantage of fingers in a hand seems to be less for manipulation than for grasping. Fingers are open kinematic chains, like manipulator arms, that form closed loops when grasping or holding. Unlike manipulators, which can have mounted actuators and motors to perform their articulation, fingers are usually small and require smaller and more precise motors. Most of the current hand design relies on cables and pulleys driven by actuator motors mounted on the arm (Figure 11.15).

11.7   Positioning a Robot in Space

Consider a three-link planar manipulator, as shown in Figure 11.16, with three revolute joints at O_1, O_2, and O_3. The local axes are defined as those associated with each link. They form a set of orthogonal axes; for simplicity in the figure, the x_i $(i = 1, 2, 3)$ ordinates are along the control axis of each link. Each local axis is fixed to the particular link and moves with it as it articulates. On the other hand, the global axes x, y, and z are defined as the base references fixed in an inertia frame.

We want to describe the position of each link and the end point of the terminal link in most cases with respect to the global reference frame. Recall from Chapter 4 that transformation matrices were used to describe the relationship between manipulated objects. In this context of robotic motion, we will use them to relate points described in the local axes to the global one. For instance, point O_2 in the local axes (x, y, z) is defined by $(1, 0, 0)$, whereas in the global frame, its components are $(l_1 \cos \theta, l_1 \sin \theta, 0)$. It is obvious that a rotation about the z-axis of the local axes (x_1, y_1, z_1) clockwise by θ_1, will make it coincide with the global axes x, y, and z. We can then write the following:

$$[l_1 \cos \Theta_1 \quad l_1 \sin \Theta_1 \quad 0] = [l_1 \quad 0 \quad 0] \begin{bmatrix} \cos \theta_1 & \sin \theta_1 & 0 \\ -\sin \theta_1 & \cos \theta_1 & 0 \\ 0 & 0 & 1 \end{bmatrix}$$

$$\underbrace{\hphantom{[l_1 \cos \Theta_1 \quad l_1 \sin \Theta_1 \quad 0]}}_{\substack{\text{Position in the} \\ \text{global frame}}} \quad \underbrace{\hphantom{[l_1 \quad 0 \quad 0]}}_{\substack{\text{Position in the} \\ \text{local frame}}}$$

(11.9)

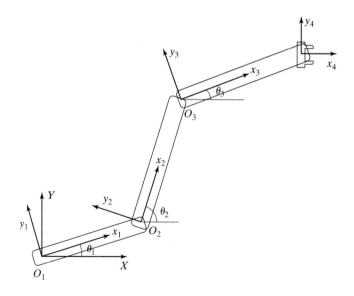

FIGURE 11.16   Three-link manipulator with end effector.

In compact form, this relationship is expressed as

$$^1PR = {}^GP$$

where ^1P denotes the position of a point in the local axes, here chosen to be the origin of link 2 (O_2), and ^GP represents the point position in the global frame.

Similarly, we can write relationships between any local axis describing the position of the robot links and the global frame.

Example 11.3   Transformation Between Local and Global Axes for a Three-Link Manipulator

---

Give the transformation matrix that relates the position of the end point of link 3 between its local and global axes of the three-link manipulator in Figure 11.17.

Solution   From Equation (11.10), we write

$$^3PR = {}^GP_3$$

where R is the transformation matrix relating the position of link 3 in local coordinates (x_3, y_3, z_3) and global coordinates. We should also note that its global components are measured from point O_2. Hence, we need to add the previous components of link 2 and link 1 to form the actual position of link 3 in the global frame.

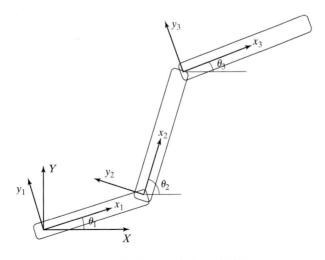

FIGURE 11.17   Three-link manipulator.

The latter is given by

$$^GP = {}^1P + {}^2P + {}^3P \tag{11.11}$$

or

$$^GP = [l_1 \quad 0 \quad 0] \begin{bmatrix} \cos\theta_1 & \sin\theta_1 & 0 \\ -\sin\theta_1 & \cos\theta_1 & 0 \\ 0 & 0 & 1 \end{bmatrix} + [l_2 \quad 0 \quad 0] \begin{bmatrix} \cos\theta_2 & \sin\theta_2 & 0 \\ -\sin\theta_2 & \cos\theta_2 & 0 \\ 0 & 0 & 1 \end{bmatrix}$$

$$+ [l_3 \quad 0 \quad 0] \begin{bmatrix} \cos\theta_3 & \sin\theta_3 & 0 \\ -\sin\theta_3 & \cos\theta_3 & 0 \\ 0 & 0 & 1 \end{bmatrix} \tag{11.12}$$

Assuming that all links are of the same length l, we obtain

$$^GP = [l(\cos\theta_1 + \cos\theta_2 + \cos\theta_3), l(\sin\theta_1 + \sin\theta_2 + \sin\theta_3), 0] \tag{11.13}$$

End of Example 11.3

Example 11.4   Placement of a Metal Block in a Small Area

A metal block with a curved opposite edge is to be positioned properly so it can be inserted in a storage area, as shown in Figure 11.18. Give the rotation(s) required by the robot link to ensure its insertion.

Solution   A rotation of the end effector alone by 90° about the x_3-axis suffices to position the object with respect to the hole of the storage area.

End of Example 11.4

Example 11.5   Geometric Positioning of the End Effector

In Example 11.4, if the dimensions of the object block are given such that the width and the height are about 1 and 3 in., respectively, what instructions should be given to make sure that the forward motion will keep the metal block in the direction of the hole?

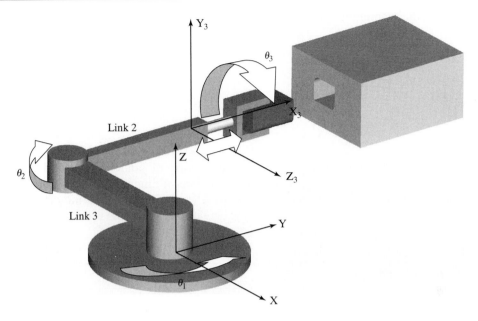

FIGURE 11.18 Positioning of a block by a two-link manipulator.

Solution The motion must be such that the position of point p remains invariant along the y_3- and z_3-axes and moves by an increment of at least 2 in. along the x_3-axis. This could be accomplished by setting the velocity components (v_x, v_y, v_z) of point p as follows:

$$v_x = \text{constant}$$
$$v_y = 0$$
$$v_z = 0$$

The velocity components are found by first deriving an expression for point p in the global frame:

$$Gp = [(l_1 \cos \theta_1 + l_2 \cos \theta_2 + r \cos \theta_2), (l_1 \sin \theta_1 + l_2 \sin \theta_2 + r \sin \theta_2), 0] \quad (11.14)$$

where l_1, l_2, and r are positions in the total frames of link 1, link 2, and the metal block, respectively.

Then, from the above two equations it follows that

$$v_x = (d/dt)(l_1 \cos \theta_1 + l_2 \cos \theta_2 + r \cos \theta_2) \quad (11.15)$$

$$v_y = (d/dt)(l_1 \sin \theta_1 + l_2 \sin \theta_2 + r \sin \theta_2) \quad (11.16)$$

$$v_z = 0 \quad (11.17)$$

These equations yield

$$v_x = -(l_1 \sin \theta_1 + (l_2 + r) \sin \theta_2) \begin{bmatrix} \dot{\theta}_1 \\ \dot{\theta}_2 \end{bmatrix} \qquad (11.18)$$

$$v_y = (l_1 \sin \theta_1 + (l_2 + r) \sin \theta_2) \begin{bmatrix} \dot{\theta}_1 \\ \dot{\theta}_2 \end{bmatrix} \qquad (11.19)$$

$$v_z = 0 \qquad (11.20)$$

Following the conditions set on the motion of point p, Equations (11.18) to (11.20) are solved for $\dot{\theta}_1$, $\dot{\theta}_2$, θ_1, and θ_2 as functions of time using an integrator. (The assumptions are v_x = constant, $v_y = v_z = 0$). The results are rather important, because they provide information about how the actuators and motors used to drive the robot links are going to perform.

End of Example 11.5

11.8   Defining the Workspace of a Robot

The workspace of a robot manipulator is an important design criterion used to determine the optimal structural configuration of a robot. The workspace is defined as the volume or space the robot occupies given its joint constraints. The workspace is also defined as an envelope bounding its minimum and maximum reach.

There are two basic approaches to the workspace problem:

1. Given the structure of a robot, what constitutes the workspace?
2. Given the workspace, what should the robot's structure be?
3. Defining the workspace of a robot

In the first approach, robot parameters, such as link lengths, joint constraints, and loads, are known. Hence, the accessible region where the robot can operate can easily be found by using a CAD system (Figure 11.19).

The second approach is more complex because the robot structure is not known, but the accessible regions are defined. This problem involves a synthesis and an optimization of the parameters chosen to define the robot. These parameters usually involve joint constraints and link lengths.

11.8.1   Accessible Region

The workspace of a robot is an important criterion for evaluating the manipulator as the volume within which every point can be reached by the hand or end effector (gripper). The workspace also defines the working area of the robot. Because of the limitations

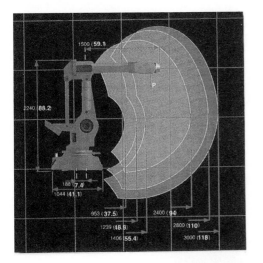

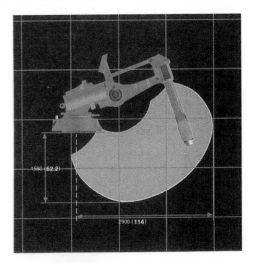

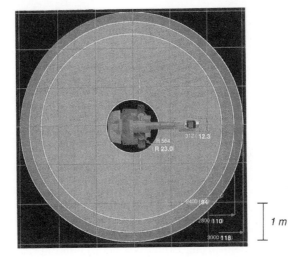

FIGURE 11.19 Work envelope of a robot. (Courtesy of ABB Robotics, Inc., Norwalk, CT.).

of the range of motion placed on the joints, the manipulator's operational capacity is restricted to a well-defined region.

The workspace of a robot can be understood through the analysis of its accessible regions. Consider a simple two-link planar manipulator with revolute joints as shown in Figure 11.20. The x, y coordinates of the end of the second link (x, y) represent the position of the hand and are given by

$$x = l_1 \sin \theta_1 + l_2 \sin(\theta_1 + \theta_2) \tag{11.21}$$

$$y = l_1 \cos \theta_1 + l_2 \cos(\theta_1 + \theta_2) \tag{11.22}$$

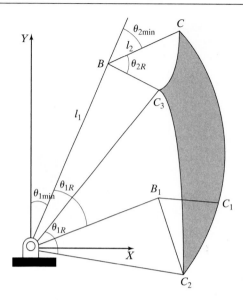

FIGURE 11.20   Two-link workspace.

Squaring and adding these equations, we obtain

$$x^2 + y^2 = l_1^2 + l_2^2 + 2l_1l_2 \cos \theta_2 \tag{11.23}$$

which represents an equation of a circle (where only O_2 is present) with a radius given by the square root of the right-hand side of Equation (11.23).

We can also reorganize Equations (11.21) and (11.22) and get

$$(x^2 - l_1 \sin \theta_1)^2 + (y^2 - l_1 \cos \theta_1)^2 = l_2^2 \tag{11.24}$$

which yields another representation of the circle with 9 only and a radius given by l_2.

In the analysis of the workspace, one would solve for B, and e_2 given the coordinates (x, y) of a point using Equations (11.21) and (11.22), respectively. (This can be done with the assumption that links l_1 and l_2 are known.) As a matter of fact, we can derive expressions for B, and 92, expanding Equations (11.23) and (11.24), which gives

$$\theta_1 = \cos^{-1} \frac{y}{\sqrt{x^2 + y^2}} - \cos^{-1} \frac{x^2 + y^2 + l_1^2 - l_2^2}{2l_1 \sqrt{x^2 + y^2}} \tag{11.25}$$

$$\theta_2 = \cos^{-1} \frac{x^2 + y^2 - l_1^2 - l_2^2}{2l_1l_2} \tag{11.26}$$

We should note that Equations (11.9) and (11.10) serve as a basis for determining the boundary of the work area by simply setting one angle to its minimum value and rotating the other through its range of values, and vice versa. Figures 11.20 and 11.21 show the construction of the work area for two- and three-link robots.

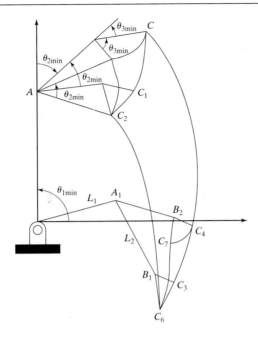

FIGURE 11.21 Three-link workspace.

11.9   Robots and Computer-Aided Design

There is an increasing trend to incorporate robots into the computer-aided design process in order to obtain maximum efficiency. This trend has immense benefits both in design and manufacturing.

The maximum efficiency from a robot can be availed if it could be task-programmed directly from a supervisory control via a hardware interface in the flexible manufacturing cell. This is possible because of the ability of the rapid changeover of work-cell activities with a minimum disruption of productive time.

Supportive software for the hardware interface would have a protocol to confirm that the robot is in a condition to receive a program before program downloading begins. On completion of the download, the software must confirm the status of data transmission, which would, among other things, confirm if the data were received correctly.

With the development of new languages and techniques such as offline programming, a robot can be directly programmed after completing the computer-aided design process. Most computer-aided design and solid modeling software available have the ability to develop programs to enable programming a robot.

However, to effectively program a robot off line, a CAD and/or CAM database is required. A CAD database provides information related to part geometry and a CAM database provides machine and tool information. The available database has to be enhanced in most cases because it requires clearance and interference-checking data and information such as weight, center of gravity, surface features, surface quality, and gripper constraints.

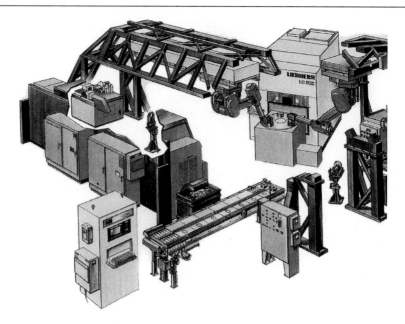

FIGURE 11.22   OLP/S software used for reach analysis and cycle time and to create the robot program.
(Courtesy of ABB Robotics, Inc., Norwalk, CT.)

Not only can robot productivity be enhanced by the inclusion of robots in the CAD process, but complex tasks can be simulated, analyzed, and refined with computer assistance for optimal performance.

Simulation of a robot task on the computer screen avoids building expensive prototypes and allows testing and safety from hazardous environments. All tasks are simulated on the screen and robot paths can be checked and optimized with computer-aided programs to verify clearances, and the interaction of machines, tools, and workpieces can be tested in the manufacturing cell. There are programs like OLP/S (Figure 11.22) that are used to assist managers to appropriately select the robot type and placement that best optimize task and productivity.

The robot task itself can be designed with computer-aided simulation. The simulation also allows the system programmer to test the procedures and concepts without tying up the work cell.

In an industrial environment, it is quite unlikely that a robot will function independently as a pure stand-alone device. Grouping of machine tools in various work cells is done in any manufacturing arrangement. The machine tools are interconnected by a workpiece transport system. Also included is a secondary transport system incorporating one or more robots. Each robot is assigned the task of moving workpieces to and between machines. Figure 11.23 is a schematic diagram of one such arrangement.

The entire system depicted in the figure is controlled by computer programs designed specifically for robotic applications. Usually, a central computer processes

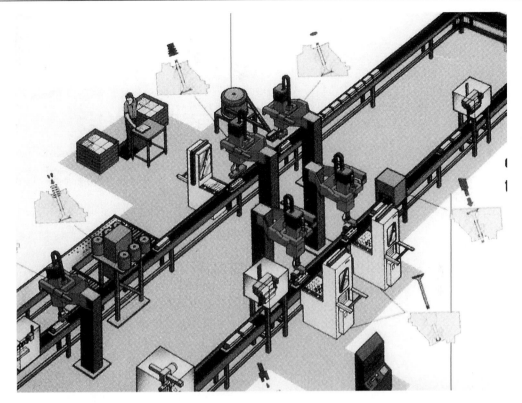

FIGURE 11.23   Offline programming simulation software. (Courtesy of ABB robotics, Inc., Norwalk, CT.)

all instructions to one system and continually monitors the system during operations. A computer system of this nature is designed and operated as a hierarchical structure.

A typical three-level hierarchy employs a top-level supervisory computer to handle general managerial functions, desk scheduling, coordination of machines, and material flow and fault management; it employs an intermediate-level host computer to generate desired trajectories, tool speeds, feed rates, and other reference signals for low-level controllers; and it employs a set of low-level computers or hardware controllers for direct digit control.

PROBLEMS

11.1. A decision has to be made on the type of robot needed to move a plate from position 1 to position 2 in such a way that face B is positioned normal to the vertical axis (Figure P11.1). Provide the robot design and the degrees of freedom required to perform the task.

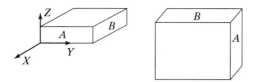

FIGURE P11.1   Positioning of a plate.

11.2. a. Justify the answer to Problem 11.1 by giving the concatenated transformation matrices to two different type of robots that could accomplish the same task.
   b. Use your computer or workstation to justify the answer to Problem 11.1.

11.3. The planar two-arm robot is to be used for painting the wall shown in Figure P11.2. If the paint gun is located at point A as shown,

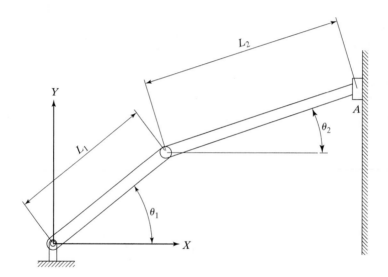

FIGURE P11.2   Two-link robot used for spraying a wall.

   a. find an expression for the tip velocity.
   b. If the vertical speeds are given by Figure P11.3, give the expressions for θ_2 and θ_2 to control tip A at such speeds.
   c. Use the results from parts (a) and (b) on your computer or workstation to yield some output of the robot motion.

11.4. a. For Problem 11.1, give the transformation matrices needed to manipulate the plate so it will be positioned as desired.
   b. Using the workstation with any appropriate application software or self-created program, determine the correct method(s) to manipulate the plate to any desired position.

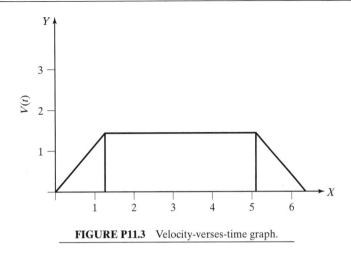

FIGURE P11.3 Velocity-verses-time graph.

11.5. For Example 11.1, a pick-and-place robot is used to carry out the operation. Explain the basic differences between the AVAL programming language and those of APT motion statements.

11.6. For a robot equipped with a wrist that has yaw, pick, and roll capabilities, give an industrial application to justify its use.

11.7. Two industrial robots are needed to collaborate on a particular task.

a. What is the optimal volume that the two robots will occupy?
b. What are the ranges of the revolute joint angles to ensure that the endpoints of the terminal links will reach the object shown?

BIBLIOGRAPHY

Amirouche, F.M.L., & Tushar, V. (1989). Accessible regions and synthesis of two-arm robots. *Journal of Robotics and Animation*, 3:3, pp. 133–139.

Ardayfio, D. (1987). *Fundamentals of Robotics*. New York: Marcel Dekker.

Asfahl, C.R. (1985). *Robots and Manufacturing Automation*. New York: Wiley.

Coiffet, P., & Chirouze, M. (1983). *An Introduction to Robot Technology*. New York: McGraw-Hill.

Craig, J.J. (1955). *Adaptive Control of Mechanical Manipulators*. Reading, MA: Addison Wesley.

Cutkosky, M.R. (1985). *Robotic Grasping and Fine Manipulation*. Boston: Kluwer.

Duffy, J. (1980). *Analysis of Mechanisms and Robot Manipulators*. New York: Wiley.

Durrant Whyte, H.F. (1987). *Integration Coordination and Control of Multi-Sensor Robot Systems*. Boston: Kluwer.

Hall, E.L., & Hall, B.C. (1985). *Robotics—A User-Friendly Introduction*. New York: Holt, Rinehart and Winston.

Koren, Y. (1985). *Robotics for Engineers*. New York: McGraw-Hill.

Lee, M. (1989). *Intelligent Robotics*. New York: Open University Press and Halstead Press.

Minsky, M. (1985). *Robotics*. Garden City, NY: Omni Press, Anchor Press/ Doubleday.

Murata, H. (1976). *Kinematic Design for Articulated Robot Arm*. Japan: Engineering Faculty.

Paul, R.P. (1981). *Robot Manipulators: Matrices, Programming and Control*. Cambridge, MA: MIT Press.

Pugh, A. (1986). *Robot Sensors*. Vol. 2. *Tactile and Non-Vision*. Kempston, Bedford, UK: IFS.

Rooks, B. (1983). *Developments in Robotics 1983*. Kempston, Bedford, UK: IFS.

Shahinpoor, M. (1987). *A Robot Engineering Textbook*. New York: Harper & Row.

Simons, G. (1986). *Is Man a Robot?* New York: Wiley.

Tsai, Y.C., & Soni, A. M. (1981). Accessible regions and synthesis of robot arms. *ASME Journal of Mechanical Design, xx*, 803–811.

Unimation Inc. (1980). *Users Guide to VAL: A Robot Programming and Control System*. Version 12. Danbury, CT: Unimation.

Vukobrakovic, M. (1989). *Applied Dynamics of Manipulation Robots*. Berlin: Springer Verlag.

Young, D.C.H., & Lee, T. W. (1983). On the workspace of mechanical manipulators. *Trans. AMSE Journal of Mechanisms, Transmission, and Automation Design. 105*, 63–69.

CHAPTER 12

Robot Economics

12.1 Introduction

Prior to the purchase of a robot system, it is important to consider its area of application, the need for it, the long-range plans, objectives of the company, and especially the social impact robots are going to have on the displacement of workers, if the robot system is purchased. The introduction of robots is justifiable when it is possible to increase productivity, improve product quality, and reduce production costs.

An economic justification for the use of robots in manufacturing can be measured by the short- and long-term profitability robots can provide. The profitability of any manufacturing operation is determined by the overall production costs. Thus, aside from the purchase cost of robots, all other auxiliary equipment and tooling costs have to be considered. Furthermore, the costs of maintenance and periodic overhaul, operating power, depreciation, special tooling, and installation have to be determined.

Robots, like any other machinery, have competitive prices. The cost usually varies from $5,000 to $350,000. Selecting the robot for the application at hand requires information such as load, speed, accuracy, repeatability, power supply, programming, and size. Traditionally, purchasing robots could be done either by paying cash or by obtaining a loan from an appropriate institution. These loans come with an annual interest rate that can be quantified on an hourly basis. All plant equipment depreciates over a period of time because of wear and tear. An annual depreciation factor is then applied to such equipment, which can also be computed on an hourly basis. The cost of the power supply for the robot system and the cost of its maintenance can also be quantified on an hourly basis. In addition to regular maintenance, a robot system might need a complete overhaul, requiring a temporary shutdown. To realistically estimate the total cost of a robot system on an hourly basis, all these costs have to be determined and added up. Note that the hourly cost of the robot system will be compared with that of manual labor.

TABLE 12.1   Hourly cost estimate of a unimate robot.

Price of Unimate robot	$50,000
Cost of installation	$12,000
Interest rate	15%
Cost on a two-shift basis in 1981($/hr)	
Depreciation	1.56
Interest payment	1.10
Installation cost	0.80
Power	0.40
Overhaul (two)	0.40
Maintenance	1.15
Total cost of robot	5.41

The comparison of hourly costs between manual labor and a robot system was carried out in 1981 by Unimation Inc. for a Unimate robot applied in the automotive industry. The various costs for the robot are listed in Table 12.1.

At the time of this survey, the gross hourly wage rate of a worker was around $20/hr in the automotive industry. Thus, the robot is cheaper. Even if we considered a depreciation period of 5 years, the robot cost was only $8/hr. Logically, if a robot is used for two shifts, its hourly cost will be significantly cheaper than manual labor. In the late 1980s and early 1990s the prices of robots dropped and so did the interest rates. This made them even more attractive to industries.

There are several other factors other than economics to justify the application of industrial robots. These include:

1. Safety and protection for workers who used to be exposed to high temperatures, such as in foundries in steel mills and with radiation and toxic waste in hazardous environments.
2. Increased productivity, especially if the robots operate much faster than humans.
3. Improved quality because robots perform at constant accuracy and the inherent fatigue factor of humans is eliminated.
4. Flexibility because robots can be programmed to perform different tasks. Although this is one function where humans are far superior, robots can possess some degree of flexibility.

The social impact of robots is another consideration we have to look at before implementation. Union representatives should be included in the discussion from the very beginning so that the inherent benefits of robots are known. This is mainly a suggestion because each company operates differently.

12.2   Economic Justification

The economic feasibility of robots can be evaluated from the viewpoints of a payback period and return on investment.

The following are the variables that pertain to the payback and return on investment equations:

P: Payback period (years)

I: Total cost of robot and accessories

L: Annual direct labor cost savings

M: Annual material cost savings

E: Annual maintenance cost and operating cost of robot

T: Investment tax credit (available from government as an incentive for robot technology implantation)

t: Tax rate

q: Production rate coefficient

D: Annual depreciation

12.2.1 Payback Period

The equation for the payback period is

$$P = \frac{I - T}{(L = M - E)(1 - T) + D*t} \tag{12.1}$$

The annual savings result from labor cost savings and material cost savings. A simpler form of Equation (12.1) used as a rule of thumb is

$$P = \frac{I}{L - E} \tag{12.2}$$

In this equation is the total cost of the robot system.

Example 12.1   Payback Returns for a T3 Robot

If the total capital investment to purchase a Cincinnati T3 robot is $75,000 and the cost of labor is estimated at $20/hr for the same task (including benefits), find the payback return for one and two shifts if the maintenance cost of the robot is $2.00/hr.

Solution   The following assumptions are made:

$$\text{One shift} = 8 \text{ hr}$$

$$\text{Number of working days/year} = 250$$

For a single shift, using Equation (12.2), we get

$$P = \frac{75000}{20(250 \times 8) - 2.0(250 \times 8)} = 2.08 \text{ years}$$

For two shifts, we obtain

$$P = \frac{75000}{20(250 \times 16) - 2.0(250 \times 16)} = 1.04 \text{ years}$$

One can easily see that if the robot is scheduled to work at least 16 hr, then the payback return is only 1.04 years. By management standards, this is a reasonable investment.

End of Example 12.1

12.2.2 Production-Rate Payback Formula

In the foregoing simple formula, the performance in terms of speed is assumed to be the same for both robots and the humans being displaced. Depending on how fast or slow a robot can perform the desired task, we can estimate the payback return to decrease or increase. To take into consideration the rate of robot speed, the following equation is used:

$$P = \frac{I}{L - E \pm q(L - z)} \tag{12.3}$$

This equation also considers savings resulting from increased productivity. The tax rate is assumed to be negligible.

Example 12.2   Payback Return Using Production-Rate Payback Formula

The following data are given for purchasing a particular robot:

   I: $75,000
   L: $20.00/hr is taken over 250 days with one or two shifts
   E: $2.00/hr is taken over the same period as *L*
   z: $45,000, or 15% of the total capital cost, which is $300,000
   q: either 20% faster or 20% slower than a human operator

Find the payback return for either q assuming a single shift of operation.

Solution   For a single shift, we obtain

$$L = 20(250 \times 8) = \$40,000$$
$$E = 2.0(250 \times 8) = \$4,000$$

Assuming the robot is 20% slower, using Equation (12.3), we get

$$P = \frac{75000}{40,000 - 4,000 - 0.2(40,000 + 45,000)} = 3.9 \text{ years}$$

if the robot is 20% faster

$$P = \frac{75000}{40,000 - 4,000 + 0.2(40,000 + 45,000)} = 1.4 \text{ years}$$

There is a drastic change in payback return if robot speed is taken into account.

End of Example 12.2

Example 12.3   Calculation of Payback Period Using Simple Formula

---

Industrial robots are to replace 12 workers in a production line. Each robot costs $80,000, including tooling. The annual maintenance cost for each robot is estimated at $5,000. The programming cost for the whole system is $18,000. What is the payback period if the workers are paid $32,000/year, including fringe benefits?

Solution

Total investment $= \$80,000 \times 5 = \$400,000$

Maintenance and programming cost/year $= \$5,000 \times 5 + \$18,000$

$= \$43,000$

Labor savings/year $= \$32,000 \times 12$ $= \$384,000$

The payback period, using Equation (12.3), is

$$P = \frac{400,000}{384,000 - 43,000} = 1.17 \text{ years}$$

We were not given the rate of production of the robot being purchased versus the human labor, and by assuming single-shift replacement, the simple formula was used.

End of Example 12.3

12.3   Justification of Robot Implementation

The principal justification for robotic application in a manufacturing operation can be carried out by studying the economics of the process. The following steps can determine the possibility of integrating a robot into the manufacturing process.

1. **Survey.** The first step is to determine the number and types of robotic applications in a manufacturing operation.

2. **Screen.** Each potential robot application is then analyzed for its economics and task limitations. The following factors are considered for the economics:

   - number of shifts per day
   - numbers of setups per week
   - major equipment to be moved
   - number of persons to be replaced

   The factors considered for task limitations are:

   - simple repetitive operations
   - visual inspection
   - part weight
   - part location and orientation suitable for a robot
   - cycle time greater than 5 seconds
   - speed and accuracy
   - reach

3. **Company Need and Priority.** Before purchasing a robot, the company's needs must be clearly stated as to whether a robot should be purchased. One approach is to look for other alternatives within the company to perform the job. An elaborate study provides an insight into the company's needs and priorities.

4. **System Development.** To minimize the risks of implementation, suitable trials should be arranged to determine appropriate toolings, workplace layout, and cycle time for the proposed application. This is a critical step. Any problems that might occur can then be addressed and corrected before a purchase is made. In addition, demonstrations and tests by various vendors should be explored to learn more about the manufacturing processes performed by the robot.

5. **Economic Feasibility.** The economic feasibility can be carried out by the payback period, return on investment, discounted rate of return, and cash flow.

The following example gives an illustration of the economic study that is usually performed.

Example 12.4   Comparison of Production Costs of Manual System versus Proposed Robotic System

---

A firm anticipating major sales increases is contemplating a $1.4 million capital investment in a system of 11 robotic paint sprayers with associated automatic spray line conveyor equipment to replace a manual spray line employing 14 skilled painters.

The existing manual system produces 90 units/hr and achieves a daily operation time of 6 hr/day, employing spray-painting personnel for a full 8-hr shift, including breaks, line servicing, and maintenance. The average cost of a human operator, including fringe benefits is $20/hr. The additional cost for maintenance for the manual system is $400/month.

The new robotic spray line simultaneously operates 11 robotic paint sprayers and achieves a production rate of 150 units/hr of operation working an 8-hr shift per day. The total cost of the robot system is $0.8 million/year. The cost of operating the system is $85/hr of which the maintenance costs of the robot are $1.3/hr for one shift and $1.5/hr for two shifts.

Compare the unit production costs of the manual system versus the proposed robotic system. Also, find the payback period for the robotic system.

Solution

Manual Spraying

The hourly labor cost is

$$\text{Labor cost/hr} = \frac{\text{no. workers} \times \text{wage/hr} \times \text{no. hours/day}}{\text{operation time/day}}$$

$$= \frac{\text{wage/hr} \times \text{no. hours/day}}{\text{operation time/day}} \tag{12.4}$$

which yields

$$\text{Labor cost/hr} = \frac{14 \times 60 \times 8}{8} = \$373.3/\text{hr}$$

$$\text{Maintenance cost/hr} = \text{Labor cost/hr} = \frac{14 \times 60 \times 8}{8} = \$373.3/\text{hr} \tag{12.5}$$

which gives

$$\text{Maintenance cost/hr} = \frac{400 \times 12}{50 \times 5 \times 6} = \$3.2/\text{hr}$$

The production rate is 90 units/hr. The unit cost is then defined as:

$$\text{Unit cost} = \frac{\text{hourly production cost}}{\text{production rate}} \tag{12.6}$$

or

$$\text{Unit cost} = 376.5/90 = \$4.2/\text{unit}$$

Robotic Spraying

$$\text{Production cost/hr} = \text{operating cost/hr} + \text{total robot system cost/hr} \tag{12.7}$$

$$\text{Total robot system cost/hr} = \frac{80000}{50 \text{ weeks} \times 5 \text{ days/week} \times 8 \text{ h/day}} = \$400/\text{hr}$$

$$(12.8)$$

We find

$$\text{Production cost/hr} = \$400/\text{hr} + \$85/\text{hr} = \$485/\text{hr}$$

We know that

$$\text{Production rate} = 150 \text{ units/hr}$$

Therefore,

$$\text{Unit cost} = \frac{\text{production cost/hr}}{\text{production rate/hr}} \qquad (12.9)$$

which yields

$$\text{Unit cost} = \$485/\text{hr}/150 \text{ units/hr} = \$3.2/\text{unit}$$

Thus, the difference in unit cost per component is

$$\text{Difference in unit cost} = \text{manual} - \text{robot system}$$
$$= 4.2 - 3.2 = \$1.0/\text{unit}$$

To compute the payback return, we use Equation (12.2), where I is the total investment (robot and accessories), L is the annual labor savings, and E is the expense of robot upkeep/year.

Using the values

$I = \$1,400,000$

$E = \$1.40/\text{hr} \times 50 \text{ weeks/year} \times 5 \text{ days/week} \times 8 \text{ hr/day} = \$2600/\text{hr}$

Hence,

$L/\text{hr} = \text{robot system cost/hr} - \text{operation labor cost/h}$
$= \$400/\text{hr} - \$373.31/\text{hr} = \$26.69/\text{hr}$

Annual labor savings are

$$L = \frac{L}{h} \times \frac{50 \text{ weeks}}{\text{year}} \frac{5 \text{ days}}{\text{week}} \times \frac{8 \text{ hr}}{\text{day}} \qquad (12.10)$$

Hence, $L = \$53,400.00$

Using Equation (12.2),

$$P = \frac{I}{L - E}$$

we get

$$P = \frac{140000}{53400 - 2600} = 2.75 \text{ years}$$

The payback return is based on the simple equation and assumes only one shift. The robot system yields a savings of $1.0/unit, which translates into a significant savings per year. To make a decision based on this analysis, one would argue that 2.75 years in payback return is high, but if we anticipate using the robots for two shifts, then its implementation is definitely justifiable.

End of Example 12.4

Example 12.5 Production per Unit Costs for a Robotic Spray System Operating on Two Shifts

Reevaluate the production cost per unit for both the proposed robotic paint spray system and the current manual system on the basis of a two-shift operation for each. Assume a 10% shift differential for all operator personnel costs associated with the second shift. Also, find the payback period for this particular case.

Solution

Manual System

The following items are given:

$$\text{Operation labor cost/hr (one shift)} = \$373.3/hr$$
$$\text{Maintenance cost/hr} = \$3.2/hr$$

Considering a 10% increase in operator costs for two shifts, we get Equation (12.11):

$$\text{Operator labor cost/h (two shifts)} = \text{labor cost (one shift)}$$
$$+ \text{ labor cost (one shift)} \times 1.10$$

Hence,

$$\text{Average operator cost/hr} = \$373.3/hr + \$373.3/hr \times 1.10\ 2$$
$$= \$391.96/hr$$
$$\text{Average production cost/hr} = \$391.96/hr + \$3.20/hr = \$395.16/hr$$

Now, we define the unit cost to be

$$\text{Unit cost} = \frac{\$395.16/hr \ I}{90 \text{ units/h}} = \$4.4/unit$$

Robotic System

$$\text{Total robot system cost/h (two shifts)} = (\text{production cost/hr})/2(\text{one shift})$$
$$= \$400/\text{hr}/2 = \$200.00/\text{hr}$$

The operation cost is determined as

$$\text{Operating cost/hr} = \frac{\$85/\text{hr} + \$85/\text{hr} \times 1.10}{2} = \$89.25/\text{hr}$$

The production cost is equal to the sum of the total cost of the robot system and the operation cost. Hence,

$$\text{Production cost/hr} = \$200/\text{hr} + \$89.25/\text{hr} = \$289.25/\text{hr}$$
$$\text{Production rate} \quad = 150 \text{ units/hr}$$

The unit cost is then obtained:

$$\text{Unit cost} = \frac{\$289.25/\text{hr}}{150 \text{ units/hr}} = \$1.92/\text{unit}$$

The new payback period for the two shifts can be obtained using the single formula, Equation (12.2):

where

$$I = \$140,000$$

$$E = \$1.3 \times 50 \times 8 \times 5 \times 2 = \$5200/\text{year (two shifts)}$$

Hence,

$$L/\text{hr} = \$400/\text{hr} - (\$373.2 \times 2)/2 \text{ hr} = \$26.7/\text{hr}$$

$$L \text{ (two shifts)} = \$26.70 \times 50 \times 5 \times 8 \times 2$$

$$= \$53,400 \times 2 = \$106,800.00$$

$$P = \frac{140000}{160800 - 5200} = 1.3 \text{ years}$$

End of Example 12.5

As expected, the payback period was reduced significantly, to 1.3 years. Hence, from the economic viewpoint, it is profitable to go along with the project. What is more important is the unit cost savings of $2.48 if the robotic system is adopted.

12.4　Robot Applications

With the advent of microprocessors and controls, the technology of robotics is advancing in all areas of industrial and space applications. Robots are especially being used in areas such as welding, painting and finishing, machine loading, material handling, assembling, and machining.

12.4.1　Welding

Welding is the largest area of application for robots. They are being used in assembly lines for automobile and truck manufacturing (Figure 12.1). Spot welding is the essential application for those robots; however, robots are now increasingly being used in arc-welding applications.

　　In welding applications, workers are exposed to risks that make their jobs undesirable. For instance, they have to wear protective clothing to move heavy equipment, which renders the job difficult and limits their flexibility.

FIGURE 12.1　Industrial robots are changing manufacturing methods. An IRB 6000 robot performs spot weld operations at Ford. (Courtesy of ABB Robotics, Inc., Norwalk, CT.)

Other reasons for using robots in welding are the quality, product uniformity, and reliability they provide.

Spot welding is an autogenous process in which two pieces of metal are joined at certain points. There are four major parameters that affect the quality of welded spots:

1. duration of the current supplied
2. magnitude of the electric current
3. pressure provided by the electrodes
4. material and thickness of the metal to be welded

The first three parameters must be appropriately selected to suit the thickness and type of welded material. These parameters are usually set and maintained throughout the process in a robotic welding system. Thus, under repetitive production conditions, high-quality welds are produced. Spot-welding robots are mounted on assembly lines that produce between 50 and 90 cars per hour. Work is performed while the car bodies are continuously moving on conveyors. Most of the work done by robots in the automotive industry is that of respotting, which is repetitive welding by several robots to the body of the automobile. These robots are under computer control, which signals the arrival of a particular body style and automatically causes the robot to switch to the appropriate task program in its memory.

Spot welding uses a point-to-point type of control. Because of the complicated shapes of automobile bodies, spot-welding robots use six axes of motion and are designed to carry a heavy gun.

Arc welding, on the other hand, is a relatively difficult task for robots to perform. The electrode has to follow a continuous programmed path while maintaining a constant distance from the ream. Arc-welding robots require five axes of motion, although in certain applications, four axes are adequate. They are designed to carry a lighter gun and to move at a constant speed along a continuous path.

12.4.2 Painting and Finishing

Robots were used in painting at an early stage in the automobile industry because of the hazardous working conditions resulting from toxic fumes. Of the various painting techniques, robots are largely used for spray painting (Figure 12.2).

Skilled human operators guide the robot through the painting task to develop the necessary database for the robot to repeat the task. Once the optimal program is attained, the robot is used in spray-painting operations with a consistency unattainable by human operators.

A spray-painting robot has to have a high level of manipulator dexterity, a compact wrist, a large working volume for a small-base manipulator, a small payload, low accuracy, and repeatability. The high mechanical dexterity of the hand is essential to enable it to reach the less accessible areas of the inside of the automobile. This is why spray-painting robots have at least six degrees of freedom. Because of the restricted space in spray booths, a spray-painting robot must occupy a small amount of floor space

FIGURE 12.2 An IRB 5000 robot used for spraying adhesive on interiors of commercial aircraft.
(Courtesy of ABB Robotics, Inc., Norwalk, CT.)

and also be able to reach the middle of the spray booth. A compact wrist enables the robot spray gun to penetrate narrow spaces. Because spray guns are lightweight, robots handle light payloads. Repeatability and resolution are not critical for spray-painting robots as each location of the endpoints is not critical.

Programming the spray-painting robot is done by a lead-through technique, in which a skilled painter leads the robot through the required painting path, which is stored and played back by the robot.

12.4.3 Machine Loading

Robots are used for machine loading to provide workers relief and safety from tasks such as loading heavy jobs on punch presses, milling machines, forging machines, and iron-casting machines (Figure 12.3). Thus, robots help to increase industrial safety.

12.4.4 Assembly

Speed, efficiency, reliability, and accuracy are the favorable criteria motivating the application of robots for assembly. Industrial robots do not make errors to which humans are susceptible, like errors of omission and substitution.

Robots are used for the assembly of small products like electric switches and electric motors and for engine assembly in the automotive industry and the electronic industry. An assembly robot system is usually very sophisticated and has a variety of tactile and/or visual feedback loops to enable the robot to monitor the results. Tactile force sensors are mounted on the robot's hand to indicate when a part is misaligned and when to back up and try again. The visual and tactile sensors also allow the use of the robot for quality control. The robot senses a defective assembly and signals for corrective action.

Assembly robots can operate in any coordinate system: Cartesian, spherical, cylindrical, or articulated. Certain tasks require only vertical assembly motions such as the assembly of printed circuit boards. For such applications, a four-axis robot is sufficient, whose arm has two articulated motions and whose wrist has a linear vertical displacement and a roll movement. Such a robot can pick up parts located on the horizontal plane, bring them to the assembly location, orient them with the roll motion of the wrist, and insert them in a vertical motion.

There are certain difficulties in applying robots to assembly. Part preparation with the right orientation is needed and the mating of parts is difficult because of close dimensional tolerances. However, new product designs have been developed to overcome these difficulties.

12.4.5 Machining

Of the various machining processes available, drilling is the only one in which robots have been successfully applied. Robots have also been applied to deburring metal parts (removal of ridges or rough edges left on metal by machine tools).

FIGURE 12.3 An IRB 3000 robot used for picking cylinder heads and rotating them prior to loading them on the indexing table. (Courtesy of ABB Robotics, Inc., Norwalk, CT.)

Robots are applied to drilling processes in the aircraft industry. Because a large number of holes have to be drilled in aircraft with close tolerances, the repeatability criterion of robots is the biggest advantage they have in this application. The robot is programmed using the manual teaching method for drilling applications.

Robots perform deburring in two ways. If the part is lightweight, the robot picks it up and brings it to the deburring tool; however, for heavy parts, the robot welds the tool and brings it to the workpiece. These robots are either adaptive or programmable servo-controlled. Robots are also used for grinding purposes, typically in automobile plants. They are also used to dispense urethane on windshields and back-light openings. (Figure 12.4)

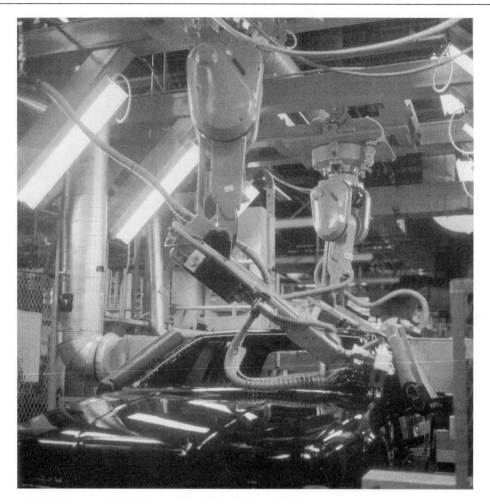

FIGURE 12.4 Two IRB 2000 robots used to dispense urethane on the windshields of cars. (Courtesy of ABB Robotics, Inc., Norwalk, CT.)

12.5   Selection and Implementation of Robots

The selection and implementation of robots are performed through four phases:

1. *Planning.* This phase requires an evaluation of the nature of the production oper-ations(s) for which the robots are being considered and a determination that robots are justifiable.

2. *Application.* A detailed study of the robot application is conducted and a specific application along with a specific robot are selected. Some specifications for the

TABLE 12.2   The Process Layout.

Phase 1	Organize the team project
	Define the objectives
	Conduct an economic analysis
Phase 2	Select the initial application
	Select the robot
	Select the initial application requirement
Phase 3	Prepare for installation
	Install and start up
Phase 4	Monitor performance
	Upgrade for new developments and applications

application are analyzed, such as layout requirements, workplace modifications, and robot accessory requirements.

3. *Installation.* This phase covers the time from the preparatory work performed on the workplace through the installation and startup of the robot.

4. *Integration.* Once the robot has begun operation, an ongoing process is required to ensure that it continues to perform its job in an effective manner.

The various steps involved in the four phases are highlighted in Table 12.2.

PROBLEMS

12.1. A firm is planning to buy a robot system for its manufacturing plant that is expected to cost $88,000. The manual labor cost for the task required at present is $22/hr. The maintenance and operating costs for the robot system is $2.00/hr. Justify the purchase of the robot system based on the simple formula of payback return for one and two shifts.

12.2. The union is trying to keep management from purchasing a robot. If the decision is based on the payback return and that the value of $P = 3$ years is not a feasible purchase to make that happen, what should the labor cost be if the robot and maintenance costs are taken from Problem 12.1?

12.3. At what rate should the robots in Problem 12.1 function in order for the payback return to be 1.2 years for both one and two shifts?

12.4. The capital cost of a spray-painting plant using robots is $400,000. $120,000 is the total cost of the robot and accessories, $25.00/hr is the labor cost savings, and there is a 20% return on the total capital cost of the plant by using the robot system. The maintenance cost of the robot is estimated at $4500/year. Find the payback return based on the production-rate equation if the robots are assumed to be 25% faster.

12.5. a. Is our estimated value of a 20% return on the capital cost low or high in decreasing the payback return for the robotic system proposed in Problem 12.4?

b. At what return rate could the payback period be kept below 1.6 years?

12.6. An automobile manufacturing plant is considering a $1.6 million investment for a robotic welding system that would use 18 robots. At present, 22 workers produce 45 units/hr, and the actual working time is 6 hr out of an 8-hr shift. The workers are paid $21/hr, including benefits. The monthly maintenance cost of the manual system is $600.00.

The robotic system has a production rate of 95 units/hr in an 8-hr shift. The annual cost of the robot system is $1 million. The operating cost is $95/hr and of this the maintenance cost is $4/hr for one shift and $4.50/hr for two shifts.

Compare the unit production costs of the manual welding system to the proposed system using robots for one shift. Also find the payback period for the new system.

12.7. The management of an automobile company wants to compare the unit costs for parts for the manual and robot systems when two shifts are used. Assume a 12% differential for all personnel costs associated with the second shift. Find the payback period for this particular case.

BIBLIOGRAPHY

Ardayfio, D.D. (1987). *Fundamentals of Robotics*. New York: Marcel Dekker.

Bein, G., & Hackwood, S. (1985). *Recent Advances in Robotics*. New York: Wiley.

Cutkosky, M.R. (1985). *Robotic Grasping and Fine Manipulation*. Boston: Kluwer.

IBM Corporation (1982). *IBM robot system: AML, reference manual*. SC34-0410-1. *IBM robot system 11: AML, concepts and user's guide*. SC34-0411-0. *IBM robot system 11: general information manual and user's guide*, 3rd ed. 0180-2. Boca Raton, FL: IBM Corporation.

Koren, Y. (1985). *Robotics for Engineers*. New York: McGraw-Hill.

McDonnell Douglas, (1981). *Robotic system for aerospace batch manufacturing, task B—high level language user manual*. Technical Report AFML-JR-79-4202. Wright Patterson Air Force Base, Ohio.

Paul, R.P. (1983). *Robot Manipulators—Mathematical Programming and Control*. Cambridge, MA: MIT Press.

Rosenburg, J. (1972). *A History of Numerical Control, 1949–1972: The Technical Development, Transfer to Industry and Assimilation*. Report no. IS I-RR 72-3. Marina Del Ray, CA: USC Information Sciences Institute.

Shahinpoor, M. (1984). *A Robot Engineering Textbook*. Albuquerque: University of New Mexico Press.

Unimation, Inc. (1980). *User's Guide to VAL, Version 12*. Danbury, CT: Unimation, Inc.

Unimation, Inc. (1983). *User's Guide to VAL-II. Part 1. Control from the System Terminal, Version X2. Part 2. Communication with a Supervisory System, Version X2. Part 3. Real Time Path Control, Version X2*. Danbury, CT: Unimation, Inc.

Unimation, Inc. (1981). *VAL Univision Supplement, Version 13, VSNO*, 2nd ed. Danbury, CT: Unimation, Inc.

Vukobratovic, M., & Stokic, D. (1981). One engineering concept of control of manipulators. *Transactions of the ASME, Journal of Dynamic Systems Measurement Control, 103*, 119–125.

Wichman, M.W. (1987). *The Use of Optical Feedback in Computer Control of an Arm*. Stanford, CA: Stanford Artificial Intelligence Laboratory, Stanford University.

Wolovich, W.A. (1987). *Robotics: Basic Analysis and Design*. New York: Holt, Rinehart and Winston.

Yang, D.C.H., & Lee, T.W. (1983). On the workspace of mechanical manipulators. *Trans. ASME, Mechanism, Transmission Automation Design, 105*, 70–77.

CHAPTER 13

Group Technology

13.1 Introduction

Group technology is a method used to optimize manufacturing processes in an orderly fashion. Its main objective is to form a database of similar parts, designs, and processes and use it to establish a common procedure for designing and manufacturing those parts. The parts grouped together form a "part family." This family is usually based on similarities in design, such as shape, or processes, such as milling and drilling operations. The benefits of this method include efficient plant floor ordering and increased production, resulting in a great cost savings brought about by proper planning and measures that avoid duplication of existing designs. Group technology is best achieved using a CAD/CAM system, taking advantage of its CPU and graphics capabilities.

The assignment of numbers, classification, and coding to parts is highly beneficial in the initial stages of a design. These are fundamental to the success of group technology. To avoid the expense that a new design requires in time and effort from engineers, and the cost for setup, and assuming a similar part exists within the company inventory, group technology allows for finding and retrieving the exact part. Making the necessary modification results in the desired design, saving the company time and money.

The part classification of a coding system is also applied in computer-aided process planning, and it involves the automatic generation of a process plan to manufacture the part. Recognizing specific attributes of a part and relating them to the corresponding manufacturing operations develop the process route sheet.

Part numbering is an important aspect of today's design and production. The design department uses part numbers as identification numbers for design retrieval. The manufacturing department uses them as references on documents such as process plans, production schedules, bills of materials, and cost estimates. The sales department uses them on invoices. No manufacturing or engineering organization is effective without an accurate and well-structured part-numbering system.

Part-numbering systems are of two types: (1) for individual components; and (2) for products and subassemblies. The numbering system used for individual components carries information helpful in manufacturing the part. All parts with similar manufacturing processes are gathered in a one-part family. This results in manufacturing advantages such as reduction in set-up time and inventory. The numbering system for products and subassemblies requires a different method of classification, and it does not carry most of the information used in coding individual components. What follows are descriptions of parts classification and coding systems and the common software available.

13.2   Part Classification and Coding

The method mostly used in classification and coding is usually based on primary and secondary code. The primary code identifies the part and the secondary code carries additional information useful in other sectors of the organization. The primary code is an address behind which the secondary code is stored. The primary code carries only the permanent attributes, such as shape, and material, which are decided when the part is designed. The details of production are not basic or permanent attributes. They form the secondary code and help in the interpretation of the design. The design is only partially implied by the shape of the component, which can change as product demand alters or production technology is improved. Thus, the primary code is more important for identification purposes.

13.2.1 Part Families

The part classification and coding system is concerned with identifying the similarities between parts and relating them to a coding system. In part classification, parts that are similar in shape and that have similar manufacturing operations form a so-called family of parts. The advantages are

1. reduced setup times
2. lower process inventories
3. better scheduling
4. improved tool control
5. use of standard process plans

These advantages are illustrated by the two layouts for the same product in Figure 13.1. Work-handling time, lead times, setup times, and in-process times are all reduced by using the group technology layout.

13.2.2 Design Retrieval

An effective design-retrieval system is very important to an engineering department with a large inventory of drawings. A designer faced with the task of developing a new

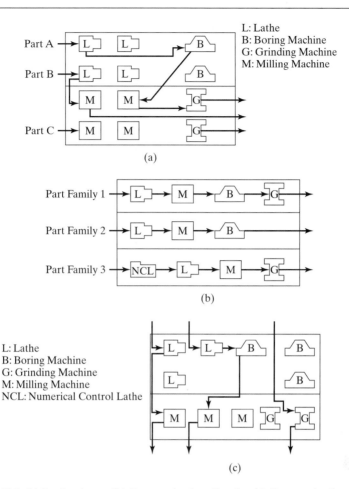

FIGURE 13.1 (a) Product layout (b) Group technology flow line (c) Group technology layout.

design has to either start from scratch or pull an existing drawing from the file and make necessary changes to conform to the requirements of the new part. Finding a similar design can be quite difficult and time consuming. So the designer may decide that it is easier to start from scratch to develop the new part, resulting in increased drafting and engineering costs. With an effective design-retrieval system, duplication can be avoided, but that requires an a priori form of coding and classification system.

13.2.3 Coding System Structure

A large number of classification systems exist whose code digit lengths range from 2 to 20 or more. The actual number of digits used only partially indicates the information carried by a particular system. Thus, it is the structure of the code and the attributes it carries that provide the information.

There are basically three forms of classification system structures used for coding:

1. monocodes (hierarchical codes)
2. polycodes (attributes of fixed-significance codes)
3. hybrid codes (mixed monocodes/polycodes)

Monocodes. The monocodes or hierarchical codes use a tree-like structure. The code is obtained through a step-by-step procedure of choosing values from a series of coding charts. Each successive value chosen leads to a different coding chart. Monocodes are difficult to construct, but they provide a detailed analysis of the nature of the classified item. Monocodes are best suited for classifying parts with a limited number of digits. This type of system is ideally suited to the identification and retrieval of similar designs.

Polycodes. A polycode is a code in which each digit is independent of all others. Thus, each digit carries self-contained information about the part. Polycodes are easier to construct and modify as needed. They are generally preferred for parts whose information is liable to change. One of the drawbacks is the limited information the code digits can carry; hence, polycodes are longer. On the other hand, polycodes allow for the convenient identification of specific part attributes, which is helpful in identifying parts with similar processing operations.

Hybrid Coding System. Most classification and coding systems used in industry are a combination of monocode and polycode systems, combining the advantages of the two. These systems have some digits arranged hierarchically and others fixed, indicating the presence of a particular attribute. Usually, the first and the second digit divide the population of items into the main subgroups, as in a monocode system. Then each subgroup has its own attribute code or series of fixed-significance digits. This system is best suited for both design and manufacturing processes.

13.2.4 Different Types of Codes

Codes can also be classified as (a) universal codes and (b) tailor-made codes.

Universal Codes. A considerable amount of effort and research has been devoted to coding. A universal code is basically an all-purpose software code that can be adapted to a wide range of applications. These programs are long and require considerable data for input. The universal codes are well received by companies with large inventories because they can take advantage of their versatility in applying them to both design and manufacturing operations. An example of a universal code is the Dewey decimal classification system, which is used in libraries around the world.

Tailor-Made Codes. These codes are designed to meet a company's particular need. They are usually an in-house development that proves to be very effective because it is designed around the company structure to perform a specific task. Tailor-made codes are the future for small companies and for those that find large-scale programs expensive and cannot use them to their full potential. They usually run on personal computers and are easy to manipulate. Information flows rapidly, and the response is immediate. The initial cost associated with tailor-made programs is high, but their benefits are overwhelming once implemented.

13.2.5 Existing Code Systems

There are a number of component classification and coding systems that have been developed for both design and production rationalization. These systems aid in the selection of families of parts and minimize the search for parts with similar processing requirements. What follows are commercial software codes used for classification.

VUOSO Classification System. This system uses four digits, three of which are arranged hierarchically to classify the part's shape, including size and proportions; the fourth digit defines the material. The VUOSO system codes rotational parts with more detail than nonrotational parts. Thus, companies with a large number of nonrotational parts find this system to be disadvantageous.

BRISCH System. This code uses four to six digits as a primary code. A series of secondary polycodes can be added to cover additional classification requirements. The code number is obtained in a step-by-step procedure through a series of coding charts. A serial number is then added for the unique identification of the part. Because this code is hierarchical, the selection of specific features from various groups is difficult. BRISCH is suited for design retrieval and shape reduction.

PARTS Analog System. Similar to the BRISCH system, this hierarchical type of code is designed to fill the client's requirements. The code is usually made up of four to six digits.

Opitz Classification System. This system was developed by H. Opitz of Aachen Tech University, Germany. Its basic code consists of nine digits; however, it can be expanded by four more. The first five digits, called the "form code," identify the production operation type and sequence. The last four digits are called the "supplementary code." The extra four digits, A, B, C, and D, called the "secondary code," identify the production operation type and sequence. The structure of the primary code is such that each of the first five digits can represent the basic shape, component class, rotational surface machining, plane surface machining, auxiliary holes, gear teeth, and forming. The five digits can represent the primary, secondary, and auxiliary shapes of the part. The four digits in the supplementary code classify the size, material, original material form, and the tolerance of the part. The first digit of the supplementary code represents the major dimension (either length or diameter). The component size can then be determined by using the dimension ratio specified in the geometry. The dimension ratio specified is from 0.8 to 80.0. Dimension ratios less than 0.8 in. and greater than 80 in. are represented by a 0 and a 9, respectively. The second, third, and fourth digits represent the material type, raw material

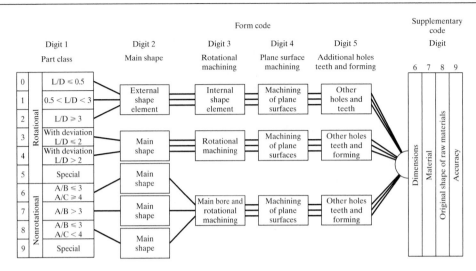

FIGURE 13.2 Basic structure of the Opitz system (Groover, M.P. (1987). Reprinted by permission.)

shape, and accuracy, respectively. The addition of a serial number to the code makes the system suitable for the identification of parts for design retrieval, provided that the distribution of parts is similar to that present in the code structure. The Opitz code system for rotational parts is illustrated in Figures 13.2 and 13.3.

CODE System.   The CODE system, developed by Manufacturing Data Systems, Inc. (MDSI), has an eight-digit code similar to the Opitz system. However, it has a mixed code structure in which each digit is represented by a hexadecimal value. The hexadecimal numbers allow more information to be represented with the same number of digits. The first six digits describe the shape of the part by considering its basic form and subsidiary features. The seventh and eighth digits provide the dimensions of the part. The structure of the CODE system is shown in Figure 13.4. The CODE system contains form and dimensional information. Size information is described more completely because one can assign more digits to auxiliary shapes. The system was originally developed for design-retrieval purposes; however, it can be used for other production applications as well.

      As an example, let us code the part shown in Figure 13.5 using the Opitz classification system and the CODE system.

Opitz Classification System (Refer to Figure 13.2)

Because the overall length-to-diameter ratio, L/D, is 2.57, the first digit is 1.

The part is stepped on one end and has threads, so the second digit is 2.

There is no hole or breakthrough present; hence, the third digit is 0.

Digit 1		Digit 2		Digit 3		Digit 4	Digit 5	
Part class		External shape, external shape elements		Internal shape, internal shape elements		Plane surface machining	Auxiliary holes and gear teeth	
0	$L/D \leq 0.5$	0	Smooth, no shape elements	0	No hole, no breakthrough	0	No surface machining	0	No auxiliary hole
1	$0.5 < L/D < 3$ (Rotational parts)	1	No shape elements (Stepped to one end or smooth)	1	No shape elements (Smooth or stepped to one end)	1	Surface plane and/or curved in one direction, external	1	Axial, not on pitch circle diameter
2	$L/D \geq 3$	2	Thread	2	Thread	2	External plane surface related by graduation around a circle	2	Axial on pitch circle diameter (No gear teeth)
3		3	Functional groove	3	Functional groove	3	External groove and/or slot	3	Radial, not on pitch circle diameter
4		4	No shape elements (Stepped to both ends)	4	No shape elements (Stepped to both ends)	4	External spline (polygon)	4	Axial and/or radial and/or other direction
5		5	Thread	5	Thread	5	External plane surface and/or slot, external spline	5	Axial and/or radial on pitch circle diameter and/or other directions
6	(Nonrotational parts)	6	Functional groove	6	Functional groove	6	Internal plane surface and/or slot	6	Spur gear teeth
7		7	Functional cone	7	Functional cone	7	Internal spline (polygon)	7	Bevel gear teeth (With gear teeth)
8		8	Operating thread	8	Operating thread	8	Internal and external polygon, groove and/or slot	8	Other gear teeth
9		9	All others	9	All others	9	All others	9	All others

FIGURE 13.3 Form code (digits 1 through 5) for rotational parts in the Opitz system. (Groover, M.P. (1987). *Automation, production systems and computer-integrated manufacturing*, p. 441. Englewood Cliffs, NJ: Prentice Hall. Reprinted by permission.)

There is no surface machining and there are no auxiliary holes present, so the fourth and fifth digits are 0.

The whole Opitz code for the part is 12000.

CODE System

The basic shape of the part is cylindrical, so the first digit is 1.

Concentric parts or diameters are sent, which when compared to Figure 13.3 gives the second digit as 4.

There are no center holes present, so the third digit is 1.

There are no auxiliary holes present, so the fourth digit is 0.

There are threads present on one end, so the fifth digit is 8.

There are no flats, slots or protrusions present, so the sixth digit is 0.

The last two digits of the code are used to define overall dimensions. The outer diameter falls within the range of 1.2 and 2 in. (O.D. = 1.75 in.), so the seventh digit is 7. The eighth digit classifies the overall length, which in this case falls between 4.4 to 7.2 in., so the eighth digit is 5.

The code of this part using the CODE system shown in Figure 13.3 is then 14108075.

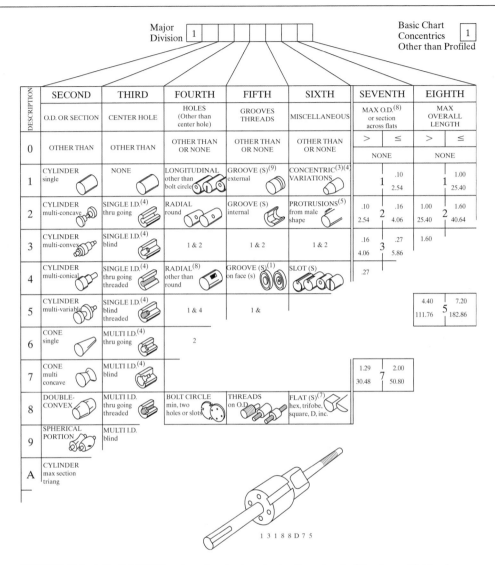

FIGURE 13.4 A Partial CODE system showing how to classify and code. (Courtesy of Schlumberger CAD/CAM, San Jose, CA.)

MICLASS System. The MICLASS system was developed by TNO (The Netherlands Organization for Applied Scientific Research) of Holland and is currently maintained in the United States by the Organization for Industrial Research. The MICLASS classification system ranges from 12 to 30 digits. The first 12 digits are universal and can be applied to any part. Up to 18 additional digits can be used for data that are specific to the particular company. These supplemental digits provide the flexibility to accommodate broad applications. For example, lot size, cost data, and operation sequence are included in the 18 supplemental digits.

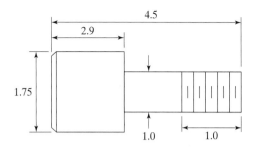

FIGURE 13.5 Coding of a part using Optiz and CODE systems.

The MICLASS system can help automate and standardize a number of design, production, and management functions, including standardization of engineering drawings, retrieval of drawings according to classification number, standardization of process routing, selection of parts for processing a particular group of machine tools, and automated process planning. The MICLASS system has been adapted in many U.S. industries, and several other application programs such as MIPLAN and MULTI-CAPP variant process planning systems are available. The MICLASS code structure is shown in Figure 13.6. An example of coding a part using the MICLASS system is described in Figure 13.7.

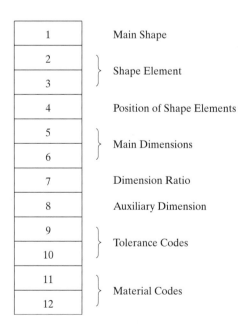

FIGURE 13.6 MICLASS code structure. (Courtesy of International Techne Group Incorporated, Milford, OH.)

ENTER THE CLASSIFICATION ROUTE (1 TO 9) •1

3 MAIN DIMENSIONS (WHEN ROT. FART D,L AND 0) :2.9375,2,0 DEVIATION OF
ROTATIONAL FORM ,NO

  CONCENTRIC SPIRAL GROOVES :• NO

TURNING ON OUTERCONTOUR (EXCEPT ENDFACES) -YES

  SPECIAL GROOVES OR CONE(S) OR PROFILE(S) ON OUTERCONTOUR ...:NO
  ALL MACH. EXT. BEAM. AND ROT. FACES VISIBLE FROM ONE END (EXC.
  ENDFACES + GROOVES) :=YES

TURNING ON INNERCONTOUR ::YES

  INTERNAL SPECIAL GROOVES OR CONE(S) OR PROFILE(S) •NO

  ALL INT.DIA. + ROT.FACES VISIBLE FROM 1 END(EXC. GROOVES)YES ALL

D1A. + ROT.FACES VISIBLE FROM ONE END (EXCL. ENDFACES ?YES ECC.

HOLING AND/OR FACING AND/OR SLOTTING :AYES

  ON INNERFORM AND/OR FACES (INC. ENDFACES) YES ON OUTERFORM NO

ONLY ENCLOSE[, INTERNAL SLOTS •NO ECC. MACHINING ONLY ONE SENSE :Y

  ONLY HOLES ON A BOLTCIRCLE (AT LEAST 3 HOLES) ::YES FORM-OF

THREADING TOLERANCE .,NO

  DIAM. OR ROT. FACE ROUGHNESS LESS THAN 33 RU (MICRO-INCHES) .,YES

SMALLEST

  CLASS .NR.= 1271 3231 3100 0000 0000 0000 0000 00

  xxxx*xxx*x*xxx***x*x*x*xxxxxx***x**x*xxx**xx*xxx*

  DIGIT TO CHANGE >

  CONTINUE (Y/N)>N

  TTO – STOP

  >

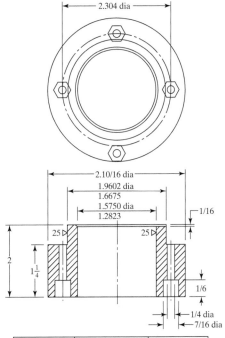

DRAWING	TOLERANCES	MATERIAL
TITLE	Fractional - 1/64	CC 15
BUSHING		125
DRAWING NO:	Decimal - 0.003	
?		ALL OVER EXCEPT AS NOTED

FIGURE 13.7   Coding session of MICLASS. (Courtesy of International Techne Group Incorporated, Milford, OH.)

DCLASS Systems.   The DCLASS system was developed by Del Allen of Brigham Young University; it is a decision-making and classification system. It is a tree-structured system that generates codes for components, materials, processes, machines, and tools. Each branch of the system represents a condition in which a code is formed at the junction of each branch. The complete code is obtained by taking multiple passes in the decision tree. For the components, an eight-digit code is used. Digits 1, 2, and 3 represent its basic shape; digit 4 represents the form; digit 5 represents the size; digit 6 represents the tolerance; and the last two digits (7 and 8) represent the material of the component. (Figure 13.8).

13.3   A Proposed Classification System

A classification and coding system developed and applicable to a manufacturing firm dealing in dies, tools, presses, and other related equipment is presented. The structure

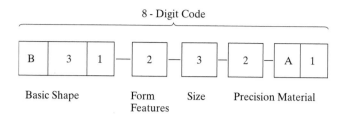

FIGURE 13.8 Sample of DCLASS code representation.

of the proposed coding system is based on a hybrid or mixed code construction. The aims of the proposed system are product identification and design retrieval. A monocode is not suitable because of the large amount of information shared by a variety of products. A polycode structure is also not suitable for this classification because of its restrictions on the numbering system itself. In a polycode structure, each digit carries information that is totally independent from the others. In this application, the commonly shared information by different products makes the use of a polycode system prohibitive. In essence, for this application, the hybrid system or mixed code structure is the optimal classification system.

The data are classified into different categories and classes using most of the documented information. The proposed method of classification and coding utilizes a 12-digit code used for information retrieval and design simplification. This system provides coding for designed and purchased assemblies, products and raw materials, and has the capability of accommodating individual components and other miscellaneous items.

Component classification is done by shape or function, and the shape feature is taken into account when individual components are grouped together by their manufacturing similarities. But classification of a product by its shape is almost impossible. When it comes to grouping products, usually classification by function is preferred. The proposed system brings similar items together by classifying them by function.

The code is a numerical code of constant length and is divided into two groups of six digits each:

$$\underbrace{\text{XXXXXX}}_{\text{General Code}} - \underbrace{\text{XXXXXX}}_{\text{Specific Code}}$$

The first group, the "general code," classifies the part into its major categories and subclasses. The second group, the "specific code," is tailored by user requirements to give additional information related to a certain product or assembly.

13.3.1 General Code

The breakdown of the general code is as follows:

$$\text{AA BC DD}$$

The first digit (AA) has 10 possible values, the second and third digits (B and C) are combined to give 99 possible subclasses of each item classified, and the last digit (DD) in the general code has 10 possible values. The general code gives a general description of the part, the type of operation it performs, and other specifications that uniquely identify the product.

13.3.2 Specific Code

The remaining half of the system, the specific code, carries specific information about a certain range of products. The breakdown of the specific code is as follows:

$$XX\ X\ X\ X\ X$$

The specific code gives us a more detailed description about a part by classifying it into subclasses. Some parts do not need all 12 digits. The extra digits are reserved for possible future expansion of the company line of products.

13.3.3 Method Used for the Proposed Classification System

The first step taken in designing the proposed classification system is to break down all of the company's components or parts into eight major design classes as follows:

1. designed piece parts
2. designed assemblies
3. designed products
4. purchased piece parts
5. purchased assemblies
6. purchased products
7. raw material
8. miscellaneous

Classification of Design Classes.   Each design divides each component into an assembly product or raw material and identifies whether the components are designed or purchased. Simultaneously, those components are divided into three classes: individual piece parts, products, or assemblies. This division is beneficial for family grouping and retrieval purposes. Each design class is then broken down into subclasses. Figure 13.9 illustrates this classification. The method uses digits two and three for this subclassification. Each design class is again subclassified into different types of products and assemblies like presses, special machines, feeders, punch and die units, dischargers, etc. Thus, all similar equipment can be grouped at the initial stage, making it easier to identify their class. The subclasses are progressively subdivided into subsubclasses to form classes of items that are similar in design.

Figure 13.10 shows a code for a designed assembly and shows the general and specific codes, giving the type of information carried for one assembly that is designed and marketed by a particular company.

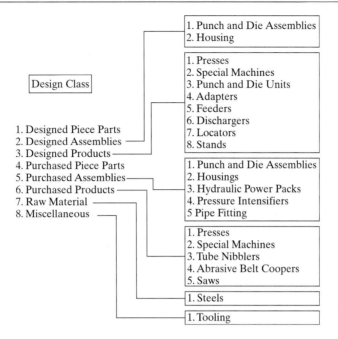

FIGURE 13.9 Division of a design class into subclasses.

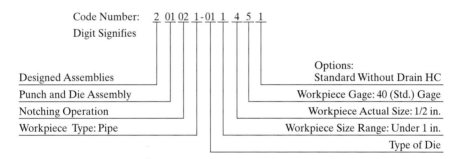

FIGURE 13.10 Construction of a proposed code.

13.4 Work Cells

Group technology can be defined as a technique of identifying and bringing together similar parts in a production process in order to use the inherent economy-of-flow production methods. In other words, when using group technology, the machines are grouped to produce a family of similar parts. Each group has the necessary machines to produce the family of similar parts. However, a certain part might not require the use of every machine. Such a system is most effective when a coding and classification system is used.

In work cells, machine layout is based on component flow, and a component enters and terminates at that cell location. Each work cell in effect can be regarded as a manufacturing unit. The number of machines in the work cell depends on the part family that is going to be manufactured. A work cell can have only one machine supported by the required tooling and fixtures. For example, a nut and a bolt are made on a single lathe machine. A work cell can have a group of machines supported by either manual or mechanized material handling. Part families with a large number of parts can be manufactured by a flexible manufacturing system (FMS), which consists of automated processing stations connected by a fully integrated material handling system. An FMS employing four T-30 machining centers, each with a two-position automatic work changer and a 90-tool automatic tool changer is shown in Figure 13.11. The system also includes automated material and tool handling systems, an automated wash station, a coordinate measuring machine for in-process inspection, and a milacron 10-station AWC for part queuing.

There are a few problems arising from work cells:

1. If the mix of the work piece requires change, then the machine layout of the work cell must also be changed.
2. Because the work cell contains several different types of machines, the supervisor must be an expert in several different machining techniques.
3. Because the machine operator is typically not an expert on several different types of machines, transfer from one machine to another can be a problem. The

FIGURE 13.11 FMS cell. (Courtesy of Cincinnati Milacron, Cincinnati, OH.)

flow of the work cell must be designed around the most complex work-piece machining route. Overloading or underloading of a single machine may occur, resulting in an uneven work balance.

4. The flow of the work cell must be designed around the most complex work-piece machining route. Overloading or underloading of a single machine may occur, resulting in an uneven work balance.

13.4.1 Types of Work Cells

Work cells are of four basic types:

1. single machine work cells
2. group machine cells using manual material handling
3. group machine cells using semiintegrated material handling
4. flexible manufacturing systems

All four types can exist together in one factory and result from the analysis of data carried out by either part-coding or production-flow analysis.

The design of a work cell can be based on the composite-part concept or the key-machine concept.

The composite-part concept groups work at a single machine tool and designs tooling to increase productivity by reducing the idle time caused by the need for resetting between batches.

When a group of components is similar in shape, size, or manufacturing requirements, a single composite component can be formed that has all the features of the individual components. Pooling and sequencing of machines are based on the composite component. Operations and tools that are not required for certain individual parts are simply dropped. Setup times can be reduced by up to 50% and floor-to-floor process times by about 40%. We should note that the concept of work cells and flexible manufacturing systems assumes that all individual components have two basic characteristics in common: (1) similar holding or clamping requirements and (2) similar surfaces for machining.

The key-machine concept designs work cells so that the most expensive and important machines have the highest use, whereas the least important have the lowest. The expensive machines are called "key machines" and the other machines are called "supporting machines." The aim is to operate key machines at maximum output at all times. In the case of supporting machines, it is important to maximize the use of labor rather than equipment.

13.4.2 Arrangement of Machines in a Work Cell

A simple method to decide on the arrangement of machines, developed by Hollier and described by Wild uses From–To charts and is illustrated in the following example.

Example 13.1   Arrangement of Machines Using From–To Charts

Five machines constitute a group technology work cell. The From–To data for the machine are

Machines		To			
From	1	2	3	4	5
1	0	10	80	0	0
2	0	0	0	85	0
3	0	0	0	0	0
4	70	0	20	0	0
5	0	75	0	20	0

   a. Determine the most logical sequence arrangement of the machines for the data given using the To–From ratio.

   b. Where do the parts enter and exit the cell? How many parts are in each place?

Solution   (a) The first step is to develop a From–To chart from the data given by summing up the "From" and "To" trips for each machine:

Machines		To				
From	1	2	3	4	5	"From" sums
1	0	10	80	0	0	90
2	0	0	0	85	0	85
3	0	0	0	0	0	0
4	70	0	20	0	0	90
5	0	75	0	20	0	95
"To" Sums	70	85	100	105	0	

The second step is to calculate the To–From ratio for each machine by calculating the ratio of the "To" and "From" sums for each machine:

Machines	To	From	To–From
1	7	90	0.77
2	85	85	1
3	100	0	00
4	105	90	1.16
5	0	95	0

Now the machines are arranged in the increasing order of To–From ratios. This concept allows machines with low To–From ratios to receive work from fewer machines and distribute it to more machines. Thus, the arrangement of machines in the work cell would be as follows:

$$5 \rightarrow 1 \rightarrow 2 \rightarrow 4 \rightarrow 3$$

We then can specify the To and From parts for each machine in the arrangement found in the first step (Figure 13.12).

(b) To determine where the parts enter and leave the work cell, we need to equate the number of parts entering the work cell at specific machines to the number of parts leaving the work cell from all machines. Thus, it is seen that 95 parts enter the work cell at machine 5, 20 parts enter at machine 1, 100 parts leave at machine 3, and 15 parts leave at machine 4 (Figure 13.13).

End of Example 13.1

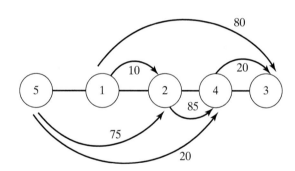

FIGURE 13.12 From–To Chart.

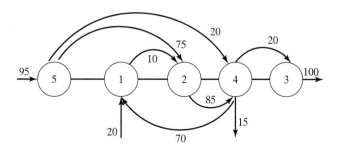

FIGURE 13.13 From–To Chart.

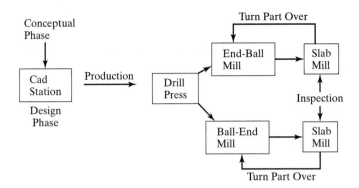

FIGURE 13.14   Work cell for circuit board support.

Let us consider a few more examples of work cells. They further illustrate how the work cells function independently. The solution provided might not be the optimal one but rather one in which the manufacturing process is described within a work cell function.

Example 13.2   Work Cell for Circuit Board Support

The work cell for a circuit board support contains one drill press; two end ball mills, with a cutter diameter of 1.82 mm; and two horizontal slab mills, with a cutter diameter of 13.6 mm, as shown in Figure 13.14.

The proposed work cell shown is very simple and there are several ways that it could have been constructed. In this work cell, no tool changes are required; however, the workpiece must pass through each mill twice. The factors determining the structure of the work cell are not discussed here.

End of Example 13.2

Example 13.3   Work Cell for Manufacturing Castings

The work cell illustrated in Figure 13.15 is used for manufacturing castings. The manufacturing process starts on conveyor 1, where the molds for the tasted parts are placed at equal distances from each other. This conveyor is controlled by a CAD/CAM machine because it starts and stops at various intervals so that the molds can end up directly beneath the molten lead valve. The valve is then opened by a CAD/CAM machine command to fill the mold. Next, the robot takes the last mold from conveyor 1 and removes the tasted part from inside it. The part is then placed on the machining

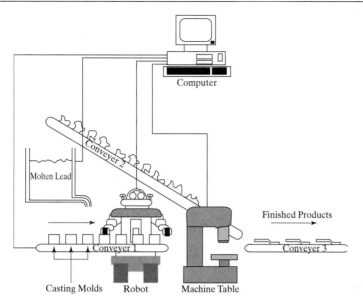

FIGURE 13.15 Work cell for manufacturing castings.

table in the proper position to enable the top of the part to be machined. While the top of the part is being machined, the robot brings the empty mold back to the beginning of conveyor 1 so that it can be used again. When the robot returns to the machining table, it proceeds to flip the part when required by the APT program. Between each repositioning of the part, the robot sweeps and scraps the lead onto conveyor 2. This conveyor carries the scrap lead back to the vat, where it can be remelted and used again. When the machining is complete, the robot places the part onto conveyor 3 (refer to Figure 13.13), where the finished products are turned out. The robot then grabs the next mold and repeats the process.

It is not necessary for the CAD/CAM machine to control conveyors 2 or 3 because they run constantly. The only precaution that is taken is to make the length of conveyor 1 long enough to ensure that the tasted parts have cooled enough to be machined. This involves doing a study on the length of time that is required to machine each part. The intervals at which conveyor 1 is turned off and on equal the machining time. The length of conveyor 1 can be determined from the machining and cooling times required for the casted parts.

End of Example 13.3

Examples 13.2 and 13.3 show how an independent work cell is used for the manufacture of similar parts.

13.5   Computerized Coding and Information Retrieval

Once part classification and other processes are completed, the information has to be stored in the computer so that it can be retrieved later. A computerized coding procedure retrieves the necessary parts by interacting with the program through a selection of items displayed on a menu.

13.5.1 Coding Parts

Parts-coding tables can be used to generate part numbers. However, if this procedure is automated, considerable savings of time and money can result. One can add information about the part after generating the code number; the database is automatically modified and updated.

13.5.2 Information Retrieval

One can retrieve information about a specific component or group of components in whichever manner is suitable. To obtain a general description of the part, the part code can be entered to retrieve information from the database. For a group of machines like feeders and presses, we can retrieve information about the numbers of units sold, their costs, etc.

The following illustrates how information is retrieved for a company manufacturing dies and tools. Suppose we want to retrieve information about all the different types of four post presses available at the company. In order to search for a component, we choose number 2 from the main program menu displayed in Figure 13.16.


```
                                    ** PART-NUMBERING SYSTEM **
                               PROGRAM MENU


                               1. PART CODING
                               2. INFORMATION RETRIEVAL
                               3. INFORMATION CORRECTION




    Type 'E' to End


              ENTER YOUR CHOICE:
```

FIGURE 13.16   Program menu for computer coding and information search.

```
                                              **PART-NUMBERING SYSTEM**

                    INFORMATION-RETRIEVAL MENU


                    1. Interactive Search for Part
                    2. Search by Code Number
                    3. Sort Part by Code Number
                    4. Specific Part Printout Menu




Type 'E' to End
Type 'P' to for Program Menu

        ENTER YOUR CHOICE:
```

FIGURE 13.17   Information-retrieval menu.

Information-Retrieval Menu.   The information-retrieval menu displayed in Figure 13.17 gives four options. There are two ways of searching for a part—using the interactive search scheme or the part code number. The other two options provide a sorted printout of either all the parts or a specific product.

Interactive-Search Method.   By using the outlined procedure, this method helps us to group items of similar type and to get a list of a particular product. We pick up the choices from the menu; at a particular level, we can select option L, listing, to get information about a particular product. From the menu displayed in Figure 13.17, we pick option 1 to carry out an interactive search; the new menu displayed in Figure 13.18

```
                                              **PART-NUMBERING SYSTEM**

This menu gives us the list of design classes in which all VOGEL products have been classified.
To begin search pick the choices from menu to narrow your search to specific component.
                    1. Designed Place Parts
                    2. Designed Assemblies
                    3. Designed Products
                    4. Purchased Piece Parts
                    5. Purchased Assemblies
                    6. Purchased Products
                    7. Raw Material
                    8. Miscellaneous

Type 'M' for Main Menu
Type 'E' to End
Type 'P' for Prev. Menu

        ENTER YOUR CHOICE:
```

FIGURE 13.18   Search menu displaying a list of design classes.

PART-NUMBERING SYSTEM

You want to search for Designed Products. Designed Products have been further classified into the following categories. Select the option that matches your requirements:

1. Presses
2. Special Machines
3. Punch and Die Units
4. Adapters
5. Feeders
6. Dischargers
7. Locators
8. Stands

Type 'M' for Main Menu
Type 'E' to End
Type 'P' for Prev. Menu

ENTER YOUR CHOICE:

FIGURE 13.19   Search menu displaying list of design products operations.

gives the design class. We are now asked to pick a choice to narrow our search to a specific component. The choice is "Designed Products," option 3, because we are searching for a designed press. This displays another menu, shown in Figure 13.19, that contains all major designed products. At present there are eight options available (other products could be introduced to the menu when the need arises). From the designed products menu, we select presses, option 1. The next menu displays four options (Figure 13.20) that subclassify the presses by their source of power, namely, hydraulic, pneumatic, mechanical, or manual. Because we are searching for a press in the hydraulic category, we choose option 1. The menu displayed in Figure 13.21 classifies hydraulic presses by their operation type given by eight different classes.

In this case, our choice is the first class; we select option 1 (i.e., hydraulic press) for multipurpose operation. This gives us the menu shown in Figure 13.22. There are

PART-NUMBERING SYSTEM

Your choice was Presses. Presses have been further classified by source or power. Select your option:

1. Hydraulic
2. Pneumatic
3. Mechanical
4. Manual

Type 'M' for Main Menu
Type 'E' to End
Type 'P' for Previous Menu

ENTER YOUR CHOICE:

FIGURE 13.20   Search menu displaying a list of different modes of power available.

Your choice was Hydraulic Presses. Hydraulic Presses are further classified by the type of operation they perform.
Select your option:

1. Multipurchase
2. Notching/Slotting
3. Piercing
4. Cutting
5. Bending
6. Reducing
7. End Forming (Multipurpose)
8. Hydroforming

Type 'M' for Main Menu
Type 'E' to End
Type 'P' for Previous Menu

ENTER YOUR CHOICE:

FIGURE 13.21   Search menu displaying a list of different press operations.

four choices available and we pick option 1 for four-post three-platen presses. This leads us to the menu listing four-post three-platen presses classified by tonnage, as shown in Figure 13.23. Now we enter "L" for a complete listing; the computer program in turn will ask if we want a list of all four-post three-platen presses or a specific one. If we need a list of all presses with a 10-ton capacity, we enter 1. The display of this information, shown in Figure 13.24, gives the particulars of the class, source of power, a list of all the four-post three-platen presses of 10-ton capacity, and additional information like bed length, width, and stroke. From here we can either get a hard copy or exit and go to the main menu.

PART-NUMBERING SYSTEM

Hydraulic presses for multipurpose operation are further classified into the following types.
Select your option:

1. Four-Post Three-Platen Press
2. Bench Arc Hydraulic Press
3. 57000 Series Hydraulic Production Presses
5. VOGEL Cage Style Hydraulic Power Units

Type 'M' for Main Menu
Type 'E' to End
Type 'P' for Previous Menu

ENTER YOUR CHOICE:

FIGURE 13.22   Search menu displaying different types of multipurpose hydraulic presses.

Four-post three-platen presses are available in the following tonnage.
Select your option:

> 1. 10 Tons
> 2. 15 Tons
> 3. 25 Tons

Type 'M' for Main Menu
Type 'E' to End
Type 'P' for Previous Menu

> ENTER YOUR CHOICE:

FIGURE 13.23   Search menu displaying the tonnage of four-post three-platen presses.

Design Class:	Designed Products			Family Code: 301011-0100000	
Unit Price:	Presses				
Operational Type:	Multipurpose				
Source of Power:	Hydraulic				
Type of Press:	Four-Post Three-Platen Press				

Part Code	Tonnage	Length	Width	Stroke	Price	Units-Sold
301011-011110	10 TONS	12 IN.	12 IN.	8	5675.00	10
301011-011120	10 TONS	12 IN.	16 IN.	8	6095.00	11
301011-011130	10 TONS	12 IN.	20 IN.	8	6445.00	13
301011-011230	10 TONS	18 IN.	20 IN.	8	6495.00	20
301011-011240	10 TONS	18 IN.	24 IN.	8	6795.00	15
301011-011250	10 TONS	18 IN.	28 IN.	8	7165.00	12
301011-011340	10 TONS	24 IN.	24 IN.	8	6995.00	14
301011-011350	10 TONS	24 IN.	28 IN.	8	7395.00	16
	10TONS	24 IN.	32 IN.	8	7835.00	13

Type 'M' for Main Menu
Type 'E' to End

> ENTER YOUR CHOICE:

FIGURE 13.24   Listing of all 10-ton four-post three-platen presses.

The interactive search for a part can be modified in many different ways, depending on the nature of the information needed and the extent by which the information is available through the database.

Search by Code Number. If we need to retrieve information from the computer's database, we can also use the part number as the entry key. For this we have to choose option 2 from the interactive-search menu, which takes us to the routine that searches for a part by its code number.

Selecting option 2, we then enter the part code. The computer then searches for the part in its database. If a part number exists, it brings up and displays all its information on the screen. Otherwise, it displays a message that says the part does not exist.

Sorting Parts by Code Number. The third option available in the information retrieval menu, displayed in Figure 13.17, is the sorting of parts by code number. At present, it prints out a sorted list of all the coded parts with a two-line description, giving a brief summary of the part.

Specific Part-Listing Menu. The last option of the information-retrieval menu is the printed list of information of a specific component. For example, it can print out a sorted list of all designed and purchased punch and die assemblies. It also gives a brief description of the component with its code number. This option is useful when searching for punch and die assemblies of a particular size or type.

Information-Correction Routine. The last option in the computerized information-storage and retrieval systems program menu is the information-correction option. This helps in updating the database of all the parts.

13.6   Benefits of Group Technology

Some of the benefits of classification, coding, and information retrieval are as follows.

Simplification. The use of group technology helps to reduce the occurrence of similar designs in a variety of ways. It minimizes duplication in manufacturing and enables the manufacturing engineer to better control existing inventory.

Identification. Once the system is learned, one can get a general description of a part by knowing its code number.

Reduction in the Cost of Design. If a suitable design already exists, the unnecessary creation of a new one is usually prevented by classification. If a new design has to be created, an approximate code number can be searched, because a final design may be achieved through the simple modification of an existing one. This reduces design cost. Group technology also promotes standardization in design.

Material Handling. There is an efficient flow of materials through the shop and reduction in idle time by applying the principles of group technology.

Storage and Inventory Control. Because all similar items have nearly related code numbers, the raw materials or individual components can be stored in code-number sequence, thus eliminating the need for bin numbers. Manufacturing lead times and work-in-process times are drastically reduced because of reduced setup times and more efficient material handling. In-process inventories can be reduced by 50% and throughput time by as much as 60% by the use of group technology.

Reduction in Tooling Cost. In computer-aided design and computer-aided manufacturing, one of the major tasks involves geometry description of the part in question. The identification of the entities that describe the mechanical part serves as a basis for generating corresponding manufacturing processes and tooling programs. The classification and coding systems help identify the parts whose manufacturing processes are already defined.

Reduction in Cost Estimates. By estimating the records of items with similar code numbers made in the past, the cost estimates can be made for new designs by interpolating from the actual costs of the old ones. Alternatively, the actual costs can be used to check the calculated estimates.

PROBLEMS

13.1. a. Give two examples that form a part family for the automobile industry.

    b. What type of process-planning technique must be used to develop a process plan for machining a new part using an existing computer database of route sheets?

13.2. Using Figures 13.2 and 13.3, develop a formcode using the Opitz system for the part shown in Figure P13.1.

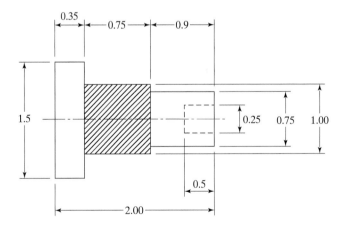

FIGURE P13.1 Form code for a robot.

13.3. Develop the form code for the same part shown in Figure P13.1 using the CODE classification system.

13.4. Using Figures 13.6 and 13.8, generate codes using the MICLASS and DCLASS coding systems. Describe the similarities between the codes and their major differences.

13.5. Four machines consist of a work cell. The From–To Chart for these machines on which 60 parts are processed follows.

Machines	To			
From	1	2	3	4
1	0	10	0	30
2	30	0	0	25
3	20	30	0	0
4	10	0	0	0

Fifty parts enter machine 3 and 15 enter machine 2; 45 parts leave machine 4 and 20 parts leave machine 1. Determine the logical machine arrangement and suggest a feasible layout.

13.6. In Problem 13.5, the numbers of parts traveling from machines 1 and 4 to machines 2 and 3 are exchanged. How would this change the machine arrangement and machine layout?

13.7. Develop the form code for the rotational part given in Figure P13.2 using the Opitz and CODE classification systems.

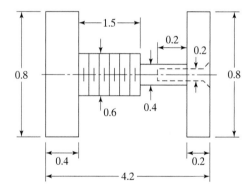

FIGURE P13.2

BIBLIOGRAPHY

Allen, D.K. (1979). *Classification and Coding Theory and Application.* Monograph no. 2. Provo, UT: Computer-Aided Manufacturing Laboratory, Brigham Young University.

Allen, D.K. (1979). *Generative Process Planning Using the DCLASS Information System.* Monograph no. 4. Provo, UT: Computer-Aided Manufacturing Laboratory, Brigham Young University.

Brankamp, K. (1970). *Objectives, Layout and Possibilities of the Opitz Work-piece Classification System*. Proceedings of the Group Technology International Seminar. Turin, Italy: International Center for Advanced Technical and Vocational Training.

Burbridge, J.L. (1979). *Group Technology in the Engineering Industry*. London: Mechanical Engineering Publications.

Burbridge, J.L. (1975). *The Introduction of Group Technology*. New York: Wiley.

Burbridge, J.L. (1971, April/May). Production flow analysis. *The Production Engineers*.

Chang, T.C., & Wysk, R.A. (1985). *An Introduction to Automated Process Planning Systems*. Englewood Cliffs, NJ: Prentice Hall.

Dautzig, G.B. (1963). *Linear Programming and Extensions*. Princeton, NJ: Princeton University Press.

Dedworth, D.D., and Bailey, J. E. (1982). *Integrated Production Control Systems*. New York: Wiley.

Edwards, G.A.B. (1971). *Readings in Group Technology*. London: Machinery Publishing.

El Gomayel, J., & Abou-Zeid, M.R. (1975, May). *Piece part coding and the optimization of process planning*. Presented at the North American Metalworking Research Conference.

Gallagher, C., & Knight, W. (1973). *Group Technology*. London: Machinery Publishing.

Groover, M.P. (1987). *Automation, Production Systems and Computer Integrated Manufacturing*. Englewood Cliffs, NJ: Prentice Hall.

Haan, R.A. (1977, March). *Group technology coding and classification applied in NC part programming*. Proceedings of the 14th Numerical Control Society annual meeting and technical conference, Pittsburgh.

Ham, I. (1976). *Introduction to group technology*. Technical Report MMR 76-03. Dearborn, MI: Society of Manufacturing Engineers.

Ham, I., Hitomi, K., & Yoshida, T. (1985). *Group Technology*. Boston: Kluwer-Miijhogg.

Hartley, J. *FMS at Work*. Kempston, Bedford, UK: IFS Publications.

Hitomi, K. (1979). *Manufacturing System Engineering*. London: Taylor and Francis.

Houtzeel, A. (1975). *Classification and coding, group technology and computer assisted process planning*. Waltham, MA: TNO. Organization for Industrial Research.

Hyde, W.F. (1981). *Improving Productivity by Classification, Coding, and Data Base Standardization*. New York: Marcel Dekker.

Kakino, Y.F., Oba, F., Meriwaki, T., & Iwata, K. (1977). *A New Method of Parts Description for Computer-Aided Production Planning: Advances in Computer-Aided Manufacturing*. New York: Elsevier North-Holland.

Kerry, T.M. (1995). Intergrating N.C. programming with machining and group technology. Proceedings of the 12th Numerical Control Society annual meeting and technical conference, pp. 149–162.

King, J.R. (1982). Machine-component group formation in group technology: review and extension. *International Journal of Production Research, 20,* 117–133.

Opitz, H.A. (1970). *Classification of Described Workpieces*. Oxford: Pergamon.

Organization for Industrial Research, MICLSS Migroup, MIPLAN, MI-GRAPHICS (marketing brochure). Waltham, MA: Author.

Orlidily, J. (1975). *Material Requirement Planning*. New York: McGraw-Hill.

Schaffer, G. (1980, May). GT via automated process planning. *American Machinist*, pp. 119–122.

Scheck, D.E. (1975, February). *New Direction in Process Planning*. SME technical paper, series MM75-908, presented in Ft. Lauderdale, FL.

Stanuffer, R.N. (1979, May). The rewards of classification and coding. *Manufacturing and Engineering*, pp. 48–52.

Woodward, J. (1965). *Industrial Organization—Theory and Practice*. Oxford: Oxford University Press.

CHAPTER 14

Computer-Integrated Manufacturing

14.1 Introduction

The competitiveness of the United States has been steadily eroded by manufacturing challenges over the past two decades. Individual companies that have adapted to the changing technological environment have fared well; however, there is much more to be done before the United States can regain its manufacturing leadership (Tables 14.1 and 14.2).

Management, labor, and government all share responsibility for the changing face of U.S. industry. It can be safely assumed that the effectiveness of design and production functions in supporting the overall business strategy is a major determinant in the competitiveness of U.S. industry. The United States has the means to regain its manufacturing leadership.

New technologies such as computer-integrated manufacturing (CIM) permit manufacturers to implement strategies and objectives to increase productivity. CIM deals with the integration of manufacturing activities and support facilities using computers. The advent of powerful low-price computers has made it practical for communications to take place between different industries. Computers used in manufacturing not only contribute to decision making, but also to the control of production and shipment of products. Integrating these computers through common databases can radically change the running of a company. CIM allows decision makers to access data on all relevant computers, enabling them to make better decisions. Further, decisions can be implemented with greater speed, and their effects can be carefully monitored. The concept of CIM is taking full control over manufacturing processes through a single

TABLE 14.1   Capital Investment as Percentage of Output[a] in Manufacturing, Selected Countries, 1965–1982

Period	United States	France	West Germany	Japan	United Kingdom
1965–1982	15.1	12.8[b]	21.2	13.6	10.5
1965–1973	16.5	14.3	25.3	14.3	10.0
1974–1982	13.6	11.2[c]	17.1	13.0	11.1

[a] Fixed Capital and output measured in constant dollars.
[b] 1965–1981.
[c] 1974–1982.

Source: Unpublished data obtained from the U.S. Bureau of Labor Statistics, 1985.

TABLE 14.2   Output per Hour in Manufacturing, Average Annual Percent Change

Country	1960–1973	1973–1983	1989–1990
Canada	4.7	1.8	2.7
France	6.5	4.6	1.1
West Germany	5.7	3.7	3.4
Japan	10.5	6.8	3.7
United Kingdom	4.3	2.4	0.8
United States	3.4	1.8	2.5

Source: U.S. Bureau of Labor Statistics, 1991.

information source. Full control implies control over the direct manufacturing process, support business practices, and enterprise goals.

14.2   CIM Objectives

CIM allows enterprises to meet higher levels of objectives that are unattainable with partially computerized industries. The objectives are as follows:

1. Develop quality products at competitive prices.
2. Integrate and control design and manufacturing operations.
3. Manage finances.
4. Increase sales by controlling product demands.

Once more, the feasibility of integrating information of all the enterprise functions is possible only through a computer network designed to meet the specifics and goals of the enterprise. Computerized industries will have two companies' demand and, second, develop a standard CIM computer architecture for a variety of different enterprises. Because CIM is still new, its implementation requires restructuring enterprise functions and computer-controlled decision making. Communication will rely mostly on computer interaction with a database that is accessible to all CIM functions. When implemented properly, CIM can realize the enterprise goals. To see how that is possible, we now examine the major areas of CIM:

- Marketing
- Engineering design
- Research and development
- Manufacturing operations
- Financial planning

The benefits that result from the implementation of CIM extend into each functional area of the manufacturing enterprise.

Marketing. Gathering information from customers is key to future product development. To satisfy customer needs, a credible database, which is possible only through CIM technology, is needed. Its purpose is to help manage customer demands, prompt responses to inquiries and assist companies in accurately predicting sales projections.

Engineering Design. The benefits of CIM are similar to those of computer-aided design (CAD); however, the speed of designing products is faster because of the enormous database available that includes current and historical product information.

Research and Development (R&D). The benefits of integrating manufacturing functions result in a broader knowledge of past and present product performance. This knowledge enables R&D departments to access future product development that best uses company resources to increase sales. The R&D function is to keep a company competitive by responding in a timely manner with newly developed products. CIM allows the enterprise to adapt quickly to market changes and provides the ultimate guidelines to future product development.

Manufacturing Operations. The advantages of CIM are also similar to those of computer-aided manufacturing (CAM) as stated in Chapter 8. However, CIM adds a new dimension to process planning, plant operations, and resources by providing a database to manage all these operations. The resources and information available through CIM allow more realistic scheduling of manufacturing operations, resulting in shorter production times and customer satisfactions. This is possible in part because of the floor organization and the computer network serving the enterprise.

Financial Planning. CIM offers better product cost tracking, more accurate financial projections, and improved cash flow for business management activities such as managing finance and accounting and developing enterprise directives and financial plans.
Thus, the benefits of CIM are

1. quick release of new products
2. shorter delivery times

3. more realistic inventories
4. shorter production planning
5. reduced lead times
6. improved product quality
7. increased responsiveness and competitiveness

The main CIM objective is to strengthen the relationship between the supplier and the customer. It assists the supplier in planning production and deliveries more efficiently and provides the customer with the benefits of shorter order-delivery time and quality products at a reasonable cost.

The benefits of CIM presented are conceptual in nature and are idealistic, serving more as goals than as guidelines. What are at the heart of CIM are the modeling of the enterprise and the restructuring of the organization to meet those goals. Restructuring requires the careful study and implementation that has the full support of management and a well-trained team of professionals.

14.3   The Enterprise and Product Modeling

CIM technology is based on an enterprise model that integrates all operations and functional management into a network to optimize productivity and profitability. The traditional enterprise is divided into several departments that are in most cases separate entities operating on their own. The lack of data sharing results in duplicated work, wasted time, and high expenses. To eliminate unnecessary and redundant work, the new enterprise model relies on its functions to work in harmony. Figure 14.1 illustrates the functions involved and their integration.

One of the objectives of CIM is organizing the manufacturing operations processes and machine tools to optimize the quality and efficiency or durability of the product. In other words, CIM designs work cells suited for company needs. This can be done only if the database provided is such that all interfaces are present; hence, the product is directed at all stages by a computer. Feedback identifies product status and decided-on concurrent operations. In the event that something goes wrong, the computer should be equipped with the best alternatives to proceed with manufacturing.

Essentially, the enterprise models the product around its CIM structure to benefit from computer-controlled process planning and manufacturing. It is often helpful to develop simple intuitive models describing the subsystem elements and their relationships. This visualization allows a better understanding of complex systems on a heuristic basis. However, it is necessary to develop more detailed system models to improve communication and learning and to study system performance.

There are broadly three types of models for viewing manufacturing systems:
(a) physical models, (b) functional models, and (c) organizational models.

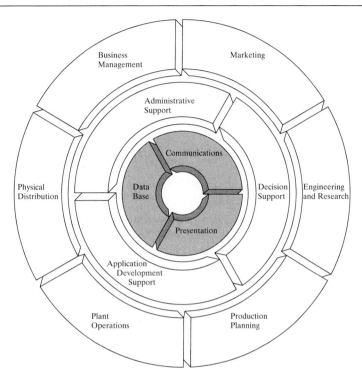

FIGURE 14.1   Functions of a CIM enterprise. (Courtesy of International Business Machines Corporation, New York.)

Physical models.   Physical models describe the visible aspects of a manufacturing enterprise. They are classified into those involving material transformation, such as manufacturing equipment and operators, and those involving hardware for information flow and system control, such as computers and operators. Subsystems are defined in terms of hardware units and the movement of material through the system.

Functional Models.   Functional models describe the manufacturing system in terms of the functions it performs. It is important to define system functions and to describe the material transformation processes achieved by the product equipment and those that describe information flow through the system.

Organizational Models.   Organizational models describe the manufacturing system in terms of the organizational relationships that exist among the people in the system. They are used to consider how informal organizations relate to one another and to overall manufacturing system activities.

Simple models are also used in all areas of a manufacturing organization to decide on the physical management of equipment, describe a process, or plan reorganization.

More formal system models can provide an in-depth system understanding, but can also be misleading if the limitations of the models are not kept in mind.

14.4 CIM Architecture

CIM architecture is a framework that provides a structure of computer hardware and software with appropriate interface for computer systems in manufacturing enterprises to integrate information and business processes. Some of the interfaces are provided by international standards, and suppliers of hardware and software determine others. CIM architecture can provide a consistent base for integrating the enterprise's product, processes, and business data. It defines the structure of the requirements.

CIM architecture has considerable advantages in enabling a system to take advantage of new business opportunities and changing technology. Paper architecture is essential to effective management and use of computer systems.

Communication is a critical aspect of the CIM architecture, because the present industrial environment, with its wide range of computer systems, makes it difficult for people and machines to communicate with each other because they format data differently. Communication has to be highly integrated to extend beyond an individual area throughout the entire enterprise and to customers and suppliers. A typical communication network in the CIM environment is shown in Figure 14.2.

In a CIM environment, local areas such as shop floors share data without passing through the central computer. The agreement that a local area network (LAN) is needed on the shop floor mainly enhances CIM environment data communication. The LAN on the shop floor has extra functions not needed in the office environment; hence, it is known as industrial LAN, or ILAN. ILANs provide a common communication system that allows suitably configured terminals and computers to be easily plugged in and disconnected. Because data are sent from one point on the network directly to another node, the switching and load-balancing functions of the central computer are avoided.

LAN technology allows the use of printers and disks so that printing costs can be reduced and common files maintained. High reliability and serviceability are provided by the flexibility of LANs. Vertical communication to mainframe computers and horizontal communication to other networks are provided by gateways, routers, and bridges.

The major mechanism used to connect different computers is international standards. Software is an important integration tool. Common operating systems are being developed for different computers. International standards are needed if different computer systems are to be connected. These standards are agreed to formally by organizations that are independent of computer manufacturers and computing nations. For example, the International Organization for Standardization (ISO) works through committees of representatives of the national standards organization of each participating country. These, in turn, are formed by representative industrial organizations within each country and not by individual companies. Physically, a standard is a document giving detailed specifications of hardware and software protocols. ISO standards usually begin as working papers that are published as draft proposals when agreed to by the appropriate ISO working group. In practice, many hardware and software products

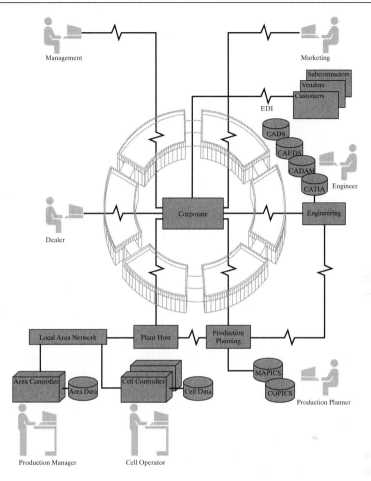

FIGURE 14.2 Communication network. (Courtesy of International Business Machines Corporation, New York.)

have become standards by virtue of their wide use and acceptance. Many suppliers of computer systems have their own proprietary interface products that may not be adapted as international standards because of constantly rising costs and the fear of loss of control. There are standards emerging that integrate these different proprietary systems, such as the OSI and MAP models.

14.4.1 Open Systems Interconnection (OSI)

The OSI reference model provides a seven-layer communication architecture that divides the complex functions needed to interface many different computer systems for different applications. Separate functions such as controlling the physical connection or providing an interface for user programs can be performed by different hardware and software. The OSI reference model is shown in Figure 14.3. Layers 1 to 4 transmit

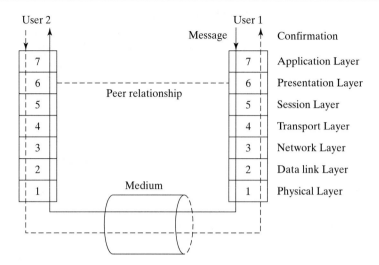

FIGURE 14.3 OSI reference model. (Courtesy of Mitchell, F. H., Jr. (1991). *CIM systems: an introduction to computer-integrated manufacturing*, p. 360. Englewood Cliffs, NJ: Prentice Hall. Reprinted by permission.)

data from system to system without error, and layers 5 to 7 interpret the data stream and present it to the user within these layers. OSI provides a selection of standards for different communication purposes.

The application layer is the interface between OSI and the application that uses it. Standards are concerned with data exchanges and the sources provided, such as remote file manipulation, distributed processing, message transfers, and manufacturing messages. The presentation layer selects the syntax used for data transfer. Syntax is precisely defined by manufacturers. The session layer provides facilities to manage and coordinate the dialogue between the application processes, including restarting a dialogue if there has been a temporary communication failure.

The transport layer provides reliable transfer of bit streams between end systems. Five classes of protocol are defined, depending on the quality of service required by the upper layers. The network layer sets up the communication path between nodes. The connection is established for the duration of the communication. The data link layer transmits the bit streams through the physical medium. It is divided into the new sublayers, logical link control, and medium access control. The physical layer activities the mechanical and electrical operations of the network.

The relevant ISO committee can change the selection of standards within the different layers; that is, new standards can be added to the OSI reference model, increasing the choice of standards available.

14.4.2 Manufacturing Automation Protocol (MAP)

General Motors initiated work on MAP in 1982 to prevent the problems of linking shop floor computers. The objective was to establish one set of LA protocols for communication between intelligent devices such as computer-controlled machine tools, engineering workstations, process controllers, factory floor terminals, and control rooms.

MAP is an implementation of the OSI model; that is, a set of standards is selected from the OSI model. MAP also requires defining some functions not available within OSI. This enables the continuation of work without developing new standards. Another function of MAP, called manufacturing message specification (MMS), assists programming in a manufacturing environment. MMS was developed by an electronic industries association (EIS) committee; it defines protocols for network services such as device status and control, program load, job queuing, and journal management. The functions of MMS affect application design and reduce the application programming required to install MAP systems.

14.5   Computer-Aided Process Planning

Process planning defines the sequence of operations that a part has to undergo during manufacture.

When developed manually, the sequence of manufacturing operations is listed on a route sheet, which also identifies the machines to be used for the processes. Additional manufacturing information such as cutting speed, feed, and depth of cut are also listed. The primary disadvantage of manual process planning is inconsistency. For example, a family of different routes of manufacturing sequences might be specified for a part instead of a single route. This is mainly due to different planners, specifying different routes for the same part. To avoid overlapping and confusion, one must use computers.

Computer-aided process planning (CAPP) devises a route for any part. There are two type of computer-aided process planning: retrieval-type CAPP and generative-type CAPP.

14.5.1 Retrieval-Type CAPP

In retrieval-type CAPP, standard processes for each part family are stored within the computer and called up whenever required. If a new part comes in, the existing database is searched for a similar process plan that can be modified. Hence, this type of process planning is also referred to as variant process planning.

The process followed during retrieval process planning is illustrated in Figure 14.4. To retrieve a part route sheet or process plan, the part code number is entered into the

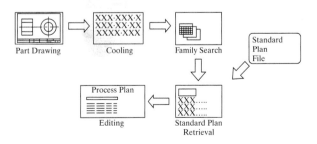

FIGURE 14.4   Variant process planning.

computer. The process-planning program then searches the part family listing to determine if a part family exists. If the part family exists, the machine sorting and operation sequences are retrieved from the computer and displayed. If no part family is found, the standard operation sequence is displayed, which can be edited and modified to make it compatible with the new part.

14.5.2 Generative-Type CAPP

In generative process planning, a new process plan is created every time, using a set of algorithms based on general rules about manufacturing routes. The input to the system is in the form of a detailed description of the part to the manufacturer, including a geometric description of the part to be manufactured and material specifications.

In a generative planning database system, process plans are created from the information available in a manufacturing database without human intervention. Technological and logistical decisions are made by the computer using a set of algorithms to achieve a viable manufacturing plan. However, knowledge of manufacturing must be captured and encoded into efficient software. Other planning functions, such as machine selection, tool selection, and process optimization can also be incorporated into the program. Thus, the system can synthesize the design of a manufacturing process. However, current generative CAPP systems fall short of the ideal and are limited to small manufacturing processes. Human intervention is also often used during decision making. Hence, generative process planning is used for a less complete system. Systems with built-in decision logic are often called generative process planning systems.

Implementation of generative process planning requires the following:

1. The logic of process planning has to be identified and captured.
2. The part to be produced must be defined in a 3D model or GT code, that is, a computer-compatible format.
3. The logic of process planning and part description must be incorporated into a unified manufacturing database.

Some of the advantages of generative process planning are the ability to generate consistent process plans rapidly, the possibility of planning new components with relative ease, and the potential of interfacing with an automated manufacturing facility to provide detailed control information.

14.5.3 Popular Process Planning Systems

Most process planning systems are of the retrieval type, such as CAPP, MIPLAN, MITURN, MIAPP, ACUDATA/UNIVATION, CINTURN, COMCAPPV, etc. Some of the generative systems are CPPP, AUTAP, APPAS, GENPLAN, and CAR. Brief descriptions of the popular process planning systems follow:

CAM-I CAPP.   The CAM-I automated process planning system is widely used. It was developed by McDonnell Douglas Automation Company under contract from CAM-I

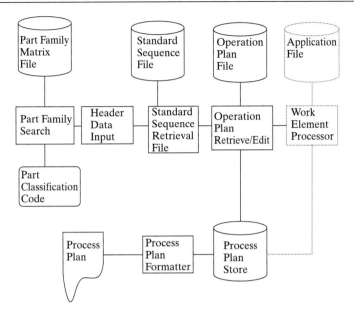

FIGURE 14.5   CAM-I process plan. (Courtesy of CAM-I, Inc., Arlington, TX.)

and was first released in 1976. CAPP is a database management system written in ANSI standard FORTRAN, and it provides a structure for a part classification and the output format to be added by the user.

A graphical description of the CAM-I process planning system is shown in Figure 14.5. The system is operated via an interactive computer terminal. The system contains a standard process plan and a sequence of operation codes for each family in an operation plan file. Standard plans and operation plans are developed for each installation, as they are a function of the machines, procedures, and expertise of individual companies. The parts are coded and classified in families outside of the CAPP system using the group technology code of 36 alphanumeric characters. These are major steps in the creation of a process plan:

1. The planned part is attributed to particular group technology part family.
2. The header information, such as part numbers, materials, part name, and revision, which can identify a process plan, is input.
3. The routing (operation sequence) of the part is specified.
4. The text describing the work performed at each operation is created.

The plan is then stored and can be printed and edited as desired.

CAPP allows the user to use an existing group technology system in the process plan search, requiring minimum modification by the user during system implementation.

MIPLAN and MultiCAPP. MIPLAN and MultiCAPP were developed in conjunction with the Organization for Industrial Research, Inc. Both are variant systems using the MICLASS coding system for part description. Process plans are retrieved based on part code, part number, family matrix, and code range. Part-code input results in the retrieval of similar parts of each process plan and can be subsequently edited by the user.

AUTAP. AUTAP, one of the most complete planning systems, is capable of material selection, process selection, process sequencing, machine tool selection, tool selection, and part program generation.

AUTAP has its own part description language. It uses primitives similar to those used in constructive solid geometry language to construct a part.

The AUTAP system is illustrated in Figure 14.6, which shows the description of a rotational component. The component is divided into three entities starting from the left. The codes, starting with "1" describe the first entity, consisting of a cylinder, a straight chamfer, and a fillet chamfer each assigned a unique description. Thus, any shape and information can be represented. Currently, AUTAP can plan rotational and sheet metal parts.

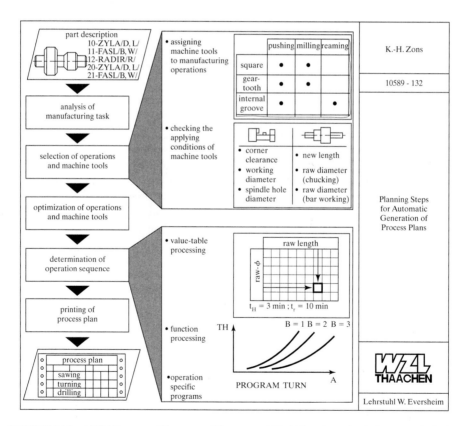

FIGURE 14.6 AUTAP system. (Courtesy of Computer-Aided Manufacturing Laboratory, Technical University of Aachen, Germany.)

APPAS and CAD/CAM. APPAS (automated process planning and selection) is a generative system for detailed process selection. CAD/CAM interfaces with APPAS using a CAD "front end" approach and decision table logic for process selection. APPAS is unique in its surface by a special code. A single machined surface is usually defined by a data string of 30 to 40 attributes and process selection multiple passes and processes for designated machined surfaces. The details of APPAS include selection of the feed rate, cutting speed, length and diameter of the tool, number of teeth, or depth of cut for each tool pass. CAD/CAM provides an interactive graphics interface.

CAPP. CAPP was developed by United Technologies Research Center, partially under U.S. Army funding, and was developed primarily for planning cylindrical parts. The system generates a summary of operations and a detailed operation sheet required for production. CAPP uses a comprehensive component containing all features of the components in one part family.

Components of an entire family can be planned by building a process model that contains the solution for every feature (Figure 14.7). COPPL is a special language used to describe a process model for CAPP. Development of a process model is necessary for every part family; hence, it is most suitable for an application that has few part families, with each family member having some variation.

14.6   Planning and Control within CIM

Planning is the process of organizing material and component availability to optimize the use of productive capacity in a manufacturing organization.

14.6.1 Material Requirements Planning

Material requirements planning (MRP) is a planning method that handles the ordering and scheduling of inventories such as raw material, subassemblies, and component parts. It identifies the individual components and subassemblies that make up each end product and indicates the required quantities and when to order them. The detailed information is obtained from the master production schedule, which is prepared by the MRP process. The structure of the MRP system is shown in Figure 14.8.

The planning system is comprised of

1. the master production schedule
2. the bill of materials file
3. the inventory status file
4. MRP software

The master production schedule is based on an accurate forecast of demand for the firm's products along with the estimate of the firm's production capacity. It indicates the final products to be produced, their number, and the time they are to be ready for customer delivery.

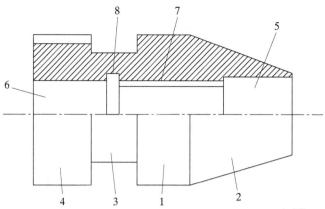

1–8 Feature Number

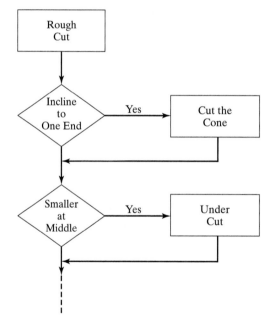

1. Rough Cut on Outside
2. Cut the Cone
3. Undercut
4. Cut External Thread
5. Drill Hole from Left-Hand side
6. Drill Hole from Right-Hand side
7. Recessing the Groove
8. Internal Threading
9. Part Off

FIGURE 14.7   CAPP. (Tien-Chein Chang, T.-C., & Wysk, R. A. (1985). *An introduction to automated process planning systems.* Englewood Cliffs, NJ: Prentice Hall, p. 181. Reprinted by permission.)

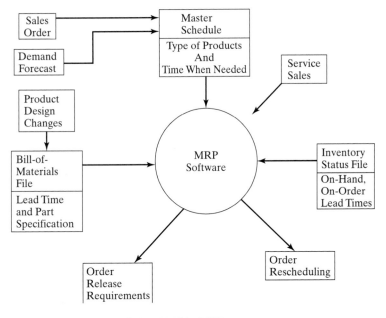

FIGURE 14.8   MRP system.

Product demand influencing the master production schedule is of three types: actual customer orders, forecasted demand from past orders, or demand of individual components from service departments.

The bill-of-materials file specifies the composition of the finished product and outlines its structure in terms of its component parts and subassemblies. This information is required to manufacture the end products listed in the master production schedule

The inventory status file provides data on how much inventory is in stock. It contains a record of the actual inventory level, lead time, ordered inventory, and backorder inventory.

The master production schedule, bill-of-materials file, and inventory status file are used as inputs for the MRP package. The software processes the information in these files to calculate the net requirements for each period of the planning cycle.

After computing the requirements of each new material and component, MRP plans the time when work must commence for each product. It does this by considering the ordering lead time and manufacturing lead time for the required product. Ordering lead time is the time required from the initiation of the purchase order to the actual receipt of the item from the supplier. Manufacturing lead time is the time required to manufacture a component part. It includes processing time, idle time, and material handling time.

Some of the benefits of MRP are

1. low inventory levels
2. avoiding possible delays

3. expediting and de-expediting orders

4. use as a long-term planning tool

14.6.2 Manufacturing Resource Planning

Manufacturing resource planning (MRP II) is a progressive evolution of material requirements planning. Priority planning is now incorporated into MRP to determine not only what part is required, but also when it is needed. Thus, MRP can deal with urgent jobs by increasing their priority and extending them ahead of schedule.

MRP II combined material requirements planning with production planning and control function and the financial system of the company.

MRP II covers all aspects of the company business, including sales, production, engineering, inventories, and accounting. It uses financial data as a common medium for the operations of each independent department. Through the common medium, various departments can work together and company management can obtain necessary information. MRP II can be used also as a simulator to consider alternative production plans management decisions, enabling the company to examine probable outcomes.

14.7   Capacity Planning

The process of evaluating the feasibility of a manufacturing plan considering production constraints such as labor and equipment is known as "capacity planning." The planned production orders from MRP are tentative manufacturing plans because capacity might not exist to make all of the desired products. Capacity planning entails a detailed evaluation of the feasibility of the MRP results. The basic information requires for capacity planning are

1. planned orders from MRP
2. in-process orders
3. routing sheet
4. facilities information
5. labor availability
6. subroutine potential

The process of evolution for the capacity requirements of a tentative manufacturing plan begins with due dates for each order. Each order is back-scheduled from the due date to determine when a particular work center will be used; it uses bills of material, routing, and lead times. The capacity requirements are constantly compared with the available infrastructure, which can change because of the breakdown of machines or overloaded conditions. Certain problems can be avoided by shifting the sequence of orders, expediting, subcontracting, and reusing manufacturing plans.

14.8   Database Management Systems

A database is a collection of interrelated data, stored so as to be efficiently available for creation, update, and deletion by as many remote and local users as the applications require. There are two main types of databases: hierarchical and relational.

14.8.1 Hierarchical Database

In a hierarchical structure, data records are related in a tree-like structure. Starting at the root of the tree, each record has a one-to-many relationship to its branches. A parent record can have several child records, but a child record can have only one parent record (Figure 14.9).

Hierarchical database systems, or preferred-path database management systems, are most suited to the well-structured, static data of business such as item data, orders, costs, etc.

14.8.2 Relational Database

In a relational database, data are stored as a collection of tables composed of rows and columns. Rows and columns in the table need not be in any special order, making it easy to add data. Data relationships are located through row-by-row searches, making relational databases more flexible. They are better suited in less-structured situations, in which many unanticipated queries might be made. A typical relational database is shown in Figure 14.10.

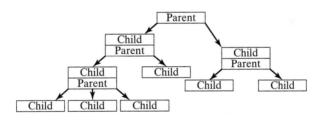

FIGURE 14.9   Hierarchical records.

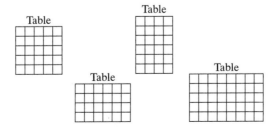

FIGURE 14.10   Relational database.

14.8.3 Database Management

Database management determines how data are defined, stored, and related, and who has access to that data. Database management is critical in today's environment because there are many different databases, formats, and storage and access techniques. Database management defines and recovers the location of data created and used by the enterprise's business function that are not accessible by current standards. It also means enabling users to get the data they need without knowing where it is located.

The accuracy of data is the user's responsibility because the computer system cannot rigorously check the data provided. Hence, measures should be taken continually to ensure the data's integrity. Security has to be built into the database software, the operating system, and the communication software. Different levels of security are needed, distinguishing between access to data, update of data, creation of new records, and deletion of data. Management of databases can be assisted by use of a "data dictionary." The dictionary contains information about data fields and records, such as which programs access and update items and which departments have responsibility for the accuracy of the data.

14.9 CIM Implementaion

For CIM to be successfully implemented, the parts to be manufactured must have certain common characteristics, allowing them to be grouped into part families. Aggregate production suitable for CIM applications ranges from 1000 to 100,000 parts yearly, but specific processes and process times determine the profitability of a CIM system. CIM is the only technology that can be used in the intermediate-volume range, compared to stand-alone numerically controlled machines, consisting of a computerized control system with its carts, pallets, shuttles, robots, and computerized control and production planning systems.

To ensure the long-tem benefits of CIM companywide, planning the implementation of CIM is necessary. The first step in obtaining a coordinated CIM effort is to set up long-term business goals. While moving down the corporate ladder, these goals have to be embedded into the goals and objectives of the functional areas. It is also necessary to understand and document the operation of the business. Documentation of business operations and information flows are carried out by business process modeling and data modeling, which show how the decisions, information, and products generated in one function have an impact on other functional areas. Additional models help document the strategic direction of process operations and information flows.

For CIM to be implemented, it is necessary to develop a plan for transforming current operations to meet the business objectives. To establish a transition plan to move from the present environment to the planned one, it is necessary to identify changes, priorities, and dependencies of the changes between the two-model versions and to organize these changes into an implementation subset.

Changes in process operations should be distributed over several implementations. The application and data plan establishes steps for data integration and new application development. And a resource plan organizes the changes in utilization of manufacturing and testing equipment, utilities, support, and information systems. The information system plan stages that implementation of processors, networks, databases, and input/output access to users and plant equipment.

Staff should be provided with ample information, education, and training to motivate them for CIM. Formatted courses are available; however, most of them do not deal with the complex problems of implementing and integrating CIM technologies into the business. Training is required to upgrade the skills of the people directly involved.

To ensure that CIM is not viewed as a threat, additional incentives should be provided to compensate for the changes, and it should be ensured that career paths will be readjusted. CIM typically creates new jobs that tend to be highly skilled—jobs like planning staff, computer hardware and software specialists, training specialists, and preventive maintenance. This results in new hiring, redeploying staff, and also lot of training and education. It is essential that the change in jobs brings about job enrichment instead of the reverse. A number of lower-skilled jobs, however, like low-level expediters, warehouse attendants, material handlers and machine operators, will be lost.

14.10 Costs Associated with CIM Implementation

The initial costs involved in CIM implementation include expenditures in application engineering, equipment procurement, site preparation, actual installation, and operation costs. The costs of CIM include machine tools, robots, material handling systems, computer hardware and software, interface accessories, computer terminals, spare parts, and special tools. Included in this cost are hazard barriers, intrusion detection devices, and other safety equipment associated with the installation. Tooling costs for special-purpose devices such as end effectors for robots, adaptor plates, part feeders, orienters, special power tools, fixtures, and positioning devices are considered during CIM implementation.

The modifications of machinery and facilities that are required to accommodate a CIM installation are considered, such as rearrangement of conveyors, chip handling systems, and changes to operator interface panels, Provision of utilities, such as compressed air, electrical power, and cooling water, that were not previously required is also in the area.

Training programs for CIM system operators and the personnel responsible for system maintenance, which are provided in advance of installation, are considered an initial cost. In addition, the cost of retraining employees displaced by the CIM system to qualify them for job reassignment and the cost of transferring displaced personnel to other jobs are also included. The cost of product changes is also chargeable to initial costs.

After installation of the CIM system, there is an additional cost incurred during programming startup and debugging, interference with production, scrapping of parts, overtime to make up for production losses, damaged or scrapped parts, and repairs to equipment damaged by program errors are other unforeseen expenses experienced with the launching of the system.

BIBLIOGRAPHY

Belby, W., & Collier, P. (1986) *New Directions Through CAD/CAM*. Dearborn, MI: Society of Manufacturing Engineers.

Chang, T. C., & Wysk, R.A. (1985). *An Introduction to Automated Process Planning Systems*. Englewood Cliffs, NJ: Prentice Hall.

Compton, W.D. (1988). *Design and Analysis of Intergrated Manufacturing Systems*. Washington, DC: National Academy of Engineering.

Crowley, O.R. (1984, December). Let's discuss CAD/CAM integration. *Modern Machine Shop*. December.

Ham, I., Hitomi, K., & Yoshida, T. (1979). *Group Technology*. New York: Kluwer-Nijhoff.

Harrington, J., Jr. (1985). *Computer Integrated Manufacturing*. Boston: Krieger.

Hirsch, B., & Artis-Data, M. (1987). *ESPRIT CIM, Design Engineering, Management and Control of Production Systems*. Amsterdam: North-Holland.

Hunt, V.D. (1989). *Computer Integrated Manufacturing Handbook*. New York: Chapman and Hall.

IBM Corporation (1989). *Computer Integrated Manufacturing*. New York: Author.

Lenz, J.E. (1988). *Flexible Manufacturing: Benefits for the Low-Inventory Factory*. New York: Marcel Dekker.

Mitchell, F.H., Jr. (1991). *CIM Systems: An Introduction to Computer-Integrated Manufacturing*. Englewood Cliffs, NJ: Prentice Hall.

Rembold, U., & Dillman, R., eds. (1986). *Computer-Aided Design and Manufacturing: Methods and Tools*. New York: Springer-Verlag.

Thompson, V., & Graffe, U. (1987). *CIM–a manufacturing paradigm*. National Research Council report DM-c06. Washington, D.C.: National Research Council.

Weatheral, A. (1988). *Computer Integrated Manufacturing from Fundamentals to Implementations*. London: Butterworth.

Zgorzelski, M. (1986). *Computer Integrated Manufacturing: Trends, Problems, Strategies*. Warrendale, PA: Society of Automotive Engineers.

CHAPTER 15

Implementation of a CAD/CAM System

15.1 Introduction

The ever-increasing demand for quality products and lower prices has manufactures turning to the new technology offered by computer-aided design and computer aided manufacturing. The successful implementation of CAD/CAM relies on the basic principles of planning. Those manufacturers that have done their homework have seen a dramatic increase in quality products made and, in turn, have built a smooth running operation to keep a competitive edge in the market. On the other hand, there have been manufacturers who rushed into integrating CAD/CAM technology before fully understanding their need and who suffered serious setbacks, thus losing their competitive edge. It is essential, therefore, that "planning" be a major step before implementing CAD/CAM.

15.2 Misconceptions about CAD/CAM

The following are some misconceptions about CAD/CAM:

1. It is an overnight success.
2. It provides magical solutions.
3. It allows a quick fix to existing problems.
4. It allows for the easy transfer of data between systems.
5. It dissolves bureaucracy and eliminates paperwork.
6. It has user-friendly software.

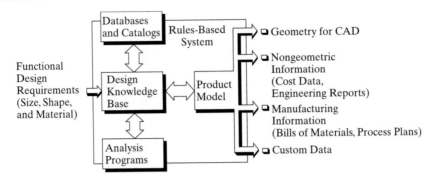

FIGURE 15.1   Example of a CAD/CAM operating configuration (ICAD Inc.).

Salespeople tend to present CAD/CAM as the key to overnight success. This is not the case, when hidden costs surface and problems arise. Management realizes that the cost of maintaining and operating a CAD/CAM system has not been fully understood. CAD/CAM technology cannot solve personnel and equipment problems nor can it make problems disappear. On the contrary, computer technology, if not used properly, can magnify problems and even produce faulty designs faster than humans can. Users have experienced difficulty integrating different hardware components. In many cases, data do not transfer easily and additional work is needed. The most challenging problem of implementing CAD/CAM technology is to convince managers that their companies have not been making profits for years without so-called fancy computers. … The dissolution of paperwork threatens managers' authority and territorial status. To think that all departments can share information through a database brings fear to workers as well as to managers, and fosters opposition to the full integration of CAD/CAM into a company (Figure 15.1).

15.3 Looking for a System

When purchasing a CAD/CAM system, the following must be considered:

1. Reason for purchase
2. Expectations of the system
3. Adjustments before and after implementation
4. Goals

It is important when planning the purchase of a CAD/CAM system that the manufacturer determine some specific reasons for the purchase. The ultimate goal is reducing lead-time in production. This is the most compelling reason for a manufacturer to implement a CAD/CAM system. For instance, if the purpose of purchasing a computer system is to improve drafting capabilities so layouts are produced more quickly, it is important to point out that in most cases drafting represents only 1% of the total operating cost. This alone does not economically justify a CAD/CAM system.

15.4   Practical Benefits

Reducing Errors in Design.   In addition to the accuracy provided by a CAD/CAM system, errors in design can be minimized if data are exchanged and transmitted via the computer network rather than through the usual approach of copying, tapes, creating from scratch, etc.

Enhancing Design Using Integrated Analysis.   This function has yet to be fully used by all manufacturers; it should be part of planning.

Graphic Simulation.   The manufacturing process can be simulated graphically to minimize errors and reduce operating costs. Graphics play a major role in checking the NC part programming, checking the clearance between different parts by simply merging them on the screen, helping select product colors, and most of all allowing the user to modify the existing design instantly.

Technological Necessity.   To stay competitive, manufacturers need to produce quality products at a competitive price. Foreign countries are becoming more and more aggressive and are determined to do what it takes to stay active in a shrinking world market. Japan had combined two very important ingredients essential to economic success: computer technology and a dedicated, skilled labor force. Japan had stayed ahead by constantly improving the quality of its products and keeping its process competitive. In addition, it had developed a system to service and maintain its products. South American and Asian countries are providing the cheapest labor imaginable. In doing so, they have attracted a large number of businesses. Western Europe is entering a new phase by developing a European Market whose main goal is to compete against Japan and the United States. To survive this strong competition, manufacturers are planning ahead, and CAD/CAM technology is becoming more of necessity than an option.

   In addition to the practical benefits a CAD/CAM system offers, its successful performance yields

1. shorter product cycle
2. integration of engineering functions such as design, analysis, and manufacturing
3. increasing design productivity
4. shorter lead times
5. efficient planning and quality control
6. better control of manufacturing processes
7. reduced manufacturing costs
8. competitive pricing of products

15.5   Costs

There are basically two kinds of systems to select when deciding to purchase a CAD/CAM system: turn-key systems and standard systems.

Turn-Key Systems.   Certain vendors usually design these systems so that the hardware, software, and operating system are integrated to function in the most efficient way. This usually creates a proprietary problem, in which the user is committed to one vendor for better or for worse. Turn-key systems are not standard and therefore do not interface with other hardware, nor do they support software other than theirs.

Standard Systems.   These systems are based on popular operating systems such as DOS, UNIX, or VMS, therefore allowing the use of a multitude of software packages. Users have the choice of selecting the appropriate hardware and software.

     The cost of a CAD/CAM system is divided into three categories: hardware, software, and training.

     Figure 15.2 and 15.3 illustrate the purchasing cost and the annual cost for stand-alone personal computers, minicomputers, and mainframe systems.

15.6   Selecting a Vendor

The first step in implementing a CAD/CAM system requires the formation of a committee. The committee's task is as follows:

1. Gather specific information on what the CAD/CAM systems to accomplish. This helps vendors with their proposals. The information should include:

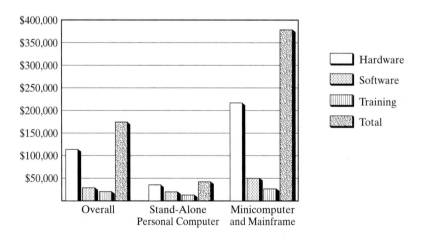

FIGURE 15.2   Purchasing cost of CAD/CAM system (*PMSJ CADD application and user survey,* as reported in Berliner, 1988).

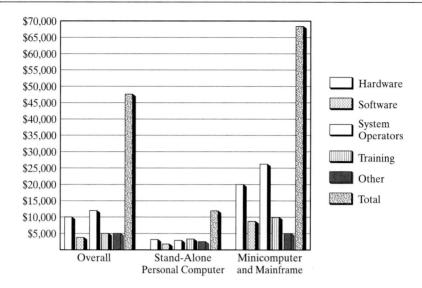

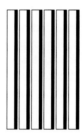

FIGURE 15.3 Annual operating costs of a CAD/CAM system (*PMSJ CADD application and user survey,* as reported in Berliner, 1988).

- Number of design engineers
- Number of draftspersons
- Number of NC programmers
- Number of shifts each department works
- Current overtime in design and drafting
- Percent of time spent generating new drawings
- Percent of the time revising drawings
- Types of NC equipment at present
- CAD/CAM systems already in use
- Competitors' use of CAD/CAM systems
- Any other useful information

2. Request proposals from vendors. This is a normal procedure in which vendors propose the most convenient system configuration for your needs, based on the information you have gathered and provided, along with an estimate of costs.

15.7 Testing the System

It is becoming standard practice to evaluate equipment by having the vendor run some of your applications. This demonstration enables you to determine the limitations, speed, labor required, and any important interfaces needed. The demonstration model must be very close, if not identical, to the one you intend to purchase. You need to keep in mind that the people giving the demonstration are usually highly skilled technicians and do not reflect the skills of your workers.

When buying a CAD/CAM system, training is essential right from the start. Many vendors provide short courses, ranging form an introduction, system operation, and drafting to advanced courses in finite elements and manufacturing. Buyers must be aware of the importance of training and decide whether on- or off-site training is need. This enhances company productivity and maintains long-term goals.

15.8 The CAD/CAM Market

The CAD/CAM market had long been dominated by the turn-key suppliers. Today's market is evolving around a complicated network of vendors serving an ever-increasing market of users. With the advances of microprocessor technology, low-cost "open" systems are becoming more popular. There are three types of CAD/CAM vendors specializing in selling hardware, software, and hardware/software.

New technology advancements in hardware opened the door to new users. What used to be a problem that could be solved only on a mainframe has migrated to the PC and workstation. The new class of hardware and its lower price attract a large number of new users. (Figure 15.4). There is an awareness by many users about CAD/CAM technology and its limitations. The limitations have made users very selective, and many turn to a custom-designed CAD/CAM system.

The future market will be greatly influenced by the power of the computer. The CAD/CAM system will be established as part of engineering departments, and thereby those departments will play a much larger function in the company.

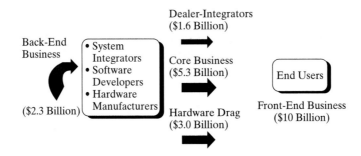

FIGURE 15.4   The CAD/CAM market (Datatech, Inc., Cambridge, MA).

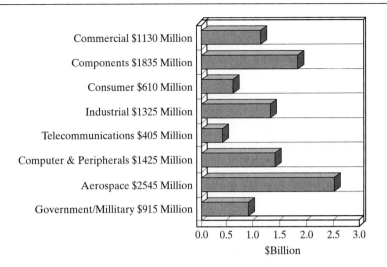

Commercial $1130 Million
Components $1835 Million
Consumer $610 Million
Industrial $1325 Million
Telecommunications $405 Million
Computer & Peripherals $1425 Million
Aerospace $2545 Million
Government/Millitary $915 Million

0.0 0.5 1.0 1.5 2.0 2.5 3.0
$Billion

FIGURE 15.5   U.S. market for computer workstations, by end users, 1990 (Report A2356 from Frost and Sullivan, Inc., San Antonio, TX).

The PC will become a vital computing power, redefining the use of mainframes and other workstations (Figure 15.5). Vector processing and parallel processing will play a major role in the next generation of CAD/CAM systems designed for real-time simulations and animation purposes.

BIBLIOGRAPHY

Bennet, R.E., Hendrikes, J.A., Keys, D.E., and Rundnickia, E.J. (1987). *Cost Accounting for Factory Automation*. (1987). NJ: National Association of Accountants.

Berliner, C., & Brimson, J. (1988). *Cost Management for Today's Advanced Manufacturing: The CAM-I Conceptual Design*. Boston: Harvard Business School Press.

CADD Aplication and User Study. (1989). *Professional Services Management*. Newton, MA: Practice Management Associates.

CAD/CAM CAE: Survey Review and Buyer's Guide. (1989). Cambridge, MA: Datatech.

Dataquest (1989). *The MCAD Evaluator*. San Jose, CA: Dataquest.

Krouse, J., Mills, R., Beckert, B., & Potter, C. (1989, July 17) CAD/CAM planning guide '89. *Industry Week*, pp. 1–63.

Medland, A.J., & Burnett, P. (1986). *CAD/CAM in Practice*. New York: Wiley.

SGI. (1989). *The Competitive Benefits of 3D Computing*. CA: Silicon Graphic, Inc.: SGI.

Taraman, K. (1982). *CAD/CAM Meeting Today's Productivity Challenge*. Englewood Cliffs NJ: Prentice Hall.

The U.S. Market for Computer Graphics Workstations (1990). Report A2356. New York: Frost and Sullivan.

Matrices

A.1 Definition

A matrix consists of a set of numbers or elements arranged in rows and columns as in double-entry tabular form. A typical matrix is

$$
\mathbf{A} = \begin{bmatrix}
a_{11} & a_{12} & \cdots & a_{1n} \\
a_{21} & a_{22} & \cdots & a_{2n} \\
\vdots & \vdots & \ddots & \vdots \\
a_{m1} & a_{m2} & \cdots & a_{mn}
\end{bmatrix}
\tag{A.1}
$$

where m indicates the number of rows and n the number of columns.

A.2 Notation and Principal Types of Matrices

A.2.1 Order of a Matrix

A matrix having m number of rows and n number of columns is said to be of the order m of n, conveniently written as m-by-n. However, m-by-n can also be called the dimension or size of a matrix. For example,

$$
\mathbf{A} = \begin{bmatrix}
3 & 2 & 4 & 5 \\
5 & 1 & 2 & -7 \\
6 & 4 & -1 & -8
\end{bmatrix}
\tag{A.2}
$$

Matrix $\mathbf{A}$ is said to be of the order 3-by-4, where $m = 3$ indicates the number of rows and $n = 4$ the number of columns.

A.2.2 Row Matrix

In the m-by-n matrix, if $m = 1$, it is called a row matrix. For example,

$$\mathbf{B} = \begin{bmatrix} 1 & 2 & 3 \end{bmatrix} \tag{A.3}$$

Matrix $\mathbf{B}$ is a row matrix. It is also known as an array of 1-by-3 dimension. That is, it is an array consisting of 1 row and 3 columns.

A.2.3 Column Matrix

In the m-by-n matrix, if $n = 1$, it is called a column matrix. For example,

$$\mathbf{C} = \begin{bmatrix} 4 \\ -5 \\ 7 \end{bmatrix} \tag{A.4}$$

Matrix $\mathbf{C}$ is a column matrix. $\mathbf{C}$ is also known as an array of 3 rows and 1 column.

A.2.4 Rectangular and Square Matrices

In the m-by-n matrix, if the number of rows is not equal to the number of columns (that is, $m \neq n$), it is a rectangular matrix. On the other hand, if the number of rows is equal to the number of columns (that is, $m = n$), it is a square matrix. For example,

$$\mathbf{D} = \begin{bmatrix} 4 & 3 & 5 & 6 \\ -9 & 6 & -8 & 4 \\ 4 & -1 & 0 & -5 \end{bmatrix} \quad \text{and} \quad \mathbf{E} = \begin{bmatrix} 4 & -3 & -1 \\ -2 & 0 & 6 \\ 0 & 4 & 4 \end{bmatrix} \tag{A.5}$$

Matrix $\mathbf{D}$ is a rectangular matrix and matrix $\mathbf{E}$ is a square matrix.

A.2.5 Identity Matrix

The unity or identity matrix is a square matrix in which the diagonal elements are ones and all other elements are zeros. For example,

$$\mathbf{I} = \begin{bmatrix} 1 & 0 & 0 \\ 0 & 1 & 0 \\ 0 & 0 & 1 \end{bmatrix} \tag{A.6}$$

Matrix $\mathbf{I}$ is an identity matrix.

A.2.6 Null Matrix

The null or zero matrix is a one in which all the elements are zeros. The dimension of the null matrix is defined according to the dimension of the adjacent matrices. The notation for the null matrix is $\mathbf{G} = \mathbf{0}$ or $\mathbf{G} = 0$.

A.2.7 Transpose of a Matrix

Let $\mathbf{A}$ be a matrix of the order m-by-n. when the rows and columns are interchanged, the resultant matrix is called transpose matrix of $\mathbf{A}$. The transpose matrix of $\mathbf{A}$ is denoted by $\mathbf{A}^T$. For example,

$$\mathbf{A} = \begin{bmatrix} 1 & 2 & 3 \\ 4 & 5 & 6 \\ 7 & 8 & 9 \end{bmatrix} \quad \text{and} \quad \mathbf{A}^T = \begin{bmatrix} 1 & 4 & 7 \\ 2 & 5 & 8 \\ 3 & 6 & 9 \end{bmatrix} \tag{A.7}$$

A.2.8 Inverse of a Matrix

The inverse of matrix $\mathbf{A}$ is written as $\mathbf{A}^{-1}$, satisfying the following relationship:

$$\mathbf{A}\mathbf{A}^{-1} = \mathbf{A}^{-1}\mathbf{A} = \mathbf{I} \tag{A.8}$$

This relationship means that the product of $\mathbf{A}$ times its inverse yields the identity matrix $\mathbf{I}$.

A.2.9 Orthogonal Matrix

A matrix is said to be orthogonal when its transpose is equal to its inverse. A matrix $\mathbf{A}$ is said to be orthogonal if the following relationship is satisfied:

$$\mathbf{A}\mathbf{A}^{-1} = \mathbf{A}^T\mathbf{A} = \mathbf{I} \tag{A.9}$$

Where $\mathbf{I}$ is the identity matrix.

A.2.10 Minors, Cofactors, and Adjoints

Consider the matrix

$$\mathbf{A} = \begin{bmatrix} a_{11} & a_{12} & a_{13} \\ a_{21} & a_{22} & a_{23} \\ a_{31} & a_{32} & a_{33} \end{bmatrix} \tag{A.10}$$

The determinant obtained by deleting the ith row and the jth column of matrix $\mathbf{A}$ is called the minor of element a_{ij} and is represented as $\mathbf{M}_{ij}$.

The cofactor of element a_{ij} is denoted as $\mathbf{A}_{ij}$. The cofactor $\mathbf{A}_{ij}$ is defined as

$$\mathbf{A}_{ij} = (-1)^{i+j}\mathbf{M}_{ij} \tag{A.11}$$

The adjoint matrix of $\mathbf{A}$ is the transpose of the matrix formed by the cofactors of all the elements $\mathbf{a}_{ij}$ of matrix $\mathbf{A}$. $\mathbf{A}$ represents the adjoint of $\tilde{\mathbf{A}}$.

$$\tilde{\mathbf{A}} = [\tilde{\mathbf{A}}_{ij}] = \begin{bmatrix} \tilde{A}_{11} & \tilde{A}_{12} & \tilde{A}_{13} \\ \tilde{A}_{21} & \tilde{A}_{22} & \tilde{A}_{23} \\ \tilde{A}_{31} & \tilde{A}_{32} & \tilde{A}_{33} \end{bmatrix} = \begin{bmatrix} A_{11} & A_{12} & A_{13} \\ A_{21} & A_{22} & A_{23} \\ A_{31} & A_{32} & A_{33} \end{bmatrix} \tag{A.12}$$

From this equation, it is apparent that the adjoint of $\mathbf{A}$ is the transpose of the matrix of cofactors of $\mathbf{A}$. For example: for the given matrix $\mathbf{A}$, find its adjoint matrix.

$$\mathbf{A} = \begin{bmatrix} 2 & 2 & 1 \\ 1 & 3 & 3 \\ 2 & -1 & -2 \end{bmatrix}$$

The minors of matrix $\mathbf{A}$ are

$$\mathbf{M}_{11} = \begin{vmatrix} 3 & 3 \\ -1 & -2 \end{vmatrix} = -3 \qquad \mathbf{M}_{12} = \begin{vmatrix} 1 & 3 \\ 2 & -2 \end{vmatrix} = -8$$

$$\mathbf{M}_{13} = \begin{vmatrix} 1 & 3 \\ 2 & -1 \end{vmatrix} = -7 \qquad \mathbf{M}_{21} = \begin{vmatrix} 2 & 1 \\ -1 & -2 \end{vmatrix} = -3$$

$$\mathbf{M}_{22} = \begin{vmatrix} 2 & 1 \\ 2 & -2 \end{vmatrix} = -6 \qquad \mathbf{M}_{23} = \begin{vmatrix} 2 & 2 \\ 2 & -1 \end{vmatrix} = -6$$

$$\mathbf{M}_{31} = \begin{vmatrix} 2 & 1 \\ 3 & 3 \end{vmatrix} = 3 \qquad \mathbf{M}_{32} = \begin{vmatrix} 2 & 1 \\ 1 & 3 \end{vmatrix} = 5$$

$$\mathbf{M}_{33} = \begin{vmatrix} 2 & 2 \\ 1 & 3 \end{vmatrix} = 4$$

The cofactors are

$$\mathbf{A}_{11} = (-1)^2 \cdot (-3) = -3 \quad \mathbf{A}_{12} = (-1)^3 \cdot (-8) = 8 \quad \mathbf{A}_{13} = (-1)^4 \cdot (-7) = -7$$
$$\mathbf{A}_{21} = (-1)^3 \cdot (-3) = 3 \quad \mathbf{A}_{22} = (-1)^4 \cdot (-6) = -6 \quad \mathbf{A}_{23} = (-1)^5 \cdot (-6) = 6$$
$$\mathbf{A}_{31} = (-1)^4 \cdot (3) = 3 \quad \mathbf{A}_{32} = (-1)^5 \cdot (5) = -5 \quad \mathbf{A}_{33} = (-1)^6 \cdot (4) = 4$$

The cofactor matrix is

$$\mathbf{A}_{ij} = \begin{bmatrix} -3 & 8 & -7 \\ 3 & -6 & 6 \\ 3 & -5 & 4 \end{bmatrix}$$

And the adjoint matrix is

$$\widetilde{\mathbf{A}} = \begin{bmatrix} -3 & 3 & 3 \\ 8 & -6 & -5 \\ -7 & 6 & 4 \end{bmatrix}$$

A.2.11 Symmetric Matrix

Matrix $\mathbf{A}$ is said to be symmetric when it is equal to its transpose matrix, that is, $\mathbf{A} = \mathbf{A}^T$. For example,

$$\mathbf{A} = \begin{bmatrix} 1 & 2 & 3 \\ 2 & 6 & 5 \\ 3 & 5 & 6 \end{bmatrix} \Rightarrow \mathbf{A}^T = \mathbf{A}$$

Matrix **A** can also be written as

$$\mathbf{A} = \begin{bmatrix} 1 & 2 & 3 \\ & 6 & 5 \\ symm & & 6 \end{bmatrix}$$

A.2.12 Skew Symmetric Matrix

The skew symmetric matrix is a matrix in which the diagonal elements are zeros and the rest are such that $a_{ij} = -a_{ij}$. For example,

$$\mathbf{A} = \begin{bmatrix} 0 & -3 & 2 \\ 3 & 0 & -1 \\ -2 & 1 & 0 \end{bmatrix}$$

where $a_{12} = -a_{21}$, etc.

A.2.13 Trace of a Matrix

The trace of a square matrix **A** is the sum of all the elements in the main diagonal. For example,

$$\mathbf{A} = \begin{bmatrix} 2 & 3 & 4 \\ 5 & 6 & 7 \\ 8 & 9 & 0 \end{bmatrix}$$

Then the trace of the matrix is defined as $tr\,(\mathbf{A}) = 2 + 6 + 0 = 8$.

A.3 Determinants

The determinant of matrix **A** is denoted by the following symbols: $|\mathbf{A}|$, $|a_{ij}|$, or det **A**. The determinant can be evaluated using Laplace's expansion:

$$\text{Det } \mathbf{A} = \Sigma_j a_{ij} \lambda_{ij} \quad (i = 1, 2, \ldots, n)$$

where λ_{ij} denotes the cofactor corresponding to a_{ij}. The determinant for a 2-by-2 matrix is $|\mathbf{A}| = a_{11}\,a_{22} - a_{12}\,a_{21}$. The following illustrates the application of Laplace's expansion to a 2-by-2 matrix.
    Given

$$\mathbf{A} = \begin{bmatrix} 1 & 2 \\ 3 & 4 \end{bmatrix}$$

find its determinant.

$$|\mathbf{A}| = (1)(4) - (3)(2) = 4 - 6 = -2$$

By applying Laplace's expansion, the determinant for a 3-by-3 matrix is found as follows. Let

$$\mathbf{A} = \begin{bmatrix} a_{11} & a_{12} & a_{13} \\ a_{21} & a_{22} & a_{23} \\ a_{31} & a_{32} & a_{33} \end{bmatrix}$$

Then

$$\det \mathbf{A} = a_{11} \begin{vmatrix} a_{22} & a_{23} \\ a_{32} & a_{33} \end{vmatrix} - a_{12} \begin{vmatrix} a_{21} & a_{23} \\ a_{31} & a_{33} \end{vmatrix} + a_{13} \begin{vmatrix} a_{21} & a_{22} \\ a_{31} & a_{32} \end{vmatrix}$$

For example,

$$\mathbf{A} = \begin{bmatrix} 2 & 1 & 4 \\ 1 & 0 & 6 \\ 2 & 3 & 0 \end{bmatrix}$$

Then

$$|\mathbf{A}| = \begin{vmatrix} 2 & 1 & 4 \\ 1 & 0 & 6 \\ 2 & 3 & 0 \end{vmatrix} = (2) \cdot \begin{vmatrix} 0 & 6 \\ 3 & 0 \end{vmatrix} - (1) \cdot \begin{vmatrix} 1 & 6 \\ 2 & 0 \end{vmatrix} + (4) \cdot \begin{vmatrix} 1 & 0 \\ 2 & 3 \end{vmatrix}$$

$$= (2)(-18) - (1)(-12) + (4)(3) = -36 + 12 + 12 = -12$$

A.3.1 Properties of Determinants

1. The value of det **A** remains the same regardless of the row or column chosen to find it.
2. If any two rows or columns are the same, the relevant determinant obtained is equal to zero.
3. If two parallel lines of the matrix are interchanged, the sign of the determinant of that matrix changes but its magnitude does not.
4. If any row or column of a matrix is zero, the value of the determinant is zero.

A.3.2 Singularity of a Matrix

A matrix is said to be singular if the value of its determinant is equal to zero.

A.4 Matrix Paritioning

If some rows and/or columns of a matrix are deleted, the remaining array is called a submatrix of the original matrix. A matrix can be considered a submatrix of itself. For example,

$$\mathbf{A} = \begin{bmatrix} 1 & 2 & 1 \\ 4 & 6 & 9 \\ \hline 2 & 5 & 9 \end{bmatrix} = \begin{bmatrix} A_{11} & A_{12} \\ A_{21} & A_{22} \end{bmatrix}$$

where **A** is partitioned into four submatrices.

$$\mathbf{A}_{11} = \begin{bmatrix} 1 & 2 \\ 4 & 6 \end{bmatrix} \qquad \mathbf{A}_{12} = \begin{bmatrix} 1 \\ 9 \end{bmatrix}$$

$$\mathbf{A}_{21} = \begin{bmatrix} 2 & 5 \end{bmatrix} \qquad \mathbf{A}_{22} = \begin{bmatrix} 9 \end{bmatrix}$$

A.5 Matrix Operations

A.5.1 Addition

Given two matrices, $\mathbf{A} = [a_{ij}]$ and $\mathbf{B} = [b_{ij}]$, the sum is defined as

$$\mathbf{A} + \mathbf{B} = [a_{ij} + b_{ij}]$$

For example,

$$\mathbf{A} = \begin{bmatrix} 2 & 2 \\ 6 & 9 \end{bmatrix} \qquad \mathbf{B} = \begin{bmatrix} 3 & 1 \\ 1 & 0 \end{bmatrix}$$

$$\mathbf{A} + \mathbf{B} = \begin{bmatrix} 2+3 & 2+1 \\ 6+1 & 9+0 \end{bmatrix} = \begin{bmatrix} 5 & 3 \\ 7 & 9 \end{bmatrix}$$

A.5.2 Subtraction

Given two matrices, $\mathbf{C} = [C_{ij}]$ and $\mathbf{D} = [D_{ij}]$, the matrix **E** is defined as

$$\mathbf{E} = \mathbf{C} - \mathbf{D} = [\mathbf{C}_{ij} - \mathbf{D}_{ij}]$$

and is obtained by subtracting the right element of **D** from **C**.
    For example,

$$\mathbf{C} = \begin{bmatrix} 4 & 3 \\ 2 & 1 \end{bmatrix} \qquad \mathbf{D} = \begin{bmatrix} 5 & 6 \\ 4 & 5 \end{bmatrix}$$

Then we obtain the matrix **E** as follows:

$$\mathbf{E} = \mathbf{C} - \mathbf{D} = \begin{bmatrix} 4 & 3 \\ 2 & 1 \end{bmatrix} - \begin{bmatrix} 5 & 6 \\ 4 & 5 \end{bmatrix}$$

$$\mathbf{E} = \begin{bmatrix} -1 & -3 \\ -2 & -4 \end{bmatrix}$$

A.5.3 Multiplication

Scalar Multiplication.   Given matrix $\mathbf{A} = [a_{ij}]$, and a scalar, then

$$\alpha \mathbf{A} = \alpha [a_{ij}]$$

For example,

$$\mathbf{A} = \begin{bmatrix} 2 & 4 \\ 5 & 6 \end{bmatrix} \qquad \alpha = 3$$

$$\alpha \mathbf{A} = \begin{bmatrix} 6 & 12 \\ 15 & 18 \end{bmatrix}$$

Matrix Multiplication.   Let **A** be a m-by-p matrix and **B** a p-by-n matrix. The product $\mathbf{C} = \mathbf{AB}$ is an m-by-n matrix and each element $\mathbf{C}_{ij}$ of matrix **C** is obtained by multiplying the correspondent elements of the ith row of **A** by those of the jth column of matrix **B**, and adding the products. The multiplication of any two matrices exists only if the number of columns of the first matrix is equal to the number of rows of the second matrix. For example,

$$\mathbf{A} = \begin{bmatrix} 2 & 4 \\ 4 & 3 \end{bmatrix}_{2\times 2} \qquad \mathbf{B} = \begin{bmatrix} 3 \\ 1 \end{bmatrix}_{2\times 1}$$

Thus,

$$\mathbf{C} = \mathbf{A} \cdot \mathbf{B} = \begin{bmatrix} 2 & 4 \\ 4 & 3 \end{bmatrix}\begin{bmatrix} 3 \\ 1 \end{bmatrix}$$

$$= \begin{bmatrix} (2 \cdot 3) & + & (4 \cdot 1) \\ (4 \cdot 3) & + & (3 \cdot 1) \end{bmatrix}$$

$$= \begin{bmatrix} 10 \\ 15 \end{bmatrix}_{2\times 1}$$

A.6   Matrix Laws

Consider that A, B, and C are square matrices of order n. Then:

A.6.1   Commutative Law

$$\mathbf{A} + \mathbf{B} = \mathbf{B} + \mathbf{A} \qquad\qquad\qquad\text{(A.13a)}$$

$$\alpha\,\mathbf{A} = \mathbf{A} \cdot \alpha \quad \text{(for any scalar } \alpha) \qquad\qquad\text{(A.13b)}$$

A.6.2   Distributive Law

$$\alpha\,(\mathbf{A} + \mathbf{B}) = \alpha\,\mathbf{A} + \alpha\,\mathbf{B} \qquad\qquad\qquad\text{(A.14a)}$$

$$\mathbf{A}(\mathbf{B} + \mathbf{C}) = \mathbf{AB} + \mathbf{AV} \qquad\qquad\qquad\text{(A.14b)}$$

$$(\mathbf{A} + \mathbf{B})\mathbf{C} = \mathbf{AC} + \mathbf{BC} \qquad\qquad\qquad\text{(A.14c)}$$

A.6.3   Associative Law

$$(\mathbf{A} + \mathbf{B}) + \mathbf{C} = \mathbf{A} + (\mathbf{B} + \mathbf{C}) \qquad\qquad\qquad\text{(A.15a)}$$

$$(\mathbf{AB})\mathbf{C} = \mathbf{A}(\mathbf{BC}) \qquad\qquad\qquad\text{(A.15b)}$$

A.7   Method to Find the Inverse of a Matrix

A.7.1   Inverse of a 2-by-2 Matrix

Given the matrix

$$\mathbf{A} = \begin{bmatrix} a_{11} & a_{12} \\ a_{21} & a_{22} \end{bmatrix}$$

Step 1:   The determinant of matrix **A** is given by

$$|\mathbf{A}| = a_{11}a_{22} - a_{21}a_{22}$$

Step 2:   By interchanging the positions of the elements in the main diagonal and changing the algebraic sign of the remaining elements, the resultant matrix is

$$\mathbf{B} = \begin{bmatrix} a_{22} & -a_{12} \\ -a_{21} & a_{11} \end{bmatrix}$$

Step 3:   The inverse matrix of **A** is obtained by dividing all the elements of matrix **B** by the determinant value of matrix **A**, which yields

$$\mathbf{A}^{-1} = \frac{1}{a_{11}a_{22} - a_{12}a_{21}} \begin{bmatrix} a_{22} & -a_{12} \\ -a_{21} & a_{11} \end{bmatrix}$$

For example,

$$A = \begin{bmatrix} 2 & 3 \\ 4 & 5 \end{bmatrix}$$

$$|A| = 10 - 12 = -2$$

$$B = \begin{bmatrix} 5 & -3 \\ -4 & 2 \end{bmatrix}$$

Thus,

$$A^{-1} = \frac{1}{-2} \begin{bmatrix} 5 & -3 \\ -4 & 2 \end{bmatrix}$$

Finally,

$$A^{-1} = \begin{bmatrix} -2.5 & 1.5 \\ 2.0 & -1.0 \end{bmatrix}$$

A.7.2 Inverse of a 3-by-3 Matrix

Given the matrix

$$A = \begin{bmatrix} a_{11} & a_{12} & a_{13} \\ a_{21} & a_{22} & a_{23} \\ a_{31} & a_{32} & a_{33} \end{bmatrix}$$

Step 1: The determinant of matrix **A** is defined by

$$|A| = |a_{11}(a_{22}a_{33} - a_{32}a_{23}) - a_{12}(a_{21}a_{33} - a_{31}a_{23}) + a_{13}(a_{21}a_{32} - a_{31}a_{22})|$$

Step 2: Find the adjoint matrix of **A** (Section A.2.10), which is denoted by **B**.

Step 3: The inverse matrix of **A** is obtained by dividing all the elements of matrix **B** by $|A|$:

$$A^{-1} = \frac{1}{|A|} \begin{bmatrix} b_{11} & b_{12} & b_{13} \\ b_{21} & b_{22} & b_{23} \\ b_{31} & b_{32} & b_{33} \end{bmatrix}$$

For example, given

$$A = \begin{bmatrix} 1 & 1 & 4 \\ 2 & 1 & 3 \\ 1 & 0 & 2 \end{bmatrix}$$

following Step 1,

$$|A| = (1)(2 - 0) - (1)(4 - 3) + (4)4(0 - 1)$$
$$= 2 - 1 - 4$$
$$= -3$$

Following Step 2,

$$\mathbf{M}_{11} = \begin{vmatrix} 1 & 3 \\ 0 & 2 \end{vmatrix} = 2 \qquad \mathbf{M}_{12} = \begin{vmatrix} 2 & 3 \\ 1 & 2 \end{vmatrix} = 1$$

$$\mathbf{M}_{13} = \begin{vmatrix} 2 & 1 \\ 1 & 0 \end{vmatrix} = -1 \qquad \mathbf{M}_{21} = \begin{vmatrix} 1 & 4 \\ 0 & 2 \end{vmatrix} = 2$$

$$\mathbf{M}_{22} = \begin{vmatrix} 1 & 4 \\ 1 & 2 \end{vmatrix} = -2 \qquad \mathbf{M}_{23} = \begin{vmatrix} 1 & 1 \\ 1 & 0 \end{vmatrix} = -1$$

$$\mathbf{M}_{31} = \begin{vmatrix} 1 & 4 \\ 2 & 3 \end{vmatrix} = -1 \qquad \mathbf{M}_{32} = \begin{vmatrix} 1 & 4 \\ 2 & 3 \end{vmatrix} = -5$$

$$\mathbf{M}_{33} = \begin{vmatrix} 1 & 1 \\ 2 & 1 \end{vmatrix} = -1$$

The cofactor matrix $\mathbf{B}^T$ is then given by

$$\mathbf{B}^T = \begin{bmatrix} M_{11} & -M_{12} & M_{13} \\ -M_{21} & M_{22} & -M_{23} \\ M_{31} & -M_{32} & M_{33} \end{bmatrix}$$

which can be

$$\mathbf{B}^T = \begin{bmatrix} 2 & -1 & -1 \\ -2 & -2 & 1 \\ -1 & 5 & -1 \end{bmatrix}$$

yielding

$$\mathbf{B}^T = \begin{bmatrix} 2 & -2 & -1 \\ -1 & -2 & 5 \\ -1 & 1 & -1 \end{bmatrix}$$

Following Step 3, by dividing all the elements of **B** by the determinant of matrix **A**, the following is obtained.

$$\mathbf{A}^{-1} = \frac{1}{-3} \begin{bmatrix} 2 & -2 & -1 \\ -1 & -2 & 5 \\ -1 & 1 & -1 \end{bmatrix} = \begin{bmatrix} -\dfrac{2}{3} & \dfrac{2}{3} & \dfrac{1}{3} \\ \dfrac{1}{3} & \dfrac{2}{3} & -\dfrac{5}{3} \\ \dfrac{1}{3} & -\dfrac{1}{3} & \dfrac{1}{3} \end{bmatrix}$$

which is the inverse matrix of **A**.

A.8   Solution of Simultaneous Linear Equations

There are several methods for solving simultaneous equations. Cramer's rule is one of the simplest approaches to solve a set of n equations with n unknowns, x and y:

$$2x - 3y = 5$$

$$x + y = 5$$

These equations rewritten in matrix form yield

$$\begin{bmatrix} 2 & -3 \\ 1 & 1 \end{bmatrix} \begin{bmatrix} x \\ y \end{bmatrix} = \begin{bmatrix} 5 \\ 5 \end{bmatrix}$$

which is equivalent to $[A]\begin{Bmatrix} x \\ y \end{Bmatrix} = [B]$. Using Cramer's rule, we solve for x and y as follows:

$$x = \frac{\begin{vmatrix} 5 & -3 \\ 5 & 1 \end{vmatrix}}{\det A}$$

$$x = \frac{\begin{vmatrix} 5 & -3 \\ 5 & 1 \end{vmatrix}}{\begin{vmatrix} 2 & -3 \\ 1 & 1 \end{vmatrix}} = \frac{20}{5} = 4$$

The matrix in the numerator is obtained by deleting the first column of **A** and replacing it with the vector matrix **B**. Similarly, in solving for y, the second column of **A** is replaced with vector **B**. Therefore,

$$Y = \frac{\begin{vmatrix} 5 & 5 \\ 2 & 1 \end{vmatrix}}{\det A} = \frac{\begin{vmatrix} 2 & 5 \\ 1 & 5 \end{vmatrix}}{\begin{vmatrix} 2 & -3 \\ 1 & 1 \end{vmatrix}} = \frac{5}{5} = 1$$

Then the solution is $x = 4$ and $y = 1$.

An example for the solution of three equations with three unknowns using Cramer's rule is shown next.

Given:

$$2x + 2y + z = 1$$

$$x + 3y + 3z = 4$$

$$2x - y - 2z = -2$$

These equations can be rewritten in matrix form as

$$\begin{bmatrix} 2 & 2 & 1 \\ 1 & 3 & 3 \\ 2 & -1 & -2 \end{bmatrix} \begin{bmatrix} x \\ y \\ z \end{bmatrix} = \begin{bmatrix} 1 \\ 4 \\ -2 \end{bmatrix}$$

Then, applying Cramer's rule, x is found by dividing the determinant of the following matrices. Note that the numerator matrix is obtained by replacing the first column of the left-hand side matrix with the column on the right-hand side.

$$x = \frac{\det \begin{bmatrix} 1 & 2 & 1 \\ 4 & 3 & 3 \\ -2 & -1 & -2 \end{bmatrix}}{\det \begin{bmatrix} 2 & 2 & 1 \\ 1 & 3 & 3 \\ 2 & -1 & -2 \end{bmatrix}}$$

$$= \frac{(1)\begin{vmatrix} 3 & -3 \\ -1 & -2 \end{vmatrix} - (2)\begin{vmatrix} 4 & 3 \\ -2 & -2 \end{vmatrix} + (1)\begin{vmatrix} 4 & 3 \\ -2 & -1 \end{vmatrix}}{(2)\begin{vmatrix} 3 & 3 \\ -1 & -2 \end{vmatrix} - (2)\begin{vmatrix} 1 & 3 \\ 2 & -2 \end{vmatrix} + (1)\begin{vmatrix} 1 & 3 \\ 2 & -1 \end{vmatrix}}$$

$$= \frac{(1)(-6 + 3) - (2)(-8 + 6) + (1)(-4 + 6)}{(2)(-6 + 3) - (2)(-2 - 6) + (1)(-1 - 6)} = \frac{-3 + 4 + 2}{-6 + 16 - 7} = 1$$

Similarly, to obtain y, we replace the second column with the right-hand side column matrix.

$$y = \frac{\det \begin{bmatrix} 2 & 1 & 1 \\ 1 & 4 & 3 \\ 2 & - & -2 \end{bmatrix}}{\det \begin{bmatrix} 2 & 2 & 1 \\ 1 & 3 & 3 \\ 2 & -1 & -2 \end{bmatrix}}$$

$$= \frac{(2)\begin{vmatrix} 4 & 3 \\ -2 & -2 \end{vmatrix} - (1)\begin{vmatrix} 1 & 3 \\ 2 & -2 \end{vmatrix} + (1)\begin{vmatrix} 1 & 4 \\ 2 & -2 \end{vmatrix}}{3}$$

$$= \frac{(2)(-8 + 6) - (1)(-2 - 6) + (1)(-2 - 8)}{3} = \frac{-4 + 8 - 10}{3} = -2$$

Replacing the third column matrix we obtain z.

$$z = \frac{\det \begin{bmatrix} 2 & 2 & 1 \\ 1 & 3 & 4 \\ 2 & -1 & -2 \end{bmatrix}}{\det \begin{bmatrix} 2 & 2 & 1 \\ 1 & 3 & 3 \\ 2 & -1 & -2 \end{bmatrix}}$$

$$= \frac{(2)(-6 + 4) - (2)(-2 - 8) + (1)(-1 - 6)}{3} = 3$$

Therefore, $x = 1$, $y = -2$, and $z = 3$.

Bibliography

CAD

Ablameyko, S., and T.Pridmore. *Machine Interpretation of Line Drawing Images.* Springer-Verlag, 2000.

Akin, J. E. *Computer-Assisted Mechanical Design.* Prentice Hall, 1990.

Amirouche, Farid. *Computer-Aided Design and Manufacturing.* Prentice Hall, 1993.

Anderl, R., and R. Mendgen. *Parametric Design and Its Impact on Solid Modeling Applications.* ACM Press, 1990.

Ault, H. K. "Modeling Strategies for Parametric Design." The 7th International Conference on Engineering Computer Graphics and Descriptive Geometry, ISGG, Cracow, Poland (Sept. 1996), pp. 390–394.

Banach, Daniel T. T., and T. Jones. *Autodesk Inventor from the Top.* Thomson Learning, November 2001.

Bouma, W., I. Fudos, C. Hoffmann, J. Cai, and R. Paige. "Geometric constraint solver." *Computer-Aided Design* (1995) 27(6):487–501.

Brüderlin, B. "Constructing three-dimensional geometric objects defined by constraints." *Interactive 3D Graphics* (Oct. 1986):111–129.

Casciola, G., F. Fabbri, and L. B. Montefusco. "An application of fast factorization algorithms in computer-aided geometric design." *Linear Algebra and its Applications* (June 2003) 366(1): 121–138.

"Combining interactive exploration and optimization for assembly design." *Journal of Mechanical Design* (March 1998) 120(1): 35–43.

"Computer-aided sketching of epicyclic-type automatic transmission gear trains." *Journal of Mechanical Design* (Sept. 1996) 118 (3): 405–411.

Computervision Corporation. *Introduction to Parametric Modeling.* 1993.

"CyberCAD: A collaborative approach in 3D-CAD technology in a multimedia-supported environment." *Computers in Industry,* in press.

Davies, B. L., A. J. Robotham, A. Yarwood. *Computer-Aided Drawing and Design.* Chapman & Hall, 1991.

Encarnacao, J., R. Lindner, and E. G. Schlechtendahl. *Computer-Aided Design, Fundamentals and System Architectures.* 2nd ed. Springer-Verlag, 1990.

Farin, G., H. Hagen, and H. Noltemeier. *Geometric Modeling.* Springer-Verlag, 1993.

Ge, X., S-C. Chou and X-S Gao. "Geometric constraint satisfaction using optimization methods." *CAD* (1999) 31(14): 867–879.

Gershenfeld, N. *The Nature of Mathematical Modelling.* Cambridge University Press, 1999.

Haigh, Martin J. *An Introduction to Computer-Aided Design and Manufacture.* Blackwell Scientific Publications, 1985.

Hazelrigg, G. A. "A framework for decision-based engineering design." *Journal of Mechanical Design* (Dec. 1998) 120(4): 653–658.

Hazelrigg, G. A. "The implications of Arrow's impossibility theorem on approaches to optimal engineering design." *Journal of Mechanical Design* (June 1996) 118(2): 161–164.

Ingham, Peter. *CAD Systems in Mechanical and Production Engineering.* Redwood Press, 1990.

Juttler, B., and M. G. Wagner. "Computer-aided design with spatial rational B-spline motions." *Journal of Mechanical Design* (June 1996) 118(2): 193–203.

Kim, H., O. M. Querin, and G. P. Steven. "On the development of structural optimisation and its relevance in engineering design." *Design Studies* (Jan. 2002) 23(1): 85–102.

Korsten, Maarten, and Paul Regtien. "Systematic and computer-assisted design of measurement systems." *Measurement* (March 2003) 33(2): 145–156.

Lee, Kunwoo. *Principles of CAD/CAM/CAE Systems.* Addison Wesley Longman, 1999.

Liu, L., G. Wang, F. Eng, H. Tay, and A. Roy. "Explicit matrix representation for NURBS curves and surfaces." *Computer-Aided Geometric Design* (June 2002) 19(6): 409–419.

Lu, S. C., A. B. Rebello, R. A. Miller, G. L. Kinzel, and R. Yagel. "A simple visualization tool to support concurrent engineering design." *Computer-Aided Design* (Oct. 1997) 29(10): 727–735.

Mäntylä, Martti. *An Introduction to Solid Modeling.* Computer Science Press, 1988.

Medland, A. J., and G. Mullineux. *Principles of CAD.* Chapman & Hall, 1988,

Nederbragt, W. W., and B. Ravani. "Design of tactile fixtures for robotics and manufacturing, engineering design." *Journal of Mechanical Design* (June 1997) 119(2): 204–211.

Owen, J. C. "Algebraic solution for geometry from dimensional constraints." *Proceedings of the Symposium on Solid Modeling Foundations and CAD/CAM Applications*, 1991: 397–407.

Sarma, R., and D. Dutta. "The geometry and generation of NC tool paths." *Journal of Mechanical Design* (June 1997) 119(2): 253–258.

Shah, J., and M. Mäntylä. *Parametric and Feature Based CAD/CAM.* John Wiley & Sons, Inc., 1995

Shu, L. H., and W. C. Flowers. "Reliability modeling in design for remanufacture." *Journal of Mechanical Design* (Dec. 1998) 120(4): 620–627.

Stickland, M. T., S. McKay, and T. J. Scanlon. "The development of a three dimensional imaging system and its application in computer-aided design workstations." *Mechatronics* (June 2003) 13(5): 521–532.

Taylor, Dean L. *Computer-Aided Design.* Addison Wesley, 1992.

Toogood, R., and J. Zecher. *Pro/ENGINEER Advanced Tutorial.* SDC, 2001.

Verroust, A., F. Schonek, and D. Roller. "Rule oriented method for parametrized computer-aided design." *Computer Aided Design* (Oct. 1992) 24(3): 531–540.

Zeid, Ibrahim. *Proceedings of the Symposium on Solid Modeling Foundations and CAD/CAM Applications* 1995: 1–12.

Zeid, Ibrahim. *CAD/CAM Theory and Practice.* McGraw-Hill, 1991.

Zeng, J., W. Chen, and Q. Ding. "A web-based CAD system." *Journal of Materials Processing Technology* (Aug. 2003) 139(1–3, 20): 229–232.

Zimmers, Jr., E. M., and M. P. Groover. *CAD/CAM.* Prentice-Hall, 1985.

Zou, H., K. A. Abdel-Malek, and J. Y. Wang. "Design propagation in mechanical systems: Kinematic analysis." *Journal of Mechanical Design* (Sept. 1997) 119(3): 338–345.

Geometric Modeling

Al-Ahmari, A. M. A., and K. Ridgway. "An integrated modelling method to support manufacturing systems analysis and design." *Computers in Industry* (April 1999) 38(3): 225–238.

Barsky, Brian A. *Computer Graphics and Geometric Modeling Using Beta-Splines.* Springer-Verlag, 1988.

Beach, R.C. *An Introduction to the Curves and Surfaces of Computer-Aided Design.* Van Nostrand Reinhold, 1991.

Bloor, M. I. G., M. J. Wilson, and H. Hagen. "The smoothing properties of variational schemes for surface design." *Computer-Aided Geometric Design* (1995) 12(4): 381–394.

Bu-Qing, S., and L. Ding-Yuan. *Computational Geometry: Curve and Surface Modeling.* Academic Press, 1989.

Case, K., and M. S. Hounsell. "Feature modelling: A validation methodology and its evaluation." *Journal of Materials Processing Technology* (Nov. 2000) 107(1-3, 22): 15–23.

Chen, W., and C. Yuan. "A probabilistic-based design model for achieving flexibility." *Design Journal of Mechanical Design* (March 1999) 121(1): 77–83.

Chiyokura, H. *Solid Modeling with Designbase, Theory and Implementation.* Addison Wesley, 1988.

"Curve and Surface Modeling with Uncertainties Using Dual Kriging." *Journal of Mechanical Design* (June 1999) 121(2): 249–255.

Farin, Gerald. *Curves and Surfaces for Computer-Aided Geometric Design: A Practical Guide.* 3rd ed. Academic Press, 1993.

Farin, Gerald. *Geometric Modeling, Algorithms, and New Trends.* SIAM, 1987.

Farin, Gerald. *NURBS for Curve and Surface Design.* SIAM Activity Group on Geometric Design, SIAM, 1991.

Faux, I. D., and M.J. Pratt. *Computational Geometry for Design and Manufacture.* Ellis Horwood, 1981.

Gao, F., X. Liu, and Z. Jin. "Study of CAD for robotic mechanisms." *Jixie Gongcheng Xuebao [Chinese Journal of Mechanical Engineering]* (April 2000) 36(4): 9–13.

Greiner, G. "Variational design and fairing of spline surfaces." *Computer Graphics Forum* (1994) 13(3): 143–154.

Howard, L., and H. Lewis. "The development of a database system to optimize manufacturing processes during design." *Journal of Materials Processing Technology* (March 2003) 134(3): 374–382.

Khalid, H. M. "Modelling and analysis of CAD expert behaviour in using manual input devices." *International Journal of Industrial Ergonomics* (Feb. 2001) 27(2): 79–92.

Lee, Kunwoo. "New concepts and approaches in various topics of computer-aided design: CAD tools and algorithms for product design." *Computer-Aided Design* (May 2001) 33(6): 487–488.

Limaiem, A., Q. J. Ge, M. Sirchia, and H. A. El Maraghy. "Computer-aided geometric design of two parameter freeform motions." *Journal of Mechanical Design* (Dec. 1999) 121(4): 502–506.

Mortenson, M. E. *Geometric Modeling.* John Wiley & Sons, Inc., 1985.

Piegl, L., and W. Tiller. *The NURBs Book: Monographs in Visual Communication.* Springer-Verlag, 1995.

Piegl, L. *Fundamental Developments of Computer-Aided Geometric Modeling.* Academic Press, 1993.

Preparata, F. P., and Michael I. Shamos. *Computational Geometry: An Introduction.* Springer-Verlag, 1985.

Ram-Mohan, R. *Finite Element and Boundary Element Applications in Quantum Mechanics.* Oxford University Press, 2002.

Ravi Kumar, V. V., P. Srinivasan, K. G. Shastry, and B. G. Prakash. "Geometry-based triangulation of multiple trimmed NURBS surfaces." *Computer-Aided Design* (May 2001) 33(6): 439–454.

Rogers, D. F., and J. A. Adams. *Mathematical Elements for Computer Graphics.* 2nd ed. McGraw-Hill, 1990.

Strasser, W., and P. H. Seidel. *Theory and Practice of Geometric Modeling.* Springer-Verlag, 1989.

Tay, F. E. H., and J. Gu. "Product modeling for conceptual design support." *Computers in Industry* (June 2002) 48(2): 143–155.

Tovey, M., and J. Owen. "Sketching and direct CAD modelling in automotive design." *Design Studies* (Nov. 2000) 21(6): 569–588.

Tu, J., K. K. Choi, and Y. H. Park. "A new study on reliability-based design optimization." *Journal of Mechanical Design* (Dec. 1999) 121(4): 557–564.

Wang, B. *Integrated Product, Process, and Enterprise Design.* Chapman & Hall, 1997.

CAE

Altan, T., and V. Vazquez. "Status of process simulation using 2D and 3D finite element method: 'What is practical today? What can we expect in the future?'" *Journal of Materials Processing Technology* (Nov. 1997) 71(1): 49–63.

Brenner, S. C., and L. R. Scott. *The Mathematical Theory of Finite Element Methods.* Springer-Verlag, 1994.

Brunetti, G., and B. Golob. "A feature-based approach towards an integrated product model including conceptual design information." *Computer-Aided Design* (Dec. 2000) 32(14): 877–887.

Burry, M., J. Coulson, J. Preston, and E. Rutherford. "Computer-aided design decision support: Interfacing knowledge and information." *Automation in Construction* (Jan. 2001) 10(2): 203–215.

Carrara, G., and Y. E. Kalay. *Knowledge-Based Computer-Aided Architectural Design.* Elsevier Science Ltd., 1994

Casciola, G., F. Fabbri, and L. B. Montefusco. "An application of fast factorization algorithms." *Computer-Aided Geometric Design, Linear Algebra and its Applications* (June 2003) 366(1): 121–138.

Chapman, C. B., and M. Pinfold. "Design engineering—a need to rethink the solution using knowledge based engineering." *Knowledge-Based Systems,* (Oct. 1999) 12(5–6): 257–267.

Chen, Y. M. "Development of a computer-aided concurrent net shape product and process development environment." *Robotics and Computer-Integrated Manufacturing* (Dec. 1997) 13(4): 337–360.

Cook, R. D. *Finite Element Modeling for Stress Analysis.* John Wiley and Sons, 1999.

Doyle, R., and K. Case. "CAE software in manufacturing engineering education." *Computers & Education* (1990) 15(1–3): 277–288.

du Plessis, J. P., J. A. van Biljon, C. Janse Tolmie, and T. Wollinger. "A model for intelligent computer-aided education systems," *Computers & Education* (Feb. 1995) 24(2): 89–106.

Elkind, J. I., S. K. Card, J. Hochberg (eds.). *Human Performance Models for Computer-Aided Engineering.* Boston Academic Press, 1990.

Elliott, W. S. "Computer-aided mechanical engineering: 1958 to 1988." *Computer-Aided Design* (June 1989) 21(5): 275–288.

Eriksson, K., D. Estep, P. Hansbo, and C. Johnson. *Computational Differential Equations.* Studentlitteratur, 1996.

Finkelstein, J. *Introduction to AutoCAD 2000I (Professional Edition).* Melbourne University Press, 2001.

Fujiwara, N. W. "Development of the total management system for distributed CAE." *JSAE Review* (Jan. 1996) 17(1): 84.

Gabbar, H. A., Y. Shimada, and K. Suzuki. "Computer-aided plant enterprise modeling environment (CAPE-ModE)—design initiatives." *Computers in Industry* (Jan. 2002) 47(1): 25–37.

Gateno, J., J. Xia, J. F. Teichgraeber, A. Rosen, B. Hultgren, and T. Vadnais. "The precision of computer-generated surgical splints." *Journal of Oral and Maxillofacial Surgery* (July 2003) 61(7) 814–817.

Harper, P. M., and R. Gani. "A multi-step and multi-level approach for computer aided molecular design." *Computers & Chemical Engineering* (July 2000) 24(2–7): 677–683.

Holsing, N. F., and D. C. Yen. "Integrating computer-aided software engineering and object-oriented systems: A preliminary analysis." *International Journal of Information Management* (April 1997) 17(2): 95–113.

Howard, L., and H. Lewis. "The development of a database system to optimise manufacturing processes during design." *Journal of Materials Processing Technology* (March 2003) 134(3): 374–382.

Hughes, T. J. R. *The Finite Element Method: Linear Static and Dynamic Finite Element Analysis.* Dover, 2000.

Jensen, C., D. D. Voisinet, J. D. Helsel. *Computer-Aided Engineering Drawing Using AutoCAD.* Glencoe McGraw Hill, 1995.

Kagan, P., and A. Fischer. "Integrated mechanically based CAE system using B-Spline finite elements." *Computer-Aided Design* (Aug. 2000) 32(8–9): 539–552.

Kagan, P., and A. Fischer. "Integrated mechanically based CAE system using B-Spline finite elements." *Computer-Aided Design* (Aug. 2000) 32(8–9): 539–552.

Klingstam, P., and P. Gullander. "Overview of simulation tools for computer-aided production engineering." *Computers in Industry* (March 1999) 38(2): 173–186.

Korsten, M., and P. Regtien. "Systematic and computer-assisted design of measurement systems." *Measurement* (March 2003) 33(2): 145–156.

Kozak, J., L. Dabrowski, K. Lubkowski, M. Rozenek, and R. Sawiski. "CAE-ECM system for electrochemical technology of parts and tools." *Journal of Materials Processing Technology* (Nov. 2000) 107(1–3): 293–299.

Kumar, V., S.-J. Lee, and M. D. German. "Finite element design sensitivity analysis and its integration with numerical optimization techniques for structural design." *Computers & Structures* (1989) 32(3–4): 883–897.

Li, Q., and W. J. Zhang. "Application of model-based reasoning to the development of intelligent CAE systems." *Engineering Applications of Artificial Intelligence* (June 1998) 11(3): 327–336.

Mervyn, F., A. Senthilkumar, S. H. Bok, and A. Y. C. Nee. "Development of an internet-enabled interactive fixture design system." Computer-Aided Design (Sept. 2003) 35(10): 945–957.

Miyoshi, A., G. Yagawa, and S. Sasaki. "An interface agent that actively supports CAE beginner users in performing analyses." *Advances in Engineering Software,* Aug. 1999) 30(8): 575–579.

Nagashima, T. "Development of a CAE system based on the node-by-node meshless method." *Computer Methods in Applied Mechanics and Engineering* (June 2000) 187(1–2): 1–34.

Nolan, P., G. Rzevski, and R.A. Adey (eds.). *Applications of Artificial Intelligence in Engineering.* Kluwer Academic Publishers, 1998.

Ostrowsky, O. *Engineering Drawing with CAD Applications.* Butterworth Heinemann, 1990.

Purser, Ronald E. "Sociotechnical systems design principles for computer-aided engineering." *Technovation* (Sept. 1992) 12(6): 379–386.

Raphael, B., and I. F. C. Smith. *Fundamentals of Computer-Aided Engineering.* John Wiley and Sons, 2003.

"Study of optimization method for structural parts using CAE: Application of structural optimization codes OPTISHAPE and GENESIS to A Suspension Arm." *JSAE Review* (Jan. 1995) 16(1): 102.

Szabo, B., and I. Babuska. *Finite Element Analysis.* John Wiley and Sons, 1998.

Tang, J., V. Ogarevic, and C.-S. Tsai. "An integrated CAE environment for simulation-based durability and reliability design." *Advances in Engineering Software* (Jan. 2001) 32(1): 1–14.

Tay, Francis E. H., and Jinxiang Gu. "Product modeling for conceptual design support." *Computers in Industry* (June 2002) 48(2): 143–155.

Thomas, Jr., M. "Concurrent engineering: Supporting subsystems." *Computers & Industrial Engineering* (Dec. 1996) 31(3–4): 571–575.

Toogood, R. *Pro/ENGINEER Tutorial (Release 2000i-2)*. MultiMedia CD, 2001.

Varsamidis, T., S. Hope, and C. P. Jobling. "An object-oriented information model for computer-aided control engineering." *Control Engineering Practice* (July 1996) 4(7): 929–937.

Vosniakos, G. C., M. Ziaaie-Moayyed, and A. G. Mamalis. "Design of a system for computer-aided engineering of manufacturing facilities." *Computer Integrated Manufacturing Systems* (Feb. 1997) 10(1): 1–7.

Zhang, G. P., Y. M. Huang, W. H. Shi, and W. P. Fu. "Predicting dynamic behaviours of a whole machine tool structure based on computer-aided engineering." *International Journal of Machine Tools and Manufacture* (May 2003) 43(7): 699–706.

CAM

Al-Ahmari, A. M. A., and K. Ridgway. "An integrated modelling method to support manufacturing systems analysis and design." Computers in Industry (April 1999) 38(3): 225–238.

Asfahl, Ray. *Robots and Manufacturing Automation*. John Wiley and Sons, 1992.

Avgoustinov, N. "VRML as means of expressive 4D illustration in CAM education." *Future Generation Computer Systems* (Sept. 2000) 17(1): 39–48.

Ayres, R. U., W. Haywood, M. E. Merchant, J. Ranta, and H.-J.Warnecke. *Computer Integrated Manufacturing*. Vols. 2 & 3. Chapman & Hall, 1990.

Bedworth, D. D., M. R. Henderson, and P. M. Wolfe. *Computer-Integrated Design and Manufacturing*. McGraw-Hill, 1991.

Bindhu, N., N. Yetukuri, V. Nagarjun, V. Yetukuri and G. W. Fischer. "SPAW: A design tool for planning a manufacturing process in a concurrent engineering environment." *Computers in Industry* (Dec. 1996) 32(1): 79–93.

Bjork, O. *Layer Manufacturing: A Tool for Reduction of Product Lead Time*. Tapin Forlug, 2000.

Dagli, C. H. *Intelligent Systems in Design and Manufacturing*. Asme Press Series on International Advances in Design Productivity, 1994.

Chang, T. C., R. A. Wysk, and H. P. Wang. *Computer-Aided Manufacturing*. 2nd ed. Prentice Hall, 1997.

Cherng, John G., Xin-Yu Shao, Yubao Chen, and Peter R. Ferro. "Feature-based part modeling and process planning for rapid response manufacturing." *Computers & Industrial Engineering* (April 1998) 34(2): 515–530.

Choi, D. S., S. H. Lee, B. S. Shin, K. H. Whang, K. K. Yoon, and Sanjay E. Sarma. "A new rapid prototyping system using universal automated fixturing with feature-based CAD/CAM." *Journal of Materials Processing Technology* (June 2001) 113(1-3, 15): 285–290.

David, M. A. *Design for Manufacturability: Optimizing Cost, Quality, and Time-to-Market*. 2nd ed. CIM Press, 2001.

Gibbs, B., and P. G. Ranky. *A Case Based Introduction to Advanced CAM*. 2003.

Grievink, Johan, and Jan Van Schijndel. *European Symposium on Computer-Aided Process Engineering*. Elsevier, 2002 .

Holt, D.R. *Integrated Manufacturing Engineering Systems*. McGraw-Hill, 1992.

Howard, L., and H. Lewis. "The development of a database system to optimise manufacturing processes during design." *Journal of Materials Processing Technology* (March 2003) 134(3): 374–382.

J. A. Stori, J. A., P. K. Wright, and C. King. "Integration of Process Simulation in Machining Parameter Optimization." *Journal of Manufacturing Science and Engineering* (Feb. 1999) 121(1): 134–143.

Jha, N. K. *Handbook of Flexible Manufacturing Systems.* Academic Press, 1991.

Jones, A., and E. Barkmeyer. "Toward a Global Architecture for Computer Integrated Manufacturing." *Proceedings of CIMCON 1990*, pp. 1–20.

Jones, P. F. *CAD/CAM: Features, Applications and Management.* MacMillan Press, 1992.

Klingstam, P., and P. Gullander. "Overview of simulation tools for computer-aided production engineering." Computers in Industry (March 1999) 38(2): 173–186.

Kljajin, M. "The role of CAD in flexible manufacturing systems." *Proceedings of the 8th DAAAM International Symposium, University of Zagreb, ICCU Dubrovnik-Croatia (1997),* Branko Katalinic (ed.), DAAAM International, Vienna, pp. 161–162, 1997.

Kljajin, M., F. Miani, R. Slatina-Celje, and K. Kuzman. "Integration of CAD/CAM and Rapid Prototyping." *Proceedings of the ICIT'99 3rd International Conference on Industrial Tools, April 22–26, 2001*, pp. 265–268, 2001.

Kumar, M., and S. Rajotia. "Integration of scheduling with computer aided process planning." *Journal of Materials Processing Technology* (July 2003) 138(1–3): 297–300.

Leondes, C. *Computer-Aided Design, Engineering, and Manufacturing: Systems Techniques and Applications.* Vol. VI. CRC Press, 2000.

Lin, A. C., and H. T. Liu. "Automatic generation of NC cutter path from massive data points." *Computer-Aided Design* (Jan. 1998) 30(1): 77–90.

Lo, C. C., and C. Y. Hsiao. "CNC machine tool interpolator with path compensation for repeated contour machining." *Computer-Aided Design* (Jan. 1998) 30(1): 55–62.

Luong, L. H. S. "A decision support system for the selection of computer-integrated manufacturing technologies, robotics and computer-integrated manufacturing." (Feb. 1998) 14(1): 45–53.

McMahon, C., and J. Browne. *Principles, Practice, and Manufacturing Management.* Addision Wesley, 1999.

Mehra, A., I. Minis, and J. M. Proth. "Hierarchical production planning for complex manufacturing systems." *Advances in Engineering Software* (Aug. 1996) 26(3) 209–218.

Mertins, K., M. Rabe and W. Müller. "Designing a computer-aided manufacturing systems engineering process." *Journal of Materials Processing Technology* (April 1998) 76(1–3): 82–87.

Patrikalakis, N. M., and T. Maekawa. *Shape Interrogation for Computer- Aided Design and Manufacturing.* Springer Verlag, 2002.

Perzyk, M., and O. K. Meftah. "Selection of manufacturing process in mechanical design." *Journal of Materials Processing Technology* (April 1998) 76(1–3): 198–202.

Shen, W., D. H. Norrie, J.-P. A. Barthes, W.-M. Shen. *Multi-Agent Systems for Concurrent Intelligent Design and Manufacturing.* Taylor and Francis, 2001.

Usher, J. M., U. Roy, and H. Parsaei. *Integrated Product and Process Development: Methods, Tools, and Technologies.* Interscience, 1998.

"Virtual 3D planning of corrective osteotomy and computer-aided manufacturing of a repositioning device." *International Congress Series* (June 2003) 1256: 295–304.

Wang, H.-P. *Computer-Aided Process Planning (Advances in Industrial Engineering, No 13).* Elsevier, 1991.

Windsor, J., A. I. Sivakumar, and R. Gay. "Computer Integrated Manufacturing." *Proceedings of the 3rd International Conference, Singapore, 11-14 July 1995,* 1995.

Xie, M., T. N. Goh, and X. S. Lu. "Computer-aided statistical monitoring of automated manufacturing processes." *Computers & Industrial Engineering* (October 1998) 35(1–2): 189–192.

Zhang, W. J., and K. van der Werff. "Automatic communication from a neutral object model of mechanism to mechanism analysis programs based on a finite element approach in a software environment for CADCAM of mechanisms." *Finite Elements in Analysis and Design* (Jan. 1998) 28(3): 209–239.

Index